Wakefield Press

ADELAIDE LAW

John Waugh is a historian of Australian law and legal education. He is an honorary fellow in the law school at the University of Melbourne.

ADELAIDE LAW

A History of the
Adelaide Law School

John Waugh

**Wakefield
Press**

Wakefield Press
16 Rose Street
Mile End
South Australia 5031
www.wakefieldpress.com.au

First published 2024

Edited by Julia Beaven, Wakefield Press
Typeset by Michael Deves, Wakefield Press

ISBN 978 1 92304 239 1

A catalogue record for this book
is available from the National
Library of Australia

Wakefield Press thanks
Coriole Vineyards for
continued support

Contents

Abbreviations

BA	Bachelor of Arts
BCL	Bachelor of Civil Law
CRTS	Commonwealth Reconstruction Training Scheme
CTEC	Commonwealth Tertiary Education Commission
DCM	Departmental Committee Minutes
EFTS	Equivalent Full-Time Students
FLM	Faculty of Law Minutes
GCLP	Graduate Certificate in Legal Practice
GDLP	Graduate Diploma in Legal Practice
HECS	Higher Education Contribution Scheme
LLB	Bachelor of Laws
LLD	Doctor of Laws
LLM	Master of Laws
LPEAC	Legal Practitioners Education and Admission Council
LSS	Law Students' Society
MA	Master of Arts
MLS	Master of Legal Studies
NLA	National Library of Australia
PALACE	(Division or Faculty of) Performing Arts, Law, Architecture and Urban Design, and Economics and Commerce
S	Series
SAIT	South Australian Institute of Technology
TER	Tertiary Entry Rank
UAA	University of Adelaide Archives
UniSA	University of South Australia

Preface

For tens of thousands of years, the ancestors of the Kaurna people of the plain of Tarntanya and Karrawirra Pari, its river, taught their law, bound up with their Country and the ceremonies and stories of its Red Kangaroo Dreaming. When European settlers colonised the area and called it Adelaide, they brought their own laws; the school they established to teach those laws is the subject of this book. During much of the history of the Adelaide Law School, the Kaurna and other Indigenous peoples were excluded from study there, by barriers of schooling, cost and culture, and the school's teachers said little or nothing about the relationship between the laws they taught and those of Australia's First Nations, despite the continuing presence of Indigenous people in Adelaide. This silence was confirmed as colonial courts abandoned early gestures they made towards the recognition of Indigenous laws. Omission and rejection continued in the Law School until teaching and activism concerning Indigenous people and the law increased among staff and students in the 1970s, and Indigenous law students entered the school in the 1980s.

As the nation's second-oldest law school, and the first to be founded on the principle of compulsory university training for new lawyers, the Law School has been the subject of several earlier histories. In 1968 a sketch of the Law School's early history by Helen Mills and Charles Bagot was published in the law student magazine,

Obiter Dicta, to mark the Law School's move to its present home. The tone was light, but the article contained glimpses of the recollections of early graduates. For the school's centenary in 1983, the university's former registrar, Victor Edgeloe, wrote a historical essay on the Law School, in a series of papers on the history of the University of Adelaide. He described his work as 'an administrator's history' that summarised university records and newspaper comment.[1] It focused on professors, curriculum, and other topics that left their mark in the university's central records.

In the same year, the centenary history of the Law School, *Law on North Terrace*, appeared. It began in a small way, intended as 'a colourful, unofficial, history' in magazine format, but the project became more substantial.[2] Authors Alex Castles, Peter Kelly, Andrew Ligertwood, Neil Ligertwood and Michael White concentrated on 'personalities and events', vividly portraying student life and former staff, and recording much of their lore. Peter Kelly collected detailed recollections from his contemporaries, the students of the 1930s, which are now in the Barr Smith Library. An oral history project, which grew out of interviews with women graduates, recorded memories from the 1910s to the 1960s. While *Law on North Terrace* did not aim to explore the broader context of legal education or the university setting, it established lasting themes in the interpretation of the Law School's history, among them the importance of compulsory university study (unusual in the common-law world in the nineteenth century), the transition from lecturers who were practising lawyers to a full-time teaching staff, patterns of student life, and the long-delayed entry of women to the law course.

Law on North Terrace was written when university tuition fees had been abolished and staff participation dominated university governance. Free education at a university run by academic staff now seems a passing phase, in a longer history of universities characterised by a high degree of central control and substantial charges for tuition. The sources for the Law School's history have also grown since 1983.

PREFACE

Digitisation of historical sources has provided new material on law student groups and public debate about legal education. Newspapers contain glimpses of the system of coaching and apprenticeship that provided legal training before the establishment of the Law School. Digital sources from recent years, such as archived email and social media, are still largely unavailable for research on the history of the Law School. They can be expected to shape future work.

Recent writing on the history of legal education, especially from North America, shows how histories of law schools have diversified from their commemorative origins. The ongoing Harvard Law School history project is an example of the study of a single school by independent historians who aim to interpret rather than glorify its history. But Harvard's influence on the historical literature can be deceptive. It is only one of a great number and variety of schools, whose diverse models of legal education are a reminder of the varying interests and groups they serve. The Canadian historian Wes Pue has queried narratives of progress in which enlightened academics struggle against reactionary practitioners, and academic training of lawyers is the ideal towards which history advances: 'The academic/practitioner dichotomy fails to capture either the practical utility of an academic legal education or the academic relevance of practical knowledge.'[3] Practitioners were a mainstay of teaching for much of the Law School's first century. In the 1920s and 1930s, when the sole law professor concentrated on teaching, South Australia's most active legal researchers were practitioners, including a group of women graduates who dominated early entries for the Law School's prestigious research prize.

This new history of the Law School reflects these changed perspectives and new sources. They enable a fresh look at the themes of earlier writing, with particular attention to controversies, broader contexts, and the way the Law School was run. Self-interest, as well as conceptions of the desirable shape of legal education, led to the establishment of mandatory university legal training in South Australia and its gradual separation from apprenticeship. Compulsion had economic advantages for the university and for those in the profession who welcomed higher barriers to entry. What form that training should take continues to be debated, as the price of a law degree rises. Expense, employment prospects, family ties and patterns of school education have shaped the Law School's student intake. Reversing the century-long exclusion of Indigenous students is one aspect of a recurring debate about admission policies and their effects. Conflict over admissions flared in the 1980s and 1990s, at a time when relations with the profession, financial pressures, internal disagreements and changes in university governance sometimes made life very difficult for the Law School. An epilogue touches on recent history, since the year 2000, but it is no more than a sketch. It will be for others, working when archival and digital sources for the period have become available, to write a narrative of these years, including the impact of the COVID-19 pandemic.

The archives of the University of Adelaide provided much of the source material for this history. The richness of the early records preserved there was recognised by their inclusion in the UNESCO Australian Memory of the World Register in 2013. The expansion of Law School management in the 1970s produced another large archive, running through to the early 2000s. These are outstanding sources for the history of the university's management and operations, but they have the limitations of official records, filtering the daily life of the Law School through what was committed to paper. The record of student experience is dominated by matters that brought students into contact with the administration, such as assessment, complaints, and student representation on committees. Student publications allow more of their voice to be heard, as do memoirs, oral histories, and responses to an online questionnaire sent to graduates for this project. Research was to have been supplemented by new oral history interviews, but owing to the pandemic, they were fewer in number than originally planned, one of several ways in which COVID-19 affected the project.

PREFACE

This history of the Law School could not have been completed without the unstinting help of the staff of the University of Adelaide Archives and the Barr Smith Library. I particularly thank Helen Sims, Andrew Cook, Mariah Long and Sue Coppin for all their work in making the wealth of material in the Archives available to me. Paul Babie and Wilf Prest supported and aided the project from the start, and Horst Lücke and John Keeler generously gave me access to personal papers and passed on many recollections of their long association with the Law School. I have benefited greatly from the work of other historians, including the centenary history of the Law School, *Law on North Terrace*, Greg Taylor's publications on South Australian legal history, Peter Moore's books on the legal profession, and Tim Reeves's publications on Dr Duncan. Judith O'Connor and Joelie Cook made available archival records at the Supreme Court Library, and Michael Ryan very kindly facilitated access to correspondence about Dr Duncan. Marina Loane and Zoe Smith provided expert research assistance. Parts of chapter 2 first appeared in the *Adelaide Law Review*, and I thank the editors for permission to republish them here. The former students and staff who participated in interviews and responded to the online questionnaire for this project gave their time and their varied memories of the Law School, enriching this history, and I thank them for their generosity.

Foundations: 1883–1896

The settler lawyers who worked in the Province of South Australia, as its constitution named the colony until Australian federation in 1901, came initially from the legal professions of England and Ireland. There, legal training was based on apprenticeship and self-education rather than courses of instruction. When, in 1850, the Supreme Court of South Australia first provided for the admission of locally trained practitioners, it followed the same model. The only training was service under articles of clerkship, the 'articles' being the formal agreement, common to law and other professions, that bound a clerk to work for a practitioner for several years, in return for instruction. A clerk, or more often the clerk's family, usually had to pay the practitioner a large sum of money, or premium, for this privilege, and clerks often went unpaid. In England, service under articles was the method of training attorneys or solicitors rather than barristers, although they, too, could serve a form of apprenticeship, through pupillage with a practising barrister. In South Australia, unlike Australia's eastern mainland colonies, the profession was unified, and barristers and solicitors were trained in the same way. The use of articles and an exam under rules of court aligned local training with the education of English solicitors, rather than the less formal system of socialisation and self-education conducted by the inns of court, custodians of entry to the English bar.

Increasingly, learning acquired through apprenticeship was tested by exams. In 1836, the year the Province of South Australia was established, new English rules of court required attorneys to pass a written exam before admission to practice. The South Australian rules of 1850 likewise required examination before admission, but they did not say what the exam would cover, and evidence of the content of the exams is scanty. Long after they had risen to eminence in the profession, Samuel Way and Josiah Symon traded stories in court about the admission exams they passed in Adelaide in 1861 and 1871. They had been questioned without warning on private international law and admiralty law, esoteric subjects for later students.[1]

To acquire the knowledge tested in the admission exams, clerks relied mainly on the practitioners to whom they were articled and on their own reading. Coaching was also available, for those who could afford it. The coaching or cramming industry was well established in England, and traces survive of its presence in South Australia. A practitioner remembered 'the old system of no teaching or assistance during articles—six weeks with a crammer and a mere form of examination'.[2] An observer wrote in 1881: 'There is one well-known legal coach in Adelaide who prepares the young men for their examination in from nine to twelve weeks' coaching, according to the density of the pupils' ignorance.'[3] One who provided such coaching was J. Walter Smith, a practitioner with a doctorate in law from the University of London, whose series of short books made legal information accessible for the general public. When, in 1881, he applied unsuccessfully for the university's Hughes chair in English, he cited his experience in preparing students for exams in law and in moral philosophy. Another coach was Frederick d'Arenberg, who later became a long-serving part-time lecturer at the Law School. The prospect of coaching barristers in classics and history attracted an eccentric Anglican priest, Alfred Ernest Spooner, to Adelaide in 1884. He wrote to the university in dismay on finding that the new law school had destroyed his prospects. How much success Spooner would have enjoyed is doubtful. Contemporary newspapers in Australia and New Zealand document his career, as he moved from one unsuccessful venture to another and accumulated fictitious distinctions, among them self-awarded doctorates in divinity and law.[4]

The patchy instruction provided by practitioners and a few coaches left a substantial unmet demand for law teaching. The University of Adelaide, established in 1874, could provide it, to the benefit of both the university and its students. The university's low early enrolments were a public embarrassment, although government grants and a substantial philanthropic endowment eased its financial burden. As one newspaper put it: 'At present the cost is absurdly out of proportion to the number of students receiving instruction.'[5] In 1877 only ten students who had passed the matriculation (entrance) exam commenced study, although another twenty-nine non-matriculated students, most of them women, attended lectures without being eligible for degrees. Law teaching could boost these numbers substantially. An opportunity came from the educationalist Charles Pearson, who had turned down the Adelaide chair of history three years earlier but in 1877 was facing unemployment, having been forced out of the headmastership of the Presbyterian Ladies' College in Melbourne because of his involvement in radical–liberal politics. He contemplated giving a series of lectures in Adelaide on constitutional law. The university tested the market by writing to potential students, and twenty-four replied that they would attend. But Pearson was soon appointed by Victorian premier Graham Berry as a royal commissioner on education ('paid by Berry for his Berryistic politics', as Adelaide chancellor Augustus Short saw it) and could not come to Adelaide.[6]

The university now had twenty-four prospective law students, one of whom had also inquired about a full degree course in law. The council began to investigate the prospects for more law teaching. It appointed a committee chaired by Samuel Way, who was both the chief justice and the university's honorary vice-chancellor. Way did not have a university education, but he devoted time and energy to the University of Adelaide, becoming its chancellor in 1883 and remaining in that office for more than thirty years. He became the central figure in the establishment of the Law School, chairing the successive committees that shaped its curriculum and, as chief justice, connecting the university with the Supreme Court, whose rules on admission to practice gave the new course its central role in training for entry to the profession. The committee sent a second circular, testing interest in a longer course. Twenty-two articled clerks said they would enrol in a degree course, an impressive figure when compared with the size of the practising profession, estimated at eighty-five or ninety in 1871. At around the same time, four practitioners volunteered to give occasional lectures for articled clerks, independently of the university. The Law Debating Society, established the previous year as the Articled Clerks' Association and recently renamed, tried to bring the practitioners and the university together, but no more was heard of their lecture series.[7]

Despite the encouraging response, the committee decided it was not yet time for a degree course. It would require a full-time professor and probably two lecturers as well, they said, and the cost was not yet justified. The council agreed. Part of the problem was the makeup of the students who had indicated their interest in enrolling. The committee checked their names and found them unsatisfactory in some unspecified way. Many were approaching the end of their articles (ten of them were admitted to practice in 1878 or 1879) and were unlikely to enrol in a three-year course. Only one, Thomas Hewitson, a schoolteacher, went on to complete the course when it eventually began. Another problem, raised by the Law Debating Society, was that many had not passed the matriculation exam, which had become a prerequisite for articles only recently, in 1876, and would be needed for entry to a degree course. The most likely law students were not clerks part-way through their articles, for whom matriculation and a three-year course could be daunting obstacles, but those who were about to begin or were in their first year. They were likely to have matriculated, and they could more easily fit the course into the duration of their articles. For these newer clerks, the admission rules of 1876 offered an incentive to enrol in a degree course, since graduation in law or arts at a recognised university shortened the term of their articles from five years to three and exempted them from admission exams.[8]

Of those who told the committee they would enrol in lectures or a degree course, twenty-five can be identified. Sons of legal practitioners, civil servants and members of other professions were over-represented; articles of clerkship were expensive, and it was difficult to find them without personal connections. The respondents' parents included a former crown solicitor (William Bakewell), the clerk of the House of Assembly (George Beresford), the deputy registrar-general (William Carter), a judge of the Supreme Court (Randolph Stow), the court's librarian (Charles Nash) and a stipendiary magistrate (John Varley). Another five respondents had parents or close relatives in the legal profession, and the fathers of two more were medical practitioners. Other parents had businesses of various kinds. Judah Moss Solomon's father, Emanuel Solomon, was a merchant and former member of parliament who had been transported to Van Diemen's Land as a convict before moving to Sydney and then Adelaide. He is a reminder of the presence of transportees in a colony where freedom from the convict taint was a point of pride.[9]

§

Willing students and the university's need to increase enrolments soon led the council to revisit the prospects for a law course. In 1881 a second committee, again chaired by Way, reported on establishing courses in law and biology, the latter as a precursor to the opening of a medical school. Its report addressed the problem of finance by turning to money already available to the university: the fund donated by Walter Watson Hughes to establish chairs in classics and English literature. The chair of English was vacant; if the terms of the gift were altered to allow its use for the general purposes of the university, the professor of English could be replaced by lecturers, and a professor of law could be appointed. Adding the one or two law lecturers foreshadowed by the committee could follow, after two years. While the necessary arrangements were made, the vacant Hughes chair could be filled by a temporary professor, appointed for one year.[10]

This plan had the great advantage of using existing finances, but there was an obstacle. The terms of the Hughes endowment had statutory force under the university's founding act of parliament, and Hughes, while generous, was a prescriptive donor whose consent to new uses of the fund could not be taken for granted. His deed of gift to the university not only designated the disciplines in which the Hughes chairs were established, but also gave Hughes the right to choose the first two professors. Hughes had rejected an attempt in 1873 to change the terms of the deed, and in response had sought to revoke his gift and redirect it to other purposes. This disaster was averted only when the South Australian government promised financial support for the university. Hughes lived in England, and approaching him about the chair of law would take time. For this purpose, Way, who did not know Hughes, enlisted the aid of Sir Thomas Elder, the university's other founding benefactor. In the meantime, the university made its plan public. This enabled the Law Society, which represented the practising profession, to consult its members in a public meeting. Encouraged by Way, who 'in an eloquent speech pointed out the desirability of members of the Bar prior to admission having a University degree', the meeting unanimously backed the university's plan.[11] But counting on Hughes's consent was risky. Communicating through Elder's brother-in-law and business partner, Robert Barr Smith, Hughes rejected the scheme, since it would allow the university to detach his gift from the named chairs—indeed, from any professorships at all—and 'possibly to dissociate his name with the foundation of the University'.[12] He was willing for his gift to be reallocated to support three chairs instead of two, but this unattractive alternative required reductions in the salaries attached to the two existing chairs, and the council did not pursue it.[13]

The remaining option was the original proposal of 1877: the appointment of a full-time law teacher, preferably a professor. The level of public support was encouraging. The *Register* had been sceptical about reconfiguring the Hughes chair, but it came around after that plan fell through. A law faculty would be 'a means of greatly augmenting the usefulness of the Adelaide University' and would probably double the number of matriculated students.[14] Others welcomed the benefits to the public that would result from improved standards of legal education. Developments were watched by the colony's flourishing regional newspapers, among them the *Kapunda Herald*:

> In the profession the law of the survival of the fittest prevails with a vengeance, but the unfitness is always demonstrated at the expense of the unfortunate client, who has some right to be protected from the young harpies who, innocent of any knowledge of law, are yet licensed to charge fees for mismanaging the business entrusted to them. One way of remedying this evil is to make the educational standard higher.[15]

The completion in 1882 of the first building on the university campus, later named the Mitchell Building, provided a permanent base for classes previously held in rented accommodation in the city. At the building's opening, the governor, Sir William Jervois, endorsed the establishment of a law course: 'It is a matter of the highest importance for the welfare of the community that law should be treated, not as a trade, but as a science. The law student should commence his professional studies in a scientific manner before he becomes lost in the intricacies of practice.'[16] Perhaps Jervois's private secretary, Frederick Pennefather, had a hand in the speech; he would later become the university's first professor of law. Presiding as vice-chancellor, Way dangled before the audience the added enrolments a law course might bring to the university, which was still sometimes reproached for having few students: 'If all the gentlemen who are studying for the legal profession in this colony became students of this University we should add at least 50, and probably 60 students to our numbers.'[17]

In August 1882 the council considered a proposal from Way's committee that included, for the first time, compulsory university study for all new locally trained lawyers:

> The Committee have the honour to report that it is desirable to establish a Law School or Faculty of Law in this University, provided that with respect to gentlemen hereafter articled as Law Students, the degree of LL.B. of this University be substituted for the present intermediate and final examinations, and be made a compulsory qualification for admission as practitioners of the Supreme Court.[18]

Compulsion would guarantee enrolments. Way later wrote: 'In no other way could we have kept the Law School going here.'[19]

Compulsory university study was a rarity in legal training in the common-law world. It was foreign to the English legal system, from which the colonial laws of South Australia were derived; English legal education was provided largely outside the universities. In Australia, only Victoria (since 1872) made all new local entrants to the profession study at university, and the University of Melbourne had the country's only law school, in the sense of educating students to become practitioners. At Sydney, the Faculty of Law was confined to examining, supplemented intermittently by lectures. Sydney's chancellor, Sir William Manning, wrote in 1887: 'Unfortunately, we have not yet a Law School [sic] in our University.'[20] A professional-entry course was established three years later, after a bequest by merchant John Challis transformed the university's finances. In New Zealand, the federated University of New Zealand took over the examining of new entrants to the profession from the Supreme Court in 1890, but law teaching was initially provided only in the South Island, at Otago University and Canterbury University College. In the United States, educational barriers to entry to the profession had been lowered in the nineteenth century, in the broad egalitarian movement identified with Jacksonian democracy, a trend that had echoes in Canada. In both countries, university law courses grew in the later nineteenth century from a small base, preparing students for external admission exams and conferring higher professional standing, but they were not mandatory.[21]

In South Australia, the reasons for compulsory university study were partly local and pragmatic, but the change was also part of broader movements towards the consolidation of professional standing and the systematisation of legal doctrine. The story passed down to Way's successor as chief justice, Sir George Murray, was that Way had to persuade practitioners of the need for university study:

> The late Chief Justice saw the advantages offered by the lectures and examinations at the University as a substitute for an examination without systematic teaching at the Court but he had great difficulty in persuading the older members of the profession who had not been at a University, and yet had become learned and distinguished lawyers, that the change was desirable.[22]

The plan met stiff resistance in the university council, led by John Hartley, inspector-general of schools and one of the university's founders. He was 'strongly opposed to any scheme which would compel all future practitioners in the Supreme Court to be LLB's of this university', he told the council, although his reasons were not recorded.[23] The council was at first evenly divided on this part of the Law School scheme, and it passed only on a second vote.

Elsewhere, Way was pushing at a half-open door. Maintaining and improving professional status was a concern of many associations of lawyers in the common-law world, as it was in other professions. Educational standards, both perceived and substantive, influenced social status and earning capacity. The council of the Law Society, when it convened the meeting of members that endorsed the university's plan for the Law School in November 1881, said that the plan would 'tend considerably to elevate the status of the profession'.[24] Barriers to entry also increased the economic value of practitioners' qualifications, by limiting the number of new entrants. At the same time, practitioners had a business interest in maintaining an adequate supply of new lawyers to recruit as employees and partners. In many cases, the interest was a close family one, heightened by the desire of fathers to see their sons established in the profession; the number of sons of lawyers who expressed interest in legal study in 1877 prefigured a recurring theme in the Law School's history.

The Law Society's evolving response to the university's plans hinted at these concerns. The broad outline of the law course, including the key principle of compulsory university study, was endorsed at the meeting in November 1881, but the Law Society's council was more circumspect when it considered the details of the proposed curriculum the following August. It now proposed that the full LLB course would not be the only qualification for admission to the profession. There would be a shorter alternative course, comprising only doctrinal subjects and without Jurisprudence, Roman Law and International Law. Way's committee agreed, recommending that students taking the shorter course 'be granted a certificate of competence conferring no academic status but for the purpose of qualification for permission to practice [sic]'.[25] This became known as the final certificate.

The creation of a shorter alternative to the LLB may have pacified Hartley (council records throw no further light on his stance), but it complicated the university's choices in framing the curriculum. In 1877 Way's committee had envisaged that legal study would begin with the first year of the BA course (including Latin, but omitting Greek, Natural Philosophy and Chemistry). Two years of law subjects, plus Logic, would follow, making three years in all. The law subjects were not specified, and when the committee turned to the details in 1882, it removed most of the arts subjects and spread the law subjects over three years. Latin remained until the Law Society opposed it, although school-level Latin persisted as a prerequisite for the LLB subject Roman Law. The committee then dropped the last of the arts subjects, Logic. The eight remaining subjects of the degree course were identical to those for the Melbourne LLB, covering Roman law, property, jurisprudence, constitutional law, obligations, international law, wrongs (civil and criminal), and procedure.[26]

Newspapers joined the debate about broadening the minds of LLB students by making them study arts subjects. The *Advertiser* was at first happy with the curriculum's balance between legal doctrine and 'those subjects which are of a more scholarly and ornate character'.[27] It endorsed the creation of the certificate course as a more achievable goal for articled clerks. After a second look, it suggested adding arts subjects to the LLB, to suit students who (like some of their Oxbridge counterparts) studied law without intending to practise, and for 'encouraging advanced culture among our embryo judges'.[28] Even ancient Greek, a sticking point for many practical-minded critics of colonial higher education, should be an option. The *Register*, often reluctant to echo its competitor, praised the 'purely professional nature' of the course.[29]

Academic matters came under the supervision of the Faculty of Law, a governing board comprising the teaching staff and representatives of the university council and the Professorial Board. Later generations might have thought this arrangement inevitable, but it was not to be taken for granted in 1882. The idea of a faculty as a disciplinary division for teaching or examining was familiar from British universities, but in Australia the word had a second meaning, a board or committee that supervised departments in the relevant discipline. In this sense, the Faculty of Law was the university's first and, for a time, only faculty. Other disciplines were governed directly by the council and the Professorial Board, until faculties were established in medicine in 1885 and in arts and science the following year. The council kept overall control, however, and the Faculty of Law's statutory function was merely to provide advice. Endorsement of its recommendations was far from automatic.

Early drafts of the faculty's founding statute survive in the handwriting of William Barlow, the Irish-born legal practitioner who had recently resigned as the university's part-time registrar and librarian. In September 1882 he gave detailed form to the scheme adopted by the university council. The faculty was initially to be chaired by a president rather than a dean, perhaps to avoid confusion with the dean of the Professorial Board, who was a faculty member ex officio. In early drafts, the professor of law, once a chair had been created, became dean automatically. Providing instead for annual election of the dean opened the way for the appointment of someone other than the incumbent professor. This opportunity came to be used frequently when a new professor was settling in. The dean (but not the professor of law) was made a member of the Professorial Board. This body was short-lived at Adelaide, but many of its functions were later performed by the Education Committee.[30]

The uncertainty about the title of the faculty's presiding officer is a reminder that the office of dean was an innovation. It did not come from Oxford or Cambridge, where deans were college chaplains, not presiding officers of faculties. At Harvard, the office was a novelty when Christopher Langdell became the first dean of the law school in 1870. The universities of Sydney and Melbourne did not immediately appoint deans or establish faculty structures when they opened, but both had done so when Adelaide followed their example in 1882. Chairing meetings was the common function of deans at all three Australian universities, but their broader roles varied. At Sydney, the law deanship seems to have been merely titular until Justice William Windeyer of the Supreme Court became dean in 1883. He facilitated the establishment of the new law course and held the deanship until it passed to the first professor of law, William Pitt Cobbett, in 1891. Melbourne quickly developed a pattern of influential, long-serving law deans, and only fifteen people held that office from the inauguration of the Melbourne faculty to 2012. The Adelaide deanship, by contrast, rotated frequently: the dean in office in 2012 was the thirty-fourth person in that role. The number was inflated by a practice of appointing full rather than acting deans during professorial absences and interregnums, but the record also reflects the collegiate nature of the faculty board and the responsibilities accepted by its external members. Down to 1950, only half of the Adelaide law deans were full-time teachers, the others being practitioners who were members of the faculty.[31]

The faculty model had special advantages in professional disciplines, by creating a formal structure for the participation of lawyers who would not otherwise be directly involved in the running of the school. At Adelaide, the university council was to choose two of its members each year to join the faculty, effectively creating places there for lawyers who were not lecturers, and any Supreme Court judges on the university council were faculty members ex officio. The professors and lecturers in law completed its membership. The involvement of the profession was strengthened by provision for the use of external examiners who (at the suggestion of the Law Society) would be vetted by the judges.[32]

Amendment of the rules of court concerning admission to practice completed the framework for the new course. The amendment, published at the start of February 1883, made the LLB or the final certificate essential for the admission of locally trained practitioners. The university's statutes and regulations for the law course were published in the same issue of the *Government Gazette*. Clerks already serving under articles were exempt from the new requirements, but the university regulations gave them an incentive to enrol, by allowing them to begin in the second year of the degree course if they had passed one of the Supreme Court's exams.[33]

§

The law course had taken shape, but who would teach it? In August 1882 the university council decided to seek two part-time lecturers, each at a salary of £200 a year, as recommended by Way's committee.

The council also agreed that the Hughes chair of English should be advertised at a salary reduced by £200, evidently to make room for the expenses of the new law school. Hope persisted that the Hughes professor might be used in the law course. Changing the Hughes endowment was now out of the question, but some law subjects might piggyback on the Hughes chair if the professor's teaching load was increased in return for extra pay. An early plan for the university's chair of English had included constitutional law among its many teaching responsibilities, alongside modern history and political economy. The scope of the chair had since been narrowed, but it still covered mental and moral philosophy (psychology and ethics, in modern terms) along with English language and literature. In October 1882 the university found a polymath willing to take the chair with the additional subjects. He was Edward Ellis Morris, an English schoolteacher who had studied law, classics and modern history at Oxford and had recently resigned as headmaster of Melbourne Grammar School. Along with the chair's core subjects of English and philosophy, he was willing to teach jurisprudence, constitutional history, Roman law, ancient and modern history, and political economy. Whether Morris could handle this encyclopedic collection was never put to the test. Within a month of his acceptance of the Hughes chair, Morris was offered a newly created professorship of English, French and German language and literature at the University of Melbourne. The Melbourne council asked its Adelaide counterpart to release him, and it generously agreed. Morris's replacement was unable to teach legal subjects, and the plan to add law to the Hughes chair was abandoned.[34]

The last of the Hughes schemes having failed, the university advertised for two law lecturers in January and February 1883, to cover the full range of LLB subjects and to begin work at short notice, at the start of April. One lecturer, for a salary of £200 a year, would cover jurisprudence, Roman law, constitutional law and international law. The other, for £300, would teach property, obligations, wrongs and procedure, subjects that demanded 'a practical lawyer', as the *Register* noted.[35] The two posts could be combined, and the duration of the appointment was two years. The salaries might attract young practitioners keen to supplement their incomes, but the workload of four subjects each was heavy, and the *Advertiser* found the pay 'absurdly low' for the labour involved.[36]

A young English lawyer who was living in Melbourne, Walter Phillips, was selected in March 1883 to fill both lectureships, becoming the Law School's first full-time teacher. Born in 1855, he was the son of a fruiterer and market gardener. After passing the University of London's intermediate law exam, he studied at Cambridge with great success, graduating LLB with first-class honours in 1878 and winning several scholarships. He was capable and popular, elected secretary of the Cambridge Union, the student club and debating society. Phillips was called to the bar in London in 1879, but the following year he emigrated to Victoria. His health had broken down, if Way's much later recollection is accurate, and his close friend at Cambridge and the London bar, George Waterhouse, was Australian. If better professional prospects had drawn him to Melbourne, he was disappointed: he had 'no opportunity of discharging any work as a Barrister', he said.[37] Like some other briefless barristers, he used his time for writing. He contributed an article on Confucius to the *Victorian Review* and perhaps published unsigned work elsewhere, as his obituarist suspected. He looked for opportunities outside the law, applying unsuccessfully for the position of registrar at Adelaide in 1882.[38]

A trip to England delayed Phillips's arrival in Adelaide until September 1883. Rather than wait for him to arrive, the university hurriedly found temporary lecturers to inaugurate a skeleton course with teaching in two subjects. Both were Adelaide practitioners in their thirties who had been called to the bar in London after studying at Oxford or Cambridge. Aretas Young, the lecturer in property, was the son of Sir Henry Young, governor of South Australia from

1848 to 1854, and his wife Augusta, after whom Port Augusta was named. Born at Government House, Adelaide, in 1849, but educated in England, he was an Oxford graduate in law and modern history (BA, 1871) and was admitted to the South Australian profession in 1879. He was praised for his skill in cricket and tennis, though hampered by lameness. His students could see his name frequently in the news in 1883, in a controversy over immigration policy and in court proceedings where he was alleged (wrongly, the court decided) to have tried to smuggle some of his luggage through a customs check on returning to Adelaide. He later became a stockbroker, and died in Adelaide in 1933. Robert Moore, the lecturer in obligations, was born and schooled in Adelaide, the son of a surgeon. He studied at Cambridge, completing the law and history course in 1873, but he did not graduate. The story was later told that he had objected to paying the university's fees for taking the degree. He was admitted to practice in South Australia in 1876, a year after being called to the bar in London. He died in Adelaide in 1890, at the age of thirty-eight, remembered as 'unassuming, studious, self-contained ... an excellent cabinet lawyer', a bibliophile, and a drafter of acts of parliament and rules of court.[39]

The teachers were not the only appointments needed to establish the new school. The council elected two of its members to the Faculty of Law: William Barlow, who had joined the council after retiring as registrar, and Frederic Ayers, son of former premier Sir Henry Ayers, who had studied at Cambridge and was called to the bar in London before practising law in Adelaide. At the faculty's first meeting, on 27 February 1883, they joined Way, who was automatically a faculty member as the only Supreme Court judge on the university council, and the dean of the Professorial Board, William Fletcher. Barlow was elected dean. Neither he nor Ayers, who also served as dean, ever taught in the Law School, but they became an important connection between the faculty, the council, and the university senate. The latter, composed of the university's graduates, had a veto over university statutes and regulations; Way became a member only in 1892, when he first received an Adelaide degree. The two lecturers automatically became members of the faculty, but they were in a minority there. Law teachers would have shared, not exclusive, control of the academic affairs of the Law School.[40]

§

The hopes of Way and others for a boost to student numbers were realised. In the Law School's first year, its students dominated the university's enrolments in degree courses, accounting for thirty-five commencing students out of a total of forty-seven. To Way's surprise, most students chose to study for the degree rather than the cheaper certificate, which initially attracted only four enrolments. Law thus made little contribution, at least at first, to the university's largest category of students, those not studying for degrees. There were 106 of these in 1883, including sixty-one women. Soon, however, law was joined by a discipline with greater needs and greater philanthropic pulling-power, when the Medical School opened in 1885. The combined enrolments in Law and Medicine led some to call the university 'the Adelaide "Pill and Brief Factory"', or so the *Register* said in 1889, but Medicine drew ahead.[41] By 1894 there were forty-one undergraduates in Medicine and only sixteen in Law (along with fourteen studying for the final certificate). The medical staff comprised the Elder professor of anatomy and sixteen part-time lecturers, while the teaching staff of the Law School numbered only three. Science, too, was growing, with endowed chairs in chemistry and mathematics (the former established as a separate chair to serve the medical course) and a lectureship in mathematics and physics.[42]

Law lectures began without fanfare on 3 April 1883, when Young took the first-year class in Property, and Moore took Obligations for the clerks who commenced in second year. The timetable suited articled clerks who were allowed an hour for classes at the start or end of the working day, but students in other full-time work would find it difficult to attend. All lectures began at 8.45 am (despite a request for evening lectures from students who had to get to court after morning classes). In 1884, when third-year subjects were added, lectures at 4 pm were introduced. Phillips quickly made a good impression, as a reporter noted: 'Mr Phillips promises to be popular with the students, as he has a pleasant manner and is an evident enthusiast in his profession.'[43] Charles Hodge, the university registrar's clerk in Phillips's time, remembered him: 'He was a jovial single man. When not obsessed with lecture work he would come into my room sometimes and give me a hand with my work.'[44] How he found the time is a mystery. As the *Advertiser* said on his departure, Phillips, 'by some extraordinary endowment of nature, possesses both the learning and the physical strength to do such encyclopaedic work—work which for extent and variety far exceeds anything anywhere else required of a single lecturer'.[45]

The class lists of 1883, published in the university calendar, record the earliest students to pass the Law School's exams. They are a cross-section of Adelaide's more prosperous families, along with a minority of junior civil servants and teachers who were able to support themselves as they studied. Of the twenty-seven students who passed one or more exams, three-quarters were born in South Australia, and the average age was twenty-one. Parents in government service were well represented, as in the university's market research in 1877. The students' fathers included two stipendiary magistrates, a government surveyor, the colony's under-secretary (head of the Chief's Secretary's Department) and the sheriff of the Supreme Court. Five students were employed in various government offices. The largest group were sons of businessmen, such as pastoralists, brokers, merchants and retailers. Two were sons of medical practitioners, two of teachers, two of ministers of religion, and two of army officers. Three were brothers of respondents to the 1877 surveys, among them Reginald Stow, son of Justice Randolph Stow. The youngest and the oldest students were more unusual. Francis Knowles, who was in his mid-thirties when he began the course, was born in Barbados, the son of an officer in the British Army commissariat. William Tucker was only fifteen when he enrolled, but he had been an exceptionally successful student at the Grote Street Public School in Adelaide, where his father taught, and at Prince Alfred College. For those without other financial support, scholarships such as those won by Tucker were the only means of access to secondary schooling, and thus to higher education. The Advanced School for Girls, established in 1879, was South Australia's only state-supported secondary school until state high schools were established in the twentieth century, and even it charged fees.[46]

All but three of the students who passed in 1883 were later admitted to practice in South Australia, but their careers were mobile and diverse. Ten practised in other parts of Australia. Francis Knowles worked in the South Australian Survey Office and, after graduating with an LLB, taught at Prince Alfred College and elsewhere. He did not practise as a lawyer (his later occupations included auctioneer and land agent), but the law held his interest, and he was an unsuccessful candidate for a doctorate of laws in 1906–10. His classmate Thomas Hewitson, who lectured at the Law School in the 1890s, also maintained an interest in research, earning a doctorate in 1922. He later became president of the South Australian Industrial Court. Law graduate William Tucker was awarded the South Australian Scholarship in 1885 for study in the United Kingdom. He had an Adelaide degree in arts as well as law, but he studied medicine in Edinburgh, with equal success, until failing health drove him to Switzerland and then home to Adelaide, where he enrolled in the Medical School but died in 1892, aged twenty-four. Another student of 1883 who turned from law to medicine was William Gething, who qualified as a physician after practising law and became resident medical officer at Port Adelaide. James Anderson, who graduated in 1884, later had the unique distinction of serving briefly as attorney-general of South Australia (in 1905) without being elected to parliament. Two of the students gained Commonwealth legal appointments, Gordon Castle as principal registrar of the High Court and Commonwealth crown solicitor, and Noel Webb as a judge of the Court of Conciliation and Arbitration. Two (Frederick Joyner and Alexander Melrose) were patrons of the arts, and James Anderson and Alfred Gill were chairmen of the South Australian Football League. Frederick Whitington became an Anglican priest and biographer of the university's second chancellor, Bishop Augustus Short.[47]

The Adelaide course quickly attracted potential students from outside South Australia. The Melbourne and Sydney LLB degrees were available only to BA graduates, but there was no such hurdle at Adelaide. In 1885 Albert Edward Jones wrote from Melbourne seeking permission to sit the Adelaide law exams without attending lectures. The Faculty of Law had not yet adopted a policy for such applications, and it consented. Jones was allowed to remain in Melbourne (aside from sitting exams) for the whole of his course. He obtained copies of Adelaide lecture notes and graduated with an LLB in 1888.[48]

Jones had originally intended to move to Adelaide, and when other students outside South Australia (among them Jones's brother) sought enrolment, the faculty usually refused. There was an exception for students from Western Australia, which had no university of its own until 1911, and no law school until 1927. The University of Adelaide, and the South Australian legal profession, had close connections with Western Australia. The university conducted school-level exams there, as it did in South Australian regional towns. Five of the Law School's successful students in 1883 were later admitted to practice in Western Australia, joining a steady progression of Adelaide practitioners who headed west for a time, many drawn by the prosperity of the Western Australian goldfields. The University of Adelaide began to hold law exams in Perth in 1898, and Western Australian residents continued to enrol in the Adelaide law course into the 1920s.[49]

Exemption from attendance at lectures was vital for absentee students, since the university enforced attendance and lecturers kept rolls. Law students were not allowed to sit exams unless they had attended three-quarters of the lectures, and only the council could excuse them, although it usually followed the faculty's advice. Students articled in offices more than ten miles from the university were excused, but those working closer to the campus were expected to attend. Port Adelaide was just within the ten-mile radius, as one student found when he was refused exemption from attendance despite working at the Port from 9 am to 5.30 pm. Running for parliament was an acceptable excuse. George Ash was already a member of the House of Assembly when he began the law course in 1891, at the age of thirty-one. He was excused from lectures in the election campaign of 1893, as was Herbert Angas Parsons, the future parliamentarian and judge, when he ran in 1897.[50]

There was little comment on the style of the early law lectures, but the high failure rate in the law exams was the subject of a flurry of newspaper debate in 1886. The two or three subjects for each year of the degree course made up a single, collective exam. Failure in one subject meant failure of the whole year, and all subjects had to be repeated. Only eight out of forty-one students completed their years by passing all subjects in November 1885, although another six passed when the exams were repeated in March.[51]

The exam papers were daunting. Like papers in other disciplines at Adelaide and elsewhere, they often contained a long series of questions that it would be impossible to answer fully in the available time. Students, who had to work entirely from memory, would answer as many as they could and hope that they gathered enough marks to pass. In 1883 none of the law papers had fewer than ten questions, and Obligations students were confronted with twenty, mixing doctrinal summaries and random points of detail:

State the general law on the validity of contracts in restraint of trade, and give the leading case on the subject. Where the restraint is partial and in respect of space, how is the distance measured from the point whence it is to be reckoned – by the nearest mode of access or as the crow flies?[52]

Even the students' prescribed text for this subject, Pollock's *Principles of Contract*, said it would be impossible to give an adequate account of restraint of trade, and its summary of 'the principles and the short results of the authorities' took up ten pages.[53] Lecture regurgitation supplied the key to many such questions, but only if the lecturer reached the topic. Writers to the newspapers complained that exam questions went beyond the lectures. The newspapers' editorial opinions were ambivalent: the failure rates were unsatisfactory, but high standards were good. Frederick d'Arenberg, the only examiner to comment publicly, was uncompromising: 'The conception of real earnest study is utterly unknown to the majority of law students', he said.[54] The fuss was loud enough for the attorney-general to ask to see the exam papers, but it soon faded.[55]

Behind the scenes, Phillips put ideas for course reform to Samuel Way. More lecturing was needed, he said, and therefore more lecturers. Fees should rise to pay their salaries. The failure rate did appear 'absurdly large', but that was because unprepared certificate students tried to pass the extra subjects needed for the LLB: 'Of course they fail and the diversion of their attention from the compulsory subjects causes failure in them at the same time.'[56] The answer was to exclude certificate students from the LLB, by adding first-year arts to the degree course. These proposals initially went nowhere, but they became part of a prolonged debate about the curriculum after Phillips's departure.

The plentiful enrolments of the Law School's early years did not last. Overall law enrolments started falling in 1887, and students shifted to the cheaper certificate course. Its enrolments outnumbered the LLB in most years from 1893 to 1898, during the economic depression of the 1890s, and total law enrolments did not exceed thirty from 1892 to 1896. These hard times put great pressure on the Law School's finances. Law was, as registrar Charles Hodge later noted, the university's only faculty without an endowment. Arts, Medicine and Science each had at least one endowed professorial chair, while all the Law School's expenses had to be met from the university's general revenue. The university's overall enrolments also fell sharply, and the council pressed hard for a reduction in the gap between the Law School's expenses and fee income. However, its repeated requests to the faculty from 1890 onwards produced little result. The faculty resisted higher fees, since articled clerks already had to pay large premiums to their employers, and a fee increase 'would cause much dissatisfaction amongst the students and their friends, and might lead to an agitation to abolish compulsory attendance at lectures'.[57] Compulsory university study for lawyers was under attack in parliament in the mid-1890s, and the faculty sought to avoid further assaults on its vital monopoly. The Law School's main expense was the salary of its single full-time teacher, and so little was spent on the Law Library and part-time lecturers that little could be saved. However, the end-of-course fees to obtain the degree or final certificate were raised, and, in a show of support from the profession, the Law School's external examiners all agreed to forego payment in 1895. The faculty offered status as a consolation, appointing them for three years and naming them in the university calendars as honorary examiners. They remained a target for cost cutting, but the faculty defended them, 'in the interests of the students, for the maintenance of the prestige of the Law School, and for the promotion of professional interest in the work of the Law School'.[58] External examiners continued to be an important link between the school and the practising profession.[59]

§

The LLB was not the only degree offered by the new law school. The university's founding act of parliament provided for a doctorate of laws, the LLD, although it was not until 1885 that regulations gave shape to the degree. It began, not as a research degree, but as a higher test of legal knowledge, assessed by exams and an original essay on an approved topic. The faculty chose to prescribe topics, as if for an essay competition, rather than leave candidates to devise their own.

The universities of Melbourne and Sydney also awarded LLDs based on subject exams, although at Sydney the exam was limited to civil law in the original Latin. The subject of the Sydney exam suggests its likely model, the Oxford doctorate in civil law, although until 1887 the Oxford DCL was available automatically, after a prescribed period, to holders of a bachelor's degree in civil law. Sydney, Melbourne and Adelaide joined a trend in which doctorates were awarded only by increasingly stringent examination. A parallel is found at Trinity College, Dublin, where assessment for the LLD comprised essays on civil law and then, from 1878, exams in designated subjects, or a thesis or book. A future dean of the Law School, Jethro Brown, earned a Trinity LLD in this way.[60]

The first candidate for the LLD exam was the resourceful Albert Jones. He asked for a book list in 1891: 'Of course you know that the junior members of the Bar have usually plenty of time on their hands which they ought to occupy in reading, and although my success hitherto has been greater than I could have expected, still I am not an exception from the rule.'[61] He was still asking nearly a year later: a candidate would be 'a madman', he wrote, to attempt the exam without knowing which books it was based on.[62] The faculty had been busy in the meantime. Professor Pennefather, who was in England, prepared a book list, after consulting authorities including the doyen of English legal history, Frederic Maitland. Pennefather thought the bar should be set high: 'Considering our LL.B. is only a pass degree, the exam. for the LL.D. shd be a stern reality.'[63] The number of exams was increased to five, and a reading list was eventually published.

Jones confronted a stern reality indeed, sitting fifteen hours of exams over three days in November 1892. His thesis on the influence of Roman law on English equity was judged 'brilliant', but he failed nonetheless.[64] Undaunted, Jones prepared for a second attempt in 1894 but withdrew, having found the subjects had changed and he was working on the wrong material. His final attempt, in 1900, was an ingenious scheme to get a certificate from Adelaide saying that his thesis had passed. He aimed to use the certificate to get a doctorate from the University of Bologna, but Adelaide declined to play along. Jones became a well-known Melbourne practitioner and eventually got his long-sought doctorate in law from the University of Salamanca.[65]

§

The university's new building was impressive, but it had little space for the Law School. A law lecture room was included in the architectural specifications, but only as part of a future extension, and law lectures were peripatetic in the early years. In 1886 classes had to move between four different rooms, and the faculty complained about the 'extreme difficulty' Phillips had in obtaining a room in which to lecture.[66] By the turn of the century, a dedicated law lecture room had been found, and in 1902 it moved to the Prince of Wales Building, whose first stage extended the ground floor of the central building eastwards. The lecture room there, in 'the semi underground dungeons', also housed the Law Library.[67] Adjoining the lecture room was the law professor's office, 'exceedingly bare, unfurnished, and uncomfortable', according to the occupant.[68] Music from the nearby Elder Conservatorium disrupted lectures, and when the frosted windows were open, the male law students could taunt the predominantly female music students as they went to and from classes. One such incident in 1905 led to a formal complaint, and the professor of law, John Salmond, called the whole Property class to a faculty meeting to be reprimanded.[69]

The university acquired a collection of law books as the nucleus of a law library. The University Library was small, its books 'rather scanty in number', as Governor Jervois observed in 1883.[70] When English barrister Clifford Holgate visited the library in 1884, he found that 'Classics, Law, History, and Medicine make a poor show'.[71] The city's principal law library was at the Supreme Court, where articled clerks were able to consult a wide range of textbooks, law reports and statutes from Australia, England and the United States. Students made such free use of the collection that in 1888 the judges warned them to return missing books, on pain of being barred from the library. Professors, but not students, were allowed to use the parliamentary library, on days when parliament was not sitting. Local booksellers had to adjust to the new demand for law books. Soon after lectures began in 1883, students complained that some of the prescribed texts could not be purchased in Adelaide.[72]

The first of the University Library's law books was Robert Phillimore's four-volume commentary on international law, a fitting first accession considering the library's later strength in international law. It remains in the library today. In 1883 a grant of £100 from the university council funded the acquisition of more textbooks, along with books of reference and Chitty's compilation of British statutes. The Attorney-General's Department sent South Australian legislation and law reports, and the governments of the other Australasian colonies sent or promised their statutes. The council granted funds for the purchase of a set of the authorised law reports of the United Kingdom, going back to 1866, which Walter Phillips obtained in London. An adequate collection of monographs was more difficult to build. The annual allocation of £50 for law books was enough to buy only about thirteen titles at 1883 prices, and in the lean 1890s the grant shrank to £20. It was just as well that the benefactions of the Barr Smith family to the University Library, which began with a munificent gift of £1000 in 1892, were partly available for law books. A pattern was established of fluctuating, often inadequate, funding for the Law Library, supplemented by occasional catch-up grants for major acquisitions.[73]

§

By November 1885, Phillips had become restless as the Law School's overburdened full-time lecturer. He gave a year's notice, saying that he would return to England to practise at the end of 1886. Unspecified news from overseas led him to offer to stay on for 1887 if his salary rose from £500 to £600, and the council agreed. He was farewelled in December 1887 with a 'most brilliant' banquet given by law graduates and students.[74] In England, he married and spent time in legal practice, but in 1898 he returned to teaching, becoming the inaugural professor of law at Yorkshire College, later the University of Leeds. He retained his widespread interests; in 1904 he was working on Assyriology. 'I am afraid that I have dreamed much of my life away', he wrote.[75] In 1918 he noticed that the chair of law at Adelaide had fallen vacant, and expressed interest in returning. His sons were living on the coast for the sake of their health, he told the chancellor: 'At times I have thought longingly of Adelaide where I think my boys would gather strength.'[76] But it was to a different warm climate that Phillips moved. The Adelaide chair was not advertised until the following year, and when Phillips was approached, he replied that he had accepted an appointment in Egypt. He became a professor at the Khedivial Law School in Cairo, where British hegemony had led to the appointment of a series of British lawyers.[77]

As the date of Phillips's delayed resignation approached, the university received an application for the lectureship from a favoured candidate, the Irish-born lawyer Frederick Pennefather. Law, theology and membership of the Irish Protestant gentry were intersecting themes in Pennefather's career. His ancestors were landowners, soldiers, parliamentarians and lawyers during the Protestant ascendancy in Ireland. His grandfather, Edward Pennefather, was lord chief justice of Ireland, and his father, another Edward, was a barrister. Study at Trinity College, Cambridge, consolidated his social standing and developed his interest in theology, the discipline in which he graduated, as a Bachelor of Arts, in 1874. He maintained strong connections with the Church of England. He became a member of the Anglican synod in Adelaide, chancellor of the Diocese of Dunedin in New Zealand, and lay secretary to the Lambeth Conference, the ten-yearly world assembly of Anglican bishops, in 1897. The extent of his qualifications in law became a point of contention in Adelaide, but they were at least as good as those of most English or Irish barristers. In 1875 he took a short law course at the University of Dublin, as required for admission to the Dublin bar, and he then returned to Cambridge, graduating in 1877 with a master's degree in law, available to arts graduates by completing a selection of undergraduate law subjects. He was admitted as a barrister in London and Dublin, and practised on the south-eastern court circuit in England. He described himself in this period as 'engaged in professional & literary occupations'.[78] Over the years, under his own name or as 'Irishman', he authored monographs and articles for newspapers and journals (notably the London *Spectator*), ranging across travel, penology and the Irish Unionist cause. In 1891, during a visit to England, he earned a Cambridge LLD, based on a short thesis and oral exam.[79]

Ill health affected Pennefather for much of his life. He travelled in search of healthier climates, and in 1881 he had visited Adelaide. Writing from the Adelaide Club, where he became a member, he applied for the Hughes chair of English language and literature and mental and moral philosophy. He was quick off the mark: his application was dated the day after the death of the incumbent professor, John Davidson. The appointment became bogged down in the attempt to use the Hughes endowment for law teaching, and in the meantime Pennefather found a different opening. The governor of South Australia, Sir William Jervois, knew the Pennefather family and appointed Frederick as his private secretary. He continued in this role when Jervois became governor of New Zealand in 1883. During this period, Pennefather wrote his only substantial legal publication, a guide to civil procedure in the Supreme Court of New Zealand, co-authored with lawyer Edward Balcombe Brown. In 1886 he resigned as private secretary and travelled to London as one of the representatives of New Zealand at the Colonial and Indian Exhibition, where he delivered a series of lectures on New Zealand topics. In February 1887 he began legal practice in Wellington.[80]

Early in November 1887, the Faculty of Law recommended to the university council that Pennefather should become the new full-time lecturer. The decision seems already to have been contentious, and it was reached only after 'considerable discussion'.[81] Many later jumped to the conclusion, with some reason, that the driving force behind Pennefather's appointment was Samuel Way. Pennefather's work as Jervois's private secretary involved contact with Way, who mixed socially with the governor, joined him and his ministers in the Executive Council when death sentences were considered, and would deputise for him in the event of Jervois's absence. Pennefather addressed his letter of application to Way, and Way was present at the faculty meeting that recommended his appointment. The two men became friends, travelling together and collaborating in the running of the Law School.

Whatever the extent of Way's influence, it did not extend to getting the university council to ratify Pennefather's appointment at the first attempt. The council sent the recommendation back to the Faculty of Law and asked for the position to be advertised. It was now one lectureship, rather than the two that Phillips had combined. Of the eight resulting applications, five were easily put aside, coming from recent Melbourne or Adelaide graduates who did not even send the usual testimonials. A sixth came from Thomas Hewitson, the former schoolteacher whose Adelaide LLB was among the first awarded by examination. Now in legal practice, he was a winner of two successive Stow Prizes, given to the best student in each year. Among his testimonials was one from the attorney-general, Charles Cameron Kingston.[82]

None of these applications greatly appealed to the faculty, which narrowed the choice to two: Pennefather, and a thirty-five-year-old Sydney barrister, William Cullen, who held a doctorate in law from the University of Sydney. Cullen's testimonials were impressive. They came from (among others) the chancellor of the University of Sydney (former Supreme Court judge Sir William Manning), the chief judge in equity of the New South Wales Supreme Court, the attorney-general of New South Wales, the editor of the *Sydney Morning Herald*, and the future prime minister, Edmund Barton, at that time a barrister and member of parliament. Cullen had lectured in mathematics at residential colleges attached to the University of Sydney. Pennefather had no teaching experience, but he was a successful public lecturer. Sir James Hector, chancellor of the University of New Zealand, testified to his 'singular ability' in this regard.[83] His other testimonials, too, were impressive, coming from Jervois (then governor of New Zealand) and two New Zealand judges. Justice William Richmond commended Pennefather's energy: 'We all know that the chair of Jurisprudence is one in which a Professor may easily go to sleep. I do not believe there is any danger of this in a man of Mr Pennefather's character.'[84] The Faculty of Law again recommended him. Still unconvinced, the council interviewed Cullen in person and then divided equally between the two candidates. Presiding as chancellor, Way broke the deadlock by voting for Pennefather. A last complication remained. The council kept open the possibility of appointing more lecturers to share the teaching load, as Phillips had proposed. Pennefather's duties, and perhaps his salary, would then be reduced, although none of this was mentioned when the post was advertised. The council offered Pennefather appointment for only one year, at Phillips's original salary of £500. He baulked at this uncertainty, but when reassured that the post would not be abolished, he accepted.[85]

Within a fortnight, criticism of the appointment appeared in Adelaide newspapers. It began with a letter to the *Advertiser* from 'Alumnus', whose information appeared to come from inside the university council, although the writer's memory, or source, was at fault on the number of applications received and the chronology of events. The letter hit hardest in its claim that Way's decisive vote for Pennefather overrode the objections of other lawyers on the council. The council's minutes did not record how members other than Way had voted, but Alumnus's description fits three likely dissentients:

Archdeacon George Farr, headmaster of St Peter's College, who had legal training and a doctorate in law from Cambridge; legal practitioner William Symon; and Adolph von Treuer, a business manager whose Estonian law degree had earned him an Adelaide LLB. The claim about the voting was repeated in leading articles in both the *Advertiser* and the *Register*, without contradiction. Alumnus went on to contrast Pennefather's record with Cullen's prizes and degrees, and denigrated Pennefather's Cambridge LLM. Another letter, from 'Magister', said the Cambridge degree was 'far inferior' to the Adelaide LLB.[86] Alumnus concluded: 'The choice made by the council and the manner of that choice are extremely distasteful both to the University and to the legal profession.'[87]

The *Advertiser* joined the attack: 'The advertisement was a farce, the applications and testimonials were disregarded by the Law Faculty, and their recommendation was in favor of a gentleman who had not succeeded in showing any sufficient qualifications.' Pennefather 'deserted the Court of Chancery to take refuge during ill-health in the agreeable occupation of secretary to a colonial Governor'. He had no experience of legal practice for the last six years. (The writer was unaware of his legal practice in Wellington.) He 'should not have been appointed'; he was 'blindly preferred to better qualified men'. Alumnus said nothing about Way's relationship with Pennefather, but the *Advertiser* implied that Way's 'private friendship' had determined his vote.[88]

Another line of attack soon emerged. The council had forgotten to renew Way's appointment as chancellor, and the *Register* claimed that Way's casting vote was therefore illegal. The council remedied this embarrassing lapse by reappointing Way and ratifying its selection of Pennefather. *The Lantern*, a persistent gadfly of Adelaide institutions, retorted that although the university might ratify Way's actions, 'there is one thing they cannot do, and that is to make a very shady transaction look OK'. Cullen 'was lugged over from Sydney only to find out that he was made a fool of'.[89] The council left the newspaper debate to burn itself out, in the absence of more fuel for the fire.[90]

The appointment of a mere lecturer may seem a surprising issue for the newspapers to pursue, but the *Advertiser* made a case for the significance of the Law School: 'This faculty is in some respects the most important in the University.'[91] Its degrees served as a licence to practice (the writer conveniently overlooked the need for articles and admission by the Supreme Court) and as training for public life. Other factors piqued public interest. The university was a focus of civic pride and of close and critical attention from graduates and other observers. Some had opposed Way's appointment as chancellor in 1883 because he had no university degree. The oversight that accidentally interrupted his chancellorship was bound to be noted by his critics and by those who relished the mishaps of tall poppies.[92]

The qualifications of Pennefather and Cullen were not as far apart as Alumnus suggested. Both were practitioners without extensive experience. Cullen's academic record was superior, but Pennefather could point to his book on civil procedure. They were separated by class and social connections. Cullen had supported his education through scholarships, against the wishes of his father, a farmer; Pennefather's father and grandfather were graduates respectively of Oxford, and Trinity College, Dublin. Cullen's later career as a barrister, parliamentarian, chief justice of New South Wales and chancellor of the University of Sydney, when compared with Pennefather's more modest record, seemed to confirm the university's critics, although it also hinted that the Law School might not have satisfied his interests and ambitions for long. Whether Cullen would have accepted appointment for only one year is uncertain; the offer was never made.

A surviving lecture on international law shows Pennefather's style as a teacher. He drew students into the rather forbidding topic, the Bering Sea arbitration of 1893. International law, he began, is

the most interesting & the most useful of all the subjects that come within the legal course ... The world is our field; the persons of whom we speak are vast nations; the new questions wh[ich] are perpetually arising take us at one time to Europe, at another to Asia, & not infrequently to the remote islands of the Atlantic & the Pacific.[93]

This engaging start is followed by long and dry quotations from the records of the arbitration, perhaps intended to be copied down at dictation speed, as was common before students had ready access to their own copies of primary sources. They were not always captivated, on Pennefather's own admission. Describing the many distractions of a visit to an Indian temple, he added: 'The worshippers, with true Oriental calmness, took no more notice of it all than a student at the University of Adelaide does of the sound of the lecturer's voice.'[94]

Illness soon disrupted Pennefather's life in Adelaide. He suffered in its hot summers and travelled regularly to gain relief from the heat, often to Yankalilla on the Fleurieu Peninsula and sometimes further afield. He was ill in December 1888 and went, on medical advice, to New Zealand, returning in March. He was in New Zealand again the following summer, this time with Way. They had travelled together before and, in 1891, they journeyed through India, supplying Pennefather with material for articles in Adelaide newspapers and a book, *A Visit to India*.[95] Pennefather did not envisage that his stay in South Australia would be a long one. In April 1889 he wrote to Jervois: 'My throat troubles me at times, but I hope I shall be able to hang on till November, by which time I shall have settled my "Broken Hills", started a few more protégés, and be quite ready to shake the South Australian dust off my feet.'[96] A few months later, these dealings in mining shares were sufficiently interesting and profitable to keep him in Adelaide, despite his dislike of the city:

I detest the place more than ever, but I rather think I shall stay; I have been turning my attention largely (& successfully) to mining affairs lately, and am as keenly interested in Centrals, and Block Fourteens, and Baker's Creeks, as I once was in Maori legends or the N.Z. Rules of Court. It does not give me the slightest pleasure, but one may as well roll money together as do anything else; at any rate, it is a form of excitement.[97]

The university valued him, accommodating his desire to travel and offering him promotion. Pennefather told Jervois: 'They have been pressing me to stay on here for another year; the bribe this time being the status of a Professor.'[98] On the motion of journalist and legal practitioner James Smith, in April 1888 the university senate pointed out to the council that Pennefather was already performing the duties of a professor and that his one-year appointment was undesirable. No immediate action was taken, but when the senate raised the question again, the Faculty of Law and the council agreed to act. In December 1890 the university's seal was attached to a grandiloquent commission making Pennefather a professor:

> Confiding in your learning, ability, and integrity the University of Adelaide aforesaid by virtue of the above mentioned Act, and by virtue of the Statutes made & passed thereunder, and by virtue of all other enabling powers doth nominate and appoint you the said Frederick William Pennefather to be Professor of Laws in our University.[99]

By a narrow margin, Pennefather was the third professor of law in an Australian university, behind Edward Jenks at Melbourne (1889) and William Pitt Cobbett at Sydney (February 1890). As an economy measure, the university did not increase Pennefather's salary of £500 a year, with the result that he received only half as much as the professor of natural science and £100 less than the lecturer on physiology. The professor of law remained the university's lowest-paid until Pennefather's successor, John Salmond, obtained an increase in 1900.[100]

§

The newly elevated status of the professor of law, and the university's confidence in him as a public speaker, were highlighted when Pennefather delivered the commemoration address at the annual graduation and prize-giving ceremony in December 1890. It was a chance to demonstrate that, despite the controversy, the university had chosen well in appointing him. As was usual at the ceremony, students made 'all sorts of foolish noises', and Pennefather was often inaudible.[101] However, the speech was reported in full in the newspapers, evidently from Pennefather's own text. He celebrated the university's progress and embraced the exclusion of professors from political debate (the university barred professors from sitting in parliament or joining political associations). Australian federation, much discussed after an intercolonial conference on the question earlier in the year, was, he said, no concern of a university professor, an attitude foreign to his counterparts at Melbourne and Sydney, both of whom joined the federation debate. Law reform, however, was a topic Pennefather was happy to address. He made an early and prescient call for an Australian federal system of admission to practice, so that lawyers admitted in one jurisdiction would be recognised in all. His suggestion that universities should merge to form 'one great Australasian university' was more fanciful. He called for the establishment of residential colleges and lamented the exclusion of 'the loftiest of sciences', theology, from the university. His most sustained argument was for the inclusion of broad contextual study in the law course: 'In order to be complete it must involve the study of ethics, of history, of politics, of economics.' English land tenure was an example: 'In order to understand it scientifically we must trace the history of the race from the time when they first emerged from the forests of Germany', along with 'the result of the contact between the rude Teutons and the effete Romans' and the history of feudalism. The law of contract had to begin with early Rome, constitutional law with the Anglo-Saxons. Pennefather envisioned a cultured university, strong in the humanities, energised by group spirit among the students, and avoiding potentially embarrassing political entanglements, as befitted a former private secretary to the governor.[102]

Pennefather deplored 'the undue prominence which is sometimes given in modern systems to natural science', but he allied law and even theology with science in some sense. This provoked the *Advertiser*, which questioned how theology could be scientific. Pennefather quoted a dictum of Edmund Burke: 'The science of jurisprudence, the pride of the human intellect.'[103] Calling jurisprudence (that is, legal doctrine, rather than legal philosophy) a science could have been merely commonplace, repeating, as it did, a phrase used by many legal writers. But Pennefather's pointed disparagement of natural science suggests more deliberation. He spoke of science in the sense of systematic knowledge, rather than empirical research. This differed from American writing that treated legal knowledge as a form of inductive, empirical science, and legal education as an introduction to the methods by which legal principles could be discovered. The centre of this thinking was the Harvard Law School, where the case method of teaching encouraged students to join in a dialogue with the lecturer and uncover legal doctrine through the selective analysis of reported cases, rather than learning settled legal rules laid out in lectures or textbooks. Pennefather's didactic historicism sat uneasily with this approach. It was not until the appointment of Jethro Brown as professor of law in 1906 that the case method received serious attention at Adelaide.[104]

§

In June 1888 Pennefather wrote to Samuel Way about reforming the Law School. Its staff, he said, should consist of a professor who 'will regard the appointment as a Profession' and at least one (part-time) lecturer, who would remain in practice.[105] The heavy teaching burden of the sole lecturer (comprising all eight law subjects) had drawn criticism from the *Advertiser* before Pennefather's arrival, and it was obviously unsustainable. As the faculty told the council: 'To carry out the work of the Law School efficiently is more than one Lecturer can perform.'[106] The council needed little persuasion. Two part-time assistant lecturers were appointed at the start of 1889 to teach Contracts and Wrongs. They were Thomas Hewitson and Alfred Gill, young practitioners with good Adelaide degrees, who had been unsuccessful applicants for Pennefather's lectureship.[107]

Other concerns raised by Pennefather were less easily addressed. He found students' knowledge of Latin inadequate for his lectures in Roman Law and said the matriculation standard should be raised. Articled clerks, who had to spend most of their time in their offices, should be discouraged from undertaking the demanding LLB course, at least in the standard time of three years. The duration of articles for LLB graduates, also three years, encouraged students to combine articles and the degree, to the detriment of their university studies. Students in the shorter certificate course had to be articled for five years, with the result that they, too, only studied part-time. But getting more students to study full-time, even if only for the first year or two, needed the cooperation of the profession and the Supreme Court, gained only after long preparation.[108]

Another of Pennefather's goals was to extend the LLB course. The faculty had previously supported such a move in principle, and reform was soon hastened, and complicated, by an emerging problem with the recognition of the Adelaide LLB outside South Australia. Each of Australia's three universities, following the British model, allowed graduates of recognised universities to take matching degrees without examination, admitting them *ad eundem gradum* ('to the same degree'), in the Latin phrase that designated the process. These degrees were commonly taken by graduates who moved to a new city and wanted to join a university senate or convocation composed of local graduates. The University of Adelaide issued open invitations for graduates of other universities to join its new senate in this way. The procedure was the basis for ceremonial awards of degrees to eminent visitors, in the absence of provision for honorary degrees, and university recognition of an external degree could facilitate admission to legal practice. The professions of the six Australian colonies were separate, and admission to practice in one colony did not necessarily entitle the practitioner to practise elsewhere. However, the colonies made periodic attempts to achieve reciprocity of admission, and holders of law degrees from universities in other jurisdictions enjoyed concessions when seeking admission. University recognition of external degrees was sometimes a prerequisite for these concessions.[109]

In 1889 the council of the University of Melbourne refused to recognise the Adelaide LLB as equivalent to its own, thus barring an Adelaide graduate, George Downer (nephew of South Australian lawyer and politician Sir John Downer), from entry to the Victorian profession. The council's reasons were framed in terms of academic standards, but they were also protecting enrolments in the Melbourne law course. The Adelaide course was shorter (Melbourne LLB students had to complete a BA first), and, as the Victorian Supreme Court was told in a related case, 'people were not likely to spend five years in Melbourne if they could get the same advantages by going to Adelaide for three years'.[110] The court ruled that the University of Melbourne had already recognised the University of Adelaide for other purposes, with the result that Adelaide law graduates could be admitted to practice in Victoria, but they were still unable to get *ad eundem* degrees at Melbourne. Pennefather wrote a detailed rebuttal of the Melbourne council's reasons, noting, among much else, that Adelaide did not readily grant exemption from attendance at lectures, so there was little risk of Victorians using Adelaide as a back door to get Melbourne LLBs. He also used a visit to Melbourne to argue Adelaide's case.[111]

Adelaide newspapers could have taken non-recognition by Melbourne as an affront, but instead they treated it as a salutary warning. The *Register* commented: 'No care is too great which tends to raise the value of degrees.'[112] The newspaper maintained its interest over the following years, using Melbourne's refusal of recognition to support changes in the Adelaide course, notwithstanding the Victorian Supreme Court's admission of South Australian graduates, which was prominently reported in Adelaide. The *Register* reviewed the university's annual report in 1890:

> We look in vain for any indication of the intention of the Council to raise the standard of the LL.B. degree to that of the same degree as conferred in Sydney and Melbourne. A Bachelor of Laws of Adelaide is a marked man in the colonies now. Whatever his own abilities he is not recognised as the equal of Bachelors of Laws in Sydney or Melbourne.[113]

The information was not quite up to date—Sydney had recently recognised the Adelaide LLB for the purpose of an *ad eundem* award—but the spur to action remained.[114]

In August 1888 the Faculty of Law had adopted a plan to extend the LLB course from three years to five, by dividing existing subjects. Two part-time lecturers would relieve the full-time lecturer of some of the increased teaching load. The plan was not proposed by Pennefather but by William Barlow. Pennefather criticised the heavy teaching load planned for the full-time lecturer and considered it was 'perfectly hopeless' to get students, especially busy articled clerks, to attend the six or more lectures needed each week in place of the current three.[115] Nor did he like the division of the existing subjects. The faculty compromised. A final scheme drafted by Frederic Ayers (serving as dean after Phillips's resignation) retained the divided subjects but renamed some, reduced the duration of the course to four years and cut the number of lectures.[116]

The council endorsed the faculty's scheme, but it met opposition in the senate. James Smith criticised the lengthened course and the increased fees it would entail. Journalist George Sutherland agreed: 'If they went on in this way it would be advisable to form a society for the prevention of cruelty to University students.'[117] The senate was equally divided, and the warden used his casting vote to refer the question to a committee. After long delays, the committee agreed to extend the LLB course, but not, as Barlow had suggested, by expanding the doctrinal subjects. Instead, it added two years of the BA course to the three-year LLB. The law faculty minutes rarely recorded strong feelings, but on this occasion, they captured Way's vehement objections:

> The Chancellor observed that he yielded to none in his desire to introduce a higher amount of culture among the students of law, and that although he should be glad to see the principles contained in the proposed Regulations in regard to the Arts Course adopted, he saw clearly that if this were done that [sic] the Law School so far as conferring Degrees was concerned would be destroyed, as the Students would with a few rare exceptions simply elect to obtain certificates instead of proceeding to the Degree. These altered Regulations if carried would be a death-blow to the School of Law.[118]

Two days later, the committee's proposals were debated in the senate, where they were introduced by James Henderson. A legal practitioner, he graduated in arts before the Law School opened and joined the university council in 1889. The refusal of recognition by Melbourne was the initial justification Henderson gave for the changes, but he was forced onto the defensive by the faculty's objections: 'It was said that they would by adopting the regulations break up the law school, but surely the University existed for something more than to enable students to become practitioners of the Supreme Court.'[119] As the debate continued at a second senate meeting, Henderson became more expansive, but less careful, saying that all the great or important universities made the BA a prerequisite for the LLB. The Adelaide degree was 'considered too cheap', he said.[120] Canon Frederick Slaney Poole tackled Way's objection head-on: 'It would be better to have the law school snuffed out than that it should lead a discredited existence.'[121] Sutherland pointed out that the changes would lift enrolments in the arts course: 'It was pitiful to see how few entered it.'[122] Only two students commenced the BA course in 1889, and seven in 1890.

Opposition to the added arts subjects was led by George Murray. Like Henderson, he was an Adelaide graduate in arts, but he went to England to study law and was called to the bar in London. His leading role in the senate debate was a foretaste of his future prominence. He was not yet a member of the Faculty of Law, but in 1891, aged twenty-eight, he became a member of the university council and a temporary lecturer, taking on a herculean teaching load of six subjects during Pennefather's absence on leave, while maintaining at least some of his nascent legal practice. Murray went on to become chief justice, lieutenant-governor and chancellor of the university. He did not, perhaps, much enjoy the pleasures of office. After he became chief justice, he confided: 'I should like to have been a painter or a singer, but it is too late now.'[123]

Murray told the senate that adding arts subjects would not help students to study law, and that it was undignified for Adelaide to attach too much weight to what other universities said about its degrees. According to the *Register*, he said that a Melbourne law degree was inferior, 'a good Arts degree, but a bad law degree'.[124] He corrected Henderson's claim about other universities: Cambridge was among the universities that did not make the BA a prerequisite, as Murray knew, being a Cambridge law graduate himself. John Hartley, the inspector-general of schools, saw self-interest behind Melbourne's decision, saying it 'was simply a species of protection'.[125] Pennefather seemed reluctant to take sides. He would not vote against the proposal, but he made a point that was usually missed in the frequent comparisons with Victoria. There, the LLB (as distinct from the shorter certificate course) was a prerequisite for admission to the bar, buttressing enrolments. Barlow took up this theme, saying that the changes could not be made unless the LLB became mandatory for professional admission.[126]

A persistent theme of the debate was culture. As Tamson Pietsch has observed, a common purpose of colonial universities was to develop the minds of their students both ethically and intellectually, and so cultivate the character of the citizenry. Murray argued that the study of law was itself a cultural education, but advocates for the inclusion of arts subjects in the LLB treated them as a desirable infusion of culture in a merely vocational course. This was a claim to the universal value of the subjects of the BA curriculum: mathematics, physics, languages and literature, logic, history, philosophy and psychology, Latin and ancient Greek. Most of these could pass as useful general knowledge, but the place of Latin and Greek in Australian school and university curriculums had become increasingly contentious in the 1880s, as they competed with the study of modern languages and science. Ancient Greek was compulsory for entry to the Adelaide BA course through the Senior Public exam, and in the BA itself, but few school students studied it: only eight of sixty-eight candidates for the Senior Public attempted it in November 1890. This filter on entry to the arts course would extend to the LLB, if it incorporated the first two years of the BA. Latin, on the other hand, was more widely taught, second only to English and Pure Mathematics in examinees.[127]

The idea that barristers should be educated in arts was an old one. In New South Wales, Queensland and Victoria, where the profession was divided, barristers were examined in a range of arts subjects, including ancient languages, science, literature and history, either in admission exams or in a degree course. Queensland barristers were still being examined in ancient Greek in 1891. The educational requirements for solicitors were lower and generally consigned non-legal subjects to preliminary exams, with matriculation as an alternative. The difference in status was a distant echo of class distinctions in the English profession, where university degrees (but not degrees in law) became increasingly common among barristers in the nineteenth century. This pattern helped to sustain social distinctions between barristers and solicitors, although mandatory educational qualifications for the bar grew only slowly.[128]

South Australia's fused profession left less scope for mandatory non-legal study. Its admission requirements were closer to those for solicitors in divided professions than those for barristers. Where the profession was divided, only solicitors undertook articles, but they were mandatory for all new practitioners in South Australia. Before the establishment of the Law School, the exams conducted under the auspices of the Supreme Court covered only legal subjects, although wider knowledge was required by making matriculation a prerequisite for articles. It was easier to extend the LLB course if the degree was mandatory for barristers and not for solicitors, thus guaranteeing some enrolments but leaving a pathway open for non-graduates. In Victoria, the partial fusion of the profession in 1891 led to the abandonment of the BA prerequisite for the Melbourne LLB, as the shorter certificate course became an option for barristers as well as solicitors. In South Australia, advocates of arts in the LLB could aim only to persuade students with more ambition or financial means to opt for the longer degree course. Students did eventually make this choice, and the final certificate course became less popular during the twentieth century, but the process was slow.[129]

Despite the dissenting voices from the Faculty of Law, the senate decided that the LLB curriculum should include at least two years of the arts course. The *Register* supported the decision: 'It will be a fatal mistake for the University to court popularity for its Law School by the device of granting degrees which are not fit to be recognised in other parts of Australia.'[130] Confronted with this division of opinion, the council sought a compromise. Barlow suggested the eventual solution. Some arts subjects would be incorporated into the LLB curriculum, which would extend to four years. The increased subject load in first year (from two subjects to four) would encourage degree students to defer articles, even if only for one year. New regulations for 1891 set out the details: the new subjects were two years of Latin (or one each of Latin and Greek), English Language and Literature, and Logic or Elementary Pure Mathematics. Mental and Moral Science became an alternative to Procedure. The doctrinal subjects would not be subdivided. To keep students up to the mark, they would sit exams at the end of each term, and they could be denied credit for class attendance if they were negligent or inadequately prepared. Fees increased, supporting the appointment of the new part-time lecturers.[131]

In the *Register*, Frederick d'Arenberg defended the plan to add two years of the BA to the LLB and attacked the 'emasculated programme' which would ensure Adelaide degrees continued to be recognised only as far as the Victorian border:

> If the young men of South Australia are so unambitious and so far behind the students of the rest of the world as to require this tender handling, they are certainly undeserving of even the shoddy degrees which have been hitherto conferred, and whose three magic letters only adorn their owners' names as far as Serviceton.[132]

Pennefather's reply questioned the benefits of a full two years of arts for law students, but he conceded that more needed to be done:

> So long as the law students continue to give up their whole working days to the offices where they are articled, making their University work a by-play, and there is no means of compelling anything more than a mere physical presence at lectures, I believe that the proportion of failures will continue to be as large as it has hitherto been; nor can I see how adding additional subjects for examination will help matters.[133]

Nevertheless, the compromise smoothed the path of the new curriculum through the senate, where it was approved with little debate. 'Thus was put to rest', the *Advertiser* commented, 'by a measure of compromise, a question which has for some time past been in agitation in local, legal, and academical circles.'[134]

§

Unlike his immediate successors, John Salmond and Jethro Brown, Pennefather did not make legal authorship part of his work at the

Law School. He continued a routine of teaching and travel, taking leave without pay in 1893 to visit Europe while Murray again replaced him. In England, he successfully lobbied for Adelaide undergraduates to get partial recognition for their studies if they transferred to Cambridge, a measure he had advocated in his 1890 commemoration address. Only a tiny number of students stood to benefit, but the concession was some compensation for Melbourne's earlier rejection. Pennefather's absences, however, were becoming troublesome. The council had initially rejected his application for leave in 1893, and after his return an anonymous writer to the *Register* criticised the 'excessively generous treatment' that had allowed him to be absent for two of the last three years.[135] When, in 1895, Pennefather again requested a year's leave to travel to England, the Faculty of Law took precautions, recommending to the council that it should reserve the right to terminate his appointment on three months' notice and that Pennefather should give six months' notice if he decided not to return. The main reason for his journey was to undergo surgery, probably for a rupture mentioned by Way. George Murray stepped in again to teach three subjects, and the rest were shared between Thomas Hewitson and two other Adelaide graduates now in practice, Rupert Ingleby and Leslie Stow.[136]

Before Pennefather left Adelaide in March 1896, he warned the university that he might have to resign while in England, and his resignation, on the ground of ill health, followed in August. There were no hard feelings. He joined a London selection committee for the vacant chair, working with South Australia's agent-general to find and vet candidates. His dislike of Adelaide had faded, and his farewell was affectionate. He presented a banner to the Law School, depicting the sword and scales of justice and the maxim that later adorned the moot court room: *'Fiat justitia ruat coelum'* ('let justice be done though the heavens fall'). He dispatched it to Way:

> I cannot send it without a certain feeling of pain, as it seems the final closing of what has been a very happy period of my life—the

time of my connection with the University. I shall always, as long as I live, watch with interest the careers of those whose [sic] I once knew as my friends and pupils.

Long may the Banner wave over a prosperous Law School and a flourishing University.[137]

Pennefather maintained links with South Australia. After serving as an acting judge of the Supreme Court of New Zealand in 1898–99, he returned to Adelaide and worked as private secretary to the governor, Lord Tennyson, for some months in 1900. During this visit, he began work on a draft criminal code for South Australia, under the auspices of the attorney-general, John Gordon. Greg Taylor has traced the evolution of this project and analysed the resulting draft, which Pennefather presented to Gordon on another visit to Adelaide. The code was introduced in parliament, but it was abandoned after Gordon left office to join the bench of the Supreme Court. In 1904 Pennefather became a reluctant landowner, on inheriting his family's property in Ireland, and he died in Dublin, unmarried, in 1921, at the age of sixty-eight.[138]

2

Scholars: 1897–1925

The future of the chair of law was uncertain when Frederick Pennefather resigned in 1896. His travel leave had been given 'on the understanding that the Council is to be free to make any arrangements for the continuance or otherwise of the Professorship'.[1] The council's repeated efforts to cut costs were one reason for this caution, as enrolments declined in the 1890s. The work of the Law School could probably be continued at less expense by abolishing the chair, as the faculty pointed out. The law course also faced a political threat. When the faculty considered Pennefather's application for leave, in November 1895, parliament was debating the Law Reform Bill, an omnibus measure introduced by the premier, Charles Cameron Kingston. It proposed to reshape legal education and abolish compulsory university study for new entrants to the profession, ending the policy that had guaranteed the Law School's enrolments. It would also allow women to become lawyers, a proposal that had broad support in the wake of parliament's decision in 1894 to give women the right to both vote and stand for election. Other parts of the bill made sweeping changes to court procedure to reduce cost and delay. Reform of this kind had been on the parliamentary agenda before, in 1892–93, in the form of two private member's bills introduced by a conservative member of the House of Assembly, Robert Caldwell. The measures were appealingly titled the Justice Attainment Bill and the Facilitation of Justice Bill. Caldwell was not a lawyer, but he had the help of Robert Homburg, the attorney-general in 1890–93. Neither bill was passed, but conciliation (or mediation) in private litigation was part of Kingston's policy platform at the 1893 election.[2]

Removing barriers to entry in the legal profession had a long history in the United States, where several states allowed anyone to practise law, within overarching restrictions of gender and race. The idea had less traction in Australia, but it did have supporters. In 1895 two members of the House of Assembly advocated opening the legal profession to every elector over the age of twenty-one, or to anyone who had 'a knowledge of law', however acquired.[3] A similar proposal surfaced in the Victorian parliament, during debate on amalgamation of the two branches of the profession in 1891. In New South Wales, parliamentarian John Neild, inspired by American experience, included the opening up of the legal profession among his many reform projects, repeatedly introducing his Law Practitioners Bill between 1891 and 1897. The bill, which would have abolished mandatory articles and simplified entry exams, passed the lower house on three occasions but failed to pass the upper house. Kingston toyed with the idea of ending the monopoly of legal practitioners over paid legal work and introducing 'free-trade in law', but the time, he said, was not yet ripe.[4]

Kingston's bill was introduced as the Labor Party made its first gains in the South Australian parliament. Labor members held the balance of power in the House of Assembly after the 1893 election, and Kingston's government, broadly liberal in composition, depended on their support. The government introduced a wave of reforms, of which the electoral franchise for women is now the best known. Law reform had special significance in South Australia, which had a long history of legal innovation. In particular, the Torrens system of titles registration had made dealings in land cheaper and more certain, partly by allowing land agents as well as lawyers to handle transactions. The memory of lawyers' resistance to that reform was used against the profession in the debate on Kingston's bill.[5]

In place of the university course, Kingston proposed to substitute a maximum of two (later three) years of articles, and exams in seven strictly doctrinal subjects, to be conducted by a board of examiners whose members included the attorney-general. 'We also declare that no examination shall be required in any dead or foreign language or constitutional law. These are of no use to the ordinary solicitor', Kingston said.[6] No candidate for admission would be required to take a degree, to attend university lectures, or to pass an exam before commencing articles. These provisions would override the admission rules made by the judges of the Supreme Court. The government, Kingston said, 'intended to provide means whereby men might become lawyers without subjecting them to unnecessary delay or unnecessary cost'.[7] He was known for his 'bludgeoning oratory', and he used it here with evident zest.[8] Kingston ridiculed the two years of Latin (or Latin and Greek) that were added to the LLB in 1890, citing a university Latin exam: 'They had to translate and comment on a passage. He could not translate it, but he could comment on it and say it was rubbish. If any one had that knowledge in his mind the quicker he got rid of it the better.'[9] 'You know the trash there is in the University education', he said.[10]

Training would be made modern, practical and useful, in contrast with the antiquities of the degree course. It would also be made South Australian. Kingston criticised the appointment of outsiders to posts in the Law School, and made an exam in the statute law of South Australia a prerequisite for admission. If it was a paradox that this up-to-date training would be ensured by reverting to the old system of instruction through apprenticeship alone, it did not trouble him. The careers of eminent lawyers proved the success of the old system: 'All our judges, all our leaders of the bar had been trained under the old school.'[11] He could have added that, in Australia, only South Australia and Victoria required new lawyers to study at university. Caldwell probably spoke for many of the bill's supporters when he told the House of Assembly: 'He respected Universities, but why should they force people to go through them?'[12]

Kingston spoke of the legal profession with the knowledge of an insider—he had been a practitioner since 1873 and a Queen's Counsel since 1888—but he had not studied at a university. His friend, the barrister Patrick McMahon Glynn, a graduate of Trinity College, Dublin, in arts and law, noted the disadvantages of low educational requirements in the United States, and traced English efforts to improve legal training, but his didacticism and moderation carried little weight with members who cheered attacks on an unpopular profession. Nor were they persuaded by an open letter from the Law Society to Kingston, which protested that 'the proposed reduction of the qualification for admission will materially diminish the protection at present afforded to the public against insufficiently trained practitioners'.[13] Such arguments had more success in the Legislative Council, which was dominated by conservative independents elected on a restricted franchise and hostile to Kingston. Among them was John Stirling, a Cambridge graduate who had been called to the bar in London but now occupied himself with his family's extensive pastoral and mining interests in South Australia. From 1896 he was a member of the university council, where he joined the leader of the opposition, Sir John Downer. Stirling reiterated many of Glynn's points in defence of educational standards. As for barriers to entry, he pointed out that the premiums paid to obtain articles cost far more than university study. James Howe, a conservative representative of Mid North farming interests, was one of the few members to show some fire in opposing the bill. The admission provisions would 'create uneducated parasites', he told the upper house. 'Very soon they would see signs down the street—"Hair cut and law advice given, 6d."'[14]

The immediate threat to the university was averted when the Legislative Council rejected the Law Reform Bill in December 1895, but Kingston promised to reintroduce it. 'We have too many lawyers and too little justice', he said in his election policy speech the following year.[15] The bill made little progress, but when Kingston tried yet again in 1898, the Faculty of Law took the unusual step of persuading the reluctant university council to petition parliament. Many of the petition's arguments had already been heard in parliament, but one was often overlooked: lectures benefited articled clerks, and the university would probably be unable to continue them if enrolment was not mandatory. As the petition put it: 'Systematic teaching is an immense advantage to Articled Clerks.'[16] Kingston took the petition seriously enough to attack it in parliament. He was sorry that the university had 'seen fit, as it were, to enter the political arena'. It had made the mistake of never appointing a local lawyer as 'chief law lecturer'. 'It was to this gentleman from outside that the petition suggested the training should be confided of those who seek admission to the South Australian bar.'[17] The bill again passed the House of Assembly, but it failed in the Legislative Council. Most of the clauses concerning entry to the profession were nullified before the bill lapsed.[18]

Kingston included the Law Reform Bill in his policies for the 1899 election, but he lost his majority in the Assembly at the end of the year, and later governments did not share his interest in legal education. The large majorities by which the bill was passed in the Assembly did not translate into a lasting impetus for change, inside or outside parliament. Few other parliamentarians advocated it in their election speeches, and the smattering of newspaper commentary and correspondence on the question divided along party lines, the *Advertiser* for and the *Register* against the government and the bill. Its failure removed a cloud hanging over the future of the chair of law and, indeed, over the Law School itself, whose already precarious finances would have suffered under a regime that encouraged law students to rely on self-education and apprenticeship alone. The Law Society was the school's ally in the defence of educational standards, which protected law firms against an influx of new practitioners. The university was well served by its connections with the Legislative Council, and by the electoral system that shielded the upper house from the voters who supported Kingston.[19]

§

There was no urgency for the chair of law to be filled on Pennefather's resignation, thanks to the arrangements already made for teaching during his year of leave. But his resignation was widely reported, and potential candidates for the chair began to ask the university for information. One was William Jethro Brown, professor of law and modern history at the University of Tasmania. The son of a prosperous farmer near Mintaro, in South Australia's Clare Valley, Brown studied as a pupil–teacher at the Moonta Mines public school on the Yorke Peninsula, where the head teacher was his uncle, William Torr. The connection was an important one. In 1886 Torr was offered the headmastership of Way College, a new Bible Christian school named after the Reverend James Way, father of Samuel, the chief justice, who took an active interest in the project. Lacking the university education expected in such a role, Torr drew on a recent inheritance from his late wife to study at Oxford, before returning to the headmastership. Brown, aged eighteen, went with him.[20]

The trip became an extraordinary academic collecting expedition, in which the two men earned seven university degrees between them (and another seven without examination, under *ad eundem* provisions or their equivalents). They began at Oxford, where Torr took a BA, with honours in theology, in 1889 and passed the Bachelor of Civil Law exam in 1891 (the degree was awarded two years later). Brown studied as a non-collegiate student, without entering a college or taking a degree, but enrolled at Cambridge, where he graduated BA and LLB in 1890, with first-class honours in law. Torr, too, passed Cambridge exams, but residence requirements prevented him from taking a degree. Then, at Trinity College, Dublin, Torr graduated LLB (1891) and worked on an LLD that was conferred in 1892. Brown gained his own Dublin LLD in 1893. The two men were both called to the bar in London, before returning to Australia in September 1891. Their acquisitive roaming took advantage of Dublin's loose residence requirements and generous credit for study elsewhere. A doctorate was a prestigious ornament for a headmaster and a valuable qualification for Brown, who was now heading towards an academic career.[21]

Like Pennefather, Brown had a connection with Samuel Way: Brown's father had been Way's neighbour at Mintaro. Pennefather, too, was a supporter. He had hoped that Brown would replace him as acting professor during his previous year of leave, in 1893, but by the time negotiations between Pennefather and the university council were complete, Brown had accepted a lectureship at Tasmania and was unavailable. He had difficulty deciding on his next move, a pattern repeated later in his career in Adelaide. He was in touch with Way, who told the university council in December 1896 that Brown would probably be available for the chair. Way invited him to apply, but a conversation with Brown left Way with the impression that he 'did not seem inclined to become an applicant'.[22] Yet, soon afterwards, Brown asked again for information about the chair. Reluctance to leave Hobart was understandable. Brown, still in his late twenties, had only recently been promoted to professor, and the salaries of the two chairs were the same (although Tasmania had made a temporary reduction, because of the university's financial difficulties). The upshot of this indecision was that Brown remained in Hobart, where he was establishing a record of productive and original interdisciplinary scholarship.[23]

Another who sought information about the chair was John Salmond. Six years older than Brown, he was working as a lawyer in New Zealand, where he had moved as a teenager from his birthplace in northern England. He combined legal practice with scholarly authorship, having already published two books, *Essays in Jurisprudence and Legal History* and *First Principles of Jurisprudence*. A scholarship had taken him from the University of Otago, where he graduated in arts, to University College, London, where he took a bachelor's degree in law. He let Adelaide's registrar know that he would apply when its council had decided what to do about the chair, and he sent copies of his publications.[24]

It was not until January 1897, after Brown's unpromising response, that the council decided to seek other applicants and advertise the chair. The London committee had reservations about all its candidates, and when the faculty recommended Salmond, the council agreed. Way was not present at the faculty meeting, but he, too, found Salmond the most eligible candidate. 'I am glad he has the appointment', he wrote.[25] The initial term was three years, and the salary remained a prudent £500, despite Way's preference for an increase to £600. Way reported favourably to Pennefather in November 1897, when Salmond had been in Adelaide for five months: 'Your successor is not much to look at, but the Registrar tells me that the students seem very well pleased with him.'[26] With longer acquaintance, Way revised his opinion of Salmond, who (perhaps not coincidentally) delivered in person some 'pungently frank criticism' of one of the chief justice's judgments.[27] Way later said that Salmond was 'a very dull dog, without the faintest gleam of humour and he is not much liked by the students. He resents any question or discussion.'[28] The editor of Salmond's text on torts, R.F.V. Heuston, sought to correct the record: 'Way was a man of rather egotistical and domineering temperament ... Those who remember Salmond testify to his friendly manner and engaging conversation.'[29]

With John Salmond's appointment, Anne Salmond became the first wife of a Law School professor. The role was significant, so much so that it could affect a candidate's chances, as it did in Vice-Chancellor William Mitchell's assessment when Coleman Phillipson applied for the chair in 1919. Anne Salmond was born Anne Bryham Guthrie in 1862, daughter of James Guthrie, influential secretary to the commissioners who managed the River Tyne and the port of Newcastle, and author of a history of the river. Anne became a schoolteacher, before marrying John Salmond in 1891. They had three children. Her talents made her well suited to Adelaide's social and intellectual upper crust. She was 'a most clever and cultured lady', an examiner in French at the university and a familiar speaker at the May Club, a women's social club that was 'taken up by all the leaders of society … It is quite the thing to belong to it.'[30] Her talk about the author and women's suffrage campaigner Millicent Fawcett showed her interest in feminist politics, as Alex Frame has observed. The fragmentary records of her life in Adelaide show her as a gifted public speaker and a regular participant with her husband in the balls and receptions that brought together the wealthy and the successful at Government House, the Town Hall and elsewhere.[31]

§

The makeshift teaching arrangements that had covered Pennefather's absence ended when the chair of law was filled. Salmond was allowed to choose the subjects that he would leave to part-time lecturers on his arrival. He divested himself of Property, and Evidence and Procedure, which were taught by a new lecturer, Frederick d'Arenberg. Salmond taught the remaining six subjects himself. D'Arenberg became the first of a group of long-serving part-time lecturers who seemed almost inseparable from their subjects. He taught Evidence and Procedure for twenty-two years, a period rivalled by Edward Benham (Property, 1910–37), Earnest Phillips (Mercantile Law, 1938–59) and Louis Whitington (Companies, Partnership, Bankruptcy and Divorce, 1938–60). Benham was a member of the Faculty of Law for thirty-eight years, and both he and Phillips served as dean during absences of the professor. Whitington and Phillips (who kept his parents' unusual spelling of his first name) had extensive legal practices, while the university was more important for d'Arenberg and Benham. Both applied unsuccessfully for the chair of law, d'Arenberg after Pennefather resigned and Benham in 1919.[32]

D'Arenberg had been called to the bar in London after graduating in arts at Trinity College, Dublin, but on arriving in Adelaide he worked mainly as an academic coach. His connections were useful: he migrated to South Australia with his brother and sister-in-law, David and Louisa Kelly, when David Kelly was appointed to the chair of classics. Later he practised in the Local Court. A student remembered him: 'Poor old Darry! The students used to tease him unmercifully.'[33] His day-to-day work in debt collection was a target for their mockery. Another student credited his high result in Procedure to his realisation that d'Arenberg repeated his exam questions after three or four years. His lectures, too, were recycled regardless of changes in the law. Edward Benham, by contrast, was authoritative, although he did little to engage his students. His biographer, Margaret Jennings, evoked his teaching:

> After turning off his hearing aid, he dictated rather dull, unin-spiring lectures, with little explanation or discussion. A hard examiner, he seemed reserved, remote and a very private person to his students, but they recognized his high ideals, his professionalism and his mastery of the law of property, and— beyond his earshot—called him Teddy.[34]

Benham left the bulk of his estate to the university, which used it for prizes, book acquisitions and a sculpture for the campus grounds, a monumental late bronze by Henry Moore.[35]

Part-time lecturers like these made up most of the Law School's teaching staff until full-time teachers began to predominate in the 1960s. Almost all were practitioners, grateful for the income from a lectureship, attracted by the status of a university appointment (a useful distinction in the career of an up-and-coming barrister) or willing to help when gaps arose through illness or sudden departures. They were not confined to the doctrinal subjects closely connected with legal practice, such as Evidence and Procedure. Jurisprudence, Roman Law and International Law were taught by practitioners for long periods. Some were on their way to greater things. Among them were four future chief justices (George Murray, Mellis Napier, John Bray and John Doyle) and eighteen future judges of the Supreme Court. These and lesser lights maintained the Law School's connection with, and dependence on, the profession it trained.

§

Outreach, to law graduates, the university and the wider community, was a theme of John Salmond's time at Adelaide. He was an advocate and organiser of the first of the university's annual dinners, in 1898, which brought together the council, staff, graduates and undergraduates and was attended by the governor. Three years later, a group of students and young practitioners organised the first of a series of annual Law School dinners. Like Pennefather, Salmond spoke at the university's annual commemoration ceremony, but his homily on keeping intellectual interests alive bored the students. They let out a 'long-drawn-out wild-beast yawn', which was 'most distressing to the Professor', according to the *Register*.[36] Salmond delivered an open lecture-course on commercial law in 1902–06 and had an interest in economics, a subject that was not yet part of the university's regular teaching program when he arrived. He proposed a series of evening lectures on political economy in 1898, but he wanted to be paid an additional £200 to deliver them, and the council baulked at the expense. The teaching of economics (aside from some incidental lecturing) began, independently of Salmond, in 1901.[37]

It was as a scholar that Salmond was best remembered. Even as a young man, he wrote with the voice of authority, citing sources sparingly and making his own path through the subject, whether it was legal history or jurisprudence. As Glanville Williams, a later editor of Salmond's *Jurisprudence*, remarked: 'Salmond's method in writing the book was to give a smooth and lucid presentation of his own point of view, mostly as though it were the only opinion in the world.'[38] *Jurisprudence, or the Theory of the Law* (1902) was the first of two books that made his name in the United Kingdom and North America. In *Jurisprudence*, as Gerald Postema has written, Salmond 'broke with Austinian orthodoxy and set English-speaking general jurisprudence on a very different trajectory'.[39] He rejected John Austin's concept of positive law as the command of a sovereign and looked instead to judicial recognition of sources of law. The second book was *The Law of Torts: A Treatise on the English Law of Liability for Civil Injuries*. It was published the year after Salmond left the Law School, but it was probably begun there; he lectured on torts as well as jurisprudence. Salmond's 'precision, coherence and system' (to adapt his own words) assured the book's longevity, even as his methods and conclusions came under challenge.[40]

Among Salmond's legacies was the start of a legal research collection in the University Library. Invited by the faculty to recommend new acquisitions, he went beyond the textbooks on which the Law Library had previously concentrated and proposed works on jurisprudence, constitutional law and international law, in Latin, French and German as well as English. Perhaps seeking to give the books a wider readership or safer custody, since the Law Library was housed in the lecture room, Salmond proposed to add them to the central library, recently renamed in honour of the Barr Smith family. For the Law Library, he proposed journals (the *Law Quarterly Review*, *Juridical Review* and *Political Science Quarterly*), an additional set of English reports (the *Revised Reports*) and textbooks. Lack of funding slowed progress, however, and some of the titles were still to be purchased a year later.[41]

By the end of 1905, Salmond wanted to return to New Zealand. In Wellington, Victoria College was about to open a law school, and, unlike any of its Australian counterparts, it was to have two professorial chairs. The college approached Salmond, found him willing, and appointed him as inaugural professor of law. New Zealand was his home, sharing the work with a second professor would be less burdensome, and Victoria College offered an additional £100 a year. But the offer came too late for Salmond to give the required notice at Adelaide, where his appointment could be terminated only at the end of a calendar year and with six months' notice. In December 1905 he asked Adelaide to release him in time for him to start work in Wellington at the end of March. The council was understandably reluctant. It attempted to stave off his departure by offering him a salary increase of £150 and by asking Victoria College not to seek his resignation. But an even heavier teaching load was a condition of the pay rise, and plans had advanced too far in Wellington for the college to backtrack. The chief justice, Sir Robert Stout, was a Victoria College council member. He could approach Way as an equal, and he appealed to Adelaide's generosity in a telegram: 'Trust you will facilitate us as you are established and we are beginning.'[42] The appeal was successful, and Salmond departed. He soon left academia, becoming successively the New Zealand government's counsel on legislative drafting, solicitor-general, and a judge of the Supreme Court, where he remained until his death in 1924.[43]

§

The university did not advertise the chair of law after Salmond's resignation. Way (now Sir Samuel, a baronet since 1899) and the university council again had a preferred candidate. Only nine days after Salmond resigned, the council offered the chair to Jethro Brown. He accepted, becoming the Law School's first full-time teacher born in South Australia. The call for the university to employ Australians, implicit in Kingston's criticism of the Law School in 1898, appeared again in the press. An anonymous writer to the *Register* disapproved of 'the want of local knowledge, colour, and ethos which is generally shown by the gentlemen who come to us from Great Britain'.[44] The university did not bow to this criticism—its choice had already been made—but Brown's origins featured prominently in reports of his appointment, and the registrar gave the *Register* a list of the university's six Australian-born professors. Brown was in many ways an ideal candidate. After he was approached for the Adelaide chair in 1896, he had taken a Cambridge LLD, and a second Dublin doctorate, in letters, for his book *The New Democracy*. He had not remained at the University of Tasmania but, always professionally restless, became professor of constitutional law at the University of London and then professor of constitutional and comparative law at the University College of Wales, at Aberystwyth. There, Brown and his wife suffered the death of an infant daughter. Way guessed that this loss contributed to Brown's decision to move again: 'I think that grief at the death of his child and the desire for a change of scene, had something to do with his determination.'[45]

Yet Brown did not find the decision to return to Adelaide easy, as he explained in a long letter to Way. There were two law professors at Aberystwyth, and taking the Adelaide chair would more than double the number of subjects he taught. Despite 'this terrorising difference in the scope of the work', Brown saw great possibilities in South Australia. 'If great Law Schools have been established in America, and if they are being established in Great Britain, why should they not be established in Australia?' He was thinking big:

> It is early days to speak of all that would be involved in this work, buildings, staff, library, regulations, schemes of study, the maintenance of close relations with the legal profession, etc. etc. ...
>
> If I come to Adelaide, it is because I have great ambitions as to the possibility of that School in the future, and because I believe that even in the immediate future, the School need be second to none in Australia.

Adelaide's Medical School, he said, had two professors and some ten lecturers for around the same number of students as the Law School. Brown hoped that the council, seemingly so generous to Medicine, might 'do substantial things' for the Law School as well.[46]

Legal education was one of Brown's research interests, and he was the first of the Law School's professors to publish on legal pedagogy. He argued that, as the case method dictated, students should develop their capacity for independent judgement by analysing cases for themselves. Visiting the 'Wonderland' of wealthy American law schools in 1904 had a profound effect on him.[47] He marvelled at their buildings, lecture rooms and libraries, and the zeal of their teachers and students. He was a perceptive observer in their classrooms and noted that the case method and other forms of teaching were not mutually exclusive; teachers used eclectic combinations of case analysis and expository lecturing. The elite schools represented an ideal unattainable at home: 'Their general excellence is almost calculated to arouse in one a feeling of despair.'[48]

He was not alone in looking to America. Harrison Moore, professor of law at the University of Melbourne when Brown was at Adelaide, said of legal education: 'What we have to learn, we have to learn from America, not the English system.'[49] Pitt Cobbett, Moore's Sydney counterpart, took the progress of American law schools as a spur to future change at his university. Some British jurists had already taken up the theme. A.V. Dicey lavished praise on the Harvard Law School after he lectured there in 1898. James Bryce, who had taught law before his career in authorship, politics and diplomacy, remarked on the 'extraordinary excellence' of many American law schools: 'I do not know if there is anything in which America has advanced more beyond the mother country than in the provision she makes for legal education.'[50] These were the opinions of visitors and admiring observers rather than insiders, although Bryce made himself an expert on the United States. None of the jurists mentioned above had studied at an American law school, and American postgraduate degrees would not become common among Australian academics for decades. Nor could American models (above all, the example of Harvard) be adopted as a blueprint for an Australian law school. The finances of the Harvard Law School depended on large and increasing enrolments, high tuition fees and a substantial philanthropic endowment, none of which was easily replicated. Australian educators did not want to copy everything they observed in American law schools, and Moore became more critical after he visited American law schools in 1911. The case method in its purest form was time-consuming for students and staff. American bar admission rules did not usually require practical training through apprenticeship, but coexistence with articles was a fact of life for the Adelaide law course. American teaching methods, research and student life were essential reference points for reformers like Brown, but they could be emulated only selectively.[51]

Earlier law professors began their professorial careers without fanfare, but in June 1906 Brown delivered what was, in substance if not name, an inaugural lecture, on legal education. He had done the same at Aberystwyth. Reported in the newspapers and subsequently discussed there, Brown's Adelaide lecture drew on his American experience to set directions for his teaching. He introduced his students to the case method: they would participate with him in the inductive formulation of underlying principles, thus (in theory, at least) composing their own textbooks and developing their abilities, rather than merely memorising information. Articles of clerkship should be shortened, to allow more time for study. Compromises were necessary in applying the case method in Australia, but students should attempt it. 'As far as possible, of course, the formulation of principles should be done at the <u>suggestion</u> of the students', Brown wrote to George Murray.[52] An appreciative *Register* editorial welcomed these 'psychologically scientific' innovations, which could benefit the public by improving legal expertise.[53] Brown's students took time to be persuaded. Way said they 'did not like him at first' but were 'now enthusiastic'.[54] 'His dry sense of humour endeared him to nearly all his students', one of them, William Norman, remembered. 'He rarely dictated anything. He would sit at the end of the table with students all round him and proceed to propound problems for discussion always analysing the students' answers and showing their fallacy or merit.'[55]

The values Brown outlined in his lecture soon took more concrete form, in a report he presented to the university council in August 1906. It was partly an explanation and justification of his teaching innovations, and partly a call for action. He tactfully omitted his usual references to Harvard as something like an ideal law school. Brown described his use of problems in exams, instead of questions asking students to summarise points of law, and explained his novel forms of assessment, incorporating class discussion and the students' notes of their reading. 'The general object of the reform is to penalise the crammer, and to ensure that a high place in the examination lists shall be a more satisfactory proof of all round mental efficiency', he later said.[56] He expected himself to be a researcher in all the subjects he taught: 'Only by constantly learning himself can a teacher hope to make true learners of others.'[57] He hoped that students would sometimes share the work of investigation with their teacher. He sent Way a report he had written at Aberystwyth: 'Every student should be compelled to study some small portion of his subject according to the same methods as his teacher—endeavouring to find out things for himself, to examine text-books critically, to refer to his original authorities, to <u>discover</u> … The research work alike of teacher and student should go hand in hand.'[58] He made the argument for more staff that he had foreshadowed to Way, urging the creation of a second chair, and called for a review of the curriculum, to lighten the students' workload. An early result was the removal of one of the three arts subjects from the degree course. Public international law also disappeared from the curriculum, leaving only private international law. It did not return to the LLB course until 1959.[59]

Perhaps most creatively, Brown urged the university to explore a wider market for the law course by going beyond the trainee practitioners who made up most law enrolments. The university, he argued, 'should seek to increase the number of callings to which that discipline may be regarded as a more or less direct preparation'.[60] A first step would be to make law subjects available as options in the arts course. Constitutional Law and Theory of Law and Legislation were added to the BA in 1907, as a single portmanteau subject, Jurisprudence. Reform of university governance and access could complement this strategy, and in 1911 Brown called for the university to be made more democratic. He joined commentators who detected a change in public attitudes to the university, as government interest grew and the extension of secondary education made university study more accessible. Brown argued that the university council should include parliamentary representatives (a change that was underway as he wrote), 'to guarantee a responsiveness to public opinion' and to increase public confidence in the university.[61] Faculty deans, too, should be members. The *Register* took up the theme:

> For a long time Parliament concerned itself little with the chief seat of learning, which was looked upon as standing in solitary aloofness from the lives and affairs of the mass of ordinary people; but the cause of secondary education has been greatly advanced in recent years by the high school movement, which has carried numerous scholars of the public schools right up to the gates of the University, which is now seen in true perspective as a part of the national system of education.[62]

Premier Archibald Peake, who was also the education minister, made similar comments, joining wider calls to enhance the national utility of universities and expand access to higher education. But Brown did not support the abolition of tuition fees, which had been favoured the previous year by the royal commission on the establishment of the University of Western Australia and was implemented there in 1912. Brown understood that the abolition of fees was not enough by itself to make the university more accessible. Support for living expenses was needed as well, he wrote; a bursary scheme would be more effective.[63]

The government had provided some financial assistance to students almost from the University of Adelaide's foundation, although on a smaller scale than the scholarships that once made up nearly one-fifth of the University of Sydney's government endowment. The South Australian government awarded three university scholarships a year from 1876, based on exam results. Their value—£50 a year for three years—amply covered fees and went some way towards meeting living costs. The number of scholarships grew, but law students were ineligible. A few lawyers who had graduated in arts benefited, among them Alfred Gill, the early law lecturer, and George Murray, the future chief justice. As the award to Murray shows, children of wealthy families could receive scholarships.[64]

More active state involvement with the university in 1909–13 included a royal commission on higher education, extensions to the state scholarship program, augmented funding for the university, and parliamentary representation on its council. The state's first director of education, Alfred Williams, had initiated reforms in school education. Adelaide High School was formed in 1908, by amalgamating older government schools, and by 1911 eighteen district high schools had been established, broadening opportunities to study for university entrance. The number of government bursaries, as they were now called, rose to ten and then twelve each year, eligibility was extended to courses including law, and a maintenance allowance of £20–£40 a year supplemented exemption from fees. Both men and women were eligible. This scheme benefited Roma Mitchell, who received a free Law School place and an allowance of £20 a year in 1931. Other miscellaneous scholarships and studentships also helped law students. Mitchell had additional support from the McCaughey fund for children of soldiers killed in World War I. University prizes could aid those who had already begun their studies.[65]

Expanding the teaching staff was one of Brown's first aims. He supported the use of practitioners as lecturers: 'They keep us from getting too academic. It is extremely important both from the point of view of economy and efficiency that we should have practising lawyers.'[66] Above all, they were sorely needed to ease the burden on the sole professor. Sir Samuel Way told Pennefather that Brown had overlooked the teaching load when he accepted the Adelaide chair and that he was later taken by surprise:

> Brown accepted our offer without noticing that it included the whole of the teaching work of the School, which Salmond would have undertaken if he had stayed, to enable us to raise his salary to £700 a year. When Brown arrived he was naturally appalled at the task he had undertaken—too much for any man.[67]

But Way had forgotten the letter in which Brown accepted his offer of the chair. There, Brown made it clear that more lecturers would be needed and offered to pay for them from his own salary, leaving him with a heavy but manageable five subjects. Happily for Brown, his report to the council in August 1906 elicited funds to pay the new lecturers, as Way recounted:

> By a remarkable stroke of luck Jethro Brown's memorandum as to the Law Chair procured from one of the Council sufficient funds for remunerating assistant lecturers to relieve him of what would otherwise have been an impossible task.[68]

The donor was Robert Barr Smith, who added to his earlier generosity by promising a donation to the Law School of £250 a year for four years (later extended to six), beginning in 1907.[69]

These gifts enabled the council to appoint three new lecturers. Like so many of the Law School's part-time teachers, they were Adelaide graduates and experienced practitioners, willing to help the university but not teachers by profession. Two of them, Percy Johnstone and William James Isbister, had helped to keep lectures going between Salmond's departure and Brown's arrival. Edward Cleland, a future Supreme Court judge, took over Wrongs, Johnstone took over Contracts, Isbister took Property Part II and d'Arenberg continued in Procedure. Isbister exemplified the interrelationship of the legal profession and the Law School. Admitted to practice in Adelaide in 1888, he then read for the bar in London, winning scholarships from the Inner Temple and from the Council of Legal Education, which coordinated training at the four inns of court. In Adelaide, he established himself as an advocate and was later appointed a King's Counsel. He was a long-serving member of the university council and a mainstay of the Faculty of Law, being dean in 1917–20 and 1925–26, although he never held a full-time teaching appointment.[70]

Most of Brown's reform agenda, however, remained unimplemented. He continued to advocate shorter articles and more full-time study, but the one year of full-time study encouraged (though not mandated) by the expanded LLB curriculum of 1891 was as much as the judges and the profession would concede. The university registrar noted succinctly on this section of Brown's 1906 report: 'Not practicable under existing conditions.'[71] Bruce Ross remembered the small prewar classes, made up of full-time articled clerks: 'You got individual attention, but you got very little of the ordinary university life.'[72] Brown looked enviously at the Sydney Law School, where students studying to be barristers in a divided profession had no obligation to serve as articled clerks and could, if they had the means, study full-time. The chair of law there became vacant in 1909. Brown applied, but Sydney preferred one of its own star graduates, John Peden. Brown wrote to Sir Samuel Way:

> One reason, perhaps the chief, which predisposed me to apply for the Sydney chair was the fact that the law students there are genuine University students who devote their whole time to the study of the law. I cannot have Sydney; and I desire, with an intensity I find impossible to express, to bring up our own school to the Sydney standard.[73]

In 1911 Brown wrote again to Way, calling for a broader curriculum and higher exam standards, to ensure 'a systematic study of Case Law on Harvard lines'.[74] Three years later he lamented that students' study of case law 'has hitherto been generally neglected for want of time'.[75] Way saw no prospect of increasing students' full-time study: 'What you propose is, I fear, a counsel of perfection which would be destructive of the Law School. It would probably occasion the passing of an Act for making the present and the new and proposed system of education at the University, non-compulsory.'[76] The Law School could not risk provoking a new attack on the admission rules that had ensured its survival.

Like Salmond, Brown managed to keep writing, despite the insistent demands on his time. In 1906 he published *The Austinian*

Theory of Law, a selection of Austin's writings accompanied by six essays by Brown himself. As Brown's biographer, Michael Roe, has shown, there was a creative tension between Austin's exposition of commands as positive law and Brown's interest in the sociological approach of the American realists. For Brown, legal theory had important implications for current politics, which he explored in both his writing and his teaching. From 1907 Jurisprudence was replaced in the LLB course by a new subject, Theory of Law and Legislation. Salmond's *Jurisprudence* remained a prescribed text, but it was now joined by Brown's book on Austin, Jeremy Bentham's *Theory of Legislation* and, tellingly, David Ritchie's *Principles of State Interference*, which defended state action to make education compulsory and impose health and safety regulations, while laying the groundwork for more far-reaching interventions, in the control of corporations and the reduction of economic inequality.[77]

Theory that could guide state action became the theme of Brown's most popular book, *The Underlying Principles of Modern Legislation* (1912), a hybrid of political philosophy, legislative policy and broad-brush history that went through six editions in eight years. The book's accessible style reflected its origins in the public lectures that Brown delivered around South Australia, as part of the university extension program. Like many of his contemporaries, he was attracted by the pseudo-scientific allure of social Darwinism. He supported eugenic policies that would prevent some people from having children, in order 'to encourage the survival of higher types', and called for better social conditions to ameliorate the supposed effects of natural selection in the population.[78] His book was ostensibly scientific rather than political, but many of his conclusions, such as his cautious endorsement of the regulation of monopolies, had obvious practical applications. He soon had an opportunity to explore them further.

In October 1911, Brown's friend, Sir John Gordon, became head of a federal royal commission into the sugar industry. Regulation of monopolies was a central question for the inquiry; the industry was dominated, many thought unfairly, by a single firm, the Colonial Sugar Refining Company. Gordon invited Brown to accompany the commission and contribute to its work during the summer vacation, officially as his private secretary. This assignment was followed by a more demanding task in August 1912, when Gordon resigned because of illness. The prime minister, Andrew Fisher, asked the university to allow Brown to become the new chair of the commission. Brown told the council that his earlier experience with the commission had been invaluable 'in ways which are very apparent to myself although they may be difficult to explain to those who have never known the dangers of academic detachment'.

> The best Law Schools have come, or are coming, to recognise how much the teaching of the more theoretical subjects of legal study gains in virility and effectiveness if the Professors keep themselves in close touch with those social and economic conditions which it is the purpose of the law to regulate and control.[79]

The university consented. The company's successful challenge to the commission's evidence-gathering power curtailed its hearings, but it nevertheless produced a detailed report. The experience provided Brown with material for another book, *The Prevention and Control of Monopolies* (1914), and drew him further into forums where he might be able to implement his legislative ideas.[80]

The outbreak of war in August 1914 led to a gradual depletion of student numbers in the Law School. Enrolments fell from fifty-six in 1914 to thirty in 1916. Many had departed for military service, but the rate of enlistment did not satisfy Sir John Gordon, who had returned to the Supreme Court bench after resigning from the sugar commission. In April 1915 he complained to the *Register* that only four out of forty-one current law students had enlisted and that the number of volunteers from the practising profession was equally low. Other correspondents contested Gordon's claims, and Peter Moore has found that, by the end of the war, enlistments from the South

Australian legal profession were in line with national averages across all occupations. Moore identified 120 lawyers, most of them former Law School students, who served or sought to enlist during World War I; eleven died.

The enlistment controversy was part of an increasingly punitive debate about university support for the intensifying war effort. In the first flush of bellicose fervour in September 1914, students bound and gagged Hermann Heinicke, a German-born teacher at the Elder Conservatorium, and threatened him with 'disaster' if he was 'unpatriotic'. Jethro Brown proposed that the university should call on the assailants to come forward and apologise for this 'gross injustice'.[81] After the Board of Discipline toned down Brown's condemnation of the assault, the students (none of whom were from the Law School) apologised. The university's own displays of patriotism grew more insistent. From 1917 until the end of the war, every student was required to declare 'absolute allegiance and loyalty to the British Throne and Empire', and in the same year the list of degree-holders in the university calendar was purged of 'enemy graduates'.[82] Arthur Blackburn, a law graduate and a recipient of the Victoria Cross, called on the senate to 'cleanse and purify the records of our University'.[83] Neither expedient was repeated during World War II.[84]

The death of Sir Samuel Way in January 1916 deprived Brown of a powerful patron, and the resulting reshuffle of judicial posts led to his departure from the university. The president of the South Australian Industrial Court, Alexander Buchanan, moved to the Supreme Court, and the Labor government of Crawford Vaughan offered Buchanan's old job to Brown. Again, he hesitated. 'As a Professor and an author rather than a man of affairs, I am naturally compelled to ask myself whether I should be justified in assuming the grave responsibility of accepting the post', Brown wrote.[85] He took a year's leave from the university, on the understanding that he would decide within six months whether to stay permanently at the court. When the time came, however, the choice was no easier. Brown was dissatisfied with his status and salary, which were inferior to those of a Supreme Court judge. The government endeavoured to improve both but met resistance in parliament, where Brown was blamed for delays in the Industrial Court. He submitted his resignation as president, withdrew it after parliament raised his salary, and finally resigned from the university in November 1916. He saw the presidency as 'civilian war work', after he was rejected for military service.[86] The university kept the chair vacant during the war, but it was not necessarily keeping it for Brown, although he seemed to think so. When he sought to return, as peace approached in 1918, the council chose to wait and then advertise the vacancy. Brown was unwilling to compete with others for the chair that had once been his. Asked whether he wanted to be considered with the other applicants a year later, he replied ambiguously, and the council passed him over. He persevered at the Industrial Court, in declining health, until his retirement, at the age of fifty-nine, in 1927.[87]

§

The University of Adelaide welcomed women students when classes began in 1876, but their entry to the law course was long delayed. In the university's first year of teaching, most students attending lectures (thirty-three out of fifty-eight) were women, but they were able to enrol only because the university opened its classes to students who had not first passed its matriculation exams. None of the women in class in 1876 had passed these exams, although they were eligible to sit them, and unless they did so, they could not graduate. The first woman who enrolled as a matriculated student was Frances Williams, who began the BA course in 1881 but left the university after passing her first-year exams. In 1885 Edith Dornwell became the university's first woman graduate and its first student, male or female, to graduate as a bachelor of science by examination. Only two years earlier, Australia's first woman graduate, Bella Guerin, had received her BA at Melbourne.[88]

A science graduate could follow an established path into teaching, as Dornwell did, but a law graduate had to break new ground to enter the profession. Catherine Helen Spence, South Australia's great feminist reformer, born in 1825, wrote that law was 'the profession that I should have chosen when I was young if it had been in any way feasible'.[89] Women were no strangers in legal offices, where they had worked as clerks since the 1880s, but qualifying as a lawyer presented more obstacles. Women graduates not only had to find willing employers and clients, but also had to make sure that the law would allow their admission. The admission rules, while referring to 'persons', also used male pronouns, and the statutory presumption that such references included women did not apply to rules of court. Test cases for the admission of women had some success in the United States, but a similar case failed in Western Australia in 1904, and acts of parliament, rather than litigation, became the means for women to be admitted in all the Australian states. The first Australian woman law graduate, Ada Evans, received her Sydney LLB in 1903 but was excluded from the New South Wales profession until legislation made women eligible in 1918. In the meantime, Australia's first woman lawyer, Flos Greig, had been admitted to practice in Victoria, in 1905.[90]

South Australian women led the Australian colonies in gaining the parliamentary vote, when royal assent to the measure was received in 1895, but the first woman did not graduate in law until 1916. This uncharacteristic delay is partly due to the misfortunes of early candidates. The first woman to enrol in law at Adelaide is usually said to have been Doris Egerton Jones, in 1911, but she had a predecessor, Emily Meredith Moulden (later Emily Egerton Warburton), who enrolled in the LLB course in 1903. Moulden came from a family of lawyers. Her father, Bayfield Moulden, was a practitioner, as were her grandfather, her uncle (Sir) Beaumont Moulden, her cousin Frank Moulden and her younger brother, Arnold, who was later a part-time lecturer at the Law School. Emily Moulden was educated at Tormore House, one of a small group of private girls' schools that facilitated university entrance by preparing students for external exams. She began the arts course in 1902, passing in Psychology and Logic, and then switched to law. She showed determination. Lacking the required school-level Latin, which was often unavailable in girls' schools, Moulden passed the November BA exams and then took the matriculation Latin exam in March 1903, successfully coached by law lecturer Frederick d'Arenberg. She duly passed LLB Latin in November 1903, but she did not pass her other law subject, Contracts, and she withdrew from the course. In 1908 she married Richard Sandford Egerton Warburton, an accountant, and she later lived in Broken Hill and Melbourne. Her departure from South Australia helps to explain her disappearance from institutional memory as the Law School's first woman student. If she pursued her academic interests in later life, it seems to have left no trace in public records.[91]

The second student, Doris Egerton Jones, switched to law in the final year of her BA course, in 1911. She was educated at the Advanced School for Girls, the public school at which Edith Dornwell had taught. During her first year in the law course, Jones campaigned for legislation to allow women to enter the profession. The proposal was not new: admission of women had been part of Kingston's unsuccessful reform proposals in 1895, just after the parliamentary franchise was extended. Introducing the 1911 bill to admit women, the attorney-general, William Denny, made the connection: 'If we had given political equality we should surely give equality in all respects.'[92] The bill was passed with broad support. Illness forced Jones out of the law course after only one year, but she used credit from her LLB studies to graduate in arts. She became a novelist, and several of her books feature women graduates or university students. In *The Year Between* (1918), the protagonists discuss Miss Rotha Lovell, BA, LLB:

'Rotha hasn't time to marry; she's a lawyer. What does she want a husband for? He'd be a nuisance.'

He enjoyed seeing Jan's eyes widen out till they seemed to fill her face. 'I didn't know women could be lawyers,' she said when her surprise became articulate.

'Women can be anything these days,' said John. 'At least such is their opinion.'[93]

And again, later in the story:

'Rotha will never marry; she is too crazy about her work. She has unfortunate women and factory girls and such like on the brain. She says they need a lawyer of their own sex, one to whom they can bring their side of things, things they would find hard to tell a man and one who'll bring a trained mind to fight their battles. She's under engagement now with some society that helps girls. She'll never give up her work to marry.'[94]

The passage suggests some of Jones's own reasons for studying law. Rotha's counterparts in real life would carry out some of this work.[95]

Legal folk memory seems to have conflated Moulden and Jones. Decades later, Roma Mitchell told a story (which she heard from Reginald Wallman, a contemporary of her father) about an unnamed woman who studied law during her father's time at university. Harold Mitchell's first year in the law course was 1903, the year Moulden enrolled. The law professor of the day, Roma Mitchell said, was going to ensure that the unnamed woman did not pass. She did not continue with law but took her revenge by writing a book about the students. Mitchell was careful to say that she did not know whether the story was true. There is an echo of the novelist Jones's history here, but the remark about the professor cannot apply to her. Jones wrote to Jethro Brown when she left the Law School: 'Goodbye Professor and thank you more than I can say for your unfailing kindness & interest while I was your student. I think you were kinder to me than you knew.'[96] In Emily Moulden's time, John Salmond held the chair of law, and she would have been in his Contracts class. Salmond's biographer, Alex Frame, records that he had 'conservative views on the place of women'.[97] But nothing more has emerged to confirm or refute Mitchell's story.[98]

The first woman to complete the law course was Mary Kitson (later Mary Tenison Woods), whose LLB was conferred in 1916. Like several other early women law graduates (Roma Mitchell among them), she was educated at St Aloysius College, in Angas Street, Adelaide, run by the Sisters of Mercy. She enrolled in law in 1912, the year after legislation confirmed women's eligibility to enter the profession. She seems to have said little about her reasons, but, like Jones, she later spoke of women lawyers' opportunities for social service. Kitson had a family connection with law, although it was different from Moulden's family of practitioners: Kitson's father, John, was a detective in the South Australian police and a frequent witness in criminal cases. The enlistment of many male clerks at the outbreak of World War I made it easier for her to find articles of clerkship, which she signed in August 1914. She remained with the firm as a partner until, like many women of her era, she was forced to resign from paid work when she married. Soon afterwards, in 1925, she joined Dorothy Somerville in what was reputedly Australia's first all-female legal firm.[99]

A chorus of early women graduates said, in public at least, that they faced no discrimination once they entered practice. 'There is no prejudice against women lawyers', wrote Dorothy Somerville, who was admitted in 1922.[100] Sheila Maddeford, who joined the profession five years later, said the same. Mary Tenison Woods said it was no more difficult for women than men to find openings in the profession. Speaking anonymously in 1929, a woman practitioner told a somewhat different story:

> If women barristers had to rely upon men solicitors for briefs ... they would starve. Their only hope would be in there being sufficient women solicitors to feed them. I do not think male solicitors would brief a woman barrister unless a client demanded it.[101]

Male lawyers barred women from social occasions, as Roma Mitchell found when she tried to attend ceremonial legal dinners in the 1930s. Some women benefited from family connections. Aileen Ingleby (LLB, 1921) was encouraged by her father to study law, and later worked for his firm. Gwendolen Ure (later McCarthy), the first woman to win the Law School's prestigious Stow Scholarship (1923), practised with her husband, as did Thelma Bleby (later Leaver) and Dorothea Pavy, who entered the South Australian profession in 1928 with an Adelaide BA, a London doctorate in sociology, and an award in the Order of the British Empire for her work in the British Ministry of Munitions during World War I.[102]

At the university, the hostility of some male students was displayed for all to see. A newspaper reported Emily Moulden's enrolment and added: 'A placard has been conspicuously displayed at Varsity [sic] intimating that "the prestige of the law school will be interred in the vaults of the medical school on Monday next."'[103] The idea that women were incompatible with male legal prestige featured in their prolonged exclusion from elite law schools in the United States. Why the Medical School was chosen for the Adelaide burial is less clear. Perhaps law students were needling the medical students, who had included women since 1887; perhaps medical students put up the placard, to annoy the lawyers. Teachers, too, could be hostile. The attitude of an unnamed part-time lecturer who taught Aileen Ingleby was all too clear: 'He stood up there and informed us before he started his first lecture that we marred his class ... Well, we just thought, silly old man. We were young enough to think we didn't mar anything ... But we never forgot it.'[104]

The most confronting disadvantage for women law students was their exclusion from the Law Students' Society. Its membership rules did not initially exclude women, but when the society was reconstituted in 1919 (when three women were studying law), only males were made eligible. The LSS was unusually strict in its segregation. The Medical Students' Society did not exclude women, nor did the University Union, although women had their own committee, clubroom and, from 1929, separate space at the Union, in the Lady Symon Building. Attempts to reverse the LSS ban began soon after it was introduced. A motion to admit women failed in 1920, and efforts continued for decades. 'Year after year the women tried. It was like the suffragette movement', said Jillien Goode, a student in the 1940s.[105] When Robert Ward proposed the admission of women in 1936, his opponents moved that he should be expelled from the society for advocating it. Both motions were lost. Women came close to being admitted in 1938, when the professor of law, Arthur Campbell, used his casting vote in their favour. Nine women became members the next day, although the LSS secretary, Howard Zelling, refused to attend the meeting, and the decision to admit women was promptly reversed. Supreme Court justice Mellis Napier chided the men of the LSS at their annual dinner: 'It is hard to see how you are justified in excluding your fellow-students from any of the privileges of the University.'[106] The supposed dampening effect of the presence of women at the men's uninhibited social events was one reason; being seen as effeminate for supporting women was another. According to the student newspaper, *On Dit*, one male student said that he 'would rather be prejudiced than a pansy'.[107] A wartime drop in enrolments led the men to invite women to join their debates in 1941, as Jillien Goode remembered: 'There were insufficient men to run their debates effectively, and they had to come cap in hand to some of the girls.'[108] By the late 1950s the ban on women was breaking down. The LSS voted to admit women in 1956, although the university calendars continued to say that only men could be members. The calendars were behind the times or reflected an LSS constitution that had not yet been updated: women were not excluded from any of the LSS's activities by 1957.[109]

Women responded to their exclusion from the LSS by forming the Women's Law Students' Society, in 1932. Their greatest need was for a program of debates or moots. Exclusion from the men's debates was a serious matter for women who aspired to work at the bar. The women arranged their own debates and found that the practitioners who devised the topics were willing to act as judges for both societies. Arthur Campbell, too, supported the women students and attended meetings of both societies. As well as debates, the women organised social functions, such as an annual dinner. The smaller number of women in the law course sometimes made organising debates hard, and the program was in difficulties in 1938–39. The Women's Law Students' Society seems to have faded away by 1949, when it disappeared from the student societies detailed in the university calendar.[110]

§

When World War I ended in 1918, the university still lacked a professor of law, although two years had passed since Jethro Brown's resignation. The council had chosen to leave the chair vacant for the duration of the war. Potential candidates could be absent on military service, and the patriotic university may have been reluctant to make a wartime appointment that would necessarily go to someone who was not serving king and country. Additional lecturers filled the gaps left by Brown's departure. They included the parliamentary draftsman, Albert Hannan, and Mellis Napier, then a rising practitioner. The demands of their legal careers would soon preclude lecturing, but they remained members of both the Faculty of Law and the university council. In 1948 Napier would emulate Sir Samuel Way and Sir George Murray by combining the offices of chief justice and chancellor.[111]

Peace and the gradual return to civilian life led the council to advertise the chair of law in August 1919. The annual salary rose to £800, £200 above Brown's commencing salary as professor and competitive with Sydney's new chair of international law and jurisprudence, advertised a few months later at £900. Nevertheless, there were few local applicants. Sydney, too, had difficulty attracting suitable candidates for its chair. Alongside Brown's ambiguous and unsuccessful expression of interest, the council considered a perfunctory application from part-time lecturer Ronald Finlayson and a longer one from Albert Hannan, now assistant crown solicitor. The most serious local contender was Harry Thomson, who had an

Adelaide LLB, first-class honours from Oxford as a Rhodes scholar and, as a major with the Military Cross, perhaps the best war record of any applicant (an important consideration for the council in 1919). But Thomson withdrew, for unknown reasons.[112]

A larger field, fifteen in all, applied in London. They were vetted by a local committee, consisting of Sir Frederick Young (a Law School graduate who had been South Australia's agent-general and was a member of the House of Commons), another alumnus, company director J.F. (Fred) Downer, and the vice-chancellor, William Mitchell, who was visiting Britain. They narrowed the choice to two. Thomas Hirst Black was a Glasgow graduate in arts, law and science who had just turned thirty. He had only one publication, a recent article on Roman law. This sparse record and his deafness relegated him to second place for the Adelaide chair, but he became professor of Roman law and jurisprudence at the University of Toronto, until his early death in 1924. The successful candidate was a barrister and international lawyer, Coleman Phillipson. Aged in his mid-forties, he had supported himself as a university student by working as a schoolteacher and now had doctorates in both law and letters, from the University of Manchester. He was the author of no fewer than six books, including his major work, a pioneering two-volume study of international law in ancient Greece and Rome. His expertise in international legal problems arising in wartime made him useful to the British government, perhaps through the intermediation of Sir John Macdonell, the well-connected professor of comparative law at the University of London, where Phillipson had been a prize-winning research student. Phillipson seems to have had no formal government appointment, but *Who's Who* recorded that he 'did confidential work' for government departments during the war and that he wrote one of the many handbooks prepared by the Foreign Office to provide background information ahead of the Paris Peace Conference, which he attended.[113]

Recommendations from two eminent British lawyers strengthened Phillipson's application for the chair. He knew Frederick ('F.E.') Smith, with whom he appeared in court when Smith was attorney-general, and the lord chief justice, Lord Reading, who spent much of World War I as an unofficial adviser to the British government. Phillipson produced a new edition of Smith's textbook on international law, and Smith (newly promoted to lord chancellor, as Lord Birkenhead) was among his Adelaide referees, along with Reading. Smith endorsed him as 'a very learned lawyer' who had done 'valuable work for the British Government' and was 'an author of much distinction'.[114] In his preface to Phillipson's edition of his textbook, Smith went further, boosting the editor, and indirectly the book, by saying Phillipson was 'generally recognised as one of the greatest living authorities upon the subject of International Law'.[115] Reading said Phillipson was 'eminently suited for the position' and 'certain to give every satisfaction'.[116]

This praise from the mighty was impressive, but their patronage does not seem to have helped Phillipson find employment closer to home. Moving to Australia was a significant change of direction, one that at best postponed further advancement in England and more likely jeopardised it. In Australia, Phillipson could have little contact with the practice and development of international law. His nemesis in Adelaide, A.G. Rymill, claimed to have asked Phillipson: 'Why did you come out to a place like this when you had London at your feet?'[117] His answer, according to Rymill, was that he was war-weary. His war had certainly been a busy one, but his response was partly a deflection of the question. He had sought an overseas academic post before the war, applying in 1913 for the chair of jurisprudence and Roman law at the Khedivial School of Law in Cairo (where Adelaide lecturer Walter Phillips became a professor). In his Adelaide application, as if aware of a need to account for his interest in such a distant place, Phillipson mentioned that he had four siblings in Melbourne and that his wife had Australian relatives.[118]

Anti-Semitism was another possible reason for Phillipson to have to apply widely to find an academic post. His family background was Jewish, and his father was a teacher of Hebrew, but the extent to which Coleman identified with this heritage is unclear. He is usually said to have been born in Leeds, where he grew up, but it is more likely that, as English census records indicate, he was born in Russian- or German-occupied Poland and came to Leeds with his parents as a child, when anti-Semitism surged in Russia in the 1880s. Jewish scholars could find academic advancement difficult. The University of Adelaide had rejected a strongly recommended Jewish applicant for the chair of modern history, the polymath Joseph Jacobs, in 1900. The legal scholar Julius Stone, who came, like Phillipson, from an immigrant family in the deprived Leylands area of Leeds, was rejected for a series of university posts in England and in 1939 accepted a chair in distant New Zealand, at the Auckland Law School. Anti-Semitism was among the motivations for a prolonged but ultimately unsuccessful campaign against Stone's appointment to a chair at the University of Sydney in 1941.[119]

When Phillipson applied for the Adelaide chair, the dean of law, William Isbister, received two warnings that he was Jewish. One came from Fred Downer, the member of the London selection committee, who informed Isbister: 'Dr Phillipson's appearance suggests Jewish ancestry[;] with this possible qualification his claims seem to us to be undoubted.'[120] The other came from John Latham, the future chief justice of the High Court, who met Phillipson at the Paris Peace Conference and wrote at Isbister's request with his impressions:

> I believe—as was generally understood in Paris—that Dr Phillipson is of Jewish race. I do not like to appear to pay attention to race prejudice, but I know that many persons would regard this aspect of the matter as highly relevant, & I therefore mention it to you. Personally, I got on well with him & found him a decidedly interesting man.

Latham found Phillipson well qualified for the appointment, 'a highly competent lawyer', 'well fitted ... for academic work', 'active minded' and 'a legal author of some distinction'.[121]

The London committee favoured Phillipson, but they were unsure. Mitchell found him somewhat odd:

> He ultimately said that his one recreation is conversation! But, he added, in literature and philosophy ...
>
> If I hadn't known that he was in Paris for four months in connexion with international questions I should have put him down for a learned book-worm such as you see at the British Museum.

Mitchell wanted to 'get better at his character'.[122] The committee provisionally recommended Phillipson, while seeking more information. Mitchell was reassured by discussions with Evelyn (Eva) Phillipson, Coleman's wife and collaborator, and with an Oxford don who knew him. Eva compiled the substantial appendix of treaty documents in one of Coleman's books and worked with him in other, unacknowledged ways. 'She has done a deal of researching for him in the British Museum', Mitchell said. Before making a final recommendation, he wanted to make sure that she, too, was a suitable candidate:

> That was in fact the direction in which my doubts existed. They were without ground ...
>
> She was a long time in France & possibly that is why she is Catholic, but she looks as Jewish as he does. She is anxious to go to Australia & have more of a home-life. And altogether the two of them will be able to hold their own in point of ability.[123]

The committee's provisional recommendation stood, and it was endorsed by the university council. The Phillipsons arrived in Adelaide in March 1920.[124]

§

Law enrolments began increasing again in 1917, after reaching their wartime low the previous year. For students who returned from military service, the Supreme Court and the university offered concessions to speed their entry to practice. Those already articled could usually count their war service as time under articles, and the Supreme Court granted so many individual exemptions as to create a 'new dispensation' for admission, in Peter Moore's words.[125] The university was not quite so generous. Curriculum requirements remained unchanged, but the Faculty of Law excused many returning servicemen from lecture attendance and term exams. The university and the federal government combined to offer fee-free places for returned servicemen in need of financial assistance, as part of the Repatriation Department's postwar vocational training scheme. Women who served overseas in the Army Medical Corps Nursing Service were eligible for assistance, but none moved from nursing into law.[126]

Reform of the curriculum was the main academic development of the postwar years. The law course was extended and, for the first time, a year of full-time study became mandatory before clerks commenced articles. The changes were a shared initiative of the professor and the four part-time lecturers. In 1920 they produced an ambitious report, with explanatory comments by Phillipson. Entry to the profession, the report said, was too easy; the LLB course should be the only pathway to admission, and it should be extended from four years to five, to raise the status of the profession, increase the value of the LLB and provide opportunities for future practitioners to extend their knowledge. Students should study full-time for their first three years. This would provide more time for study, discourage cramming, allow more contact with the professor and encourage more practical training, through Law Students' Society debates. A faculty meeting largely agreed, although it cut full-time study from three years to two.[127]

The plan needed broader support, not least because the admission rules would have to change. The teaching staff referred the question to a special meeting of the faculty, attended by the chancellor (Chief

Justice Murray), the vice-chancellor (Mitchell), Justice Thomas Slaney Poole (a former lecturer) and, for the first time at such a meeting, official representatives of the Law Society. The matter was then thrashed out by a committee, where the university and the Law Society had equal numbers. Much of the extensive reform program did not survive this winnowing. The period of full-time study was reduced to one year (first-year subjects became a prerequisite for articles). The final certificate course continued, but the term of articles for certificate-holders would drop from five years to four. The longer LLB course was abandoned, but there was a new introductory subject, Elements of Law and Legal and Constitutional History. Napier had argued for such a subject since he first lectured in Brown's absence in 1916, and Law Society representative Harry Thomson, who presented the revised scheme to the faculty, had been an advocate for legal history. Making the necessary amendments to the admission rules dragged on until 1925. The outcome was not what the teachers had hoped, but the year of full-time study could be extended in future. The Law Society, newly energised after its incorporation by statute in 1915, was for the first time a partner in curriculum reform.[128]

Outside the university, Coleman and Eva Phillipson were active in cultural and social circles where business, professional and university families mingled. Unlike Jethro Brown and Arthur Campbell, his successor as professor of law, Coleman was not a member of the Adelaide Club, which had few Jewish or Roman Catholic members. Eva sang at the Alliance Française and joined the board of management of the Adelaide Repertory Theatre. Her membership of the organising committee for the Artists' Ball, a charity event held under the patronage of the state governor, led indirectly to the conversations that ended her husband's Australian career. Coleman wrote feature articles for the newspapers and was a frequent, and popular, public lecturer. His subjects ranged far beyond international law, to include penology, art, literature, music and other topics of general interest. He was a British Empire loyalist, an advocate of reformative prisons and the abolition of capital punishment, and a supporter of the League of Nations. Fluent, engaging and prickly, he was slow to let a matter drop. On the other hand, the stream of scholarly publications that poured from his pen dwindled. While he was at the Law School, his only publication was *Three Criminal Law Reformers*, an appreciation of the work of Cesare Beccaria, Jeremy Bentham and Samuel Romilly. The manuscript had been completed before he came to Australia.[129]

§

A controversy over the coaching of law students ended Phillipson's time at the Law School. Coaching of university students was nothing unusual. Frederick d'Arenberg, the Law School's long-serving lecturer in evidence and procedure, got the faculty's permission to coach law students in 1898, and professional coach G.G. Newman prepared students in subjects including LLB Latin in the 1920s. Newman's advertisements in the *Adelaide University Magazine* in 1919 began: 'How about your next exam?'. After Phillipson's time, graduates W. Anstey Wynes and David Hogarth both coached law students. None of these teachers, however, offered coaching in subjects in which they lectured at the university; d'Arenberg's permission from the faculty was explicitly limited in this way. A university statute restricted private coaching by professors, but it was ambiguous. It stated that, unless the council approved, no professor could 'give private instruction or deliver lectures to persons not being students of the University'.[130] The ban on private tuition of students from outside the university was clear, but the clause's bearing on private tuition of university students was uncertain.[131]

Before his Adelaide appointment, Phillipson was essentially a freelancer, and he continued to pick up work where he could. Victor Edgeloe guessed, plausibly, that he was paid for his contributions to the newspapers. With the council's approval, Phillipson taught Italian at the Elder Conservatorium of Music in the evenings, but the council rejected his request in 1923 for permission to enter legal practice in Adelaide. None of the earlier professors had practised while they held the chair of law, and the university's statutes required professors to give all their time to the university during term. However, Phillipson's successor, Arthur Campbell, another barrister who wanted to continue practising, made a right of limited practice a condition of his acceptance of the chair. In the face of this insistence, the council gave permission, so long as any court appearances were approved in advance.[132]

Detailed records kept by the university document the events leading to Phillipson's downfall. They began in December 1923, when John McLeay, father of law student Marshall McLeay, offered Phillipson £250 to tutor his son. It was a substantial, even startling, amount of money, as much as many people earned in a year. The sum was far more than the total fees for the LLB course (about £66) but comparable to the premiums paid to obtain articles of clerkship. When McLeay was later questioned, he was not asked about his motives for offering such a large amount, and they remain obscure. Phillipson himself gave no indication that he saw the sum as anything other than an appropriate recognition of his expertise and the value of his time. It had once been common for students' fees to supplement professors' salaries. Adelaide's early professors received their students' term fees, as did their counterparts in Sydney. Joshua Ives, Adelaide's professor of music until 1901, received up to £250 a year from the fees of his students, and Phillipson himself received the bulk of the fees paid by his students at the Elder Conservatorium. In all these cases, however, professors received the fees through the university, not directly from the students.[133]

Phillipson turned down McLeay's offer, but in June 1924 he approached another parent, the dentist John Trotter Hardy, and offered to coach his son, John Scott Hardy, for £90 or more, another substantial sum. Again, nothing eventuated, but in March 1925 Agnes Rymill and her husband Arthur Graham Rymill wrote to the vice-chancellor complaining that Phillipson had told them, in separate meetings, that he was willing to coach their son Arthur (known as 'Lum') in Contracts, for a fee of 200 guineas (£210). Phillipson himself was the lecturer in this subject. The Rymill family was wealthy and well known. A.G. Rymill was a pastoralist, land agent and director of companies including the Bank of Adelaide. His father, too, had been a director of the bank. Agnes Rymill was a friend of Eva Phillipson, at least until their conflicting recollections put them on opposing sides in the inquiry that followed.[134]

The university council established a high-calibre subcommittee to investigate. Its members were two Supreme Court judges (Thomas Slaney Poole, who was acting chief justice and warden of the university senate, and Herbert Angas Parsons), and William Isbister, the former dean. The subcommittee met in Poole's chambers at the Supreme Court, taking witness statements over three days in March and May 1925. According to the Phillipsons, Agnes Rymill asked Coleman, during a social visit to the Phillipsons' house, whether he would coach her son. Agnes Rymill raised the subject again, Eva Phillipson said, a few months later. Soon afterwards, Agnes Rymill met Coleman Phillipson, at his suggestion, and he told her he was willing to coach her son for a fee of 200 guineas. Phillipson later said, and Agnes Rymill denied, that he said he would first need to consult the Faculty of Law or the university council. A.G. Rymill then met Phillipson, with the admitted purpose of trapping him by getting confirmation of his conversation. Phillipson initially confirmed his willingness to coach Lum Rymill but changed his mind when A.G. Rymill said he would consult the chancellor. Phillipson asked both A.G. Rymill and Hardy to keep their meetings with him confidential.[135]

Phillipson conceded the most important points: he had named a fee of 200 guineas for coaching Lum Rymill, and he admitted that such coaching was undesirable. On other matters, however, the witnesses disagreed emphatically, notably over who first suggested coaching (Agnes Rymill said it was Coleman Phillipson) and whether

Phillipson said he would need to consult others before proceeding. The question of who initiated the proposal was a sensitive one. If Phillipson was the first to suggest coaching for a fee, he might seem to have demanded money to let the student pass, as A.G. Rymill implied when he told his wife that Phillipson's offer was 'like a case of refined blackmail'.[136] On the other hand, if the idea came from the Rymills, they might appear to have sought preferential treatment for their son.[137]

In April, before the subcommittee completed its inquiry, Phillipson found an anonymous note pinned to his office door:

> Coleman Phillipson, Blackmailer
> Get out you dirty swine.

He wrote to Poole to inform him, adding:

> I beg you to bring the enquiry to a speedy conclusion. My health is suffering through the protracted enquiry, through gross misrepresentations and distorted accounts scattered about the town, and through such an attack as the present one, which is probably a result of these misrepresentations and distortions and which will, no doubt, be followed by similar attacks in the dark.[138]

Often outspoken in matters of controversy, Phillipson now aimed his barbs at the Rymills. Concerning A.G. Rymill's reference to blackmail, Phillipson told the subcommittee: 'This is the construction of one who is possessed either of the mentality of an imbecile or the malicious spirit of a hooligan.'[139] Rymill had 'not the least element of a gentleman'.[140] When the anonymous note appeared on his door, Phillipson took its reference to blackmail as an indication that Rymill had something to do with the incident, an implication rejected by Rymill and by Justice Poole, who called the posting of the note 'a dastardly thing'.[141] The culprit was never identified. Phillipson also claimed that Agnes Rymill had told him the Rymill family 'had always had more money than brains'. She denied the claim.[142]

The subcommittee sifted the evidence with judicial care. Their report concluded that Phillipson had offered to coach J.S. Hardy and Lum Rymill, and that he had not made his offers conditional on approval from the university. On the other hand, he had 'never agreed to coach any student', meaning, it seems, that he had not agreed that coaching would go ahead. The Rymills' statements, the report commented, 'lose weight from their obvious indignation and animus'; in court A.G. Rymill's evidence 'would be open to strong comment as being the evidence of a "trap" witness'. The report identified the essential problem with what Phillipson had done: he would face a conflict between interest and duty if he coached one of his students.

> It was his duty as a Professor examining to see that none passed unless they reached the proper standard. As a paid coach his business of coaching would be injured if the student he coached did not pass, and his interest qua coach would be in conflict with his duty as an examiner.[143]

Coaching would be an improper use of Phillipson's position, the report said, regardless of whether it breached the university's statutes and regulations. It did not recommend what action the university should take, although an unsigned note, probably originating from the subcommittee, suggested tentatively that offering to 'enter into transactions' creating a conflict between duty to the university and personal interest justified a professor's summary dismissal.[144] Nothing indicated that Phillipson had gone ahead with any coaching or received any money from parents. His offence was his willingness to do so, coupled with doubts about his honesty.

An incident that occurred during the inquiry proved particularly damaging to Phillipson. After the appointment of the subcommittee, Phillipson met again with J.T. Hardy. They discussed Hardy's son, although little else about the meeting is clear. Five days later, speaking to the inquiry, Phillipson had difficulty remembering his discussions with Hardy and said, in answer to a direct question, that he had

had only one meeting with him. The subcommittee concluded that Phillipson 'has not, it appears to us, been at all times candid. He affected to recollect with difficulty whether there had been any offer to coach the student Hardy, although within a few days of our meeting he had been to Mr Hardy with reference to the very matter.'[145]

On 11 May the council considered the subcommittee's report. The findings were apparently too damaging for it merely to warn Phillipson that he should not undertake private coaching. Instead, the council began moves to dismiss him, through notice of a motion to give him immediate leave and terminate his appointment at the end of the year. In the meantime, it gave him the chance to resign. Two days later, he did so, citing 'an attack recently made on me, which I consider unjustifiable, and the unpleasantness thereby caused'.[146] He wanted to return to research and to the legal practice that the council had denied him in Adelaide. These parting shots stung the council into rejecting the terms of his letter, but it authorised Vice-Chancellor Mitchell to accept the resignation, if he found the terms acceptable. No amended letter of resignation appears in the records, and Mitchell seems to have decided to overlook Phillipson's choice of words. He wrote immediately to Phillipson, saying that his resignation was accepted and that he could remain on leave until the end of the year. His tone was conciliatory: 'This will leave you free to resume the valuable work which you gave up to come to Adelaide.'[147]

Phillipson told his side of the story to the newspapers: 'The crux of the whole matter was my willingness to give private tuition to one or two backward students. The council objected to my doing so. There is nothing dishonourable or wrongful in it.'[148] The university had overreacted: 'The initial suggestion I made may, perhaps, have been inexpedient or an indiscretion, as you like, but surely it did not merit the application of a sledge hammer wielded in the dark.'[149] But there was no campaign on Phillipson's behalf, and he was without supporters in positions of influence when he needed them. Crucially, he had no defenders in the council.

On his departure from Adelaide, Phillipson thanked his supporters and the groups of law students who had visited him. He gave the subcommittee a copy of a letter from one of the few women in his classes, Eleanor Wemyss:

> May I be permitted to express the feelings which are shared by every right-minded student, of the strongest sympathy with you, and of intense indignation at the base and cowardly attack made upon you by some unknown person, (who, we may hope, will soon be discovered and dealt with as he deserves).[150]

Others viewed him less favourably. John Ewens, who enrolled at the Law School the year after Phillipson left, seems to have known him only by reputation: 'He had little or no interest in the students, and so far as teaching students at the university was concerned, he was a dead loss.'[151] Jethro Brown and his family became friendly with the Phillipsons, but Brown's son Cyril described Phillipson as 'a man almost completely lacking in tact, good form or sense of humour'.[152]

The Phillipson family returned to Europe. On the way, Eva and her daughter Margaret, the Phillipsons' only child, visited Coleman's brother in India. There Margaret died of enteric fever, aged eighteen. Coleman remembered her in the preface to his next book:

> I may perhaps be permitted to add that this work was written just after I lost one in whom my hopes had been centred, and who, notwithstanding her youth, often manifested a great interest in my dry writings.[153]

In 1930 he had a chance encounter with the South Australian artist, Arthur d'Auvergne Boxall, in Italy. A report of Boxall's meeting appeared in the Adelaide press:

> He approached a man he thought to be a rather voluble Italian, who spoke English well, and discovered after a few minutes' conversation that it was Professor Coleman Phillipson, formerly of the Adelaide University. His wife was wintering in the Riviera,

he explained. He was engaged in writing a series of trials to show the difference between Roman, mediaeval, and Rabbinical law. The three trials were those of Jesus Christ, Julius Caesar, and Joan of Arc. 'Perhaps,' he added, with a sardonic smile, 'I may be permitted to write my own some day and show the ideals of modern justice.'[154]

Phillipson never again held a university post. Predeceased by his wife, he died in retirement in England in 1958.[155]

He suffered at the hands of some later authors. The diplomat Walter Crocker, who had been a first-year arts student in 1925, recalled inaccurately that Phillipson had been paid, not just offered, the contentious coaching fees. Victor Edgeloe, who enrolled in arts in 1926 and began his long career in the registrar's office the following year, wrote that Phillipson was 'deeply interested in money', but Fred Downer, who met Phillipson, had the opposite impression:

> One first is inclined to wonder how it is that a man with such attainments should be prepared to accept a salary such as that offered by the Adelaide University, but he looks upon the Chair of Laws as an occupation which would not debar him from literary work, and, like so many scholars, he has little regard for financial considerations.[156]

Mitchell remarked on the smallness of the Phillipsons' London house, 'packed among others' at Putney.[157] Edgeloe made no such criticism of Walter Phillips and John Salmond, both of whom sought higher pay while at the Law School. Phillipson's scholarship, on the other hand, continued to command respect and find readers. His Adelaide successor Daniel O'Connell used his work, and O'Connell's colleague Ivan Shearer praised Phillipson's 'magisterial' book on ancient Greece and Rome.[158] The Law School included Phillipson's portrait in its gallery of former professors, assembled in the 1970s. He looks away from the viewer, with a faint smile.[159]

3

Community: 1926–1957

The era of professorial scholarship that began with John Salmond ended when Coleman Phillipson resigned from the Law School. The council reverted, for a time, to safer choices for the chair of law, opting for a reassuring personality and a proven ability to get on well with students, rather than a record of productive research. It did not advertise the chair. When it was last filled without advertisement, on John Salmond's resignation in 1906, the appointment was urgent, and the council had a preferred candidate to approach. This time, however, it had a potential problem with the university's reputation, as Phillipson vigorously defended himself in the newspapers. Darnley Naylor, the professor of classics, warned the vice-chancellor: 'After what has happened, no matter how well justified we were, it is certain that mischievous rumours will be spread in England; in consequence it will be very difficult, if not impossible, to persuade any lawyer of distinction to become a candidate.'[1] Howard Zelling, who entered the Law School in the 1930s, believed that Adelaide was blacklisted, much as the University of Tasmania was after the dismissal of Sydney Sparkes Orr in 1956: 'Of course all other law faculties did an Orr on us as a result, and that's why we got Arthur Campbell.'[2] But this thinking is from a later era, when candidates for chairs frequently came from the staff of other Australian law schools. In 1925 the only full-time teachers in Australian law schools were the five professors, and recruitment covered a much wider field.

William Isbister, stepping in again as dean of the Faculty of Law, travelled to Sydney and Melbourne, asking around in search of likely candidates. The choice came down to two, who came to Adelaide to be interviewed. The committee wanted someone under forty, and both candidates were in their thirties. Wilfred Fullagar was a Melbourne barrister and a part-time lecturer in law at the University of Melbourne. He had the strong backing of John Latham, the future chief justice, who had taught at the Melbourne Law School and was now rising in federal politics. Latham wrote to Isbister about Fullagar: 'I regard him as the best student I ever had … My earnest advice is—Don't miss this chance.'[3] After only three years at the bar, Fullagar was already in demand (his Adelaide interview had to be fitted in around a big Supreme Court appeal), but he was willing to move to academia and begin an LLD, if he could keep a limited right of practice. However, the committee had doubts about the quiet Fullagar's ability to influence students. He remained at the bar before becoming a notably scholarly judge of the Supreme Court of Victoria and the High Court of Australia.[4]

The successful candidate was Arthur Lang Campbell, a barrister who was vice-principal of the University of Sydney's Presbyterian residential college, St Andrew's. He had bachelor's degrees in arts and engineering, which he studied at Sydney, winning first-class honours and many prizes. His lack of a law degree was not unusual for a New South Wales practitioner, but it was less common for a barrister and remarkable in a professor of law. Campbell explained that he studied law and engineering concurrently and, when the timetables clashed, he was unable to get the exemption from attendance that he would need in order to be eligible for a law degree. He qualified as a barrister through the exams of the Board of Examiners, which were independent of the university. The combination of law and engineering was apparently the idea of Campbell's uncle, the barrister (and future judge) James Lang Campbell, who saw a future for his nephew as a barrister specialising in cases where engineering expertise was an asset. In an earlier generation, John Monash and Victorian judge Leo Cussen combined law and engineering qualifications, with benefits for their careers. Campbell was associate to Sir George Rich, a justice of the High Court, in 1914–15, and a translator and senior assistant censor (a civilian appointment in the army) for the remainder of World War I, leaving with the honorary rank of captain in 1919. Like other censors, he was honoured with an award in the Order of the British Empire (in Campbell's case, an MBE, in 1921). A good war record was important, at a time when returned servicemen were routinely given preference in employment. News reports of Campbell's Adelaide appointment noted that (as he told the university) he had been rejected for overseas service because of his censorship work. His only experience as a law lecturer was an appointment at the University of Sydney for one term in 1925, and his one publication was an annotated edition of the New South Wales *Companies Act*. But the Adelaide committee liked his force of character and robust personality. He was genial and had ample experience handling students. The council appointed him to the chair of law for an initial term of five years from the start of 1926. A substantial pay rise, from £800 to £1100 a year, was facilitated by recent increases in the university's state grant.[5]

Within a few months of Campbell's appointment, the university was relieved of the need to pay his salary by the Law School's largest philanthropic benefaction thus far, a gift of £20,000 from Sir John Langdon Bonython to endow the chair of law. Bonython was the owner of the *Advertiser*, which he had made the foundation of one of Australia's largest personal fortunes. As he aged, his lifelong interest in education was increasingly expressed in philanthropy. In 1921 he promised £40,000 for what became the university's Bonython Hall, although payment was deferred for ten years, by which time he presumed the then-current debate about moving the university from its cramped city campus would be settled. He was a member of the university council and hence familiar with its needs, but why he singled out the Law School for such a large gift is unclear. Law lacked an endowed chair, but so did Engineering, which had just as many students. According to the letter in which Bonython made the offer, it had been represented to him that endowing the chair of law 'would be a great advantage to the university'.[6] The representation seems to have come from the dean, William Isbister. A draft survives of Bonython's letter of offer in Isbister's handwriting, although it was not the text that Bonython eventually used. The *News*, not one of Bonython's papers, noted that he had two lawyers in the family: two grandsons were law students (one at Adelaide), and Justice Herbert Angas Parsons was his son-in-law. Parsons had been a member of the committee that investigated Coleman Phillipson, and if he had a role in Bonython's show of confidence in the Law School after that controversy, it was one the university could be grateful for.[7]

§

The postwar surge in law enrolments was sustained in the 1920s, as growth in the economy and the population fuelled expansion of the legal profession across the country. By 1933 the number of lawyers in the national census had increased by nearly 50% over prewar levels. The onset of the Depression lifted enrolments, as some of those with the means to do so chose to study rather than chase diminishing prospects of employment. LLB enrolments rose from seventy-nine in 1928 to a new high of 118 in 1933, a level not reached again until after World War II. Henry Katekar graduated in 1937:

> Work opportunities were negligible. The alternative to doing nothing or of [sic] taking a place in long queues waiting for apprenticeship or other form of occupation, was to enter the Law School which was regarded as providing tertiary education not only needed to become a legal practitioner, but also of great use for most other occupations.[8]

Salaries for new practitioners were low, and some found work outside the legal profession. The range of graduates' occupations was broadening. Alumni of the 1930s included broadcaster Keith Macdonald, broadcaster and actor Rex Dawe, diplomat Colin Moodie, and cricketer and journalist Richard Whitington.[9]

The new admission rules of 1925 encouraged law students to undertake a year of full-time university study, but not all could afford to do so. Articles could not begin until the first year of the law course was completed, but other employment could, and some students worked full-time from the start. The future Supreme Court librarian, Llewelyn Bevan, enrolled in law in 1927. He was not one of the few who received a bursary:

> The rest of us had to get our degrees under our own steam, with a very few helped by scholarships given by their schools. Law students, for instance, very often in those days, went into a law office at the same time as they began their university course, and were given time off to attend lectures; and were soundly rated by their principals if they were back at the office late after the time, well known in the office, of the end of the lecture.[10]

Bevan worked as a law clerk in first year, before starting articles. His limited budget determined his sporting activities. Unable to afford the gear required for cricket or tennis, he joined the Rifle Club, which met after the working week finished at lunchtime on Saturday:

> The Club provided rifles and ammunition; the Defence Department provided free train travel to Port Adelaide; one's oldest and least valuable clothes were the most suitable for the mud and/ or grass-seeds of the Port Adelaide Rifle Range; and the Rifle Club shot on Saturday afternoons.[11]

Articled clerks such as Anstey Wynes spent their working days in their offices: 'Law students were tied to a desk all week. We had our articles to serve.'[12] But most found the experience valuable. As John Ewens put it: 'That was really serious work. You learned an awful lot.'[13] Some clerks did not get a fair go, he remembered, but not many.

Despite the demands of articles and other employment, the rising number of students and the deferral of articles to second year gave new energy to student life. Societies for law students and law clerks were older than the Law School itself. In the 1980s, the Law Students' Society claimed historical priority: 'Today the society continues to play an important role in the life of its younger brother, the Law School.'[14] The line of succession was interrupted, however, by the founding and re-founding of short-lived student societies in the nineteenth century. An attempt to form an association for articled clerks was made in 1858, but it failed to attract sufficient interest and led instead to the establishment of a general debating club not confined to legal topics. A Law Students' Society was first established in 1863, to hold debates on legal questions and to meet the clerks' need for law teaching, by hosting lectures by practitioners. Chief Justice Sir Richard Hanson became its first president. Interest seems to have waned, and a revival of the society in 1870, initiated by Paris Nesbit and Charles Cameron Kingston, lasted only four years. Other, short-lived societies for articled clerks came and went until, in 1898, the Adelaide University Law Debating Society was formed. Unlike its predecessors, it met at the university. Meetings seem to have lapsed in 1900, but a revival in 1901 finally proved durable, and the society has continued to the present day. It continued the debates (moots, as they would later be called) that had been the main activity of its forerunners. In 1919 it was renamed the Adelaide University Law Students' Society, in the reorganisation that formally excluded women from membership.[15]

The society's activities grew. Each year, a printed program included the topics for the planned moots, along with details of an annual dinner, a freshers' debate and an address by a judge. Cricket matches against the profession began in the mid-1920s, and an annual dance and a criminal trial—an entertainment rather than a debate—in 1938. Fostering connections with the profession was an important part of the society's role. Practitioners attended the LSS dance, and they set and judged most of the society's moots. Roderic Chamberlain, crown prosecutor and lecturer in criminal law, presided at several LSS criminal trials, anticipating his later rise to the Supreme Court bench. The patron of the LSS was the chief justice, other judges were vice-patrons, and practitioners made up a large body of vice-presidents.[16]

Evening moots were enveloped in 'a low-hanging pall of blue cigarette smoke'.[17] Proceedings could drag on for hours, as they did when Arthur Campbell devised an ingenious problem concerning restrictions on news coverage of election campaigns in 1934:

> After the discussion had been proceeding for some time the dignified legal ritual was interrupted by the caretaker of the building, who came into court and said that as the hour was late he would like to go home and to bed, if no one minded ...
>
> It was far into the night before a procession of bleary-eyed law students tottered down the iron fire-escape at the back of the main building.[18]

Mooting complemented the campus culture of student debating. *On Dit* told new students in 1939: 'Debating is the sauce of life at the 'Varsity, and is highly encouraged; do what you can, and don't hold back.'[19]

Other student activities melded carnival, satire, inverted power relationships and riotous entertainment. Student demonstrations, 'more or less silly ebullitions of mirthfulness', had long disrupted or enlivened annual degree-conferring ceremonies, at Adelaide as at other universities.[20] These outbursts spread from the campus into the city streets, where students held a procession in 1905. Law students staged a mobile mock trial on the back of a cart. For some, the entertainment consisted in seeing privileged youths break the rules. An onlooker overheard one young newspaper vendor say to another: 'Why, the fun of it is they're all toffs!'[21] City processions were held intermittently in the 1920s and 1930s, and were revived after World War II, becoming the centre of a recurring controversy about student behaviour. Peter Kelly recorded the Law School's contributions to these kaleidoscopic pranks, stunts and rags: a car driven across the university footbridge, a fire lit in an interstate train carriage, disruption of Union meetings, and much else.[22]

What the students did out of the public eye was sometimes equally raucous. Graduates of the mid-1930s remembered having great difficulty finding venues willing to take the risk of hosting law student functions. 'No one would take on a second Law Students Dinner', Keith Edmunds said.[23] Most of the trouble does not seem to have occurred at the annual LSS dinner, which was usually attended by a judge and senior practitioners (and remained at the Southern Cross Hotel throughout the 1930s), but at the more casual smoke socials. *On Dit* reported on the 1932 social: 'The proceedings, while not orgiastic, were yet quietly and continuously riotous.'[24] On campus, the Law Library was sometimes chaotic, 'a pretty good imitation of Bedlam', according to *On Dit*.[25] The many complaints to Campbell and the LSS included noise, smoking, unauthorised borrowing, defacing of books, damage to a fire hydrant (apparently after it was turned on a lecturer), smashing of desks, and the hoisting of library chairs to the ceiling. In November 1936 the Law Library was closed in the evenings, a serious matter for articled clerks, whose only opportunity to work there was after office hours. The council considered moving the law collection to the Barr Smith's new building, where it could be more closely watched. The Law Students' Society responded by establishing a discipline committee, 'to control turbulent spirits'.[26] This 'petty prefect system' was resisted by some.[27] But evening opening resumed when supervision was available, and the disorder subsided.[28]

Long after the dust settled, Peter Kelly assessed the mayhem and its place in student life:

> All these wrecked hotels, burnt-out train compartments, smashed desks, chairless libraries, riotous dinners, assaulted judiciary, water-impregnated lecturers, car-crossed footbridges, disturbed Union meetings, squabbles over the admission of women and

countless other things not done by the model undergraduate—
was this then the life of the Law School? In the nine months of
the academic year, in the twelve months year [sic] of the student in
articles (as all were after first year), these things were isolated and,
except in one or two cases for one or two students, trivial. The year
for most was busy and hardworking.[29]

The damage done in 1936 was attributed to a handful of students. As
they graduated, some of the riotousness went with them.[30]

Initiations were another feature of student societies, entertaining
and bonding the group, subjugating newcomers, and giving students
a brief chance to tyrannise over their teachers. These rituals were
widely practised in Australia and elsewhere, and they persisted despite
official discouragement, usually after horseplay had escalated into
violence and victimisation. At Adelaide, evidence emerged in 1932
that participants were flogged during initiations at the university's
Roseworthy Agricultural College. The council asked students not
to hold initiation ceremonies, but, like the city procession, they
flourished after World War II. Don Dunstan, the future premier,
protested at an arts student meeting in 1948 that initiations were 'a
relic of medieval customs', but the majority were against him, and a
'short and painless' ceremony followed for the freshers.[31] (Dunstan
was in fifth year.) The nearby River Torrens was a tempting and
potentially dangerous arena into which the ceremonies spread.
Engineering students who had avoided an earlier initiation were
tarred and thrown into the water in 1948, and a tug-of-war across
the river ended with the losing side being pulled in. Police watched
the 1949 event, but in 1951 a medical student, John Neill, drowned
when he was thrown into the river during an evening initiation. Four
students were convicted of manslaughter as a result. The university
would hear more about people being thrown into the Torrens.[32]

Even before Neill's death, the Law Students' Society had voted
to abolish initiations of freshers, but, as cohorts of students came
and went, initiations were revived. A 'long and riotous initiation of

freshers took place' at the LSS annual meeting in 1956.[33] Staff, too, were initiated. The welcome given to Professor Norval Morris in 1958 included a choir and orchestra, along with

> many speeches in threatening doggerel, two songs of warning & dark foreboding, my arrest and subsequent reprieve, three gas-filled balloons tied to my coat as the freedom of the University & through which I had to make a speech, the whole enterprise on the lawns observed by over 200+ students. It was a delight. The choir then carted me off towards the Torrens, but became respectful & deposited me once we were out of sight of the crowd.[34]

Leo Blair, father of Tony, the future British prime minister, was elaborately farewelled on his departure from the Law School in the same year. He lectured on Roman law, which set the theme for the ceremony, as John Basten recounted. Blair was tied to a bedstead and carried through the grounds. The east doors of the Barr Smith Library were unlocked, opening the way through the imposing portico into the reading room, 'and the hallowed hush of the precincts was disrupted by a raucous mob of Ancient Romans in togas'. The procession continued to the student refectory. In Basten's recollection, staff initiations, or 'reception campaigns', ended partly through the quick-wittedness of Alex Castles, who joined the staff in 1958. Students invaded one of his lectures, asking questions and singing songs. 'But Dr Castles proved altogether too smart for them and they came off a poor second best.'[35] An initiation lost its appeal, and perhaps its point, if the lecturer got the upper hand.

§

In the 1930s, lawyers' professional organisations took an increasing interest in legal education, with consequences for the Law School. The Law Society of South Australia was particularly active at the time. Under the presidency of Herbert Mayo, in 1932 it proposed that Australian legal professional associations should hold their first national conference, and that a federated Law Council should be established to represent the disparate state organisations of barristers and solicitors. Both proposals were implemented the following year, and Mayo became the Law Council's first president. Defence of professional privileges and more effective lobbying of governments were among its main purposes. In Victoria, the Law Institute, which represented the state's solicitors, began calling for reforms in university training, arguing that law students should spend more time on subjects of value in practice. The resulting proposals— some preliminary training in accountancy, and expanded teaching of company law, bankruptcy and conveyancing—resonated in South Australia, where the Law Society took them up in 1935. There, however, similarities between the two states ended. In Victoria, the advocacy of the Law Institute collided with plans by the University of Melbourne for students to study more of the social and theoretical context of law, resulting in a prolonged struggle. In South Australia, the Law Society supported the non-doctrinal side of the law course, and the university welcomed proposals for new subjects. It was the judges of the Supreme Court who disrupted this amicable agreement on most aspects of curriculum reform.[36]

The Law Society proposed that Roman Law, Jurisprudence and the two arts subjects should be retained in the LLB, and that new areas of instruction would be added by extending the course from thirteen subjects to sixteen. Legal Ethics, Mercantile Law, and the portmanteau subject Companies, Bankruptcy and Divorce would be added. Most importantly, the final certificate would be abolished, and the LLB, coupled with three years of articles, would be the sole qualification for practice. Arthur Campbell was receptive, although he disagreed with the society's suggestion that Elements of Law should comprise only legal history and move from first to final year. The judges, however, had other ideas. The question of compulsory university study would be revived 'with certainty', the chief justice told Herbert Mayo, 'if the degree is made the only passport into the profession, and the course prescribed for it is made more difficult'.[37] In other words, if university study became a greater obstacle, critics would call for it to be bypassed, as Kingston had in the 1890s. The faculty heeded the judges. The result was a degree course of fifteen subjects (Roman Law merged with Jurisprudence to become one subject); the certificate course expanded from seven subjects to ten. The students' load was lightened a little by requiring only their 'satisfactory interest' in Legal Ethics, without passing an exam.[38]

The question of limiting the number of new lawyers loomed in the background of these discussions. The number of practitioners in South Australia dropped from 252 to 230 between 1928 and 1932, but stories of overcrowding and an oversupply of lawyers appeared during the Depression. The point was debated at the Australian Legal Convention of 1936. South Australian practitioner Robert Homburg, son of the attorney-general of the same name, told the convention that the university should warn parents about the poor job prospects of law graduates before they enrolled their children. The vice-president of the Law Society, Charles Abbott, told the *Mail* that young lawyers had little work and their salaries were very low. On the other hand, the president of the Law Society, George Ligertwood, did not think the profession overcrowded, and told the convention that student numbers should not be restricted. Statistics indicate that overcrowding was unlikely. Law enrolments and the number of practising lawyers both fell in South Australia in 1935. Eighteen students completed the law course that year.[39]

The future of the final certificate course remained contentious. Mandatory degree courses were supported by a national meeting of law students in Melbourne in 1938, and Campbell urged the faculty to discourage enrolment in the certificate course, but the judges maintained that it should be preserved, to broaden access to the profession. The shorter course was popular with returning servicemen after World War II, and awards peaked in 1949, when thirteen students received final certificates. New admission rules in

1955 reduced the appeal of the certificate course by allowing LLB students to complete articles in two years rather than four, if they worked full-time for a year after graduation. Certificate enrolments grew again in the 1960s, when overall law enrolments jumped, but the course was phased out after the Australian Universities Commission withdrew funding in 1970. The judges maintained their longstanding support (the admission rules still allowed articled clerks to enter the profession after passing specified subjects), but the Law School no longer offered this alternative.[40]

§

How law students should be taught was increasingly debated after World War I. The case method continued to spread far beyond its Harvard origins, and lecturing came under attack in Australia and elsewhere for its reliance on unilateral exposition by lecturers and silent transcription by students. Arthur Campbell followed the common practice of reading his notes. The effect was soporific, as Beryl Linn found: Campbell 'spoke in a monotonous voice through almost closed lips'.[41] At least he allowed students to ask questions. Ronald Finlayson, who began lecturing during World War I, 'was one of the few who would suddenly shoot a question at you in class', Dorothy Somerville said.[42] Some lectures consisted of nothing but dictation, and students wrote down the text word for word. This was John Salmond's method. Speaking at the annual Law School dinner in 1903, he 'perfectly admitted that the students were spoon-fed. That was the only way in which the operation could be performed.'[43] A student in Frederick d'Arenberg's Evidence class completed a volume of lecture notes with a heartfelt last line: 'The End Thank God'.[44]

The growing pedagogical debate extended beyond the Law School. In 1920 an anonymous writer to the *Advertiser*, who had returned to study after twenty years, lamented the hasty scribbling of notes, rote learning, cramming, and the exclusion of discussion and questions in university lectures. *On Dit* later took up the theme, as students (especially in Law and Arts) complained about dictation. They asked for printed course notes and an end to compulsory attendance at lectures. After a feature article highlighted the issue in 1937, a student committee sought improvements. Vice-Chancellor Mitchell gave them a sympathetic hearing but pointed out that action was up to their lecturers. Edward Benham closed his twenty-five years of lecturing in property by visiting British law schools in 1935–36 to investigate teaching methods. He found that his own practice of strict dictation had been abandoned everywhere, but he still favoured exposition by the lecturer, and made no mention of questions or discussion.[45]

Printed notes became more common, but expository lecturing was hard to dislodge. Its results could seem more reliable than an improvised classroom dialogue that placed new demands on teachers and students, especially if (as the case method required) students were expected to prepare carefully ahead of time. Students emerged from dictated lectures with a reassuring corpus of notes that synthesised the information on which they would be examined, even if their understanding of it was uncertain. It was cheaper and easier to get them to write their own subject outlines in lectures than to shift the burden to the university by producing printed notes. Campbell reportedly 'heartily endorsed' student criticisms of lecturing, but his own practice seems to have changed little.[46]

One who made the attempt was Martin Kriewaldt, the only graduate of an American university among the law teachers. His parents migrated from the United States before his birth in South Australia in 1900, and he travelled to America as a teenager. Kriewaldt graduated in arts at the University of Wisconsin, where he completed a year of law studies, and coached the debating team at the University of Missouri. He returned to study law in Adelaide, entered practice, and became a lecturer in property. He was quick to support the student campaign for lecture reforms. His students, he announced, would receive printed notes, and he would 'use the hours he spends with his students as they should be used—in helpful discussion'.[47] These good intentions were hard to keep. Within a few months, *On Dit* commented in verse:

> A big legal noise from the States
> Might have helped us a lot in debates,
> But the premature praise
> For his changed lecture ways
> We retract, because still he dictates.[48]

Kriewaldt's printed notes circulated among students for decades. In the 1960s they were still being sold by 'various entrepreneurs around the Law School'.[49] By that time, printed course materials were common. Students in Elements of Law and Legal Method in 1963 received a full-length set of cases and materials, printed by the Law School. The paucity of Australian casebooks, especially those covering the innovative statute-law of South Australia, increased the need for such notes, and by the end of the 1970s the Law School was operating 'what is in effect a full-time printing office', producing over a million pages of course materials a year.[50] Good sets of lecture notes were still in demand as exams approached, and students formed their own groups to share notes from missed classes. Producing printed materials remained a major operation for the Law School until the system moved online in the new millennium.[51]

After World War II, more law teachers tried variations on the old method of 'the expository lecture and the dogmatic textbook' (as the Martin report on higher education put it).[52] Louis Whitington, who began teaching company law in 1938, used the Socratic method of elucidation by questioning, as did Alex Castles. Colin Howard (1960–64) was known for 'his devastating ritual of questions' fired at named students, in Harvard style.[53] Interrogation was intimidating, and gentler methods of initiating a dialogue sometimes failed. The ethos of Australian classrooms was one reason, as Jeff Goldsworthy found when he moved from Adelaide to the University of Illinois's graduate-entry law school:

American law students were more competitive, more willing to prepare for classes, more willing to answer questions ... Classes here, when I was a student, were not like that at all. I remember David Kelly, when he taught Elements of Law, desperately tried to get a bit of student engagement and student participation, desperately tried to get us to do some reading in advance of classes, and I think most students did not do any. They weren't willing to play ball with the Socratic method.[54]

Teachers' didactic rigour had to contend with student pragmatism. Rick Sarre was in Horst Lücke's Contract class:

Horst (to the class): 'Now, I presume you have all read the cases for today. Let's look at *Lewis v. Averay*. (Now looking at me) Mr Sarre, was the contract void for mistake?' Me (quickly): 'Yes.' Horst: 'You answered quickly, Mr Sarre, in an endeavour to indicate to me that you had read the case. If you had hesitated, I would have known you had not. That was very clever, because you knew you had a 50/50 chance of getting it right. Sadly, you chose wrongly. The contract was not void for mistake. Please prepare for class next time.'[55]

An occasional student might seek more direction, or even compulsion. 'It is only too easy to let most of the year go by without doing much work, because the threat of exams is so far away', one student wrote in 1977. 'The Law School has to learn to be more forceful with students.' A covering note observed mildly that these opinions were 'atypical'.[56]

§

Research was a low priority for the professor of law after Coleman Phillipson's departure in 1925. Phillipson's *Three Criminal Law Reformers* (1923) was the last book published by an Adelaide law professor until Daniel O'Connell's *International Law* in 1964, although O'Connell and Norval Morris had published books before becoming professors. This drought was a change from the days of

John Salmond and Jethro Brown, but Australian universities did not necessarily expect monographs from their law professors. John Peden and Kenneth Bailey, who held chairs at Sydney and Melbourne respectively, were among the highly regarded and otherwise productive professors who did not write books. John Bray's verdict was that Arthur Campbell was 'no scholar'.[57] And yet research in the wider Law School community flourished as never before in the 1920s and 1930s, thanks to structural changes in the university's postgraduate degrees, and the interest and determination of a group of researchers, women prominent among them.

In the early decades of the twentieth century, the doctorate of laws changed from its Australian beginnings as a test of general legal knowledge and emerged as a research degree, a function that it performed until the PhD supplanted it after World War II. The key development was the introduction of the thesis as the basis of the degree, which occurred at Melbourne in 1889 and at Sydney in 1924. At Adelaide, the essay that had supplemented the LLD exams since their inception became 'an original thesis' in 1906, and the exams were dropped altogether the following year.[58] There had so far been no successful candidates. The first to attempt the LLD since Albert Jones failed in 1892 was Francis Knowles, whose varied working life since his LLB graduation in 1888 included teaching and coaching. When he attempted the LLD in 1906–10 he seems to have been working as a chaff merchant and then as an auctioneer. Knowles was depending on the LLD 'for some remunerative work'; perhaps he planned a return to teaching, although by the time he submitted his thesis in 1910 he was in his early sixties.[59] The thesis, on recent developments in international law, was judged inadequate by Professor Pitt Cobbett of Sydney. Knowles soon tried again, with a thesis on the constitution of South Australia, but it too failed. Rupert Stuckey, an Adelaide legal practitioner, suffered the same fate when he submitted a thesis on the Roman law of obligation. It was mainly a translation of Friedrich von Savigny's *Das Obligationenrecht*, and although the examiner, Harrison

Moore, judged it to be very useful, and commended Stuckey's careful and conscientious work, it did not measure up as original research.[60]

The first successful LLD candidate was (Francis) Leslie Stow. He had become the Law School's first Stow scholar, when he received three successive Stow Prizes for outstanding results in the LLB course; the prizes were named after his father, Supreme Court judge Randolph Stow. Leslie Stow's thesis topic, the criminal liability of the insane, was approved in 1908. He spoke for many doctoral candidates when he explained his delay in completing the thesis:

> I was not able for a considerable period to devote sufficient time to it, &, besides, it demanded more research, involved problems of greater difficulty & complexity & extended to a much greater length than I had at first anticipated.[61]

He did well to submit only a year after his topic was approved. The faculty appointed Pitt Cobbett as examiner, and set a high standard:

> In the granting of the highest degrees, a young University would be well advised, both in its own interests and the interests of the candidate, to avoid all suspicion of a low standard by deputing the responsibility of conducting the examination to individuals entirely beyond the sphere of local influences.[62]

Cobbett thought the thesis 'a serious although minor contribution to the discussion of an important problem'.[63] Stow's LLD was conferred in 1909. He practised law in Western Australia, where he became crown solicitor, commissioner of titles, and a part-time lecturer at the University of Western Australia's new law school in 1929.[64]

In the doctorate's first sixty years, to 1945, fifteen candidates had thesis topics approved, nine submitted theses, and six passed. They were a diverse group. Some were established practitioners who had no obvious professional need for the degree but apparently sought the cachet of a doctorate. For the younger graduates, a doctorate could be a useful (and rare) distinction in establishing themselves in practice and, potentially, as university teachers. Some candidates never surmounted the challenge of writing alone, without supervision, in the face of more pressing demands on their time. Judah Moss Solomon applied, like Stow, from Western Australia, where he had entered practice after graduating at Adelaide with degrees in arts and law. His topic, the law of conspiracy, was approved in 1908, but the thesis never materialised. Solomon showed no special aptitude for legal research, but the same could not be said of two other unsuccessful candidates of the 1910s, Albert Hannan and Herbert Mayo. Hannan had a prize-winning record as a student in arts and law when he gained approval in 1916 for a thesis on the constitutional law of South Australia. He was working as assistant parliamentary draftsman. Unfortunately for his doctoral aspirations, his work rapidly became more demanding, first as parliamentary draftsman, and then as assistant crown solicitor, part-time law lecturer, and crown solicitor (1927–52). He never submitted a thesis. Mayo's attempt at the LLD was disrupted by World War I and then, it seems, by his growing legal practice. He became a King's Counsel in 1930 and a judge in 1942. Another future judge, Howard Zelling, proposed no fewer than five alternative LLD topics in 1941, on contempt of court, charities, constitutional law, administrative law and mining law. Zelling was a recent graduate who was beginning his career, but he, too, failed to complete a thesis. His doctorate had to wait until he received a DUniv in 1983.[65]

The six successful doctoral candidates before World War II were prize-winning Adelaide LLB graduates now in legal practice. Thomas Browne worked as a teacher in Western Australia before he took his bachelor's degree at Adelaide in 1908. His thesis, 'Public Policy as a Ground for Legal Decision', lacked critical analysis, in the opinion of the examiner, Harrison Moore, but it passed nevertheless. Donald Kerr's legal practice was interrupted by his enlistment in the Australian Imperial Force in 1915, the year after his LLB graduation. He served as a stretcher-bearer and won the Military Medal. His thesis on the judicial interpretation of the Commonwealth Constitution was submitted only two months after the topic was approved in August 1919. Kerr became the first of the Adelaide graduates to turn an LLD thesis into a book, when he published *The Law of the Australian Constitution* in 1925. A survey and synthesis rather than an original analysis, it was soon prescribed as a student text. Thomas Hewitson, the former law lecturer, was a stipendiary magistrate when he received his LLD in 1922, at the age of sixty-nine. His topic, suretyship, took him deep into ancient history, inspired by Henry Maine's *Ancient Law*. Two years later, a rule change made the new LLM a prerequisite for the doctorate, shrinking the pool of eligible candidates, and it was not until after the change was reversed that the next LLD was awarded. Anstey Wynes, like Kerr, took federal constitutional law as his topic and used a successful thesis as the basis for a book. Wynes received his LLD in 1933, at the age of twenty-five, and later worked in the federal Department of External Affairs, before becoming South Australia's parliamentary draftsman. His *Legislative and Executive Powers in Australia*, published in 1936, ran through five editions over ensuing decades, as a standard reference on the federal distribution of power. The last of the prewar LLDs went to John Bray in 1937, for a thesis on bankruptcy and the winding-up of companies in private international law. Bankruptcy was topical in the hungry 1930s, and the influence of Roman law on private international law was probably an attraction for Bray, a classicist. Aged only twenty-four when the degree was conferred in 1937, he showed in his thesis a precocious ability to grasp and explain even the most tangled and conceptually obscure areas of legal doctrine.[66]

Bray's LLD was the last awarded by thesis at Adelaide. Few candidates sought the doctorate after World War II, at Adelaide or elsewhere. Sydney conferred no LLDs (excluding automatic, *ad eundem* awards) from 1945 to 1969; Melbourne conferred only two LLDs in the same period. The degree lost much of its appeal, as the PhD began its rise as a professional certification for academic employment. The PhD was first offered at Adelaide in 1950, but in law it was a qualification mainly for a high-flying minority until the 1990s. At the time of the Law School's centenary in 1983, the only PhD that had been conferred in law was Colin Howard's, in 1963. (Daniel O'Connell received one, in 1953, as an *ad eundem* award, on the strength of his Cambridge PhD.) At the same time, overseas study was increasingly available for dedicated legal researchers. Given the chance, aspiring doctoral candidates in the 1960s looked to gain international experience. Ivan Shearer was one such graduate who completed his doctorate overseas (in the United States) and returned to Adelaide. John Finnis took his doctorate at Oxford and stayed on. The LLD became an award for an eminent graduate, based on a record of scholarly achievement, a change confirmed when it was subsumed into university-wide rules for higher doctorates in 2008.[67]

The doctorate of laws was also a ceremonial award, conferred on important visitors to the university who had no connection with law. Other universities used the LLD in the same way. However, the University of Adelaide made no provision for purely honorary degrees, awarded *honoris causa* ('out of respect'), unlike an increasing number of its counterparts. Adelaide stuck with the earlier practice of making ceremonial *ad eundem* awards, conferring local equivalents of degrees that visitors had received previously from other universities. The university's three royal visitors between 1901 and 1927, the future Kings George V, Edward VIII and George VI, all received Adelaide LLDs, to which they were entitled thanks to their ceremonial Oxford or Cambridge law doctorates. They were, notionally at least, the law faculty's graduates, so it fell to Arthur Campbell to present the future George VI for his conferral in 1927, as his predecessors had presented earlier royal graduands. Other LLD recipients included state governors, prime ministers, and other high-placed visitors from government and academia.[68]

The question of honorary degrees was much debated at Adelaide in the 1970s. They could be very useful as ceremonial compliments, but they might undermine the value of degrees earned by examination. The Faculty of Law opposed the awarding of honorary degrees, and favoured alternatives such as making recipients fellows or companions of the university. The council agreed. But honorary awards were too widely used for the university to renounce them. The university's governing act of parliament was amended in 1978 to enable it to grant a distinctive honorary degree, Doctor of the University. It was at first conferred only in recognition of service to the university, but its ceremonial function grew when creativity in other fields was included in 2004. From 2013, service to society in general qualified recipients for the DUniv (*honoris causa*), and scholars of exceptional eminence could be granted honorary doctorates in their own disciplines, including law.[69]

The new honorary degrees began, very slowly, to redress the LLD's long bias towards men. No women received LLDs in the Law School's first century. But Dame Roma Mitchell received a DUniv in 1985 (she followed the physician Annie Wall, whose DUniv was conferred in 1982). Other women lawyers to receive the DUniv, for university or public service, included First Nations community leader Andrea Mason, and parliamentarians Amanda Vanstone, Julie Bishop, Julia Gillard and Penny Wong. Honorary LLDs went to Justice Margaret White and Chief Justice Susan Kiefel. Women were still in the minority, however, in the university's list of honorary graduands.[70]

§

The history of the doctorate in the 1920s and 1930s is intertwined with that of the research prize named after the Law School's benefactor, Sir Langdon Bonython. The two are so closely connected that a controversy concerning the prize—a failure by a well-regarded entrant in 1936—is sometimes ascribed to the doctorate. To the university, however, the prize and the LLD were distinct. They have different histories in another way. No women were candidates for the doctorate in this period, but the first three candidates for the

Bonython Prize, including the first winner, were women. Lacking master's degrees, they were ineligible for the LLD at the time, but the prize was open to them.

The Bonython Prize was established as an indirect consequence of the endowment of the chair of law, but it was not part of Bonython's gift. The university created the prize independently, as a way of honouring Bonython's generosity. The idea emerged in the Faculty of Law soon after Bonython made his donation, but remembering a benefactor was not the only motivation. As the faculty told the council: 'It would increase the efficiency of the Law School if provision were made to encourage extra research in legal work.'[71] The prize, £100, was awarded for a thesis on a legal subject approved by the faculty or the council, or for a published book on a legal subject. Candidates had to be Adelaide graduates.[72]

The first candidate for the prize, and the first winner, was Thelma Bleby. She was a young Adelaide practitioner when she submitted a thesis on the law of trusts, in 1929. The examiners, Arthur Campbell and Edward Benham, thought the thesis just short of doctoral standard, 'in point of co-ordination, extraction of principle and critical dissection of the cases'.[73] The problem, as Benham explained, was that Bleby had spent too much time quoting from judgments and summarising the facts of cases, and not enough on 'original comment and criticism'.[74] But the thesis would have been good enough for a master's degree, the examiners decided. The faculty recommended that Bleby should receive the prize, despite its earlier advice that winning theses should be of doctoral standard. Her work reads now as a cogent synthesis of current law, with a family resemblance to the law students' textbooks and lecture notes.[75]

The next two applicants were less fortunate. Sheila Maddeford graduated with an LLB in 1927 and was in sole practice in Adelaide when she applied for the Bonython Prize three years later. Her thesis on new aspects of the law of insanity was not retained by the university, but her career as a barrister showed her interest in criminal law and family law. The examiners judged the thesis inadequate for the prize, for unspecified reasons, as they did when Mary Tenison Woods submitted a thesis on the laws relating to women and children, also in 1930. Tenison Woods's thesis, too, was not preserved, although it is likely that parts of it were incorporated in her later publications. The entrants faced a demanding task, producing theses despite an uncertain prospect of winning the prize and with no chance of a doctorate. Perhaps the prize was seen as a professional distinction (and a useful sum of money) for women establishing themselves in legal practice. It would have been natural for Bleby's win to encourage others, and for the failures of Maddeford and Tenison Woods to dampen interest. The next two winners, Anstey Wynes (1933) and John Bray (1937), received their Bonython Prizes for their successful doctoral theses.[76]

In her entry for the prize, Tenison Woods pursued an interest in social policy that would shape her working life. She left her legal partnership with Dorothy Somerville after a personal crisis: she was deserted by her husband in 1927, after he was struck off the roll of practitioners for unprofessional and illegal conduct. When proceedings against him began, Tenison Woods sought refuge in Sydney, where she gave birth to their son. Returning to Adelaide, she resumed legal practice. Laws relating to women and children had been a concern of Tenison Woods since her earliest work as a lawyer took her into the Children's Court, and in 1933 she received a grant from the Australian Council for Educational Research, funded by the Carnegie Corporation of New York, for research on juvenile delinquency. It drew on her collaboration with an expert committee on this subject that was established by the Women's Non-Party Association in 1929. She sought approval for another Bonython Prize topic, on juvenile delinquency, in 1934, but she seems not to have gone any further. The faculty, wary of innovation and sharing a longstanding professional distrust of criminology, queried how much law she would discuss. In 1934 a second ACER grant took her to the eastern states to report on institutional treatment of young offenders. She published her report in 1937 in a short monograph; it emphasised rehabilitation and the welfare of children.[77]

Tenison Woods's work on child welfare continued, alongside employment as a legal editor, after she moved again to Sydney in 1935. With her colleague Marjorie Robertson, she wrote *Leaves from a Woman Lawyer's Casebook*, a book of popular legal advice presented through fictionalised anecdotes, in the style of legal advice columns in contemporary newspapers. Activism on national and international issues affecting women occupied Tenison Woods after World War II. She was a member of the anti-communist Catholic women's group, the St Joan's Social and Political Alliance, which successfully opposed the reappointment of (Lady) Jessie Street as Australia's representative on the United Nations Commission on the Status of Women. Tenison Woods joined the United Nations secretariat in 1950, as chief of the section on the status of women in the Human Rights Division of the Department of Social Affairs. Her office supported the work of the Commission on the Status of Women, through research, policy formation, monitoring and budgeting. She retired from the United Nations in 1958 and died in Sydney in 1971, honoured as a noted reformer in child welfare and 'an outstanding fighter for women's rights'.[78]

The failures of Maddeford and Tenison Woods to win the Bonython Prize attracted little attention, but the failure of a prominent male lawyer, Ralph Hague, became controversial. Hague worked briefly as a journalist before he started the Adelaide law course. By the time he graduated in 1932, he had, as he later said, won 'every prize and scholarship then available in the Faculty of Law'.[79] Four years later, while in legal practice in Adelaide, he sought to add the Bonython Prize to the list. Like Bray, he later kept his academic connections alive through part-time lecturing in the Law School. Hague and Bray both applied for the chair of law when it became vacant in 1949.

Hague's topic, the legal history of South Australia from 1836 to

1867, was close to his heart. As his biographer, Helen Whitington, observed, commemorative history burgeoned during the centenary of South Australian colonisation in 1936, and Hague may have known of Charles Currey's Sydney LLD (1929) on the legal history of colonial New South Wales. However, it was the prize, not the doctorate, for which Hague applied, first seeking the necessary council approval of his topic. He provided a synopsis, which may have made his project seem antiquarian rather than scholarly:

> The thesis is an attempt to collect such information as can now be found relating to the establishment and development of the law in South Australia, the Courts, the Judges, and the Legal Profession, from the founding of the colony to the removal from office of Mr Justice Boothby in 1867.[80]

The Faculty of Law had 'some doubts as to whether the subject may be treated merely historically or critically and philosophically'; it was prepared to approve the subject if it was 'treated critically'.[81] It sent the dean to consult two judges (Sir George Murray and Sir Herbert Angas Parsons), who saw a biographical extract from the manuscript, printed by Hague as a pamphlet. Its entertaining style made its scholarly foundations easy to miss. His topic was Australian, but that was not in itself a disqualification. The two previous winners of the Bonython Prize, Bleby and Wynes, both wrote about Australian law. However, Hague did not write about legal doctrine, as Bleby and Wynes did, but about Australian, and specifically South Australian, legal history. So little academic work had been done in this field that Hague's pioneering research could be mistaken for a mere archival chronicle, resembling other commemorative histories, an error that his modest outline left open. With Murray presiding as chancellor, the council rejected Hague's topic, without recording its reasons.[82]

It was the topic, not the thesis itself, that the council rejected. Although the manuscript was written, the university did not allow its submission, and the council never discovered what examiners might have thought of it. Whitington shows how the university's decision wounded Hague and was regarded as an injustice by the Law School's later legal historian, Alex Castles. Hague deposited his manuscript in the Public (later State) Library in 1937. Excerpts appeared as short monographs, but Hague resisted all efforts to publish the manuscript as a whole. The entire monumental work, of some 800 pages, was published after his death.[83]

§

The degree of Master of Laws, the LLM, had a delayed beginning and a more uncertain place in the university than the LLD. The nineteenth-century acts of parliament that established the universities of Sydney, Melbourne, Adelaide and Tasmania did not authorise them to grant master's degrees in law or, for that matter, in any discipline other than arts. The LLD was the only higher degree in law. The universities gained authority to award the LLM when parliament extended the range of degrees they could confer, but by 1920 it was awarded only at Melbourne and Tasmania. Their LLB honours graduates became eligible for it automatically, in much the same way as Oxford or Cambridge arts graduates became entitled to an MA. Adelaide gained the power to confer the LLM when, in 1924, parliament authorised the university to decide for itself which degrees it would award, freeing it from the legislative list of permitted degrees that had previously hindered the teaching of new disciplines, such as dentistry.[84]

The lack of consistency in Australian degrees attracted the attention of the biennial conference of Australian universities in 1922; the master's degree in law was one of the examples discussed. The conference was able to do little other than recommend uniformity, but it alerted the Faculty of Law, and the LLM was established as soon as the university gained the necessary power. As Phillipson explained to the university senate, many LLB graduates wanted to continue studying, but a doctoral thesis was too much for them. For the LLM, they would sit exams in three out of five broad subjects: the history of English law; public international law; common law and statute law; equity; and Roman law. Like the subjects initially prescribed for LLD exams, these descriptions provided little guidance. When two prospective students (Martin Kriewaldt was one) wrote asking about the syllabus, the faculty asked Arthur Campbell to prepare booklists. From 1931, to achieve consistency with other disciplines, a thesis replaced the exams, but candidates who lacked an honours LLB had to do both. Since the honours LLB was conferred only from 1931, and then in very small numbers, most prospective LLM candidates fell into this category. The exams were a formidable barrier: one unfortunate student failed twice in 1935–36. As a demanding junior research degree, less prestigious than the LLD, the master's had little appeal. It was not until 1955 that Gerald Fridman, senior lecturer in law, became the first candidate to earn an Adelaide LLM.[85]

§

The Law School encouraged research through the doctorate, the LLM and the Bonython Prize, but it was the Law Students' Society that established a journal in which scholarly articles could be published. *Obiter Dicta*'s half-joking subtitle, 'A Journal of Persuasive Authority', staked a claim to a place in legal debate. The year of publication was given only in Latin, in the style of an act of parliament, causing confusion ever since. The first issue, which appeared in April 1939, contained articles on legal doctrine, jurisprudence and judicial biography, by practitioners and students. The editors were Howard Zelling, who had recently graduated, and students (Duncan) Campbell Menzies and Elliott Johnston. All three contributed articles. Menzies won a Rhodes Scholarship, but it was deferred on the outbreak of war; he would die as a prisoner of war in 1943. Johnston, initially rejected for military service because of partial blindness, was a force in student politics, where he was aptly said to 'touch nothing without setting off an explosion'.[86] President of the University Union in 1941, the year he joined the Communist Party, he resigned after being censured for his criticism of student strikebreaking. It was an unlikely start for a future judge, but Johnston was appointed to the Supreme Court in 1983, after a distinguished career in legal practice.[87]

Obiter Dicta was Adelaide's first law journal since the brief appearance of the *South Australian Law Journal* in 1884. In concept, it resembled Australia's first scholarly law-school journal, *Res Judicatae* (later the *Melbourne University Law Review*), established by the Victorian Law Students' Society in 1935. In a foreword for the first issue of *Obiter Dicta*, Arthur Campbell lamented that many lawyers saw the university as a mere 'technical college'.

> It is therefore not only a relief, but a delight to find the students of any Faculty of the University, and more so those who are approaching the so often ignorantly disparaged profession of the law, looking beyond the mere mechanics of their training to serious consideration of difficult problems, which have already roused their interest and to a treatment of them which may perhaps prove an important contribution to their science.[88]

The third issue, in October 1941, bore witness to the growing impact of World War II. It listed law students who had joined the armed services, and paid tribute to H.M. (Monty) White, a gifted student who died while serving in the Royal Australian Air Force. It was the last issue, as wartime conditions brought publication to an end. A student-edited scholarly journal was re-established when the *Adelaide Law Review* appeared in 1960, and the title of *Obiter Dicta* was revived for a commemorative magazine in 1968, to mark the Law School's move to a new home.

§

By 1939 the state bursary scheme, the main source of scholarships for law students, was under pressure. Only twelve bursaries were awarded each year for the whole university, although concessions were also available for evening students and for trainee teachers studying arts, alongside other, miscellaneous scholarships. Delegates at a national student conference criticised the bursary scheme, and a young economics lecturer at Adelaide, John La Nauze, analysed it in detail, first in *On Dit* and then in a monograph. There were too few bursaries, and the usual living allowance, £20 a year, was not enough to live on, leading some winners to decline their awards. Selection was based on performance in the Leaving Honours exam, which students could sit twice, in successive years, to improve their results. Those who did so came predominantly from private schools, which dominated the bursary scheme as a result. Less than half of all school students aged sixteen and over were at private schools, but they won three-quarters of the bursaries. As La Nauze saw it, only the brilliant or wealthy would stay on at school, perhaps to the age of eighteen, on the chance of winning bursaries given only to the state's top twelve students.[89]

The lists of bursary winners, published in the university calendars, show how heavily these factors weighed on prospective law students from state high schools. Early in the Law School's history, the lack of state secondary schools made the predominance of private-school students inevitable, but the pattern continued as the number of government high schools increased. Between 1909, when law students became eligible, and 1939, only 17% of students granted bursaries to do law came from public high schools. The vast majority came from private schools, and nearly half, or 47%, came from one school, St Peter's. The grip of the private schools was strongest from 1922 to 1939, when no public high-school students received bursaries to study law. On La Nauze's figures, from 1927 to 1937, only about 22% of male students completing the Adelaide law course came from state schools. In Medicine, the figure was even lower, at 14%. Bursaries rewarded the top matriculants in the Law School, but they made little difference for state school students, especially those living outside Adelaide, unless they had won scholarships to continue at private schools.[90]

The state government alleviated the shortcomings of the scheme in 1939, by creating twelve bursaries for students in the Leaving exam that preceded Leaving Honours. The university remitted the students' fees (although it received no reimbursement from the government) and the same living allowance would be available. For the first time, bursaries would be means-tested, based on parental income. Means-testing was progressively extended as the state bursary schemes grew in the late 1940s, but the state schemes were soon eclipsed by the arrival of large-scale Commonwealth support for university study.[91]

§

Many of the effects of World War II on the Law School would have been uncomfortably familiar to those with memories of World War I. Enrolments dropped by nearly 60% between 1939 and 1942, and lectures were suspended in some subjects. Arthur Campbell returned to the censorship work that he had performed in the last war, serving successively as district censor for South Australia and New South Wales. He remained the titular dean of the Faculty of Law, but acting deans, Geoffrey Reed and then Charles Abbott, performed his duties during his absence in Sydney. Both were senior counsel soon to be appointed to the Supreme Court, and Abbott was also a member of parliament. Their seniority reflected the faculty's standing in the profession and the willingness of lawyers on the home front to add to already heavy workloads.[92]

Some features of the wartime experience were new. During World War I, Mary Kitson was the only woman practitioner in South Australia, and only two women (Clare Hannan and Aileen Ingleby) followed her into the law course during the war. At the outbreak of war in 1939, seven women had practising certificates. They took over some of the work of men who left on war service. Beryl Linn took sole charge of the firm in which she was a partner; Roma Mitchell and one remaining (male) partner did the work of four lawyers in their firm. In the Law School, of the students who passed one or more subjects in 1942, a quarter (six in all) were women. They collected all the prizes awarded that year.[93]

Conscription, rejected in the previous conflict, presented novel difficulties for the university during World War II. Although the Second Australian Imperial Force, raised for overseas service, consisted of volunteers, the Citizen Military Forces, known as the militia, were conscripted for home defence. Women and men could be called up for civilian work by the Manpower Directorate. A complex and ever-changing system of requirements and exemptions controlled what university students were permitted to do. The main issue confronting the Faculty of Law was the reservation of students from military or civilian conscription, to ensure a minimum supply of new entrants to the profession. Putting names on the reserved list raised awkward questions. The faculty was initially reluctant to nominate any students, but after much discussion, it eventually selected students based on academic merit, regardless of gender. The prize winners of 1942, Betty Moffatt and Aline Fenwick, were placed on the list. Nomination for a reserved place gave students the option of continuing their studies, but it did not force them to do so. Some of those who were eligible for the armed services chose enlistment over reserved study. They included the future judges Sam Jacobs and W.A.N. (Andrew) Wells, and the future Bonython professor, Richard Blackburn.[94]

Some students continued their studies despite enlistment and even captivity. The Army Education Scheme supported serving personnel who were stationed in Adelaide and could attend lectures. Clarrie Harders, later head of the federal Attorney-General's Department, was one. Others studied by correspondence. For some, wartime study and postwar assistance opened a pathway into the law that had been closed when they left school. Len King, the future chief justice, passed the first (arts) subject of his LLB course while serving in the Royal Australian Air Force in New Guinea. Pilot Douglas McLeod, a police officer in civilian life, passed University of London matriculation exams while a prisoner of war in Germany, and then used his results to enter the law course on his return to Adelaide.[95]

Increased financial assistance for students featured in Common-wealth plans for essential wartime study and the return of service personnel to civilian life. Financial assistance began in 1943 for students who had reserved places. It provided fees and a living allowance, and was means-tested, based on income. The principle of means-testing provoked a strongly worded protest from the Faculty of Law:

> The effect of such a limitation will be to restrict the privilege to one section of the community, to impose a double burden on another section, to pauperise the recipients, to foster class distinctions and in view of the present incidence of taxation to deprive many worthy students of needful assistance.[96]

The motion was proposed by the lecturer in company law, Louis Whitington. It was unusual for the faculty to protest about a matter outside the university's control, and means-testing was politically charged. The Liberal Party opposed its use for social security benefits. By contrast, the faculty merely forwarded to the council a request from the University of Amsterdam to protest against the persecution of minorities in Germany, after the Kristallnacht pogrom of 1938. The council replied to Amsterdam that 'idle protest' would make matters worse.[97]

Commonwealth financial assistance reached only a handful of Adelaide law students during the war, but many more benefited as they returned from wartime service. The Commonwealth Reconstruction Training Scheme, or CRTS, supported men and women returning from the armed services, along with those incapacitated by service in the merchant navy or by farm work in the Women's Land Army. Eligibility depended on the student's age at enlistment, previous occupation, service record, and earlier studies, but the criteria were applied generously. Like the earlier financial assistance scheme, the CRTS paid fees and a living allowance, but, unusually for the time, the allowance was equal for men and women. University study was only a small component of the scheme, and most participants undertook technical training for trades and industry. The Commonwealth's financial assistance scheme for civilian students continued after the war, although it was much smaller than the CRTS. As after World War I, the required curriculum did not change for those returning from the services, but the faculty was generous with other concessions, such as lecture attendance. The university and the Law Society organised refresher courses on recent developments for lawyers returning to practice, but one returned airman found them 'pretty hopeless as a practical means of bringing you up to date'.[98]

In 1946, the peak year, more than two-thirds of the Law School's students were supported by the CRTS. The scheme enabled Len King to study law; Sam Jacobs said CRTS support enabled him to get married. The historian of postwar reconstruction, Stuart Macintyre, noted that the social composition of the CRTS university cohort is unclear, although available studies 'suggest a strong appeal to former private school boys of modest means who might otherwise have settled for office jobs'.[99] The description fits Len King, who was expecting to return to office work at the Shell oil company after the war, but not Sam Jacobs, who was at university before he enlisted and whose father, Roland, was a prominent businessman. It appears that no returning servicewomen did law at Adelaide. The number of women in the law course dropped after the war, and none graduated in 1950–52, when the bulk of the CRTS students took their degrees. Jillien Goode remembered 'a very different feeling in the Law School. They were all very keen to get admitted, very keen on their careers, after those years away. All living on a government pension, as it were, very small incomes … Full of fun, and out to enjoy themselves.'[100]

§

Arthur Campbell returned from his wartime work to resume duties that had outwardly changed little. He was still the Law School's sole full-time teacher, even when enrolments reached a new peak of 122 in 1948. He made a rare appearance in public affairs as a member of the royal commission on South Australia's electricity supply in 1945. Premier Thomas Playford had clashed with the privately owned Adelaide Electric Supply Company over his plan to reduce South Australia's dependence on imported black coal, by generating power from brown coal mined at Leigh Creek, in the state's north. A royal commission was originally the company's idea, but when its terms of reference were extended by the Legislative Council, Playford took full advantage. Campbell, the only commissioner with an engineering degree, was the company's nominee—its chairman and managing director were fellow-members of the Adelaide Club—but the choice backfired. He joined with the other commissioners in recommending nationalisation of the company. The outcome was the state-owned Electricity Trust of South Australia, which supplied South Australia's power until the end of the century.[101]

In March 1949, after twenty-three years as professor of law, Campbell died of heart failure at his home, aged fifty-nine. As chairman of the University Union council and a participant in university hockey and fencing, he was known to many students outside the Law School, and lectures in all faculties were suspended for his funeral. Students lined the path to the West Terrace crematorium and served as his pallbearers. No will could be found. Those who knew him left many descriptions: 'urbane, convivial, friendly and unassuming', 'plump, retiring, a bachelor and a renowned culinary expert', 'a very happy fat and round little man who loved food and drink and mankind'.[102] Ralph Hague's recollection was more unsettling:

> Campbell told me that he acquired his phenomenal capacity for consuming great quantities of liquor without showing the slightest sign of mental or physical unsteadiness through being started by his father on beer at about 7 or 8, on wine at 9 or 10, and on spirits at about 13 or 14, so that by the time he went to the University he was a very experienced toper.[103]

His affections were enigmatic, and in the absence of any acknowledged relationship, rumour filled the gap. Roma Mitchell heard that Campbell married 'in the South Sea Islands' and later had a child with his German housekeeper: 'He went over to Melbourne with her and they registered the child, but he didn't marry her.'[104] The South Seas marriage has a touch of Somerset Maugham, and the clandestine birth partly resembles Samuel Way's hidden relationship with Susannah Gooding. But Campbell did have two housekeepers, sisters, with German surnames, although they were Australian-born. If he was married, the administrators of his estate were unaware of it; they regarded his sisters as his only next of kin.[105]

The university advertised the vacant chair, for the first time since 1919. The field of applicants was strong. Some were Adelaide lawyers who had lectured part-time in the Law School: Ralph Hague (now at the crown solicitor's office), David Hogarth, Martin Kriewaldt, John Portus (a Commonwealth arbitration commissioner), Andrew Wells and John Bray. Keith Aickin applied from Melbourne; he was, like Wilfred Fullagar when he was approached in 1926, a barrister and future High Court judge. Others were already in academia, notably John Fleming (lecturer in charge of the law course at Canberra University College) and James Williams, professor of law at Victoria University College, Wellington. Williams had previously been professor and dean of law at the Sydney Law School.[106]

As it did when it appointed Campbell, the university opted for a candidate whose research record was thin but who would be, as vice-chancellor Albert ('A.P.') Rowe put it, 'a great asset with regard to general student life'.[107] The new professor was Richard Blackburn, an Adelaide arts graduate who took up a Rhodes Scholarship after serving (like his father, Arthur Blackburn) in the Second Australian Imperial Force. At Oxford, Richard graduated as a Bachelor of Civil Law with first-class honours. Now aged thirty-one, he had published nothing, but he had the support of the chancellor, Sir Mellis Napier. Rowe would have been happy to appoint him without advertisement.

Blackburn completed pupillage at the London bar and visited British and Irish law schools before returning to Adelaide in mid-1950. The following year, he married (Bryony) Helen Curkeet, aviator, skier, shell-collector and sister of novelist Geoffrey Dutton. Blackburn published little more—a handful of journal articles—but he was well received by students and the wider community. He was a public lecturer for the Workers' Educational Association, and in 1955 toured the state's south-east, to drum up support for a university fundraising appeal. Bruce Debelle, judge and royal commissioner, remembered a speech by Blackburn (at St Peter's, Blackburn's old school) as his inspiration to study law. Blackburn ably fulfilled Rowe's purpose, but, for him, teaching was not a long-term career.[108]

§

Blackburn's most enduring effect on the Law School was to encourage full-time study and the expansion of the full-time teaching staff, objectives that he was quick to advocate on his return to Adelaide. The curriculum had changed little since 1936: nine subjects for the final certificate, fourteen (including Latin) for the LLB, and, for all students, an additional course in legal ethics, assessed only by attendance. Students could commence articles after their first year of university study, and most completed the LLB in five years, finishing the degree and articles together. Although it was a shorter course, most students avoided the final certificate. The shorter period of articles (three years as against four) was an incentive to choose the LLB.[109]

Curriculum reform had the backing of a new organisation that brought together the staff of Australia's law schools. After many years of slow growth, there were enough Australian law teachers to support a permanent organisation that would further their interests and allow them to meet in regular conferences. The idea was not new: Martin Kriewaldt had proposed such an association in 1939, but practical difficulties thwarted him. A fresh initiative from Melbourne in 1946 was more successful. Thirteen teachers from the six law schools, Campbell and Kriewaldt among them, gathered in Sydney to establish the Australian (later Australasian) Universities Law Schools Association. The new organisation advocated expansion of the so-called cultural subjects (such as Jurisprudence), longer periods of full-time study, and greater uniformity in law courses.[110]

The Adelaide faculty was receptive. In July 1946 it adopted a statement of principles for the future direction of the law course. The overlap between articles and university study, the faculty said, should be as brief as possible, and students could do more university work before starting articles. The 'so-called background subjects' should be reorganised and probably increased. Degree subjects should be grouped in years, and advancement from each year to the next should depend on adequate academic progress. The length of articles (currently four years, or three for LLB graduates) should be reconsidered, after the length of the law course was addressed. The judges needed to be kept onside, and the faculty sent the dean to confer with Napier, who suggested that a judge should attend future meetings about the plans.[111]

Implementation of the reform agenda began in 1952. The LLB expanded to seventeen subjects plus Legal Ethics, although its length remained four years. Two portmanteau subjects, the legacy of earlier compromises, were split: Criminal Law was separated from Wrongs, and Roman Law from Jurisprudence. Arts subjects were reduced from three to two, and Latin was no longer compulsory (but still required at matriculation for entry to law). Constitutional law was spread over two subjects. Prerequisites for advancing from one subject to another became more elaborate. The course rules envisaged, but did not mandate, that articles would continue after graduation. This model was implemented by new admission rules in 1955, which encouraged students to start articles in final year and complete them after leaving the university. LLB graduates who did so would need only two years under articles. Later, and shorter, articles became the norm.

Another target for restructuring was the law honours degree, the

LLB (Hons). It was introduced in 1931, as a by-product of the switch from exams to a thesis for the LLM, in line with other faculties. The honours degree was intended as a pathway to the LLM, but it attracted few students. Honours demanded high results in the ordinary course, followed by an exam in English legal history. By 1955 only seven students had graduated, and there had been none since 1941. New regulations introduced a broader final exam, during which candidates would have access to the Law Library. The number of honours graduates began slowly to increase.[112]

The faculty board that considered these changes had grown, and an increasing range of interest groups were represented there. Its minutes became longer and its processes more deliberative. The days were long past when its quorum had to be reduced to two, as it was in 1900, to ensure that business could be transacted. In 1950 a review of faculty memberships by the Committee of Deans led the law faculty to propose adding the president of the Law Society and all the judges of the Supreme Court (not just those who were members of the university council, as in the past). As reconstituted in 1952, the faculty also included all teaching staff of the level of lecturer and above, the chancellor and the vice-chancellor, the dean of Arts, and the professor of classics. Another two members were chosen by the council from among its own members, and three were recommended by the faculty itself. One of the first to be co-opted in this way was Jean Gilmore, an Adelaide graduate and practitioner, who became the faculty's first woman member in 1956. The increased representation of the judges allowed them to share their participation as the bench grew, but it also created the opportunity for them to attend as a group to make a point, as they would in a celebrated debate about the curriculum in 1971. They also retained their veto over the choice of examiners in subjects required for admission—and exercised it in 1967, when they forced the appointment of an additional examiner (in Family Law) with experience in local practice.[113]

§

The staff expansion advocated by Blackburn became more attainable as the South Australian government's grant to the university rose. It increased tenfold between 1948 and 1958, providing more than half of the university's total revenue. The university aligned its goals with the state government's policy of industrialisation. 'Our main intention is directed to the industrial development of the State', the chancellor, Sir William Mitchell, said at the annual university commemoration in 1947.[114] In this regard, as in many others, the state government meant Thomas Playford, who was in the audience when Mitchell spoke. According to A.P. Rowe, who became the university's first salaried, full-time vice-chancellor in 1948, the premier increased university funding only to forestall embarrassing comparisons with other states; he otherwise had no interest in the university, although he was quick to object when he thought it strayed into politics.[115]

The state government had another incentive to maintain its support. In 1951 the Commonwealth began regular grants to the states to be spent on universities, but the money was available only if state grants and student fees continued to provide most university funding. State support had to be maintained, in order to receive this welcome infusion of federal cash. State grants and fees continued to provide the bulk of the university's recurrent revenue, until the Commonwealth took over full responsibility for tertiary-education funding in 1974.[116]

New funding also benefited students. In 1951 a more comprehensive program replaced the earlier Commonwealth student assistance scheme. Commonwealth scholarships, as the new awards were called, were allocated on merit, as judged by results in matriculation exams. They were particularly significant for law students, who tended to get higher matriculation results (although there was no quota or cut-off score for entry to the course). A living allowance was available to those who qualified under a means test. It could enable university access for students who would otherwise be unable to support themselves, but there were recurring complaints from students about its inadequacy.[117]

The funding increases enabled, for the first time, an expansion of the Law School's full-time teaching staff. The first new post to be established was a readership, filled in 1951 by Francis Donovan, a Queenslander who came to Adelaide from the Crown Law Office in Sydney. As the council noted, Donovan's career resembled Blackburn's: army service, a Rhodes Scholarship and an Oxford BCL. But Donovan was still under thirty when he was appointed, and, unlike Blackburn, he had spent time in the United States (as a teaching fellow at the University of Chicago). His time in Adelaide was brief. The creation of a new chair of commercial law in 1952 drew him to Melbourne, and his later career was in trade diplomacy in Europe. His replacement was Daniel O'Connell, a young New Zealander with a Cambridge PhD on international law, who had recently missed out on appointment to a chair at Auckland University College. He joined a new full-time lecturer, English-born Gerald Fridman, another Oxford BCL graduate. Fridman was awarded the Law School's first LLM by examination, with a thesis on standards of proof, but he departed in 1956 for a graduate fellowship at the University of Pennsylvania. In 1950 the teaching staff were supported only by the part-time secretary–librarian and, in faculty matters, by the faculty secretary in the registrar's office. More full-time secretarial staff were on the Law School's wish list.[118]

Blackburn did not remain long as professor to see the results of these changes. It was not at the university but in private practice that he saw the next phase of his career, and he resigned with effect from September 1957. He remained in Adelaide and maintained his connection with the university, which appointed him a part-time lecturer in contract. When that role ended in 1961, he continued as an external member of faculty, until he became a judge of the Northern Territory Supreme Court in 1966. There he earned an ambivalent place in legal history through his decision in *Milirrpum v. Nabalco Pty Ltd*, the first ruling by an Australian judge on common-law recognition of Indigenous rights to land. Blackburn acknowledged Yolngu law with an openness to Indigenous forms of governance that harked back to fleeting colonial recognition of First Nations laws in South Australia. Kirsty Gover and Eddie Cubillo later commented:

> In many respects, Justice Blackburn's decision is an enlightened one, less dogmatic on the link between sovereignty and law than the High Court would later be in its native title findings. Blackburn J recorded his scepticism about 'Austinian analys[es] of the nature of law', refusing the Commonwealth's insistence that a recognisable 'sovereign' was necessary, instead recognising the Yirrkala-based Gumatj and Rirratjingu clans as a 'definable community' governed by what was undoubtedly law.[119]

Recognition of ownership within the common law of property, however, was a different matter. Blackburn rejected the Yolngu owners' title to land, a finding that stood until the High Court's decision in *Mabo v. Queensland (No. 2)* in 1992.[120]

§

Enrolments fell in the early 1950s, as students from the postwar surge completed their courses. At the bottom of the dip, in 1954, law enrolments were around half the level of 1948. The drop was much sharper in law than in overall student numbers or in law enrolments at Melbourne and Sydney over the same period. A discouraging outlook may have turned some students away. The president of the Law Society warned in 1949 that the profession was overcrowded. From the registrar's office, Victor Edgeloe echoed the warning, and law students said they were 'regularly reminded of the meagre prospects awaiting them on graduation'.[121] The warnings turned out to be badly timed, since the glut of graduates was short-lived. Sam Jacobs was a young practitioner: 'Then there was a drought ... It did affect the profession quite materially.'[122] By 1955 Blackburn was pleading for more students to enrol. For a moment, the students (totalling sixty-two in 1954) seemed amply provided for by the three full-time staff and six part-time lecturers. But numbers rose again, and the postwar peak was exceeded in 1960.[123]

Economic growth, aided by an ambitious migration program, drove the expansion of the profession, but the wave of postwar European migrants found it hard to make their way into the strongly Anglophone legal culture of Adelaide. In law, as in many professions, qualifications from continental Europe got little credit. Three students with doctorates in law from Prague and Budapest were allowed to attend lectures after the war, but neither they nor several others with European law degrees completed the Adelaide course. One of the first European migrants to do so began law in Australia, rather than seeking credit for earlier study. He was Stasys Cibiras, who worked as a labourer and hospital orderly in Adelaide before graduating with an LLB in 1958, still bearing a bullet scar as a reminder of the violence in his home country of Lithuania.[124]

4

On the Move: 1958–1967

By 1958 the Law School had been housed for seventy-five years in the university's original building, soon to be named after the former vice-chancellor, Sir William Mitchell. Its tenure there was precarious, as the central administration, the Law School's immediate neighbour, sought room for expansion. Law had moved from the basement to the top floor, after an extension gave the university some badly needed additional space in 1912. Reconfigured after the Barr Smith Library moved to its ornate new home in 1932, the Law School's accommodation consisted of a lecture room and the Law Library, which had a partitioned office for the professor and a cubicle for the Law School's secretary–librarian. The rooms were unheated, to the discomfort of the audience at a Women's Law Students' Society debate:

> The discussion went on for a very long time, and while the argument grew warmer and warmer, the court and the attendants at the court grew steadily colder and colder. Unfortunately the Law Library and the Law Lecture Room are made that way. The cold penetrates and penetrates till it reduces the whole body of a Law student to one numb shiver.[1]

By the end of World War II, the rooms were draughty, run-down, and leaky in wet weather. The teaching staff were accommodated wherever space could be found; Horst Lücke, on his arrival in 1959, was given a desk in the attic.[2]

The faculty knew that a move was inevitable, and in 1958 it

prepared a wish list of accommodation, based on doubling the full-time teaching staff to eight. The registrar, Victor Edgeloe, wanted the Law School to move to an extension of the Barr Smith Library, then under construction. The library would occupy the northern half of the extension, and academic departments, Law among them, would temporarily occupy the rest, until construction of what became the Napier Building. Despite the shortcomings of the Mitchell Building, the law faculty objected strongly. Led by Daniel O'Connell (who stood in as dean after Blackburn's resignation), it complained that the space offered to the Law School, on the lowest two floors of the extension, would be dark and cramped, hemmed in at the base of the escarpment that divided the campus. In new premises, the Law School might drop down the list of accommodation priorities and find itself marooned. O'Connell aimed to stay in the main building 'and use our own and the Registrar's future inconvenience as the lever to get our final building allocated in the minimum time'.[3]

Faculty members used all their ingenuity to resist the determined registrar. Some claimed that the 200-metre walk from North Terrace would add twenty minutes to the travel time of city-based articled clerks and part-time lecturers. O'Connell argued that a low ceiling in the library breached the *Building Act*. Nothing availed. The new professor of law, Norval Morris, arrived during the dispute. He wrote to his friend, the Victorian judge John Barry:

> I came into a building crisis here. A new law school, handsome & sufficient, is promised for 1964 by the Council. Everything is ready except the money but they urge me not to doubt that it too will be given to the patient. In the meantime, it is desired to kick the law school out of its present quarters at the end of 1959, to allow Administration to spread into them, and to house the law school in the intervening years on two floors of the new library extensions … To my mind all this is fine—the space is adequate. However, whipped up by Dan O'C & by a sense of injured <u>amour propre</u> the entire Law Faculty has been agreed in writing angry and

inaccurate letters to the Council, lobbying the C.J. (Acting Gov., Chancellor, Ld H. Exectnr), and generally stirring up bitterness.[4]

Adaptable, upbeat and willing to trust the council's promises, Morris had little interest in continuing a losing battle.[5]

The Law School moved to the Barr Smith extension late in 1959. The Law Library occupied the southern half of the ground floor, and a lecture theatre and staff offices filled the area immediately above it. Fears about the quality of the accommodation were realised, as Morris's successor, Arthur Rogerson, found: 'The Law Library and Law School were packed up and off, vainly protesting, to a deplorable area "at the back of the Barr Smith". Here up to 300 students took turns in fainting in the unventilated and windowless lecture room, and queued up, in noisome conditions, for seats in the Library.'[6] The building's stark red brick had none of the elegant ornamentation that made the university proud of the first stage of the Barr Smith. In the opinion of On Dit, the extension was 'a jarring obscenity all too incompletely hidden by a fortuitous tree'.[7] It did at least have a common room for law students, much frequented by card players but otherwise unloved:

We boast the commonest common room imaginable. Thirty feet by eight, it serves a multiplicity of purposes. It is a gracious foyer to the library, the men's lavatory and to the cleaner's cubby-hole. It is cloak room, bag rack, umbrella dryer and major thoroughfare, combined. It boasts dirty handmarks on a comment covered wall, a fire extinguisher and a 'Smokers Please' [ashtray]. The only common law expounded in the common room is simply a curt but authoritative 'If you want to talk, go outside.'[8]

The new accommodation was soon overwhelmed by a steep rise in enrolments, but Morris's trust in the council's plans proved well founded. Construction started in 1960 on the Napier Building, to house Arts, Economics and Law. On the building's completion in 1964, the Law School occupied level three, around the inner courtyard. The Law Library faced outwards in the northern wing. At the end of 1963, in anticipation of the move, the library was named after Sir John Salmond, in recognition of the 'considerable fame and distinction' he brought to the Law School.[9] Salmond's liking, even reverence, for law libraries made the name apt. A law library, he wrote, 'is not a mere dead record of a dead past. It is something far more than a collection of historical materials. It represents in large part a living, operative authoritative [sic], expression of the human spirit.'[10] The Law School's new accommodation was far superior to the Barr Smith extension in appearance and comfort, even if it fell short of the architects' aspirations when they submitted their plans:

> The public spaces in this faculty are larger than normal, as we wished to emphasize the dignity of this discipline and the importance of the profession in human affairs. This floor should have something of the atmosphere of the courts of law.[11]

What it lacked was space for the Law School's relentless expansion. The library and staff accommodation were inadequate from the start, and a planned moot court room had already been sacrificed to make additional offices. The school would have to move again.[12]

The Law School's wanderings were driven by the rapid rise in enrolments, a trend repeated across the university and, indeed, across Australian higher education. When the Law School's enrolments had exceeded 100 in the past—during the depression of the 1930s, and after World War II—they had dropped back after a few years. But when they topped 100 again, in 1957, they kept growing, passing 300 in 1964, 400 in 1971 and 1000 at the end of the century. The increases occurred despite a doubling of Law tuition fees between 1957 and 1960; the high proportion of law students on Commonwealth scholarships softened the blow. Population growth and the long-term shift to greater participation in tertiary study drew more students to the university. But the growth was neither smooth nor painless. Managing it presented the Law School with problems it had barely had to consider in its first seventy years.[13]

One of the most pressing questions was whether student numbers would have to be limited in some way. Enrolment quotas were unpopular, since they frustrated the choices of students (and their parents) for their studies and careers. The vice-chancellor said quotas were unthinkable when the university's accommodation shortages became particularly acute in 1956. The law faculty rejected quotas or regarded them as a last resort, but the question became more insistent, as demand for places continued to rise. The crunch came in 1966, when grants recommended by the Universities Commission for the 1967–69 triennium were reduced by the federal and state governments. An entrance quota already applied in the medical course at Adelaide, and in law courses at Melbourne, Monash and Sydney. Adelaide now imposed quotas across the board. Allocation of places would be based on results in matriculation exams. The law faculty, its hand forced by the central administration, set an entrance quota of 100 students for 1967. Excluded from the state's only law school, some students found quota-free entry elsewhere, at the University of Tasmania and, later, at the Northern Territory University.[14]

§

In common with other Australian law schools, Adelaide took many years to appoint women to its teaching staff, long after they began graduating and winning Law School prizes. Patterns of exclusion were durable, and candidates for staff appointment faced the barriers of limited access to postgraduate study, if contemplating an academic career, or glass ceilings in the profession, if seeking to combine practice with part-time teaching. It was the exceptionally well-qualified Roma Mitchell who was the first woman to be appointed a part-time lecturer, in 1960. Her subject was Family Law, often treated as a feminised area of teaching and practice. In 1966 the English criminologist Mary Daunton-Fear became a full-time senior lecturer, and Margaret Doyle, a recent graduate, became a tutor. Neither chose to stay on the staff over the longer term. Daunton-Fear resigned in

1973 to work at the Australian Institute of Criminology, and Doyle left in 1970 to join the staff of the royal commission on the Vietnam moratorium demonstration of that year.

To fill the Bonython chair left vacant by Richard Blackburn's departure in 1957, the university reverted to a familiar type of candidate: an outsider, young, energetic, with a promising research record, and male. When the chair was advertised, the applicants included Daniel O'Connell, who had been a reader for four years and had recently published the first of his books on international law. But the council was not satisfied with any of the applicants. It consulted Melbourne's dean of law, Zelman Cowen, who suggested Norval Morris. Born in New Zealand during a stay there by his Australian parents, and now in his mid-30s, Morris studied law at Melbourne and had a PhD in criminology from the London School of Economics. He held joint appointments as an associate professor in criminology and a senior lecturer in law at the University of Melbourne. Morris had international experience: he had been a teaching fellow at Harvard for a year and visited other American law schools. He accepted the Adelaide chair despite an encounter with A.P. Rowe, then at the acrimonious end of his otherwise successful term as vice-chancellor. Morris wrote: 'Literally, within minutes of my arrival for an interview here he was pouring out violent criticism of my colleagues, much of which I later found to be inaccurate and all of which was certainly ill-timed.'[15] A criminologist was an adventurous choice, since the discipline was newly established in Australia and was 'suspect in a number of places', in Cowen's words.[16] Morris's merits evidently outweighed such qualms, although his commitments in Melbourne made him unable to take up the appointment until August 1958, nearly a year after he was selected.[17]

Even before he arrived, Morris's opinions made news in Adelaide. He criticised flogging and hanging, both of which were still on the statute book in South Australia. In Melbourne, he appeared in court representing a convicted murderer who was sentenced to be flogged for wounding a warder; the Adelaide headline was 'Professor Appears for Killer'.[18] A journalist commented: 'That his views on penal reform and society's responsibility for its own misfits may be a little too advanced for South Australians of ingrained attitudes … seems highly probable.'[19] Morris had already clashed with Sir George Ligertwood, a Supreme Court judge and university council member, who took issue with Morris's criticisms of the judiciary at the Australian Legal Convention in 1953. More controversy was to come, when Morris joined the heated debate surrounding the conviction in 1959 of Arrernte man Rupert Max Stuart for the murder of a child, Mary Hattam. Morris's Law School colleague, Alex Castles, quickly became involved in the campaign on Stuart's behalf. Law staff took Thomas Dixon, the Arrernte-speaking Catholic priest who took up Stuart's case, to meet Morris: 'We came back from a party late at night and waiting at the gate to our house was a black figure, which turned out to be Father Dixon.' Dixon 'loudly announced that he's innocent … I didn't know what he was talking about but I said, "Come on in".'[20] Morris wrote to John Barry when Stuart's case was under appeal to the Privy Council in London:

> We are entering upon a blood bath here. They seem grimly determined to execute Stuart though the trial was most unsatisfactory, and despite the lack of any evidence other than Stuart's confession … I had two hours with the Attorney General on this case; his most wonderful irrelevancy was a proposition that two murderers not executed in New South Wales had come to South Australia and severally committed murder here. He was fascinated by photographs of the victim in the Stuart case and refused to turn his mind from the horror of the crime and the woolliest inaccuracies about capital punishment.[21]

The case culminated in the commutation of Stuart's death sentence and the prosecution of Morris's friend, newspaper editor Rohan Rivett, for the crime of seditious libel.[22]

Morris relished the memory of the campaign, despite its grim context—it 'made life bright'—but Adelaide never felt like home.[23] He told Barry of 'the sense of banishment that I often have here', far from colleagues working in his field.[24] Despite being a good organiser, he disliked 'the brown marshy wastes of administration'.[25] When invitations came to travel overseas, he took them. He was in Ceylon in the summer of 1958–59, chairing a commission of inquiry that advised against the reintroduction of capital punishment. While he was a visiting professor at Harvard in 1961–62, the informal approaches he received to stay on or move to Melbourne or Chicago made it unlikely that he would return to Adelaide. But the offer he accepted was from left field. Morris had been the Australian delegate at a United Nations seminar in Tokyo on human rights and criminal law in 1960, and the following year he was offered the directorship of the new UN Asia and Far East Institute for the Prevention of Crime and the Treatment of Offenders, in Tokyo. He began work there in June 1962. Two years later, he joined the University of Chicago's law school, where he remained for the rest of his long career in criminology.[26]

The university appointed more Melbourne graduates in 1958–59. They were collectively known as the 'Melbourne mafia', although the stay of two of them, Igor Kavass and Frank Maher, was relatively brief. A third, Alex Castles, remained, despite receiving tempting offers from other universities. He had worked as a journalist, and came to Adelaide with a Chicago doctorate. He became well known to the public through his media appearances; a student guide to the staff called him the 'Law School's pundit on any subject, but especially politics (strictly non-committal as to allegiance)'.[27] As a scholar, he published foundational works in Australian legal history, though he modestly disclaimed the title of doyen of that field, in favour of John Bennett of Sydney.[28]

In 1961, prompted by Morris, the faculty again recommended the establishment of a second professorial chair. It would lighten the onerous workload of the single professor, but chairs were also needed to address the emerging problem of career progression for the new cohort of full-time legal academics. Without the creation of more senior positions, able staff were frustrated by the lack of opportunities for promotion. As the faculty later said: 'Recent graduates realising the establishment bars at present existing in Australian law schools are not prepared to devote themselves to twenty years at senior lecturer status.'[29] An instalment of this liberalisation came through the appointment of Daniel O'Connell to a personal chair in 1962, on the recommendation of the faculty. O'Connell's growing reputation in international law was founded not only on authorship but also on regular travel, which sometimes caused friction with less-mobile colleagues. He was again dean in 1961–63, when Morris took leave and then resigned, but it was the last time he held that office. When tensions grew among the senior staff in the mid-1960s, O'Connell 'withdrew to the periphery, worked hard and experienced possibly the most productive years of his life', in Horst Lücke's words.[30] He became steadily more attractive to other universities as a potential recruit.[31]

§

The law curriculum, entrenched by its connection with the admission rules, was slow to change and infrequently updated. The reforms of 1952 had only divided and expanded existing subjects, and the course lacked adequate coverage of areas that were increasingly important in legal practice. In 1955 the three full-time teachers (in a joint submission to the faculty, where they were still a small minority) flagged the need for more teaching in taxation, estate and company planning, family law, and industrial law. Their preferred solution— adding a year to the LLB course—was rejected, but in 1959 taxation law became available as an optional evening course, outside the LLB. In its first year, most of its students were practitioners. The following year, Family Law (taught by Roma Mitchell) entered the curriculum as an alternative to Private International Law.[32]

Latin became anomalous in the updated curriculum. It had been removed as a compulsory LLB subject in 1952, without controversy, but matriculation-level Latin remained a prerequisite for entry to the Law School (and Latin or Greek was required for entry to Arts). Following a general reform of university matriculation requirements, in 1958 matriculation Latin was no longer needed for entry to the final certificate course, but it was still mandatory for the LLB. Its study had two common justifications. One was utilitarian: it was needed for the study of ancient texts in Roman Law, and it aided understanding of the many Latin tags used by lawyers. The other justification was cultural, harking back to the former role of the Greek and Roman classics in English school and university education. It was this role that some lawyers regarded as the most important. As Chief Justice Murray said in court, compulsory Latin was 'a question of the standard of general education'; it could be waived on proof of an equal cultural level (in the case before him, an articled clerk's knowledge of ancient Greek sufficed).[33] Social class was involved, too, since only well-resourced schools, few of them state-run, were able to teach Latin, and students elsewhere usually needed private coaching. Many in the profession supported it as an entrance requirement, as the Law Society did in 1957.[34]

The following year, a convergence of related questions brought the debate to a head. A wider plan to shift subject prerequisites out of inflexible university regulations and into subject guides necessitated a revision of the Law School's Latin requirements. At the same time, the proposed reintroduction of public international law (untaught since 1907) put compulsory Roman Law in doubt. The respective champions of these two subjects squared off in submissions to the faculty. International Law should become an alternative to Roman Law, Daniel O'Connell argued. Compulsory Latin, he said, was resented by many students, and the study of international or comparative law could introduce students to 'the growth of law, its systematisation, its points of comparison with English law, its practical treatment of familiar modern problems'. John Bray, now a QC and lecturer in legal history, asserted the value of Roman Law for understanding comparisons and contrasts, 'fundamental classifications', and the foundations of later legal developments. Progressive on social questions such as censorship, Bray was a traditionalist in education. O'Connell's propositions, he said, 'like others in other branches of learning, seem to me to offer up an excessive sacrifice on the altar of contemporaneity'.[35] The faculty agreed with O'Connell and decided that students could study either International Law or Roman Law. Mandatory Latin now hung by a thread, relying on its status as a prerequisite for the compulsory LLB subject Jurisprudence. The anti-Latin forces (led, it seems, by Norval Morris) lined up the Law Society, now in support, and removed the Jurisprudence prerequisite. Only students in (optional) Roman Law would need Latin, and school leavers unable to study it could enter the degree course.[36]

The restoration of International Law to the curriculum came as the subject was established, or re-established, as a distinctive strength of the Law School. Daniel O'Connell quickly became Australia's foremost scholar in the discipline. He published two major works in the 1960s, a general treatise on international law in two volumes in 1965, and a study of state succession, also in two volumes, two years later. His work on post-colonial state succession was part of a decade-long project funded by the Ford Foundation, under the auspices of the International Law Association. Around the same time, O'Connell, Castles and the Law Society developed a proposal for an institute, or school, of international law, focusing on questions of overseas trade. The university council endorsed the scheme, but it failed to secure funding. 'Thus failed the first of a number of O'Connell's attempts to set up his "own show" in Adelaide', Horst Lücke wrote.[37] As a teacher, he could find students disappointing. Bill Othams was in first year: 'Daniel O'Connell subjected us all to a general knowledge test early in his 1969 lectures to us (as part of the Elements of Law course), and then wrote an article for *Quadrant* about what he considered the deplorable results showed.'[38] O'Connell departed to the Chichele chair of international law at Oxford in 1972, but he was reluctant to give up his life in Adelaide, and returned for extended visits in 1973 and 1974. He kept the option of returning to his Law School chair after three years, but, when the time came, after much uncertainty, he chose to stay in England.[39]

Adelaide's prominence in international law continued, first through O'Connell's student, Ivan Shearer, and then through James Crawford. Crawford credited O'Connell with steering him into international law, but he asserted his independence by choosing a different doctoral supervisor at Oxford:

> I decided to do postgraduate work before I decided what I would do it in, which is a bit curious. It was fairly obvious that I was going to get a scholarship of some sort. I was casting around for what to do when Professor O'Connell looked up from the newspaper he was reading (I guess it was the *Australian*) and said, "Of course you've got to do international law. There's nothing else worth doing." For the lack of any more emphatic view presented by anyone else that's what I ended up doing, though fortunately not under Professor O'Connell.[40]

Returning to Adelaide, Crawford was a member of staff from 1974 to 1986. After appointments to chairs successively at Sydney and Cambridge, he became a judge of the International Court of Justice in 2015; on his death in 2021, his place on the court was taken by another former Adelaide staff member, Hilary Charlesworth, a professor from 1993 to 1997.

§

After *Obiter Dicta* succumbed to declining enrolments during World War II, the Law School was slow to revive a scholarly journal. Other universities soon established their own, emulating American law schools. The oldest of these, Melbourne's *Res Judicatae*, survived the war and was renamed the *Melbourne University Law Review* in 1957. Such journals, produced by students and staff collaborating in varying proportions, became an important alternative to the commercial legal press, which was dominated by the *Australian Law Journal* and was published mainly for practitioners. By 1958 Adelaide was the only Australian law school without a journal, a situation that could not long continue. Norval Morris and Alex Castles took the initiative to fill this gap; Castles provided much early momentum and assistance. The *Adelaide Law Review* appeared in 1960, published by the Law Review Association, an alliance of students and staff. After publication lapsed for a year in 1965, Brian Greaves, a recent recruit to the lecturing staff, became editor. Greaves's energy and experience in publishing made him 'the driving spirit' behind the *Review*, even after the editorship returned to student hands in 1968.[41] His resignation from the Law School in 1970 was a serious blow. In 1971–72 the association was taken over by the staff, although student participation remained its 'lifeblood'.[42] The association's precarious finances depended on a university subsidy, on regular donations from John Portus, who lectured in industrial law, and on grants from the Committee on Postgraduate Legal Education, derived from the fees charged for its courses.[43]

The Committee on Postgraduate Legal Education was an initiative of Norval Morris and Keith Sangster, at that time a Law Society council member. Beginning in 1961, the committee brought together representatives of the Law School and the Law Society, to meet the profession's growing interest in continuing education. An example of its regular lectures and seminars was an all-day conference in 1967 on proposed legislation, law reform and recent developments, attended by over 150 practitioners, judges and academics. Three years later, the committee co-sponsored a conference on sentencing, to be attended by the chief justices of New South Wales and South Australia. A novel feature of this Sentencing Institute, as it was called, was the discussion of hypothetical sentencing scenarios in groups, each chaired by a judge. The organiser was Mary Daunton-Fear. Such was the committee's success that by 1972 it had accumulated a large financial surplus, even after its generous donations to the Law Review Association. It sought a firmer organisational basis for its work and was reconstituted as the Committee for Continuing Legal Education, under the Law Society council. The Law Society's control of its profitable activities would become a source of friction with the university, when the practical legal training of new graduates came under discussion in the 1990s.[44]

Traditional forums, such as the *Adelaide Law Review*, brought the Law School's work to the wider scholarly community, but the Law School television project was a more innovative way of engaging with the world outside the university. Beginning in 1967, a group of law students filmed short dramatisations of common legal problems, followed by discussion of the relevant law. For the first program, concerning purchases on credit, students lent their cars to create what must have been a convincing used-car yard. Other episodes covered unfriendly neighbours and radar speed detection on the roads. The films were broadcast on Sunday mornings on Adelaide commercial station Channel 10, and shown in class and at university open days. Warren Jarrett, Justin O'Halloran and Rod O'Brien formed the camera crew; Jarrett directed. Staff assistance came from (John) Neville Turner, 'the Law School's answer to Cecil B. de Mille', and Alex Castles, whose television work as a commentator facilitated the link with Channel 10.[45] Some ten episodes were made in 1967–68, before students completed their courses and moved on, and the project wound down.[46]

Performance of a different kind made the law revue a local theatrical institution. It had forerunners in law students' participation in commemoration day processions and the university revue, Footlights. A successful cabaret at the 1958 law ball inspired a more ambitious stage show the following year, which became the university's first faculty revue. The script was by Ivan Shearer, Gervase

Coles and W.R. (Bill) Cornish (later one of the Law School's eminent Oxbridge exports), who also provided the music. *On Dit* commented: 'The general effect was happy go lucky and enthusiastic, although artless. The show hovered on the brink of mediocrity.'[47] Revived in later years, the Law Revue left strong memories: a 'blissfully creative, funny and demanding' time for one participant; for many more, a chance for students to come together and celebrate, or satirise, their shared experience.[48]

§

Research and teaching depended heavily on the Law Library as the repository of print in the pre-digital era. Its modest early collections were maintained by the University Library, in consultation with the professor of law. The Law School had no library staff of its own until, in 1932, the university appointed a part-time library assistant and typist, Edwin Olssen, who became the law librarian. The son of a labourer, Olssen worked as a clerk for the South Australian Railways, until he was retrenched during the Depression. His bridge to university study was the Workers' Educational Association, which ran adult-education courses in a broad range of subjects, with the university's support. Olssen's employment in the Law Library gave him a small income and allowed him to attend arts lectures at the university without paying fees. Able and determined, he graduated in arts in 1937, aged twenty-nine, and won the Tinline Scholarship in history, a postgraduate scholarship in arts, and a John L. Young research scholarship. He later married an Adelaide law graduate, Nancy Newland. Olssen maintained his links with the Workers' Educational Association and moved to New Zealand to work for it as an organiser, before going on to lecture in political science at the University of Otago.[49]

Olssen and later Law Library assistants combined secretarial work for the professor of law with their library responsibilities. The combination became harder to maintain as the demands of managing the Law Library grew, and in 1958 the University Library appointed the first full-time law librarian. The appointment went to another of Norval Morris's imports from Melbourne, Gwenda Sargeant (later Fischer). She was Morris's secretary at the University of Melbourne, while she completed a BA degree as a mature-age student, in her late thirties, after working as a secretary in Melbourne and London. Soon after she began work at Adelaide at the start of 1959, she organised the Law Library's move to the Barr Smith extension, the first of three relocations she managed as librarian. Her colleague and successor, Richard (Dick) Finlay, remembered her as 'a courageous, humorous, indomitable fighter'.

> She had taken a small collection of books and organised them into a law library, with the collections arranged so that the law lecturers and students could find their way about in them. Many of the University's non-law librarians found this bewildering and regarded Gwenda with suspicion, and sometimes with awe.[50]

Sargeant was officially a mere assistant librarian, subordinate to the university librarian. But, as Finlay witnessed, she was an effective advocate for the needs of a specialised law library, even if they did not suit the University Library's standard practices:

> I think that at the time Gwenda must have been regarded as a sort of devil, or a person with unusual powers, by some of the 'right-thinking' in the main Library. There she was, with very little experience in libraries, and that only in law libraries, standing up to the establishment of the University library. What was more, she was winning.[51]

Sargeant's skills and advocacy were bolstered by dual qualifications that were rare, if not unique, in Australian law librarianship at the time. She completed the LLB course while working in the library, and understood the sources and structure of law from the point of view of the library's users. In 1961–62 she undertook a master's degree in librarianship at the University of Washington, in Seattle, with funding from the Carnegie Corporation, the University of Washington and a Fulbright travel award. The 'professional content of librarianship' was little known outside the library profession, she wrote.

> I was, therefore, not surprised when university colleagues, and others, asked 'What on earth is it going to take a year to learn?' when I announced my intention of taking a year off, without salary, to study librarianship in school here, rather than by self-directed study at home.[52]

Nevertheless, her unusual qualifications were soon recognised by other universities looking for law librarians. She turned down approaches from the Sydney and Monash law schools, but by 1968 she was more receptive, frustrated with the rapid turnover of junior library staff at Adelaide. Horst Lücke regarded her possible departure with dismay. 'Please try to hang on to Gwenda, whatever the cost. We'll be sunk without her', he wrote to Alex Castles.[53] But personal and professional considerations persuaded her to move. She left Adelaide in 1968, when her husband, Gerald Fischer, the state archivist, became the archivist of the University of Sydney. Seeking more time to pursue opportunities that she saw emerging in legal bibliography and indexing, she became the compiler of the *Current Australian and New Zealand Legal Literature Index*, a forerunner of later indexing databases. After the Fischers returned to Adelaide in 1980, she pursued this work as a visiting research fellow at the Law School until her death in 1998.[54]

§

Happily for the Law School, its overcrowding in the Napier Building coincided with a period of relatively generous government funding for universities, before the financial stringencies of the late 1960s. It did not have long to wait before moving, yet again, to a larger home. In 1966 widespread accommodation problems led the Universities

Commission to recommend no fewer than five new buildings for the nation's eight law schools. At Adelaide, construction of a new law building was already underway. The university's detailed brief for the architects painted an idealised picture of the lives of students and staff:

> Within the Faculty of Law, the student's life is centred around the Law Library. During a normal working day a law student will, on arrival, make straight for the Library and stake a claim to a reading space. His functions from that time involve excursions from his Library place to lectures or tutorials, to lunch or to obtain some form of refreshment, returning to the Library immediately afterwards, he will work in there until the end of the day …
>
> Academic staff spend most of the normal working day in the building; they come and go by car, lunch in the Staff Club, visit the Barr Smith Library as well as the Departmental Library, and less frequently, the Administrative Building. However, many want access to their rooms at irregular hours in the evenings and at weekends.[55]

There were other things to bear in mind: 'Universities are chronically talkative and sensitive to disturbance. This suggests great attention to acoustic design in all areas.' The plan envisaged two stages of construction, allowing floors to be added in future. In later years, the faculty frequently invoked the figure of 600 students as the maximum for which the building was planned, but the brief to the architects told them that there would be about 500 users in the building's first stage and 650–700 in stage two.[56]

The site was awkward: narrow, sloping, and bounded on one side by the university's new underground carpark. The plaza on the carpark roof acted as a forecourt to the main entrance. It was softened by a large pond, 'glowing faintly green in the crisp morning air'.[57] The pond was plagued by leaks and algae until its removal in the 1990s. Below the entrance level, the Law Library occupied two floors. Vertical panels on the façade, finished with sandy-coloured pebbles, shielded angled windows from the western sun and complemented the stone of Bonython Hall across the plaza. The dean, Arthur Rogerson, commented:

> The Napier variegated matchbox was already in continuous and violent quarrel with the Banker's Gothic of the adjoining Bonython Hall, and the Law School, which was to occupy the east side of the open square of which the earlier buildings formed the west and north sides had to attempt to reconcile the two. In some eyes it has succeeded in doing so, though inevitably at the cost of some loss of internal efficiency.[58]

The greatest challenge to internal efficiency was movement between the building's five levels. On the one hand, a lift was available for those unable to climb the building's many stairs, and an additional entrance, from the carpark, served disabled users. On the other hand, the lift and the stairs were too small for the heavy traffic between the entrance and the lecture theatres on the upper floors. Crowding when students moved between classes, to say nothing of emergency evacuation, would prove a persistent difficulty.[59]

The Law School moved to the building early in 1967, but it was not the only occupant. The needs of the University Library and the central administration had forced Philosophy out of the Barr Smith extension and Classics from the Mitchell Building. As a temporary measure, they moved in with the Law School, taking the top floor. Despite these inconveniences, many were pleased with the 'glorious new building' for 'our Law School', as the president of the Law Society put it.[60] At the faculty's request, the council named the building after Sir George Ligertwood, who had recently retired as the university's chancellor.

Construction proved more expensive than the university expected, and savings had to be made, with lasting effects. Substitution of cheaper asbestos-based floor tiles left a dangerous legacy for future renovators. The planned permanent roof, which could be jacked up when additional floors were constructed, was replaced by a steel roof, causing 'furnace-like temperatures' on the top floor during Adelaide's hot summers.[61] Only the Law Library had air conditioning when the building first opened. Air conditioning in academic offices was outside the Universities Commission's guidelines, and, as an economy measure, it was removed from the plans of the Ligertwood lecture theatres. Experience of 'the Sauna Baths', as a student called them, led to the installation of air conditioning in the theatres in 1968.[62] Staff had to share telephone numbers, but parsimony with telephones was almost a campus tradition. The author Michael Innes (the pen-name of J.I.M. Stewart, professor of English language and literature) incorporated the university's peculiar shared telephones in the solution of his murder mystery, *The Weight of the Evidence*, in 1940. Most Law School staff still shared telephone numbers forty years later. John Keeler had the misfortune to share a number with Alex Castles, and had to field his many callers, from the media and elsewhere. The Law Library telephone became an unofficial message line for students, receiving 'continuous calls' for them.[63] The capacity of the electrical system was reduced during construction, and power would be cut if staff used too many bars in the portable radiators that provided their only heating. Even these were banished during drives for energy-saving and cost-cutting in the late 1970s, when staff were expected to warm themselves on small heat-lamps under their desks. They could take breaks to restore circulation, the university counselled: 'You may thereby be able to forgo the use of any space heating.'[64] The meagre wiring hampered efforts to extend air conditioning in the 2000s, when room air conditioners were allocated by lottery. Extreme heat or cold sometimes drove staff from their rooms. It was not until a general refurbishment in 2009 that the building's users were protected throughout against the summer heat.[65]

The Ligertwood Building became a settled home for the Law School, after a decade of moves, but it aroused mixed feelings. 'This was seen as a very fine building and a vote of confidence by the university in the Law School', said a student who arrived in 1969.[66] But it had limitations, as Bill Othams, another student in the early 1970s, found:

> It wasn't designed for anything except attending lectures and tutorials, meetings with lecturers and tutorials in their rooms, and studying in the library. Any socialising with other law students (or lecturers or tutors!) had to be conducted elsewhere ... The Ligertwood seemed a very narrow building to me, designed to encourage you to leave it to resume real life as soon as possible ... It certainly didn't promote a connection between the law and life, and it seemed a very hierarchical building, with the lecturers and tutors remote from the students in their upper floor aeries, and the library where the students were supposed to toil in the 2 lowest levels.[67]

It had aged when Callum Di Sario arrived in 2013: 'A forward-looking building in 1960s terms, sure, but after almost 50 years of continuous use ... well, it wore every minute of those 50 years on its pockmarked and stained cream-coloured walls.'[68]

The greatest shortcoming was a lack of room for growth. As the temporary occupation of the top floor by Classics and Philosophy extended into a second decade, tutorial rooms and the staff tearoom were sacrificed to make offices for law staff. Accommodation across the university was tight, and moves depended on space becoming available elsewhere. One such rearrangement allowed the Law School to take over Philosophy's space in 1980. The building still lacked the top two floors that made up Stage Two of the original design, but when reforms in higher education triggered a wave of building on Australian campuses, two floors were added in 1990–91. They provided more (shared) space, but staff and students faced punishing levels of noise, dust and heat during construction. Conditions were so bad in March 1991 that the Law School's occupational health and safety officer briefly closed the building. Lasting relief from the perennial lack of space for staff came in 2015, when the Law

School occupied the entire building for the first time. Informal space for students, however, remained marginal. Remedies for these and other shortcomings would require entirely new accommodation. Demolition of the Ligertwood Building and relocation of the Law School featured in a campus master plan released in 2016, but it remained unrealised.[69]

§

By 1969 the Law School's full-time teaching staff had expanded to fifteen. Alex Castles and Horst Lücke had applied for chairs at the University of Queensland (Castles by invitation) but withdrew when Adelaide made them professors in 1967. Differences in style and outlook were emerging. As a student, Geoff Lindell divided staff into 'O'Connellites' and 'Castleites', distinguished by their degree of formality and their interest, or lack of it, in Australian topics.[70] O'Connell lectured in an academic gown, while Castles preferred not to; O'Connell was an internationalist, while Castles was an enthusiastic Australianist, despite his use of comparative methods and his writing on international topics. Castles described himself as 'talkative ... a Deakinite, radical, a non-respecter of authority for its own sake'; O'Connell was a knight of honour and devotion in the Catholic lay religious order, the Sovereign Order of Malta.[71]

More abrasive differences emerged between O'Connell and the new Bonython professor, Arthur Rogerson, who replaced Norval Morris in 1964. Born in England in 1925, Rogerson was the last Bonython professor to have served in the armed forces in World War II. A scholarship took him to Oxford, where he won first-class honours in jurisprudence. He was called to the bar in London and became a fellow of Jesus College. F.H. (Harry) Lawson, the Oxford professor of comparative law, was one of his referees:

> As becomes a native of the North of England (more precisely Carlisle) he is outspoken and even abrupt; but he thinks before he speaks, and is at pains to understand other people's points of view.

He is quick-witted and lively in conversation, but does not waste words. He has above all intense vitality and great powers of work. I can strongly recommend him for your chair.[72]

Rogerson did not make a formal application but was approached by the vice-chancellor, Henry Basten, on a visit to England in 1963.[73]

Rogerson, like many English legal academics, had no research degree. He published little and concentrated on undergraduate teaching, curriculum reform and the mentoring of junior staff. O'Connell had an international reputation as a scholar, and in the 1960s he was publishing the major works that made his name. His personal relationships could be tense, as even the peaceable Lücke found: 'Professor O'Connell appears to have inspired unfriendly feelings in some colleagues in this University; indeed I can remember moments of personal tension between him and myself.'[74] As head of department, Rogerson was responsible for staffing the teaching program, and he disliked what he saw as O'Connell's habit of departing overseas at short notice. Castles wrote to Lücke after one such incident in 1968:

> We've had another confrontation between Dan and Arthur (per media of letters) re Dan's absence without leave at the beginning of second term but the worst of this seems to have blown over now ... I did my best to smooth over what David [Kelly] may have told you, promised to become a major and open rift in the School. (Perhaps this is too strong, but I think feelings, particularly those of Ivan [Shearer], were deeply hurt by the business.)[75]

Lücke replied: 'The tension between our two senior professors is certainly the most intractable problem in the Law School.'[76] As the staff grew, internal friction became a new and disruptive feature of Law School life. The rise of staff democracy soon gave these disputes new scope and significance.

Law lectures began in 1883 in the University's new building, seen here circa 1890.
State Library of South Australia, B 13285.

Professor Jethro Brown (at end of table) and gowned students
in the law lecture room. *Critic,* 11 July 1906.

John Salmond on his appointment as
professor of law in 1897.
Adelaide Observer, 29 May 1897

A controversial departure:
Professor Coleman Phillipson.
Mail, 8 September 1923.

A temporary home: the Barr Smith Library extension (at right, circa 1970),
'all too incompletely hidden
by a fortuitous tree'. UAA, S695, item 127.

Emily Moulden (at right) with her family in 1896. The daughter and grand-daughter of lawyers, in 1903 she became the Law School's first woman student. State Library of South Australia, B 30395.

Mary Kitson, the first woman to graduate from the Law School. Law Society of South Australia.

Irene Watson, the Law School's first Indigenous graduate, in 1985. UAA, S695, item 993

Soon outgrown: the Napier Building, 1966. UAA, S695, item 120.

Pens and paper: the Law Library, 1983. UAA, S1151, item 972.

'A glorious new building': the first stage of the
Ligertwood Building, circa 1981, with Henry Moore
sculpture. UAA, S695, item 185.

A home of its own: the Law School became the sole occupant of the enlarged
Ligertwood Building, seen here in the 1990s. UAA, S695,item 399

5

A First-Class Fight: 1968–1979

Law students of the late 1960s could seem conservative to their contemporaries. The Law School's image, to a student who enrolled there in 1966, was 'a bunch of young men in ties and sports jackets with furled umbrellas'.[1] 'From deep in the heart of Houndstooth Land your idiom is cynicism', *On Dit* advised law freshers.[2] Final-year students, who studied part-time while working as articled clerks, were 'a conspicuous presence about the building, all in suits in those days'.[3] But clothes were changing, more women were enrolling, and the articles system was in decline. Law students joined a campus-wide shift towards student participation in decision-making. Such campaigns had a long history. Medical students sought regular consultation on curriculum changes as early as 1914, and students called for representation on the university council in recurring campaigns over ensuing decades. In 1968 the university began a long process of consultation and drafting that culminated in the enactment of the *University of Adelaide Act 1971* (SA). Among other changes in university governance, it added student and staff representatives to the council.[4]

As this movement accelerated in the late 1960s, the Law Students' Society called for the establishment of a law curriculum committee that would include student representatives, as in Arts and Economics. The faculty responded favourably. A meeting of students and staff in April 1969 (attended by 140 students) broadened the committee's proposed remit to embrace 'general matters of Law School policy', and decided that its members should meet directly with the faculty, giving the students a voice in faculty meetings. After some resistance from the Education Committee (the central board composed of deans, professorial heads, members of other central committees and the university leadership), a Student Liaison Committee, composed of three elected student members, was established for this purpose. Meanwhile, the faculty invited students Helen Wighton and Robert Whitington to attend its meeting in September 1969, to discuss a Students' Representative Council resolution against compulsory attendance at lectures. They were the first students to participate in a meeting of the Faculty of Law. Three students were elected to the Liaison Committee in time to attend the next faculty meeting, where their first item of business was the appointment of students as full members of faculty, taking advantage of new provisions in the university's internal statutes. The three student representatives became full members of faculty in 1970.[5]

In the Law School, this was a peaceful process in which staff were closely involved. Student activism across the campus was generally quieter than at many other Australian universities, Flinders among them, and Adelaide students resorted only rarely to the common protest tactic of invading council chambers or administrative offices. Philip Broderick, president of the Students' Association, said in 1974: 'Adelaide avoided the "occupation syndrome" where students have taken over administration buildings to draw attention to grievances and press for claims. I feel this was due more to the agility of this administration than to lack of purpose from the students.'[6] Broderick was speaking at the annual university commemoration, where a conciliatory tone might be expected, but the opinion was a common one. Horst Lücke gave some of the credit for the relative calm to Alex Castles, who advised Vice-Chancellor Geoffrey Badger on responses to student activism. Opening the closed doors of faculty and department meetings entailed a changed perspective on the part of some of the staff. Lücke wrote in 1971: 'Staff/student committees have been formed to discuss both teacher and student performance and this (though perhaps embarrassing at first) is proving most helpful ... We do not believe that we should preserve the fictional aura of perfection which we have inherited from our predecessors.'[7] Social events also brought students and staff together. Staff hosted students at post-exam parties in the 1960s, and male students played cricket against the Law School's staff cricket club, the Gilbert Jessop Society (named for the English all-rounder), which flourished from the early 1960s to the 2000s.[8]

Despite this goodwill, students were not full participants. Student representation on American law school committees in this period has been called 'magnanimous tokenism'.[9] An Adelaide law student representative, Michael Davis, had few illusions: 'A sense of frustration has led students to believe that they are exercising not <u>effective</u> participation but <u>token</u> participation.' The student representative 'feels that his main function is to ease the collective conscience of the Faculty by having him present when decisions are made which vitally affect his fellow students'.[10] These shortcomings could be alleviated, Davis argued, by making more students members of faculty. When the faculty discussed this proposal in 1972, the minutes recorded a variety of (unattributed) opinions: 'The governed should have a say in their government', and 'the presence of students on the Faculty helped to prevent any injustice being perpetrated'; on the other hand, 'students should not have a decisive voice on how they should be taught'.[11] Davis's motion was lost by seven votes to ten. A call for student membership of the increasingly important Departmental Committee led only to the establishment in 1978 of a new Liaison Committee, composed of students and staff. Yet opportunities for participation grew. Two elected students joined the faculty's new Curriculum Committee in 1972, the advisory Assessment Committee established in 1976 had equal numbers of students and staff, and the Departmental Committee decided to include student representatives in its meetings in 1983.[12]

Vibrant and occasionally anarchic student publications accompanied the rise in student activism. A Law Students' Society newsletter appeared in 1963, taking its title, *Lux Gentium*, '(Law is) the light of nations', from the motto used since the 1920s for the society's badge and publications. Newsletter titles came and went, but the ethos was captured by the editors of *Cobwebs*, published from 1977 to 1980:

> In its short span of life, Cobwebs has successfully balanced both comedy and commentary in its pages. There appears not only the mass of lurid prose, legal melodrama and verse … but also critical articles in which aspects of the Law School and assumptions behind the law and legal education are placed under the analyst's microscope.[13]

The dean, Michael Detmold, sent a greeting:

> May Cobwebs remain scurrilous, shameful, disgraceful, despicable, unbecoming, unworthy, derogatory, scandalous, unmentionable, arrant, shocking, outrageous, notorious, dirty, vile, beggarly, low, unrighteous, naughty, unprincipled, improper, base, scurvy, flagrant, incorrigible, diabolical, Stygian, fiendish, foul and scrubby …
>
> But may you be good-humoured. May you (as the collective student) look upon our failings with the same charity that we apply to yours.[14]

Criticism of teaching remained an occasional point of friction over the newsletters and the *Little Law Handbook*, published by the Broad Left Law Group from 1989, but the publications became a lasting feature of Law School culture.

§

Staff, too, wanted a greater role in university decision-making. Their efforts were more successful than the student campaigns, although the beneficiaries were mainly teaching rather than professional staff. The Law School was an early mover in this trend, as the staff made a concerted effort to change the way the school was run, but the transition was difficult. The original forum for staff involvement in Law School management was the faculty board, the Faculty of Law. All full-time lecturing staff were members, but in 1968 they were still outnumbered by representatives of the profession, the Supreme Court and the wider university. The board had never confined itself strictly to its statutory function of advising the council on studies, lectures and examinations. Its heft was evident in its involvement in such policy matters as the triennial planning rounds overseen by the Australian Universities Commission. Its advisory role did, however, limit its power of direct decision-making. Implementation often depended on the uncertain cooperation of the Education Committee, the university council and other bodies. The faculty's large meetings muted the influence of the teaching staff, although they could have more control in its ad-hoc committees.

Day-to-day management devolved from the council, the registrar and the university's central committees to the deans of the faculties and the heads of departments. Under the university's internal statutes, the dean was elected by the faculty from among its members and exercised 'a general superintendence over the Faculty's administrative business'.[15] The duties, but not the selection, of the head of department were also prescribed by statute. Heads were responsible to the university council (not, it should be noted, to their faculties) 'for the proper functioning of their Departments'. Academic staff worked under the heads' 'general direction'.[16] The wide powers of the head included a decisive role in promotions, research support and study leave. The statutes implied that selection of the head, unlike election of the dean, came within the council's general power, under the University of Adelaide Act, to appoint officers of the university.[17]

In the Law School, which had only one department, the headship had gone automatically to the Bonython professor. This arrangement was part of Arthur Rogerson's terms of appointment: 'The Bonython Professor of Law will be the Head of the Department of Law and responsible to the Council for its work.'[18] To Horst Lücke, Rogerson was 'automatically the head of the Law Department for life, as far as we knew'.[19] This life tenure became contentious as the number of full-time teaching staff grew (from seven in 1960 to sixteen in 1970, and from one professor to four). Lücke expressed a common perception:

> However suitable the notion of a permanent headship might have been to a small Law School, comprising no more than one or two full-time staff members, it was already inappropriate to the Law School of 1964 and has become wholly indefensible as the Law School has grown to its present size.[20]

Speaking for the Staff Association, Lücke wrote: 'There is nothing so confining as to be subjected to the jurisdiction of an all-powerful Head of Department more or less in perpetuity.'[21] Personal factors increased the impetus for change. In John Keeler's recollection, Rogerson's style became less popular as the teaching staff matured and younger academics developed their careers. The staff 'became more separate, and it was from there, I think, that people saw that Arthur's somewhat mentoring and nurturing style, which came from a background that distinctly saw research as secondary to teaching, didn't necessarily match their career ambitions'.[22]

Rogerson went on study leave in 1969, setting off a train of events that shifted the centre of power. Daniel O'Connell, the senior professor, was an obvious candidate to become head of department, but Lücke wrote to Castles: 'Does Dan expect to be Dean while Arthur is away? Personally I doubt whether this would be a happy solution. I'd be happiest to see you take over, which doesn't mean that I wouldn't be happy to shoulder some of the actual work.'[23] O'Connell lacked the support of the registrar, as John Keeler remembered:

> Vic Edgeloe, who was very powerful and influential, was very clear that he thought that Dan had directed too many resources that

were given to the Law School into international law, when he had been acting dean in 1962–63 … And he simply said he wasn't going to have Dan as the acting dean.[24]

The university appointed Castles as head of department (after consulting O'Connell, Rogerson, Castles and Lücke), and the faculty elected him dean. Management practices changed. Staff meetings, first held when Norval Morris was dean, had been in abeyance under Rogerson, but Castles agreed to revive them. Regular meetings began in March 1969, buttressed with formal agendas and minutes.[25]

What would happen on Rogerson's return in 1970 was unclear. Satisfaction, or otherwise, with his role as head was only part of the issue. The trend towards wider staff participation in decision-making was gaining support across the university, informed by similar developments elsewhere. The Staff Association was the forum for much of this debate, in which law staff, with their characteristic interest in process and in structures of governance, were prominent. Some of the impetus came from the informal group who customarily lunched together at Table Four in the staff club. Rogerson was a member. So was John Keeler: '"Table Four" was one of the places where the move towards elected heads of departments took off.'[26]

Around the middle of 1969, proposals for change in the Law School were put forward by seven members of staff: Mary Daunton-Fear, Michael Trebilcock, Neville Turner, Michael Harris, David Kelly, Brian Greaves and Ivan Shearer. Together they made up most of the full-time lecturing staff below the rank of professor (Brent Fisse and John Keeler were the only absentees). All had been appointed during the expansion of the staff in 1963–66; all except Harris were now senior lecturers. Collectively they were restless. Of the seven, none remained on the staff ten years later, although David Kelly would later return, as a professor. They were unhappy with the current administrative structure, but the reasons they gave had more to do with its inefficiency than with the inherent merits of democracy. There was an 'unsatisfactory demarcation' of the functions of faculty board, dean and head, they said. Power was concentrated in the hands of the combined head and dean, who represented the faculty in the university and made decisions on appointments, promotions and leave. The resulting administrative burden was a heavy load for one person. Supervision of the Law School by the faculty board was inadequate, and many functions of the head of department were outside the board's jurisdiction.[27]

The remedies proposed by the group of seven lay mainly in clearer demarcation of responsibilities, sharing of administrative burdens, and greater staff participation. The offices of head and dean should be separated and should rotate among the professors. More responsibilities should be delegated, and regular staff meetings should continue. The department, not the faculty, was their main concern, but they also proposed wider staff representation on faculty committees. The tutors and the law librarian should be members of the faculty board. These changes, the seven argued, 'would lead to better decision-making processes, better decisions, fairer distribution of administrative burdens, a more involved, informed and enthusiastic staff, and, in result [sic], a better Law School'. John Keeler added a marginal note: 'Most likely a much more openly divided one too. The price of progress!'[28] A committee of sub-professorial staff took the proposals further. Their report recommended annual election of the head, who would usually be a professor, although any member of the full-time academic staff would be eligible. Staff should take collective responsibility for decision-making. The reasons were utilitarian rather than philosophical: broad participation would share administrative burdens, provide more 'watch-dogs' and instil a greater 'sense of responsibility in us all'. If the administrative structure was to change, it should be done 'as expeditiously as possible to promote the smooth running of the Department and to avoid frustration, discontent and even resignations from the staff'.[29]

During these deliberations, Lücke wrote to Shearer: 'The whole exercise will, I hope, be an attempt to sort out practical problems amongst friends.'[30] But the speed recommended by the committee meant that matters would be resolved in Rogerson's absence. Michael Trebilcock warned: 'The need for haste is not explained or apparent, and an adverse interpretation could very readily be placed upon it.'[31] Rogerson regarded the headship as his for as long as he wanted it. He supported democratic management in principle, but in practice he favoured consultative autocracy, under the general supervision of the faculty board. He explained his views to the staff: 'When I came to Adelaide I was determined that the Department of Law should, so far as the limitations of the University's system would permit it, be a self-governing, democratic society of equals.' Matters of principle should be decided by the faculty; the only staff committee he contemplated would be confined to allocating university research funds within the department. Aggrieved staff could complain to the Staff Association. He favoured rotation of the headship, or alternatively 'the good old Tory principle of informal consultation'. 'I would be violently opposed to elections: the dangers should be obvious, and must far outweigh the benefits to be gained.'[32] He would relinquish the headship when the new administrative structure and a new curriculum had been established. Until then, he was entitled to the post under his contract of employment.

In a private letter to the vice-chancellor, Rogerson hinted at legal action: 'I would not like you to be in any doubt that I regard this matter of the sanctity of a staff member's contract of service as being one of principle which I am prepared to go to any lawful lengths to uphold.'[33] He argued against making Lücke head, or so Lücke heard. 'Arthur apparently told the Council that I was unfit to be H. of D. for long because of my foreign background', he told Castles.[34] Lücke himself, reluctant to be drafted, remembered putting the same argument to the vice-chancellor. 'I thought I might escape a fate worse than death in this way', he said, but to no avail.[35]

The headship was ultimately a matter for the university council. It took legal advice, which backed Rogerson and confirmed that he was entitled to remain head of department for as long as he was the Bonython professor. However, confronted with the views of the staff, Rogerson asked to be released as head, although he retained the Bonython chair. Castles, away on study leave, was unavailable; the council made Lücke head for 1970 and sought further consultations between the vice-chancellor and the law professors (but not other staff) about the future.[36] The faculty elected Lücke as dean. Castles wrote to him:

> It was certainly a great relief to learn that there had been some change in the situation at the Law School ... The result of course is the right one and the only one which gives some guarantee that the Law School can be held together effectively. At the same time, I can't help feeling sorry for Arthur. It must have been a hard and difficult decision for a person of his temperament to make. If he had decided otherwise, however, I feel sure that he, as well as the Law School, would have suffered serious long term damage, both in terms of prestige and with respect to the day to day teaching and research activities carried on there.[37]

But tensions remained. Lücke mentioned 'the deep divisions which are still all too apparent in the Department'.[38]

The combined workload of dean and head was becoming too onerous for any one person to manage, especially without the assistance of associate deans or an executive officer. Castles wrote to Lücke:

> As we both know the burdens are considerable and most particularly the administrative hackwork which goes with both the Deanship and the Headship. The position in the Law School, as I see it, is exacerbated by two factors. A Dean–Head has to sit on an innumerable number of University Committees, attend the Law Society as best he can and carry out functions which in other parts of the University would be shared by at least two people. Added to this, he serves in effect as the Assistant to the Dean in interviewing

students, dealing with their troubles etc. in a way which really doesn't have any parallel in other parts of the University. This, in addition to trying to carry out teaching and research functions is an impossible long term task for anyone who wishes to carry out his functions to the best of his ability.[39]

The solution, he suggested, was to spread the burden, by splitting the headship from the deanship. Castles added: 'As I would envisage the Law School being run co-operatively it doesn't matter to me who holds what title and I'm easy about this.' The vice-chancellor consulted the sub-professorial staff, and Lücke was reappointed head for 1971, while Castles returned to the deanship.

Other reforms advocated by the Law School committee in 1969 waited until the university introduced its campus-wide Departmental Government scheme four years later. The scheme's rationale was outlined in a report to the Education Committee. Some staff were frustrated by a lack of participation and communication, it said. Where departmental committees had been established, they were working well, and most staff supported them. Under the new arrangements, heads of department were renamed 'chairmen', to signal diminished authority. Although departmental committees officially had only advisory powers, and their establishment by staff was optional, the breadth of their remit and their power to elect chairmen now gave their deliberations decisive weight. Lücke observed: 'I believe that an overwhelming majority of staff still support the principle that resolutions duly passed at staff meetings affecting departmental policy (as distinct from administrative detail) should be fully binding upon the Chairman.'[40] With the vice-chancellor's approval, law teaching staff anticipated adoption of the scheme by electing a chairman in 1972, for the 1973–75 triennium. They chose Castles, whose name was forwarded to the council for formal appointment. Administrative burdens were shared further, through the appointment of associate deans, 'to spread the considerable decanal load of administrative work and meetings'.[41]

Departmental Government and the breaking of the link with the Bonython chair initiated two decades in which the deanship rotated among the teaching staff. Professors were not the only incumbents. The twelve deans between 1970 and 1991 included three readers and three senior lecturers. Staff were expected to take their turn. The division of responsibilities between the dean and the chairman of the Department of Law persisted into the 1990s. As a Law School report said: 'The Dean was responsible for ensuring that the Faculty set strategic directions for the Law School, for allocating and monitoring the Faculty budget and for external relations'; the chairman was responsible 'for implementing academic programmes and for dealing with staffing issues'.[42] A Law School response to a Tertiary Education Commission questionnaire gave a sense of the daily reality: the chairman 'liaises with and supervises full-time staff (cajoles, implores, manipulates, struggles manfully and fitfully, pleads, grovels, ignores and, generally, endeavours to raise morale)'.[43] 'Our system of multiple kingdoms' was the description by department chair Tony Moore in 1979.[44]

Under the system of central administration introduced in 1981, following an inquiry chaired by political scientist David Corbett, university decision-making was concentrated in the Executive Committee of the Education Committee, 'a functioning experiment in industrial democracy', in Wilf Prest's words.[45] In the words of one administrator, the Executive Committee 'seemed to meet all day, every day'.[46] All deans were members, and in partial compensation for the dean's move to central administration, the Law School received funding for a half-time lectureship. The reforms aimed to strengthen academic representation, 'so that policy-making in hard times can have the best possible understanding and confidence and sense of participation among those whom it concerns'.[47] Andrew Ligertwood saw the new system come and go in the Law School: 'They were the halcyon days where the university community was running the university.'[48] Convention made the Executive Committee influential; in the system's first year of operation, all its recommendations were approved by the Education Committee and the council. But, strictly speaking, the Executive Committee had no executive authority, as John Keeler, one of its members, observed. The Corbett system was easily dismantled when the vice-chancellor and the council took more control in the 1990s, and the university gradually reverted to a more centralised system characterised by consultation and command.[49]

The deliberations of Law School committees were detailed and, at times, laborious, on matters both large and small. Often, the system produced principled and informed debate on curriculum, pedagogy and governance. But occasionally it drew staff into protracted arguments in which even minor matters generated strong divisions of opinion and clear outcomes were hard to discern. In 1975 the Departmental Committee debated the creation of a student lounge in the Ligertwood Building. 'The ensuing motions, foreshadowed motions, amendments, amendments to amendments were somewhat confused', the minutes recorded.[50] The only decision reached was that approval of the lounge should be deferred until more information was available.

§

In 1971 the academic staff had what Lücke called 'a first class fight with the Supreme Court'.[51] The dispute tested the limits of the judges' influence over the Law School and exposed disagreements about the importance of history and theory. The context was a curriculum review, driven in part by the desire of many staff to broaden the range of subjects in the LLB syllabus. Taxation, administrative law and intellectual property were among the areas that lacked adequate coverage, although Taxation was offered as a postgraduate subject in alternate years. The rapid growth of these areas of legal doctrine and practice made their absence from the course increasingly glaring. As a first instalment of expansion, seminar courses became available for third- and fourth-year students in 1971, and Legal History (a survey course of English and Australian history) became optional, to ease the added load. Lücke explained:

> Such a program would at least sustain, for one further year (in my own case, it will be the eleventh year), the hope of the staff members involved that important areas in which they possess special interest and competence will at last be recognized by the Faculty and by the University as having a claim to existence and to some academic attention.[52]

The powerful line-up of seminar teachers for 1971 included John Finnis on natural law and Daniel O'Connell on the law of the sea.

Further curriculum expansion required freer options in the last two years of the course, when students had to study either Roman Law or International Law and make two other choices between alternative subjects. Jurisprudence was compulsory. In April 1971 the faculty decided unanimously that, in place of these limited options, students would choose four subjects from a list of nine, including Jurisprudence, International Law and Roman Law. Seminar courses and the rest of the curriculum remained the same.[53]

The judges opposed the diminished role for history and jurisprudence, although the strength of their concerns became apparent to the faculty only gradually. They presented a united front, and any differences of opinion they had among themselves are unknown. One of the judges, Howard Zelling, was present when the faculty voted to approve the course changes, but the records do not disclose whether he spoke up in the debate. He abstained from voting, but this was not necessarily a warning sign; the judges routinely abstained when the faculty voted on matters that might require amendment of the court's rules concerning admission to practice. The new curriculum proceeded smoothly through the university senate. The Chief Justice's Committee on Legal Education then 'suggested that consideration be given' to making a pass in Roman Law, Jurisprudence or an expanded Legal History a precondition for the LLB.[54] This, at least, was Castles's interpretation of the committee's conclusions, when he reported back to the faculty. If it was a mere suggestion, the faculty was free to reject it, which it duly did. Lücke summarised the reasons of the majority:

> They wonder how academically respectable it is to inflict Roman Law upon students who have no knowledge of Latin; they wonder why one should force a student to study Jurisprudence or Legal History when he may well lack the special interest in speculative thinking needed for Jurisprudence or the dogged determination needed to understand the now irrelevant legal procedures of past ages.[55]

But the judges had not intended to accept the changes, at least without further debate, and they dug in when the matter reached the university council. Its members included Chief Justice John Bray (the chancellor) and Justice Roma Mitchell, who told the meeting that more discussion was required. An unnamed council member retorted that 'control of the Law degree was the Faculty's business, and that any form of external pressure on the educational views of Faculties ought to be resisted'.[56] But the council deferred a decision, to allow the discussions to take place.

As a difference of opinion about optional subjects, the dispute was a storm in a teacup, but it stirred deeply held convictions about legal education among the judges and touched a nerve among some of the full-time teachers. At its next meeting, the faculty recorded its concern about the council's action, confirmed its decision on the three subjects, and sought more information about the judges' opinions. David Kelly wrote a letter of protest to the vice-chancellor: 'The amendments in question were approved and passed by the Faculty after adequate discussion, yet have been delayed in their operation, possibly for twelve months, owing to the influence, so I am informed, of some members of the Supreme Court of this State.' There was, he argued, 'no room, within the University structure, for the influencing of University committees and the Council itself on grounds which might have been debated and voted upon by interested parties at meetings of the Faculty'.[57] (All the judges were faculty members.)

Delay at this stage might make it impossible to introduce the changes in time for the 1972 academic year.[58]

The question was thrashed out at a faculty meeting in October 1971. Four of the court's eight judges attended, including the chief justice. They were conciliatory. Neither Castles nor the faculty was to blame for the confusion about what the chief justice's committee had decided, they said. Bray harked back to his earlier losing battle for compulsory Latin and the later dropping of the two arts subjects from the course: 'It had been argued that the cultural content of the course would be maintained by such subjects as Legal History.' But Jurisprudence and Roman Law 'were of value in their own right, contributing a type of study not encountered in the other subjects'. The meeting hinted at the shift in the faculty's identity as the full-time staff rose to dominance. An unnamed speaker objected to outside influence: 'The proposal should be opposed as it involved an attempt to impose direction on the Faculty by external power sources.' But were the judges outsiders? The response came from another unnamed speaker: 'The members of the Faculty present had all been associated with the Faculty for many years and many had taught in it.'[59] All the judges present were Law School graduates, and three (Bray, Mitchell and Andrew Wells) had been lecturers. They were defending the kind of legal education that they themselves had received.

In its third vote on the question over as many meetings, the faculty rejected the judges' idea that Legal History, Jurisprudence or Roman Law should be compulsory for the LLB, but by the narrowest of margins, fifteen votes to fourteen. The result affirmed the teaching staff's wish to give students greater choice from a wider range of subjects, but it also asserted the Law School's independence. It is hard to imagine the faculty in earlier years opposing the apparently united wishes of the chief justice and three of his colleagues. Decades later, Sam Jacobs (who was present) had forgotten what the fight was about but remembered the vote against Bray: 'He was the Chief Justice and a very distinguished scholar in his own right, and these people just wouldn't listen to him.'[60] As introduced in 1972, the new curriculum had eleven compulsory subjects, four options (from a list including Administrative Law, Associations, Family Law, International Law, Taxation, Jurisprudence and Roman Law) and two seminar courses, one of which could be replaced by Legal History. The judges were not entirely defeated, however. They encouraged study of their favoured subjects by adding an extra year of articles for graduates who had not passed Legal History, Jurisprudence, Roman Law or Comparative Law.[61]

In contrast with the judges' enthusiasm for history and philosophy, the Law Society was likely to object if students could graduate without studying subjects needed in legal practice. Lücke attempted to head off such concerns by reassuring the society that the dean and his academic assistant would guide students' choices:

> Professor Castles and Mr. Ligertwood will do their utmost to ensure that students exercise their new freedom sensibly, but the fact remains that prospective practitioners, if they are sufficiently ill-advised and obstinate, could choose combinations such as International Law, Roman Law, Jurisprudence and Industrial Law.[62]

Lücke gave the society an opportunity to tell students which subjects it viewed as essential for practice. A notice duly advised students of the Law Society's preferred subjects and topics. But the society's president, Cedric Thomson, wrote: 'It is now possible for a person to obtain an LL.B. degree without a substantial course on companies. This is rather like qualifying as a surgeon without passing a course on anatomy!'[63] The curriculum changes left both the Law Society and the judges dissatisfied. The sense of common endeavour between the university and the profession was fading.[64]

§

The course changes were not the only point of friction between the Law School and the judges. In 1971 legal education in South Australia was under discussion in a plethora of committees: the Faculty of Law; the Chief Justice's Committee on Legal Education; the Committee on Postgraduate Legal Education; a Liaison Committee established by the Chief Justice's Committee; the Board of Examiners, established under the admission rules; and the Legal Education and Articled Clerks' Committee of the Law Society. A national review was proceeding under the auspices of the Australasian Universities Law Schools Association. From the Law School's point of view, the obvious risk of confusion and contradiction was only part of the problem. Staff voiced their concern that 'legal education was being considered by Committees on which we have little representation'.[65] The faculty deputed Castles and Lücke to investigate means of improving cooperation. The outcome was a Coordinating Committee, drawn from the faculty, the judges and the Law Society.[66]

Coordination, while desirable, did not change the regulatory framework for admission to the profession, which remained under the control of the Supreme Court. Indeed, when the judges agreed to the establishment of the Coordinating Committee, they explicitly rejected any fetter on their power to alter the admission rules. But this power came under challenge, since mooted reforms in matters such as practical training depended increasingly on the cooperation of the Law Society and the university. Some Law School staff proposed transferring the rule-making function to a council of legal education, composed of judges, practitioners and representatives of the university. Lücke wrote in May 1972:

> The Adelaide Law School has been suffering from somewhat strained relations with their Honours, the Judges of the Supreme Court. In an effort to improve matters the Faculty has suggested that a Council of Legal Education be established ... Their Honours have voiced some anxiety lest such a body could curtail their traditional exclusive jurisdiction over the admission of practitioners.[67]

The idea went no further for the time being, but the Law School was not its only advocate. In 1975 the president of the Law Society, Rod Matheson, put another proposal for a council of legal education to the judges and the Faculty of Law. The judges' prerogatives would be protected by giving the chief justice a veto over any new rules. Matheson cited English and New Zealand models; Victoria, too, had such a council, but it was large and unwieldy. The faculty endorsed the proposal, provided that the new council had no authority to prescribe the content of the LLB course or 'prejudice the autonomy and integrity of the University'.[68]

In a sign of the growing importance of student representation in decision-making, the faculty took a stand on the addition of a student representative to the proposed council. A student would be better informed than academics about law teaching, it said. A member of the public should also be included, since the public had a stake in the work of the council. The Law Society resisted: 'Such persons would not have the experience or knowledge to play a useful role on the Council of Legal Education as we conceived it.'[69] But its opposition to a student member softened, and the faculty reconsidered its call to add a member of the public. The state government included a council (or commission) of legal education in a wide-ranging Legal Practitioners Bill introduced in parliament in 1976, after consultations extending over several years. The bill lapsed, but the idea of vesting control over admission in a new body was periodically revived, until the establishment of the Legal Practitioners Education and Admission Council in 1998.[70]

§

As the number of applicants excluded by the LLB quota grew, so too did discussion about an alternative pathway for entry to the profession. When the quota was introduced in 1967, no qualified first-preference applicants were excluded, but ninety-six were excluded in 1972, and the figure rose to around 168 in 1973. The Selection Committee noted: 'Competition for entry to the law course has now become very intense.'[71] The exclusion of so many students caused concern in the profession: Law Society president Cedric Thomson warned that not enough lawyers would qualify over the next decade to meet community needs. After discussions in the new Coordinating Committee, Chief Justice Bray raised the possibility of allowing would-be lawyers to sit admission exams after studying privately. To provide these students with teaching, the Law Society backed the establishment of a non-degree course leading to admission to practice. It was to be no more than a stopgap, planned to operate only until the opening of a law school at Flinders University, then seen as imminent.[72]

University study had been compulsory for entry to the profession since the Law School's foundation, and the faculty opposed any such new course: it was 'most undesirable that there should be provision for admission to practice in this State without a University degree in Law'.[73] A Law Society comment about ensuring that family practices could pass to the next generation raised the hackles of some faculty members, who voiced concern that the new course might be used in this way. But it went ahead, operating in 1974 and 1975 with an enrolment of about thirty. The extended period of articles served by students in the new course—five years instead of one—was said to make them attractive to law firms; Horst Lücke reported that Law School graduates were finding it difficult to get articles as a result. The course was neither intended nor able to continue indefinitely, and when lecturers and premises became hard to find in 1976, it stopped taking new students, although the opening of a law school at Flinders was as far off as ever.[74]

The extended clerkships of the Law Society course went against the trend, as articles became more difficult to find and their educational value was increasingly questioned. 'Since 1967 at least, training for legal practice has been in an acute state of crisis', Horst Lücke wrote in

1970.[75] In that year, the Articled Law Clerks Association was formed, marking a new level of activism among clerks on such matters as pay and conditions (and confirming their severance from the Law Students' Society, which had long outgrown its origins as a society of law clerks). Aiming to alleviate the deficiencies of training under articles, the Law School and the Committee on Postgraduate Legal Education sponsored a lecture course on legal practice, delivered by practitioners. Lücke reported: 'About 70 articled clerks and junior practitioners (as well as two members of the Law School staff) have enrolled and the venture shows all signs of health, vitality and potential growth.'[76] Tutorials supplemented the lectures the following year, and attendance at the course became a prerequisite for completion of articles in the minimum time.[77]

The lecture course was a stopgap, and in 1972 the Law Society floated the idea of a legal workshop course as an alternative to articles. Students would learn through practical training rather than lectures and tutorials alone; a similar course at the Australian National University was a model. The judges supported the proposal, and Law Society president Sam Jacobs argued that university support for the workshop would be a suitable 'quid pro quo' for concessions made to the Law School in the extension of the curriculum and the reduction of time spent in articles.[78] The course would also address the Law Society's concern that the compulsory part of the LLB course did not adequately cover subjects needed for practice. Jacobs told a faculty meeting: 'The system of Articles which provided for practical training was now under strong criticism and, he thought, on the way out.'[79] Some staff were wary of Law School involvement in a practical course. John Keeler warned that subjects 'would be taught differently from the questioning, problem solving, techniques of academic treatment of law subjects'.[80] Teachers might not meet the criteria for academic appointments. Nevertheless, the faculty approved the workshop in principle. Difficulties with funding, accommodation and divided control caused the faculty to postpone introduction of the course until the 1979–81 university triennium, at the earliest, but the problem was urgent, and the South Australian Institute of Technology took over the initiative. It proposed to offer a Graduate Diploma in Legal Practice as an adjunct, rather than an alternative, to articles.[81]

Student reactions to the plan were mixed. Training under articles was flawed, but most clerks were paid, unlike workshop students. Indeed, part of the rationale for the workshop was that pressure for increased pay was likely to reduce the number of practitioners taking articled clerks. At a student meeting in October 1974, when the Institute of Technology's suburban campus at the Levels (now Mawson Lakes) was a possible venue for the workshop, many were unhappy at the prospect of spending 'nine months without money at the Levels, on top of previously anticipated commitments'.[82] Students sought restricted admission to practice on completion of the workshop (instead of first having to work under articles) and the introduction of assessable practical work in academic subjects in the LLB. Grant Mathiesen, the student who chaired the meeting, estimated that as many as half of those likely to seek articles in 1976 would be unable to find places; the Law Society put the shortfall somewhat lower, but nevertheless regarded the situation as critical. Despite such misgivings, the SAIT proposal went ahead, with state government funding, and a pilot program commenced in 1976. It got off to a slow start. As part of its efforts to minimise the number of students who missed out, the Law Society encouraged firms to take on articled clerks, with the result that the predicted shortfall shrank. Where they had a choice, students favoured articles over the legal practice course, since, in addition to the salary most received, clerks gained work experience and useful connections. Only twelve students began the GDLP in its first year, and nine the following year. But in 1977 the judges endorsed the Law Society's proposal to phase out articles altogether. After a transitional period, only students who were unable to gain entry to the diploma course could enter articles. Numbers in the GDLP course swelled, and articles declined.[83]

The Law School was on the periphery of the practical legal training scheme, although students of the diploma course became familiar users of the Law Library, causing the Law School some concern as numbers grew. It was the Law Society that drove the initiative forward. Its interest is at first sight paradoxical, given the profession's historical support for the articles system as immersive practical training and (less often acknowledged) a source of cheap labour. But the campaign by the Articled Law Clerks Association for higher pay threatened to increase the firms' costs, while the reduction of the minimum period of articles to one year in 1973 reduced the value of the clerks' labour. The Law Society was aware of the old system's shortcomings. Some clerks learned a great deal, some learned very little, and good training put burdens on practitioners that they were not always willing or able to support. The society's admission course, which required clerks to be articled for five years, was a last hurrah rather than a commitment to articles in the long term.

§

The introduction of the LLB entrance quota complicated decisions about funding and staffing in the Law School. In the past, student numbers had been largely beyond the faculty's control, and enrolments figured in negotiations over staffing as an outside force that the Law School and the university had to cope with as well as they could. Now, decisions about the intake became critical to the university's allocation of resources. The faculty did not control the quota—final decisions were made by the university council—but its agreement was always sought, and proposals for quota numbers were part of its triennial planning submissions. Threats to withhold faculty consent to quota changes could put pressure on the university to lift staff numbers, but their effect was limited, as the faculty was to find.

The size of the intake was uncontroversial until 1970. When the quota was first introduced, the university's Education Committee projected an unchanged intake of 100 in 1968 and 1969, followed by steady increases to reach a quota of 150 in 1972. The faculty agreed, relying on what it saw as a previous assurance by the council that the Law School's student population would not exceed 600. When the time came to increase the intake, as planned, to 130 in 1970, the faculty's attitude had changed, and so too had the context. Staffing levels had not risen, thanks to the financial stringency imposed by the federal government in the 1967–69 triennium. The result was the first of several prolonged battles over the size of the quota, with consequences for the Law School's relations with students, the profession and the university.[84]

The faculty objected loudly to the quota increase for 1970. It sent a resolution to the chairs of seven university committees, including the Education Committee:

The Faculty is dismayed by the present staff/student ratio in the Department of Law, the lack of adequate secretarial and research support for members of staff and the inadequacy of the funds presently made available for the purchase of library books and periodicals ...

The Faculty is therefore of opinion that, for the time being at least, there can be no increase in the present quota for the admission of students. It is also of opinion that, unless significant and immediate improvement is made in library holdings and in the staffing, both academic and ancillary, of the Department of Law, the Faculty will be forced to recommend a decrease in the quota for 1971. It will be compelled to do so in an attempt to bring the staff/student ratio within reasonable limits and to decrease the well-nigh impossible pressure on a library which is both under-stocked and under-staffed.[85]

Students, too, were feeling the pressure of low staffing levels, as the faculty meeting heard:

A member of the Student Liaison Committee said that, at present, they considered that Law students were not getting sufficient attention from staff for teaching purposes, especially in regard to written work and seminars. Not enough written work was set and there was usually such a gap between handing in and receiving back marked work that the criticism on the paper could not be related to its preparation and was therefore of little benefit to the students. Any increase in the quota, especially for first year students, would be detrimental.[86]

The university defused the protest with an offer of new lectureships, on condition that the planned quota increases were implemented, and the faculty agreed to the intake of 130. But lines had been drawn, and the faculty reserved its right to revise the figure in future. In 1970 it warned again that it would not approve an increased quota and might recommend 'a drastic reduction', unless staffing improved.[87]

The chair of the university's Staff Development Committee, mathematician Renfrey (Ren) Potts, attended the next faculty meeting. The Law School's submissions focused on its poor student–staff ratio, but the Staff Development Committee, Potts said, looked more to teaching loads (a theme that often recurred in later years). The committee 'had not been convinced by submissions from the Law School that the teaching load of the Law School was at tremendous odds with those of other departments'.[88] Because of 'problems within the Faculty' in 1969 (Potts may have had the battle over the headship in mind), the committee had been unable to obtain some of the information it needed. The Law School was not helped by its lack of representation on the Staff Development Committee, where it shared a seat with Economics, alternating each year.

Despite these reservations, Potts was sympathetic, calling for a better understanding on university committees of the Law School's problems, but the underlying disagreement remained. The faculty sought a deputation to the university council, an independent review of university staffing needs, and discussions with Flinders on the establishment of a second law school. Lücke sent the news to Alex Castles, who was on study leave at the United Nations in New York:

Possibly somewhat incited by my own displays of pessimism the Faculty has gone on another rampage ... I am happy to say that we are all beginning to adapt ourselves to a new atmosphere of stringency which, unhappily, is going to affect the Law School very much more than it will departments which have been a little more prudent in their planning for the future.[89]

Castles, who had been offered a chair at the University of New South Wales, was ready to rejoin the fight.

I wouldn't mind either if you felt it might serve a purpose if you let it be known that my 'disgust' (and that is a mild word) with the treatment of the Faculty has made me seriously consider taking an offer to go elsewhere ... No doubt the University would be more than glad to see me go. I'm just a troublemaker to some of them and perhaps this, as well as other factors, which are more personal, helps me to want to stay in Adelaide, at least for a few more years ... Even in Security Council proceedings there is little of the blatant opportunism which manifests itself in the operations of the University of Adelaide.[90]

A compromise proposed by the vice-chancellor placated the faculty, which agreed to maintain the quota for 1971–72 at 130, calculated as equivalent full-time students rather than individuals. (When part-time students were included, the intake would amount to 140 individuals.) In 1973 the quota would increase to 140 EFTS, or 150 individuals. Improved staffing had to wait, as a faculty committee reported: 'Our chances of attracting further staff development are slight, since the present "financial blizzard" which has hit the University is likely to continue.'[91]

The tone of assertiveness, even stridency, was new in the faculty's dealings with the central university, but it lacked power to back up its fighting words. The faculty had no overall budget, and its resources depended mainly on the central allocation of staff positions, supported by a range of ancillary funds or grants, for such things as maintenance, research, conferences and equipment, each with its own formula or selection process. Fortuitously, more generous federal funding in the 1973–75 triennium, and favourable responses from the university administration, improved the Law School's position, bringing a decade of sometimes tense equilibrium to the quota from 1973. Castles wrote: 'The University Staff Development Committee has begun to see the light about our needs.' Five positions had been made available in the last four months, he said. 'This is something of an embarrassment of riches as far as we are concerned, and obviously it is going to take us time to fill these places satisfactorily.'[92] Simultaneous expansion at other Australian law schools made recruitment difficult, as the Law School competed to attract suitably qualified candidates for multiple vacancies.[93]

Competition for inclusion in the quota intensified. Between 1967 and 1976, the number of applicants for entry to the law course jumped from 145 to 656. At the end of that period, only the top 19% of matriculants were selected for entry. The abolition of university tuition fees in 1974 and the expansion of financial support for students contributed to the increase, which was experienced across the university (indeed, across the higher-education sector). Rising demand ruled out cuts to the quota, even when the university's Committee of Deans encouraged faculties to save money by reducing their intakes in 1977. Law staff fielded the complaints of disappointed applicants and their parents, including those keen for family succession in the profession but unable to reach the entry cut-off point.[94]

The main policy response, from the faculty and others, was to consider establishing a second law school, at Flinders University. In the past, the faculty had been cautious about the idea, since a new law school might divert resources from Adelaide, leaving 'two Law Schools of inferior quality', as a faculty committee put it.[95] A new law school should be deferred until numbers became impossible to accommodate at North Terrace, it said, which would happen when enrolments exceeded 750. In David Kelly's later paraphrase, 'it was better to have one poor Law School than two very poor ones in South Australia'.[96] But by 1970, attitudes were changing, as Lücke wrote to Castles: 'Development is going to be a big fight in May; there is one card which will be played at a convenient time: abandonment of our policy against a second Law School at Flinders. It mightn't be such a bad idea, either.'[97] The following month, the faculty resolved to open discussions with Flinders. As Castles found when he had a chance meeting with Flinders's registrar, a new law school was a distant prospect at best, and Adelaide's strategic reasons for raising the issue were obvious:

> As far as I could gather Flinders has no intention, into the foreseeable future, of setting up a Law School and he seemed to be more than well informed on affairs in the Adelaide Law School, which suggests to me at least, that a lot of ground work would have to be undertaken before the proposal would even be given serious consideration. The view taken seems to be the proposal to go to Flinders is only a ploy related to internal politics at Adelaide.[98]

In November 1970 Adelaide's Education Committee chose not to take the idea any further, since the effects of the rising quota were yet to be seen and the Law School's student population had not yet reached the limit of 600 for which (as the faculty believed) the Ligertwood Building had been planned.[99]

By 1973 attitudes at Flinders had changed, and public pressure was growing for action to accommodate applicants excluded from the Adelaide quota. A Flinders University committee chaired by its chancellor, Supreme Court judge Charles Bright, recommended that the university should open a law school at the start of the 1976–78 triennium. It would satisfy the unmet demand for legal education and the likely future need for law graduates, both inside and outside the profession. The committee chose not to emulate the Adelaide LLB: the new course 'should evolve its own individuality. It should set out to supplement the programme at the University of Adelaide and not merely to duplicate it in details.'[100] However, establishment of the new school depended on funding from the federal government. Although the Australian Universities Commission supported the project in principle, subsequent budget difficulties caused it to be abandoned, for the time being.[101]

Concern about employment prospects was another reason for deferring a second law school. The Adelaide dean, John Keeler, reported in 1976: 'In recent months publicity has been given to the possibility that the market for lawyers in South Australia is becoming "saturated".'[102] In the same year, the Australian Universities Commission gave the ratio of lawyers to population in South Australia (although slightly under the national average) as a supplementary reason for deferring funding of a law school at Flinders. The problem, if there was one, was partly a matter of perception. In 1973 Charles Bright wrote to the dean: 'I am worried in case increasing numbers coming out of your Law School saturate the profession here with a consequential lessening of pressure by new students for Law School places.'[103] But in the same year, the president of the Law Society saw a chronic shortage of lawyers in South Australia. Statistics on employment of law graduates were reassuring. When the university's Careers Advisory Board surveyed the destinations of those who graduated with LLBs in 1975, it found that seventy-eight of the 106 respondents were in full-time employment, and thirteen were studying full-time. None said they were unemployed and seeking full-time work. The level of concern was sufficient for cautionary information about employment prospects to be included in the Law School's *Student Guide* from 1979 onwards, although fears of gross oversupply proved unfounded.[104]

The quota slowed the deterioration of the Law School's student–staff ratio, although it was consistently worse than those of other faculties. From 1967 to 1977 the number of full-time academic staff in the Law School doubled, from fifteen to thirty, but enrolments increased nearly as quickly. In 1971 the Law School ratio, at 19:1, was the worst of any

Adelaide faculty. Three years later, affected by the rising intake and unfilled staff vacancies, it had blown out to 25:1, while the average for the university as a whole was 11:1. The situation was as bad, or worse, at several other Australian law schools, and comparisons undercut Adelaide's claims for more staff. In 1974 the Law School's ratio of 25:1 could seem adequate when compared with the national average for law, 23:1, the Sydney and Melbourne law schools (33:1) or the dire situation at Queensland, where the ratio was nearly 36:1. Newer law schools, established since World War II, did better. In 1974 Monash had the most favourable staffing ratio, at around 14:1. Adelaide, Melbourne, Queensland and Sydney were, in Lücke's words, 'a quartet of ancient paupers, compelled to compete with a larger group of more modern institutions whose staffing approximates that of normal University departments'.[105] Not all old law schools were understaffed (Tasmania was only just behind Monash) and the figures fluctuated, sometimes from year to year (Queensland appointed six new staff in 1975), but Adelaide's ratio was hard to shift, leaving it 'floundering at the bottom of the academic league' with Melbourne, as Lücke put it.[106] A jump in staffing was out of reach, as university enrolments rose and disciplines competed for support.[107]

Administrative staffing barely kept pace with increasing workloads. Secretaries were essential collaborators for academics who dictated or wrote in longhand for transcription by typists. Daniel O'Connell's writing method was well honed: research assistants would fetch a trolley-load of books from the library, which were then marked-up with paper slips; O'Connell would walk up and down his office, dictating to a secretary and reaching for a book from time to time to supply a reference; research assistants would check the citations in the draft text. The most pressing need at the start of the 1970s was for a senior administrator to assist the overburdened dean and head of department. Castles wrote: 'It is vitally necessary to have an Administrative Officer, preferably along the lines in NSW, Sydney, Melbourne, ACT and Monash, to order the work of seeing students, preparing memos, staff meetings etc, in conjunction with other staff members.'[108] Illa Nicholls, an Adelaide LLB graduate, was appointed executive officer in 1972, initially working half-time, but the routine work lacked interest and secretarial support was inadequate. Nicholls voiced her concerns to Lücke, who was understanding: 'Obviously, the tasks which you have been carrying out so far have been somewhat mundane—no one could expect you to find them too inspiring.' He outlined more challenging projects that she could become involved in, and reassured her that her position was not envisaged 'as a way of relieving the head of department of unwanted drudgery'.[109] But she soon resigned, although she later worked briefly as a law tutor.

In 1974 Castles used the most recent report of the Australian Universities Commission to show the registrar that Adelaide had the lowest level of administrative support, for its size, of any Australian law school. He suspected the situation was affecting recruitment; Nicholls had left because of the lack of typing support, he said. The university appointed a full-time executive officer for the Law School, Rex Hunter, in 1975. A recent law graduate, he not only handled student and staff administration but also served as business manager of the *Adelaide Law Review* and manager of the moot court program. In 1980 he visited law schools in New South Wales and Victoria to investigate their introductory subjects, as part of the Law School's review of its own first-year subject, Elements of Law. In 1982 he moved to the university's central administration, becoming secretary of the Executive Committee and later director of planning and director of industry liaison, responsible for the university's Thebarton precinct, while others continued his role in the Law School.[110]

§

The student activism of the late 1960s and early 1970s may have touched the Law School only lightly, but student interest in social justice and the role of law in society grew. Seminar courses encouraged enquiry of this kind; in 1972 they included Human Rights in International Law, Environmental Law, Accident Law, Criminology, Parent and Child, and Law and Social Justice. Law students formed a Legal Aid Group in 1971, continuing a long history of such services in South Australia. The Law Society operated a legal assistance scheme from 1933 to 1972, providing legal aid at reduced fees, or for no fee, to those unable to pay the usual cost of a lawyer. The oldest and longest-running legal aid scheme in Australia, it demonstrated the willingness of the Law Society to provide a public service, while at the same time retaining the work in private law firms, rather than allocating it to the government's overburdened Public Solicitor. The student Legal Aid Group provided, on different days or evenings, a Legal Aid Bureau at the Port Adelaide Central Methodist Mission, a clinic in Carrington Street in the city, and a bureau for students in the University Union. Law School staff took some dock briefs from unrepresented prisoners at the monthly jail clearance at the Central District Criminal Court; students provided research assistance. The group burgeoned and branched out. In 1973 law students joined a campus campaign against mock auctions, a deceptive selling technique that lured customers at a nearby Rundle Street shop into buying mystery goods at inflated prices. Students formed a Consumer Protection Group, which investigated complaints, researched general consumer problems, and advocated environmental protection. By 1974 the Legal Aid Group was operating at Port Adelaide, Elizabeth, the university and the Citizens Advice Bureau in the city.

> The work involved usually requires only that the student be genuinely interested enough to follow up particular cases and be prepared to make enquiries and negotiations for the legal aid client. If situations arise requiring more than an enquiry or basic advice, then the client is referred to a solicitor or other appropriate body.[111]

The work continued, and in 1985 students assisted or ran legal aid clinics in central Adelaide and six suburban locations.[112]

§

In 1972 the violent death of a Law School staff member, Dr G.I.O. Duncan, became the flashpoint for a protracted public controversy about policing and homosexuality in South Australia. Duncan's time in Adelaide was brief, but the university became involved in efforts to ensure a full investigation of his drowning, and he has become, in death, one of the best-known former members of the Law School's staff.

George Ian Ogilvie Duncan, who was known by his second name, Ian, was born in London in 1930. He came to Australia with his parents as a child. He was head (dux) of Melbourne Grammar School and studied at the University of Melbourne, before withdrawing from the arts course when he fell ill with tuberculosis. His university studies resumed at Cambridge, where he graduated in arts and law and completed a PhD in legal history. His thesis was the basis for his book on early modern English legal history, *The High Court of Delegates*. It shows Duncan's gift for handling technical subject matter in engaging prose, and it continues to be cited by scholars. After teaching at the University of Bristol, Duncan accepted a lectureship in law at Adelaide, arriving in March 1972. Unmarried, he was 'intensely shy and taciturn', in the words of his biographer, Tim Reeves.[113]

On the night of 10 May 1972, Duncan visited the bank of the River Torrens, near the university. The area was a homosexual beat, where men gathered for social and sexual encounters. Duncan's possessions, impounded after his death, included copies of *Spartacus* gay travel guides (which listed the Torrens beat) and a membership card for London's Gaytime Friendship Society. A pen-and-paper version of later online dating, the society provided members with 'gay pen pals and introductions'.[114] Men seeking sexual encounters were not the only people drawn to the Torrens beat. Police were also in the area that night. Sex between men was a criminal offence, and police sometimes entrapped suspects by posing as potential partners and then making arrests. Gay men at beats were vulnerable to violence and harassment, some of it from predators who knew that their victims, deemed to be criminals, were unlikely to go to the police. Sometimes, the attackers were the police themselves.[115]

At around 11 pm, Duncan was pushed or thrown into the river by a group of men on the riverbank. He quickly got into difficulties and drowned. The same group of attackers pushed another man, Roger James, into the water, breaking his ankle in the process, but he survived to make a statement to the police and to give evidence at the ensuing inquest. A third man testified that he, too, had been thrown into the river, not long before Duncan and James. Statements at the inquest and to police investigators showed that as many as six police officers were near the riverbank and the adjacent road during the evening, including three members of the Vice Squad. However, no witnesses identified the attackers of the three men, leaving a gap in the evidence that bedevilled efforts to bring the assailants to justice.[116]

Law School staff soon became involved. Duncan was without family or close friends in Adelaide, and so Alex Castles identified his body. Ten days later, the press reported the presence of Vice Squad members in the vicinity on the night of Duncan's death. Horst Lücke became concerned: 'When it seemed as though the investigations into the Duncan case were petering out, nobody seemed very interested to work out just who had committed this deed.'[117] In a public intervention, on 28 May he wrote to the commissioner of police. Duncan, Lücke wrote,

> does not appear to have had any close relations and I feel that it is incumbent upon me, as head of the Law Department, to ensure, as far as it is within my power to do so, that those responsible for his violent death are brought to justice.[118]

In form, the letter was cautious, even reserved. Ostensibly, Lücke sought only an answer to a respectful question: 'What steps are being taken to further reassure the public of the integrity of the Police Force?' But in other ways, the letter pulled no punches. Lücke took up reports that police were implicated in Duncan's death and that some officers had refused to join an identification parade or answer questions. What was more, he made sure that the letter could not be ignored, by copying it to the attorney-general and the chief secretary; news of the letter immediately appeared on the front page of the *Advertiser*. Within days, the attorney-general called for a progress report on the police investigation and then ordered an inquest. Later, Lücke publicly defended Duncan against the slurs that many, at the time, associated with homosexuality.

> It should be pointed out that there was no evidence that Dr Duncan intended to commit any offence on the night of May 10, or, that he ever committed any criminal act anywhere.
>
> Whether Dr Duncan had been a homosexual or not, he had been a courteous and likeable colleague and a meticulous, dedicated scholar.[119]

Castles, too, entered the debate, calling for scrutiny of the Vice Squad and investigation of the prevalence of violence against homosexuals.[120]

The university council was sufficiently concerned to send its own legal representative to the inquest, but the coroner concluded that there was no evidence to identify Duncan's assailants. The South Australian police called in detectives from London's Metropolitan Police, for a fresh investigation. The senior London detective, R.W. McGowan, concluded that 'it would seem more than likely' the three men from the Vice Squad were the men who attacked Duncan.[121] Over a decade later, when new evidence emerged from a police witness, the three were charged with manslaughter, but the case against one was dropped and the other two were acquitted at trial.

Finding Duncan's assailants and investigating the actions of the police were only a part of the public debate that followed his death. Laws criminalising sex between men were already the target of calls for reform by groups such as the recently formed Adelaide branch of the Campaign Against Moral Persecution, CAMP, which worked for decriminalisation and better understanding of homosexuality. CAMP was active on the university campus, and the student press in Adelaide and beyond was at the forefront of the decriminalisation debate. *On Dit* published an opinion piece attacking laws against homosexuality in 1961, and similar articles followed throughout the 1960s. Arts student Paul Paech wrote about the Duncan case for *On Dit*, *The Review* and *Nation Review* in the months after the tragedy. Responses in the Law School community varied, sometimes reflecting the prevailing homophobia. Duncan's death was treated as a subject for humour in law student newsletter *55%* in 1981–82, but later Duncan was commemorated by a photograph in the law student lounge, a student scholarship, and ceremonies on the anniversary of his death.[122]

Growing calls for reform led, with surprising speed, to moves in parliament. Tim Reeves observed: 'The Duncan murder was such a powerful catalyst to homosexual law reform that legislation had been announced within two months and introduced in eleven weeks.'[123] The resulting act fell short of full decriminalisation, by putting the onus on the accused to prove that the alleged crime took place between consenting adults in private. It was, however, the first legislative step towards decriminalisation in Australia, and a legacy of Duncan's violent end.[124]

6

Gatekeeping: 1980–1989

The approach of the Law School's centenary in 1983 coincided with a change, long delayed, in its relationship with the First Nations of the university's home. Indigenous people were powerfully affected by the laws taught at the Law School, including the legal foundations of colonisation, which rejected their laws, and the colonial law of property, which supported the expropriation of their lands. They had no access to the Law School as students, still less as staff, so long as limited access to higher schooling and other patterns of discrimination made entry to tertiary education difficult or impossible. First Nations people sought access to schooling despite these obstacles. Education was among the opportunities that drew Aboriginal people to Adelaide from the 1940s onwards. On the university campus, some of the earliest initiatives for change came from students. Funds raised at the annual student procession through the city were regularly used to support Abschol, the long-running Aboriginal scholarship fund established by students in 1951. But the many obstacles to higher schooling limited Abschol's results. 'Our scheme is more a gesture than a remedy', the local coordinator wrote in 1962.[1]

The Indigenous-led Aboriginal Legal Rights Movement was established in 1971, to provide legal representation and to advocate for civil and legal rights. It became an early bridge between the Law School and First Nations communities. Links of this kind, and the growing interest of non-Indigenous staff in laws affecting Indigenous people, led to the development of new courses for the law curriculum.

A seminar course, Aborigines and the Law, was offered in the LLB program in 1975, and an optional subject with the same title entered the curriculum in 1984, aiming to foster understanding of Aboriginal law and culture, the impact of colonisation, and possibilities for law reform.[2]

Entry to the law course remained very difficult for Indigenous students. In 1973 the law faculty adopted an aspirational goal of admitting each year two or three Aboriginal students who would not otherwise qualify for entry. However, they would need to have completed matriculation, a requirement that excluded many Indigenous students. Another obstacle was that the Law School's broader special-entry programs were initially ineffective, hampered by narrow selection criteria.[3]

The Law School's first Indigenous graduate was Irene Watson, of the Tanganekald, Meintangk and Boandik peoples of the south-east of South Australia. Working at the Aboriginal Legal Rights Movement sparked her interest in law. Watson enrolled in the law course in 1979, after completing a diploma in Aboriginal studies at the South Australian College of Advanced Education. It had established Australia's first Aboriginal teaching program, and it developed a distinctive strength in Aboriginal studies and research. Australian law curriculums of this period had little recognition of First Nations, and when they were considered, it was often to trace their dispossession, as in discussion of Richard Blackburn's judgment in *Milirrpum v. Nabalco* in property law, or the taxonomy of British colonies in legal history. Watson has written:

> As a law student, I was confounded by the persistent construction of the Aboriginal person as a British subject, and the lack of acknowledgement that there had never been a dialogue between us and the British on the question of our legal and political status.[4]

The colonial inheritance underlay much of the legal doctrine that Australian law students were taught:

I studied Australian law while knowing and feeling how onerous it was to shift the power of colonialism. However, I knew that I could nevertheless learn and understand how colonisation legitimised and justified the theft of Aboriginal territories, and enabled an attempted genocide. I learnt how the colonial logic prevailed, while knowing how an Aboriginal way of being survived, holding on to life under the duress of it.[5]

The racism Watson encountered at the Law School as an undergraduate was expressed in a distinctive way:

Can you say an openly polite racist way? ... It was the colonial frontier. It was hostile, it was aggressive, it was doing me a favour, enabling or allowing an Aboriginal woman to enter the Law School and to sit amongst them, study them ... It was the kind of general Aussie ocker racism of the time, you know, but it had a kind of refined way of being within, you know, Adelaide establishment law school.[6]

She graduated in 1985 and went on to complete a PhD on First Nations law and the impact of colonialism. Her thesis won the Bonython Prize for legal research in 2000 and became the basis for her book, *Aboriginal Peoples, Colonialism and International Law: Raw Law*, which studied the ongoing clash of Indigenous and non-Indigenous laws. Her career in legal academia included appointments at several universities, and she became professor of law and pro-vice-chancellor at the University of South Australia. In 1989, on the initiative of the Law Students' Society, the new student lounge in the Ligertwood Building was named in her honour, and her portrait was incorporated in the relaunched lounge in 2016.[7]

Law was among the disciplines with very low participation rates targeted for improvement in the national Aboriginal and Torres Strait Islander Education Policy adopted in 1989. Such policies had limitations; they were better at getting students in the door than at lifting completion rates or changing institutional culture. At the Law

School, the number of Indigenous students grew, particularly after the commencement in 1988 of an Indigenous special entry scheme and, in 2012, a pathway into the LLB course through the Aboriginal Law Program at the vocational education provider TAFE SA. In 2018 the Law School had twenty-seven Indigenous students, mostly in the LLB program; higher-degree enrolments remained persistently low, as at other law schools. Andrea Mason, of the Ngaanyatjarra and Kronie peoples, has written of her experience studying at the Law School:

> What unfolded for me there was the concept that Australian 'modern' laws are a *malpa*—the Pitjantjatjara word for friend— to the ancient protocols, manners and rules I had learnt about in my Aboriginal community and life education. And I realised that these rules needed greater prominence when talking about Australian laws.[8]

The incorporation of Indigenous knowledge in the curriculum began gradually to reverse the exclusion that had characterised the law taught in the Law School since its foundation.[9]

§

During the 1980s, the first significant efforts were made to redress the gender imbalance that had long characterised staffing at the university. Students and staff also worked to incorporate the growing body of feminist analysis of law into the curriculum. The early participation of women students at Adelaide provided a benchmark against which the university showed new willingness to be measured. The university's annual report for 1982 noted that more than half the university's students in its first year of lectures, 1876, were women. 'By 1981 this rough parity between the sexes had given way to a serious under-representation of women both in the student and academic staff sectors of the University.'[10] Women made up 38% of students and 12.5% of staff (and only 9% of teaching positions at lecturer level and above). A working party on women at the university reported in

1981, and the following year the council adopted policies to increase the proportion of women among the academic staff.

One of the recommendations adopted by the council was consultation with students and staff when either gender made up less than 25% of a department's tenured positions. In 1982 there were only two women in the Law School's full-time teaching staff of twenty-nine. The consultation that followed, under the council's policy, overwhelmingly supported the appointment of a woman to a vacant lectureship. The appointee was Kath McEvoy, an Adelaide graduate who had been working as a tutor and temporary lecturer. The Law School's first woman professor, Marcia Neave, was appointed in 1986; three years later, she was still one of only two women professors in the university. She was a member of the review of university governance that in 1990 recommended setting targets for membership of women on key university committees. She also chaired the university's Equal Opportunity Board, established in 1986 to formulate an affirmative action program, as required by federal legislation.[11]

Women students and staff came together for support and collective action on issues of mutual concern. In the early 1980s, eighty years after Emily Moulden first enrolled in law, women made up about 40% of LLB enrolments and around 20% of the practising profession, but only about 10% of the full-time teaching staff. After a quiz in the Law Students' Society newsletter used violent misogyny as a subject for humour in 1984, a new group was formed, Women in the Law School, with broad aims:

- identifying ourselves as women in the profession
- supporting each other
- working actively together to bring women's issues to the fore
- presenting a feminist critique of the legal system.[12]

The group's newsletter, *40%*, took its title from the proportion of women in the law student population. Awareness of gender, class and the power of language informed its articles, which highlighted problems on campus and tapped into networks of research and activism. The shortage of childcare featured after a law student was humiliated in class because she had to bring her child to a lecture. The newsletter found an increasing readership off campus, but members of Women in the Law School faced 'constant abuse and harassment'; in 1983 hostile students burned copies of 40% on the Law School plaza.[13] The newsletter (renamed *Portia* when rising enrolments overtook the original title) ended as students graduated and moved on, but a new group, Women and Law, soon emerged. In 1995 the Law Students' Society established the Gender and Law Society, to provide support, discussion and networking. It was launched by a Law School graduate, Senator Amanda Vanstone. The following year, Gender and the Law Week brought to the Law School speakers on transgender people and the law, the Hindmarsh Island royal commission, and young male offenders in the justice system. Convenors of core subjects in the law curriculum were surveyed on whether they included material on how the law affected women and reflected their experience, as recommended by the recent Australian Law Reform Commission report on Equality before the Law. Responses went to the Law School Equal Opportunity Committee.[14]

New trends in research and teaching complemented this activism. Feminist students and staff in the Law School connected with counterparts in Arts, where the Research Centre for Women's Studies was established in 1982. Hilary Charlesworth joined the Law School staff in 1993: 'There was this very lively, to me quite cutting-edge set of feminist scholars ... For me it was a marvellous place to be, because of this wonderful group of women scholars, who I learnt enormously from.'[15] Judith Gardam and Ngaire Naffine taught the LLB subject Feminist Legal Theory. Its students helped change teaching and campus culture, but they also faced resistance, as Gardam remembered:

> They were a distinctive set, and I think they had to be extremely committed, because they had faced enormous obstacles to get this up and running. So they were not really representative, in a

way, of all feminists, but they were very brave and courageous and determined. But they also had extremely strong views, and why shouldn't they?[16]

In 2021, in the aftermath of the misconduct case that led to the resignation of his predecessor, Vice-Chancellor Peter Høj said: 'Sexual assault, sexual harassment and other inappropriate behaviour are found across our society—and Australia's higher education sector is no different.'[17] The Law School was no exception. A woman student remembered the law students' Smoke Socials of the 1960s: 'You just got used to being accosted when people got drunk.'[18] Classrooms, too, could be hostile environments. Women students were singled out for questioning about sexual assault cases in Criminal Law: 'You had to brave it out', one recalled.[19] Targeting of women sometimes went further. In 1981 the Law Students' Society newsletter observed: 'It seems that a number of academics, all male, are not above suggesting to some students, all female, that diligence, hard work and intelligent thought are not the only keys to high grades in their legal studies.'[20] Later, a male law teacher continued his sexual harassment of women students despite repeated incidents and at least one official warning, until he was eventually asked to leave. In the 2000s a prolonged campaign of misogynistic online bullying targeted women staff and a widening circle of their colleagues. University policy was little protection against such incidents. The council established a committee to investigate sexual harassment as far back as 1982, coincidentally the year when a national student conference on the problem was featured in 40%, but the cycle of reports and policy responses continued nearly forty years later. In 2021 Høj apologised to victims, and the university again attempted to improve its handling of reports of sexual assault, sexual harassment and other inappropriate behaviour.[21]

§

The long postwar expansion of the Law School's staff and enrolments slowed in the 1970s. In 1975 the Universities Commission classified

Adelaide as one of the nation's 'developed' universities, which were expected to have little or no growth in enrolments.[22] In the words of the dean of Engineering, Robert Bogner, the era was likely to be one of 'development without growth'.[23] The forecast proved accurate: the University of Adelaide's total enrolments barely changed for a decade, trending upwards again only in 1988, as new federal policies encouraged expansion. Demand for places continued to rise, but Adelaide's intake shrank, to accommodate growth at Flinders and rising completion rates. In 1982 Adelaide accepted around 52% of the school leavers who made the university their first preference; two years later, the figure had dropped to 35%. The limited intake hit hard in Law, where around 22% of first-preference applicants gained entry in 1984. Only Architecture and Electrical Engineering had lower admission rates, and even Medicine accepted a slightly higher proportion of applicants. By 1986 South Australia had the nation's lowest number of LLB course places per head of population.[24]

The university's federal funding (the source of almost its entire revenue in 1975) declined consistently, when adjusted for the high inflation prevailing at the time. From 1981, staged reductions in teaching staff were managed through the Compact, an agreement negotiated chiefly by the university's eleven deans. It deployed early retirement, leave without pay, conversions to fractional appointments, and exchange lectureships, aiming at a net loss of 15% of lecturing staff between 1976 and 1985. Heavier cuts in staff numbers were made in administrative roles. The Compact was endorsed by the university council, but it was unpopular in the two faculties that took the largest staff cuts, Arts and Science, and resentment of it persisted. Academic staff departing from the Law School would not be replaced until at least the end of 1983. Cost-savings were widespread, and the long-established system of central approval gave the university administration a veto over expenses both large and small. Even the purchase of a kettle for the Law School required central approval in 1981; the bursar's office refused, on the ground that it was an entertainment item and therefore outside the scope of the maintenance fund.[25]

When renewal of the Compact came under discussion in 1984, the faculty argued that the Law School was unfairly treated and deserved better resources: 'Law receives less money and staff per student than <u>any</u> other Faculty.'[26]

> The consequences of the Faculty of Law receiving the lowest resource allocation per student in this University are proving to be disastrous for law students and law staff. Students are deprived of the personalised, intensive education that their counterparts in other disciplines receive. Law staff are being worn down in their efforts to meet the teaching and research expectations of themselves and the University.[27]

The faculty quoted an earlier departmental report:

> This situation seems to have arisen from the difficulties of transition from a more narrowly professional school to a fully academic discipline, and to have been exaggerated by the increase in the Law quota and the subsequent increase in the student load.[28]

The implication was that staffing levels dating from the days of part-time students and practitioner–lecturers were inadequate, now that full-time academics were researching and publishing as well as teaching full-time students. In 1984 the Law School's student–staff ratio was 20.5:1, still the highest in the university. Economics came a close second, at 19.7:1.[29]

The faculty blamed 'historical perceptions of law as a "cheap" university discipline', but the underlying reasons for disparities in staffing were far from clear.[30] The structure of legal academia probably contributed: law teachers could work as generalists across subject areas, long after the era of generalists in science or the humanities had ended, and law schools did not have multiple departments requiring specialist staffing. Philanthropic support was hard to attract for law, particularly when compared with medicine. Once they became entrenched, relative staffing levels between disciplines were hard to change, but newly established law schools generally attracted greater support. Low staffing at older law schools undermined the case for change at Adelaide, since the Law School's student–staff ratio was slightly better than the national average for law (around 22:1 in 1984). The faculty aimed for a ratio of about 15:1 by 1991, a target that would require twelve additional staff. A transformative increase in staffing was next to impossible through renegotiation of the Compact, if it had to come at the expense of other faculties. Compact 2 eventually set a target for Law of thirty tenurable staff, an increase of three on the Compact 1 target.[31]

If a large increase in staff was out of reach, improvement in the student–staff ratio could be achieved only by reducing enrolments. Efforts to change this side of the equation triggered a searching debate about the Law School's aims, methods and social obligations. Michael Detmold, dean from 1979 to 1981, had negotiated the inclusion of a proviso in the original Compact:

> Recognising that the Faculty of Law has a staff–student ratio unsuitable to a University, the Faculty has the right under this agreement to reduce its undergraduate intake to 100 students. If it is necessary, other faculties will make up the difference.[32]

Detmold sought to invoke the proviso by reducing the quota for 1982 from 150 (where it had stood for nearly a decade) to 100. Putting his case to the faculty, he concentrated, not on metrics such as staffing ratios, but on mood and pedagogy: 'The truth, I think, is that we are not overworked by our teaching, but overburdened: a fair number of us are alienated from it, afflicted by a deep malaise', he told faculty members.[33] Desirable teaching methods, Socratic in the sense of developing capacity rather than instilling doctrine, required smaller classes: 'I am proposing a reduction in the quota in order to make it possible to increase the amount of time that a teacher can give each student.'[34]

When the teaching staff met, most disagreed with Detmold's reasoning and, for the time being, with his recommended quota. The debate did not go smoothly. Detmold described as 'slimy' the departmental meeting's dissent from his assertion that the Law School's current position on teaching 'seemed to be not one defensible by any academic principle'. He said his position had been 'totally misunderstood'.[35] While the meeting agreed that reducing the quota would produce an appropriate student–staff ratio, it nevertheless concluded that the reduction was undesirable. It would lead to lower demand for optional subjects (threatening their viability) and conflict with the Law School's 'overriding social obligation to give as many people as it reasonably can the opportunity to study law'.[36] A rough survey of student opinion favoured a quota of around 100. Students cited employment difficulties, overcrowding, 'the lack of personal contact with teachers and the feeling of mass production'.[37] 'The stairs and foyer are so jammed between lectures that it is difficult to move', a student representative told the faculty.[38] But students also observed that a cut would favour applicants from private schools, who were more likely to get high Year 12 results and so qualify for entry. The Law Society supported a quota of 150: 'All students who wished to do so should have the opportunity of a legal education', its president said.[39] The faculty noted that, unlike its counterparts in medicine and dentistry, the Law Society aimed to increase rather than restrict the number of graduates. It sought to maintain breadth of opportunity and an adequate supply of new practitioners.[40]

The 1982 quota remained at 150, although combined-course enrolments were re-weighted, to give a small reduction in equivalent full-time students. But the question was soon revisited. A new dean, Jim Hambrook, explained that maintaining the quota hindered claims for more staff: 'Some deans have responded sceptically to the explanation of why Faculty has not yet engaged in self-help by reducing its first year intake to 100 ... I believe that the deans (indeed the rest of the University) will not take Law's plight seriously until we do reduce the quota to 100.'[41] Staff and faculty agreed in 1984 to trigger the Compact proviso and cut the quota to 100, leaving open the possibility of a staged reduction. Faculty members on both sides saw much at stake. Lecturer Kath McEvoy was quoted in the *Australian* as saying the cut would 'entrench the exclusive, elitist notion of law' and reinforce the perception that the Law School was 'a little cradle of elitism'.[42] She favoured better use of resources instead.[43]

A sign of trouble ahead was the opposition of faculty member Sam Jacobs, now a judge of the Supreme Court, who proposed reducing optional subjects as an alternative. 'Some concerns he had were, he admitted, based only on hearsay. These included the poor standing of the Faculty in the profession and the community and low staff contact hours.'[44] Staff rebutted his information about teaching hours (which stood at eight per week), but Jacobs was a member of the university council, which had the final say on the quota. When the council considered a staged reduction over two years, Jacobs and another judge, Trevor Olsson, sought to defer a decision, and Jacobs told the council that the chief justice would consider reviving a training course independent of the university if the cut went ahead. Robert Culver, who had been elected to the council by the staff, protested against special pleading by unnamed members and pointed out that Law was not alone in its difficulties. Engineering had cut its intake (council reduced the Engineering quota by ten at this meeting) and suffered from understaffing and staff resignations. Registrar Frank O'Neill opposed the cut, as did Vice-Chancellor Donald Stranks. The cut might accelerate the establishment of a law school at Flinders, Stranks said: 'He feared that the end result of the University's action with respect to the Law School could be existence [sic] in S.A. of two lesser law schools. The establishment of a second law school was a very fundamental issue.'[45] Chief Justice Len King wrote to Stranks: 'Any reduction would be intolerable.'[46] Hugh Hudson, chairman of the Commonwealth Tertiary Education Commission, warned Stranks that Commonwealth funding might be reduced if Adelaide did not maintain its current level of opportunities for undergraduates.[47]

By thirteen votes to twelve, the council rejected the quota reduction, although the Law School later received the small consolation of emergency funding for a tutor for one year. The post-mortems were acrimonious. Hambrook and Deputy Chancellor Harry Medlin quarrelled over whether the council had been misled, but at the bottom of their involved and angry correspondence was the problem that what the Compact said about the law quota was unenforceable. When the proviso was negotiated, Hans Lücke warned presciently 'that behind the Compact are vested interests and that the proposal was not a legally binding contract'.[48] Implementation depended ultimately on the council, which would not be bound by past decisions, and the case for a cut in the intake had to be made afresh.[49]

§

The impasse over staffing was broken with the help of creative thinking about admissions and the curriculum. Some law staff had long doubted whether matriculation or Year 12 results, used for selection into the quota, were a good predictor of aptitude for the law course. As early as 1973, the law faculty's Selection Committee noted the advantages of selection based instead on university results: 'On the whole tertiary performance is a better guide to academic ability than is secondary school performance.'[50] Staff also questioned the quota's effects on equality of opportunity, as students of private schools continued to make up a large proportion of law enrolments. A perception that only insiders had good prospects in the legal profession could discourage potential students. Rob Fowler told his family that he wanted to study law, 'only to be told by my parents that you can't possibly do that, we don't know anybody in the law and you'll never get a job. And they were half right, in a way. Getting articles was very difficult … And it was a tight profession.'[51] Fowler persisted, and he was admitted to practice in 1971. Another student, who enrolled in 1979, was the first in their family to go to university: 'Overall I felt an outsider—I came from a government high school in the western suburbs. The first year especially felt like everyone else knew someone from school. There was a lot of snobbery—it lessened as we went further in the course.'[52]

Information about the school backgrounds of law students featured in a study by John Bradsen, a lecturer in the Law School, and John Farrington, the assistant registrar. In 1984 most of South Australia's Year 12 students (two-thirds) were at government schools, but they made up only one-third of Law School entrants for the following year. Just four independent private schools provided 40% of entrants. Former students of St Peter's College were sure to meet others in the Law School, as Jay Weatherill, the future premier, found when he was a student in the 1980s: 'I came from a public school, so all the "Saints Boys" would hang around with each other, and all the other people made friends with each other. Me and my friends used to sit up the back of the lectures with the Greeks and Italians.'[53]

Entry for school leavers also came under pressure from an emerging trend in the Law School's intake. The number of students applying to transfer into law from other tertiary courses grew rapidly, as the rising cut-off score made entry straight from school more difficult. In 1985 about 40% of the LLB intake had completed at least one year of a tertiary course before entering the Law School. Comparing and ranking applicants from these two categories was difficult. Bradsen and Farrington examined the performance of the various groups of entrants and found that, while matriculation results were a valid predictor of the performance of law students who entered direct from school, the matriculation results of students who transferred into law from other tertiary courses had a weaker correlation with their Law School performance. 'It would seem that pre-Law tertiary experience, though not Law itself, thoroughly shuffles the matriculation pack.'[54] Although high matriculation results accurately predicted good performance in law, students with lower matriculation results but good pre-law tertiary results would also perform well. Bradsen and Farrington concluded: 'In highly competitive circumstances selection would be more fair and equitable if it were based upon performance in circumstances in which all potential applicants share similar educational facilities and a common environment in which to develop their aspirations.'[55]

Led by Hambrook, the Law School began moving towards a different system for entry to the LLB course. The faculty's Curriculum Committee recommended that students should no longer enter direct from school. Selection would not be based only on matriculation results. Instead, most students would complete a year of another university course before beginning law, and selection would be based mainly on their tertiary results. A combined-degree course would become mandatory, and students would graduate with degrees in law and another discipline of their choice. The committee cited later-year entry to law at the universities of Western Australia and Tasmania, and mandatory double-degree courses at Macquarie and the University of New South Wales. Later entry would reduce the influence of schooling on selection, the committee argued, and first-year results were a better predictor of later performance than matriculation results. Law students would have a wider perspective and greater maturity. To make space for the mandatory double degrees, the LLB curriculum would need to be reduced, through cuts to optional subjects.[56]

These plans helped to resolve the dispute over the quota. Since combined-degree students would do fewer law subjects, the new, shorter curriculum would indirectly improve staffing ratios. With that change in prospect, and with the benefit of the three extra staff allocated under Compact 2, the faculty compromised on its desired intake of 100. The council accepted an intake of 120 for 1986, reassured by plans for an increase once later-year entry commenced, and by the willingness of Arts and Science to raise their intakes (and so maintain the federal funding that was tied to student numbers). Jacobs now supported the cut, as a short-term solution. Five special-entry places were provided, outside the quota. Approval of the curriculum proposals was largely uneventful, and later-year entry commenced in 1987. The president of the Law Students' Society was optimistic about the new intake: 'They should breathe some new life into the Law School, bringing with them friends and contacts from the rest of the University, and hopefully reducing some of the cliqueness [sic] that has tagged the Law School "elitist" and "separationist".'[57] As planned, the quota rose again, reaching 160 in 1989.[58]

For some of the staff, the promise of later-year entry was fulfilled. Andrew Ligertwood reflected: 'I think it made a great difference to the attention and quality of the students that we had. And also, in social terms, it brought in a bigger spread of students, not only from private schools, but also from state schools as well.'[59] This effect was strongest in 1987, when most new students came from state schools and there was an increase in enrolments of women, students with matriculation scores under 400 and students aged twenty or older. The proportion of state school students then fell again, although in 1989 it was still higher (at 34%) than it had been before later-year entry. The Law Society was ambivalent about the change. Officially, it supported a short-term cut in the intake, so long as graduate output was maintained (through higher completion rates among later-year entrants, for example). But the society warned that the supply of graduates was failing to meet demand. Its president in 1987–88, Rodney Burr, regarded the double-degree course as elitist and encouraged Flinders University to establish a law course. Competition from a new school offering direct entry was a looming difficulty for the Law School's plan.[60]

§

The Law School's fiftieth and seventy-fifth anniversaries passed without formal commemoration, but its centenary in 1983 was marked with celebrations, fundraising and high-profile events. Sir Richard Blackburn, the most senior surviving Bonython professor, delivered an address at a commemoration ceremony for law graduands, and a centenary law revue revived old sketches and added new ones. A fundraising appeal to support periodical subscriptions proved a lifeline for the Law Library, as budgets were cut and currency devaluation inflated the prices of overseas journals. A special issue of the *Adelaide Law Review* contained articles by prominent staff and graduates, and faculty members voted to choose 'a distinguished lawyer to participate in the Centenary celebrations'.[61] Former prime minister Gough Whitlam narrowly beat former chief justice Sir Garfield Barwick to become the centenary visiting professor. Whitlam spent several weeks in Adelaide, where he gave a public lecture on reform of electoral machinery, lectured to classes in Constitutional Law I and II, and led human rights seminars. The anniversary also prompted work on the Law School's history. The largest of these projects was the centenary history, *Law on North Terrace*, while the commemorative issue of the *Adelaide Law Review* contained historical essays by Blackburn and the university's chronicler, Victor Edgeloe, now registrar-emeritus. Horst Lücke delivered a talk for students that grew, through later revisions, into an unpublished, article-length study of the faculty's deans.[62]

The centenary was the occasion for a sobering reflection by the dean, Andrew Ligertwood, on the paucity of higher-degree research students in the Law School: 'In our first 100 years six have qualified for the LL.D., one for the Ph.D. and 15 for the LL.M.'[63] Postgraduate study was late to develop in Australian law schools. According to the Universities Commission, only thirty-seven research higher degrees in law were completed in Australia in 1974. The number was even lower in architecture, dentistry and veterinary science, where the pool of potential candidates was smaller. Significantly, all were professional disciplines. Conventional pathways into the legal profession provided little support or recognition for further university study, and the few graduates who aimed for academic careers had a strong incentive to study overseas, if possible, because of the value attached to qualifications from leading law schools in Britain and North America.

As the law faculty put it in 1976: 'It is rare for a student who has gained First Class honours in the LLB to proceed to postgraduate work in the Faculty rather than to pursue further studies overseas, and very few students who have gained Second Class honours think it worthwhile to devote themselves to full-time postgraduate work at the possible expense of their professional career.'[64]

A partial solution to low postgraduate enrolments had been found at the University of Sydney, where Australia's first Master of Laws by coursework was introduced in 1965. A program of this kind had several advantages. It allowed graduates, especially practitioners studying part-time, to earn a further qualification without the daunting challenge of a thesis. Staff gained opportunities to teach specialised subjects in areas of research that did not feature in the undergraduate curriculum. Connections with the profession were strengthened, through the participation of practitioners as students and teachers, and the coursework degree provided a pathway into subsequent higher degrees by research. Coursework master's programs were favoured by the Universities Commission. Its support was essential after 1974, when postgraduate students did not pay tuition fees and the number of places in postgraduate programs had to be approved by the commission. By 1976, coursework master's degrees in law were offered at Sydney, Melbourne and Monash. South Australia's Committee on Postgraduate Legal Education had laid a foundation for future coursework degrees by demonstrating that practitioners would support a fee-based program of continuing legal education. When, in 1972, the committee's financial success dictated that either the Law Society or the Law School would take full control, the Law School had withdrawn, although its staff continued to collaborate as presenters. A coursework program allowed the Law School to re-enter the field by providing specialist study leading to a degree, alongside the seminars and workshops run by the Law Society.[65]

The faculty created the framework for a coursework master's degree in 1976, to be activated when resources permitted. It was keen to maintain a high academic standard, by aiming the program at its best graduates rather than the broader market served by continuing legal education. An unusual title, Master of Legal Studies, differentiated the Adelaide degree from the LLM by thesis. Unlike the oversubscribed LLB, the MLS had to attract students, as the Curriculum Committee warned: 'No courses will be viable unless the subject matter covered is sufficiently interesting to young practitioners from whose ranks it is expected that most candidates would be drawn.'[66] In the first year of the MLS, 1980, only four subjects were offered (in taxation, competition law, insurance and criminal procedure), although students could substitute one subject from the undergraduate curriculum. Candidates needed to be LLB graduates with an honours degree, an above-average record or substantial professional experience, but the Law School still expected a withdrawal rate of at least 30%. Experience elsewhere showed that the research component of the degree—typically a minor thesis—delayed completion for many candidates.[67]

The success of the MLS depended on a balancing act. It had to attract students, but they needed good academic and professional records, to maintain the intended high standard. Because it was supported by federal funding and by staffing allocated by the university, rather than by fees, the program had a quota, set initially at twenty-five full-time equivalent students (although most students would study part-time). Three staff were allocated to the MLS under the 1981 Compact, and their continuation would depend on its success. A broad curriculum would attract students, but the more subjects there were, the greater the commitment of resources. The plan envisaged that, within a few years, at least six subjects would be offered each year, from a total of about eighteen. But staffing constraints affected enrolments: 'The Department has not had the staff or resources to mount both a changing variety of courses or [sic] the most popular courses regularly. Consequently, many MLS candidates have intermitted or withdrawn.'[68] Benefits to graduates also fell short, as the degree made little difference to advancement in the profession. Of the 115 students who enrolled from 1980 to 1985, eight had graduated by 1986, and fifty-four had withdrawn.[69]

Faced with these difficulties, the faculty proposed wide-ranging changes. The name of the degree was a sore point, as a meeting of current and past MLS students showed: 'It was argued that the title M.L.S. was not well known to the general public, required constant explanation, implied study of sociologically based areas, and, generally, by bearing a name different to the LL.M., implied inferior status.'[70] On the other hand, graduates who had met the faculty's exacting standards for the LLM by thesis could be unhappy to find their achievement equated with a coursework degree. Rob Fowler argued that the MLS had not reached 'standards concomitant with those to be expected at a postgraduate level' and should not be given the title LLM. 'Of course, the truth is that I am sensitive to the issue because I (and a few others in recent history) have obtained an LL.M. by thesis at Adelaide. I know the standards that were expected and the demands which that exercise imposed on me. Only the most rigorous coursework degree at the postgraduate level could equate.'[71] But it was difficult to hold out against the coursework LLMs offered by other law schools. Only Tasmania, an Adelaide committee reported, also used the title Master of Legal Studies. In 1988 the MLS became an LLM, awarded on completion of six half-year subjects and a minor thesis. Two specialisations were offered, the LLM (Companies and Securities) and the LLM (Commercial). There were tentative signs that recognition by the profession would improve, and that the new degrees might become attractive to young lawyers seeking to establish themselves in their preferred areas of practice.[72]

§

In 1985 the Commonwealth Tertiary Education Commission initiated a review of Australian law schools. The three-member panel was chaired by Dennis Pearce, an Adelaide graduate who had become a professor of law at the Australian National University. Conceived as the first of a series of discipline reviews, the inquiry had a sweeping remit, a short timeline and little administrative support, but, despite these obstacles, in 1987 the panel produced a five-volume report. It was stronger on evaluation of current performance than on future trends, but it highlighted the meagre resources allocated to law courses, especially in the older law schools, and welcomed what it portrayed as the recent transition of legal education from narrow vocational training to a broader academic discipline.

A national survey of recent law graduates was part of the inquiry. Student feedback on the quality of education was a growing trend. Such questionnaires were not new; Adelaide zoology students were asked to rate their lecturers as early as 1954, on the initiative of the head of department. But the practice had grown, aided by the establishment of university centres for teaching development, such as Adelaide's Advisory Centre for University Education, which opened in 1973. In the 1980s such surveys became management tools, used for internal and external appraisal of teachers and departments. For the Pearce inquiry, graduates were asked to rate their law courses on a range of criteria, covering teaching and the curriculum. Like other older universities, Adelaide did not perform well. Its graduates 'dealt with the course in a most unkindly manner', as the report put it.[73] The LLB course was ranked below average for intellectual stimulation and above average for rote learning. Less than half of the Adelaide respondents said the course gave them a good general education. (Whether this was the task of a law school was another matter, but some universities scored much higher.) These figures, the report commented, pointed to 'a dissatisfaction with the intellectual calibre of the course' and 'a lack of effort being put into the course by staff members'.[74] Considering the work then underway on curriculum reform, these remarks were disappointing, but two of Lücke's other 'ancient paupers', the Melbourne and Sydney law schools, did even worse. Only 16% of Melbourne respondents said their law school took a genuine interest in students' educational needs; at Sydney, the figure was 12%.[75]

The Pearce report was quickly overtaken by changes in higher-education policy. Reforms spearheaded by John Dawkins, the federal education minister, drove renewed growth in higher education, reorientation of management within universities, and the introduction of undergraduate student charges, payable on enrolment or later, plus interest, through HECS, the Higher Education Contribution Scheme. Postgraduate coursework students would pay full fees, intended to cover the cost of providing their courses. The Pearce report had made (in Dennis Pearce's words) 'the Canute-ish recommendation that no further law schools be established'.[76] This advice proved ill-timed, as universities sought additional revenue by lifting enrolments and new law schools proliferated. Competition took on new importance, and performance assessed in the new metrics of evaluation could be rewarded or penalised. Targets would be set, and the Law School's work would be judged.

7

School and Faculty: 1990–1999

By 1990, articles of clerkship, the basis of practical training for the legal profession for more than a century, had almost disappeared. That year, there were only two articled clerks in South Australian law firms. However, the structure and, above all, the funding for a replacement system of practical training were unsettled. Articles had been funded by the premiums formerly paid by clerks, by their discounted labour, and by the firms for which they worked, but practical training courses suffered in the funding upheavals that were reshaping higher education. The Law School had vacated the field of post-degree practical training to the South Australian Institute of Technology in 1976. For most graduates, SAIT's Graduate Diploma in Legal Practice became the final stage of training before entry to the profession. However, the GDLP was underfunded, and in 1990 student dissatisfaction and the need to accommodate rising enrolments led to the first of a series of reviews that continued for much of the following decade. Temporary funding kept the program going, but SAIT had to turn applicants away. Some twenty-five graduates had to find articles in 1991, after they missed out on balloted places. Under the admission rules, only graduates who were crowded out of the GDLP were eligible for articles, which could be very hard to secure. Further funding shortfalls led to the replacement of the GDLP by a shorter Graduate Certificate in Legal Practice in 1994, at the new University of South Australia, into which SAIT had merged. The Law Society provided top-up training, to cover admission requirements that the GCLP now omitted.[1]

The hybrid GCLP – Law Society model was yet to find either a secure funding base or a place in the affections of many students. John Keeler observed in 1994:

> Practical Legal Training courses are not often highly regarded by students. The USA course has been unpopular because although it has insisted on punctual and consistent attendance as a training for employment its practical classes are not for real clients; that its students call it 'play school' represents frustration at both points which is common to all such courses.[2]

Commonwealth subsidies for such courses ended in 1992, and federal policy allowed the charging of full fees. The cost to graduates rose. A GCLP fee of $5000, under discussion at UniSA, was among the catalysts for a broader student protest in March 1994. Students picketed the Australian National University's law school in August to protest against a similar fee for practical legal training. UniSA averted the mooted fees by allocating Commonwealth-supported (HECS) places to the GCLP, but a review by Justice Edward (Ted) Mullighan concluded that the system of practical legal training was a failure. Mullighan's preferred remedy, the revival of articles of clerkship supplemented by a training course, found some support in the Law Society, but not enough to reverse the long-established trend away from articles. Meanwhile, graduate numbers continued to swell, after the new law school at Flinders University took its first intake in 1992.[3]

The increase in graduates threatened to overwhelm the supplementary training provided by the Law Society. Lawyers objected that graduates could start work as sole practitioners without any practical experience other than that incorporated in the training programs. The Law Society's response to these problems was to propose employment in a law firm as a co-requisite for entry to its post-GCLP program. For many students, the need to find a place in a law firm in order to complete their training threatened to revive one of the most unpopular features of the articles system. The law students' societies at Adelaide and Flinders protested. Craig Pett, president of the Adelaide LSS, said: 'It is inevitable that those with connections in law will displace others who are as equally deserving [sic], but don't have the contacts.'[4] The Law Society dropped the plan after reassessing the likely demand for training, but uncertainty surrounding admission requirements remained a problem for students.[5]

Flinders and Adelaide began in 1995 to move towards offering their own practical legal training courses. Flinders had an opportunity to build on the practical side of its LLB, which was already a featured selling point, and to allow students to complete all their training using HECS. At Adelaide, motivations were more complex. A reallocation of Commonwealth-funded places from the LLB to a possible GDLP was part of a new strategy for postgraduate teaching and staff recruitment, at a time when postgraduate coursework applications were declining and the LLB was seen as overcrowded. A partner such as UniSA would be needed in order to provide a full training course, and fees would have to supplement Commonwealth funding. The central administration of the university was supportive, even over-enthusiastic; a remark by the registrar about Adelaide 'capturing' practical legal training was seen at the Law Society as provocative.[6]

The Law Society had reason to be wary. It was committed to training provided by senior practitioners, and a university course would compete with its successful program. As the society's executive group saw it, the need to raise money and reform the LLB seemed to be driving the Adelaide proposal. Adelaide dean Rob Fowler saw financial imperatives at work in the Law Society as well: 'Essentially, the Society is providing an inadequate product at a significant profit and, rightly, feels threatened by the Law Faculty initiative.'[7] After long and tangled negotiations, during which the Commonwealth moved HECS places away from postgraduate courses, a result emerged in 1998. The Law Society would provide a shortened GDLP for Adelaide students, and a revised LLB curriculum would meet some of the requirements for practical training. GDLP students would pay fees, reminiscent of the premiums once charged for articles. At Flinders, to attract HECS funding, subjects taught by the Law Society were incorporated in a Bachelor of Laws and Legal Practice, later taught wholly by the university. UniSA closed its GDLP program at the end of 1998. The Law Society's Legal Practice Centre, which opened in 1999, became a significant part of the society's activities and cemented the transition, also seen in other Australian jurisdictions, of mandatory practical training from apprenticeship to centralised teaching programs.[8]

§

The judges were sidelined in the rapid changes in post-degree training, despite their control of the admission rules. Justice Mullighan's support for articles, and a call by Chief Justice John Doyle for a single, cooperative scheme of practical training, had little effect. Outcomes were largely determined by the Law Society and the universities. As higher-education policy changed and new national standards emerged, the state lacked a suitable framework for the development of admission standards. Much of this work had been done, since 1967, by the Chief Justice's Committee on Legal Education, but (in the words of Justice John Perry) 'it was convened only when a crisis developed'. Most of the judges, Perry said, recognised that 'they can no longer be expected to address in an ongoing, satisfactory fashion the issues surrounding legal education, practical legal training, admission requirements, mutual recognition and the developing push for a national profession'.[9]

In 1995 the judges proposed a new 'single representative body' to determine the academic and practical requirements for admission and to ensure the provision of practical training.[10] It would comprise two educators, two students and the nominees of the chief justice, the attorney-general and the Law Society. An implementation committee composed in the same way would negotiate with interested parties. The inclusion of students as voting members was contentious, as it had been when a similar body was under discussion in the mid-1970s. Perry wrote: 'I am unable to accept the proposition that somebody who has never practised in the profession is qualified to take part in the process of defining the qualifications for admission.'[11] He did, however, support a non-voting student representative. The Law Society was 'strongly opposed to the creation of a body which is designed to be "representative" of the "stakeholders"', although a student had been added to the society's Education Committee in 1989.[12] Student representatives from Adelaide and Flinders stressed the importance of full membership: 'Given the unwillingness of the Law Society and others to listen and respond to student concerns in the past, if the student on the proposed board is not given voting rights then their voice can, and in all probability will, be unimportant and unheard.'[13]

The judges' power to make admission rules was as old as the Supreme Court itself, and some of the judges were reluctant to relinquish it. However, Doyle reported to the attorney-general that the new admission body would not be able to work effectively if judges retained control; they lacked the necessary time and expertise. Support from stakeholders and the government allowed the plan to proceed, and the *Legal Practitioners (Qualifications) Amendment Act 1998* (SA) established the Legal Practitioners Education and Admission Council (LPEAC). Judges and practitioners made up most of its membership, which also included the attorney-general, the deans of law at Adelaide and Flinders, and a non-voting law student appointed by the chief justice. In practice, the presidents of the law students' societies at Adelaide and Flinders alternated each year. LPEAC would make the rules governing the admission of practitioners and the issuing of practising certificates. In an acknowledgement of an emerging national professional framework, it would also participate in developing uniform national standards.[14]

Under the new system, law courses needed accreditation from LPEAC for their degrees to be recognised for entry to the profession. Accreditation was far from automatic. It involved detailed scrutiny by the council and an external academic consultant, as well as considerable work by the Law School to provide information and respond to queries. An initial review, for interim accreditation, began in 1999, at the same time as a new LLB curriculum that would, among other things, coordinate skills teaching with the new GDLP. The Law School received interim accreditation the following year, despite LPEAC's concerns about semesterisation and a reduction in student contact hours, as more teaching moved to small groups. When final accreditation followed in 2001, it came with a rider: 'LPEAC has a real concern that the resources provided are not adequate having regard to the number of students and the more intensive approach to teaching through seminars.' Accreditation was conditional, 'subject to LPEAC being satisfied, by the end of 2002, that the University has made a commitment to providing adequate on-going resources on a continuing basis ... LPEAC has formed the firm opinion that the Law School is under-resourced.'[15] Accreditation became unconditional in 2003, but LPEAC requested a further report on Law School resources. Correspondence between the vice-chancellor and the chief justice, who chaired LPEAC, kept pressure on the university to fund the Law School adequately, and the dean, Paul Fairall, was able to report that resources were satisfactory. Rolling reviews of accreditation would maintain LPEAC scrutiny in future.[16]

§

The opening of new law schools at Flinders and at Bond University in Queensland drained staff from Adelaide. Five members of the teaching staff left in 1988, to help establish the law school at Bond. They included Bond's first dean, Tony Tarr. Three more left to join the founding staff of the law school at Flinders. Among them was Adelaide's dean, Rebecca Bailey-Harris, who became the first professor of law at Flinders. Moving to a new institution had long been a path to promotion, especially in the days when, as at many law schools, promotion to professor required appointment to an existing chair or the creation of a personal chair. Unsuccessful applications for promotion could intensify discontent, especially if disappointed applicants thought that their achievements had been discounted by panel members from other disciplines who were unfamiliar with the distinctive patterns of legal academia. In the longer term, academic lawyers would adapt to common university criteria for research income and publishing. The Law School sometimes gained staff who achieved promotion by moving to Adelaide, but now the opening of new law schools presented other opportunities for advancement, and the Law School suffered a loss of experience and talent.

Developments at Flinders had other effects. In the late 1980s, as higher-education policy changed to favour rapid expansion, the Law School adopted a strategy for significant increases in its undergraduate intake. It aimed to lift the quota from 175 in 1990 to 250 in 1993. The extra students would bring additional income, and the expansion of the Ligertwood Building would provide more space for staff and teaching. But such a large increase was difficult to justify to the university or the federal government, when a growing number of students were accommodated at Flinders. In 1993 the Adelaide law intake had risen only to 190.[17]

As required in the new Unified National System of higher education, in 1989 the university adopted a strategic plan. It also initiated a continuing cycle of planning and review in its faculties. The Law School's first strategic plan, in 1992, served both to inform outsiders about the work of the Law School and to guide future efforts. It set out sixteen goals. Most were common in such documents, among them improvements in teaching and research performance, and efficient administration. The Law School also undertook to 'conduct its affairs according to democratic processes', to 'ensure the accessibility and accountability of academic staff' and to 'maintain independent status as a Faculty, but to participate fully in the affairs of the University', this last goal being more of a message to the university than a matter under the faculty's control.[18]

The plan projected a modest increase (7%) in LLB enrolments between 1992 and 1995.

'To internationalise the Law School' was the first goal in the strategic plan. Similar aims appeared in the plans of many universities, with the encouragement of a federal government keen to foster international engagement and awareness. International experience enhanced the standing of staff, and travel opportunities attracted students. Student exchange programs became a feature of the law course, as they did in many universities in this period. On the initiative of the Law Students' Society, the faculty adopted guidelines for student exchanges in 1986, and the first formal agreement for such exchanges, with the University of Marburg in Germany, was adopted in 1993. In the next few years, the Law School set a rapid pace in negotiating bilateral exchange agreements with six universities in the United States, Canada, France and Germany. The College of William and Mary, in Virginia, sent American law students to the Law School for month-long intensive courses over the Australian summer break. Links with Germany were particularly strong, drawing on both the long history of German migration to South Australia and the growth of the Centre for European Studies at Adelaide, which taught in German and other European languages and had many law students among its double-degree enrolments. In addition to the exchange agreement with Marburg, in 1998 the Law School entered an agreement with the University of Mannheim for a distinctive joint master's degree in comparative law. The degree was awarded jointly by the two universities, and students spent a semester at each campus, completing coursework and a minor thesis. The joint master's degree ran alongside undergraduate student exchange between the universities. The master's program was popular with German students, although it was harder to attract Adelaide students to Mannheim. The program proved durable (unlike the William and Mary summer school) and was still operating twenty years later.[19]

Another goal was active cooperation with Flinders, including cross listing of subjects and joint appointments of staff. This aspect of the strategic plan reflected lingering concern about the division of scarce resources on the opening of a second law school. Some cooperation eventuated—a joint legal advice clinic and a joint internship program were later examples—but there was also competition, as some had hoped and as the Unified National System encouraged. Many in the profession supported a new law school as a spur to better performance. Mike Rann, state minister for employment and further education in 1989–92, recalled that the government 'decided to survey law firms and others around town about whether there was a need for the Law School at Adelaide University to have some competition, and the message we got back … was that it badly needed some competition'.[20] Soon both law schools were seeking to lift postgraduate enrolments, introduce programs in practical legal training and continuing legal education, and attract fee-paying international students. Hilary Charlesworth came to Adelaide soon after the Flinders Law School opened:

> Flinders quickly began to be a very happening place … I think it was seen as a place where, perhaps, ambitious people from Adelaide, who perhaps were blocked for promotion, would want to go … It didn't strike me there was a clear rivalry, but there was a sense that they were less encumbered with the ghosts of the past, and they could do new and interesting things.[21]

The Law School's student journal, *Hilarian*, said Flinders was 'gaining currency as a vital, innovative, and pragmatically oriented legal institution'.[22]

Annual, national surveys of recent graduates for the Graduate Careers Council produced embarrassing comparisons. The surveys asked graduates, among other things, how they rated teaching at their universities, on a scale of 1 to 5. For publication, the early results were converted to a more eye-catching scale, ranging from –100 to +100. Students who graduated in 1993 gave the Adelaide Law School a teaching score of –31, ahead only of the University of Queensland's law school, which scored –38. The national average for teaching in law and legal studies was –10; only five of the sixteen programs surveyed reached positive figures. All five were newer law schools, established since World War II. Law students corroborated the Adelaide results. Katherine Dellit, president of the Law Students' Society, addressed the Departmental Committee in August 1996 on problems perceived by students, including quality of teaching and a feeling that students were not valued by staff. The level of student dissatisfaction was sufficiently concerning for the Law School to undertake its own survey. Its results were interpreted by the faculty as reassuring, but bad results in national surveys continued. As Michael Detmold put it: 'We have to reverse our terrible graduate survey record. In 1997 the figures were Flinders 60, national average 30, Adelaide 6.'[23] Students were aware of these figures, as a meeting with a student focus group revealed: 'The news of the recent survey which put Flinders ahead of Adelaide has caused deep concern.' The group's opinions about the quality of teaching were scathing. 'Staff display cynicism and arrogance towards students' was one comment.[24]

Deteriorating finances shrank the teaching staff, through resignations and voluntary redundancies. 'It is hardly surprising therefore that staff feel under enormous pressure, that morale is low and that there is growing evidence of student dissatisfaction with the LLB', the dean reported.[25] The number of permanent and contract teaching staff fell from thirty-four in 1994 to twenty-four and a half in 1998, although a round of appointments in 1998–99 offered hope of renewal at junior levels. A chair was advertised in 1998, but it proved difficult to fill. No appointment was made from the initial round of advertising, which had been delayed because of financial concerns (meeting the salary would have added to a budget deficit in the Law School). The advertisement stated that the appointee would become dean, and this stipulation was thought to be 'a major reason for lack of interest'.[26] The chair was readvertised without the stipulation in 1999, but with the expectation that the appointee would become dean 'at some time'.[27] The appointment process dragged on, compounded by a legal dispute. The Law School was without a third professor from the start of 1998 until the appointment of Ngaire Naffine in 2000.[28]

§

Students' experiences of the Law School needed to be improved, but how to do so was less clear. One initiative was a broad review of the curriculum and teaching methods of the LLB course. The need to retain certification of the degree for professional admission constrained curriculum choices, as it had throughout the Law School's history, but it was now affected by a new level of national coordination. In 1994 the Consultative Committee of State and Territory Law Admitting Authorities, under the auspices of the national Council of Chief Justices, released model admission rules, which listed areas of knowledge and practical skills required for entry to practice. Taking their name from the chair of the committee, Justice Lancelot (Bill) Priestley of the New South Wales Court of Appeal, the areas of knowledge became known as the Priestley Eleven, and the practical skills as the Priestley Twelve. The eleven subject areas, fleshed out by detailed descriptions, were criminal law and procedure, torts, contracts, property, equity, administrative law, constitutional law, civil procedure, evidence, company law, and professional conduct. Soon adopted by most state admitting authorities, the list codified the doctrinal core of the law curriculum for the next three decades, with little alteration.[29]

The Adelaide curriculum review arose from the need to fit subjects into the university's new academic year of two semesters, in place of three terms. Student dissatisfaction led to the expansion of the review into 'a full-scale enquiry into the LLB', conducted by a working party.[30] Its 'overriding concern' was 'to address a profound sense of alienation which exists mutually on the part of academic staff and students within the Law School'.[31] Another aim was to combine the teaching of skills with the legal doctrine that dominated the curriculum. In the Pearce inquiry's survey of law graduates, 71% of Adelaide respondents agreed with the statement that the course did not adequately relate theory to practice. Rachel Spencer graduated as the inquiry began its work:

> There was nothing practical about the degree back then. We learned black letter law and that was it. No-one ever mentioned the word client ... It didn't teach me anything about resilience in the workplace or the need to have empathy for clients or how to manage the ebb and flow of legal work.[32]

As adopted in 1997, the new curriculum had a compulsory core consisting of the Priestley Eleven, three new legal skills subjects, and a research unit, which later became optional. The legal skills subjects would cover about half of the Priestley Twelve practical training areas by combining practical skills with substantive doctrine in contract, administrative law and procedure. These subjects would dovetail with the new Graduate Diploma in Legal Practice. Interactive, seminar-based teaching would replace lectures, where feasible. The plan required additional teaching staff, but perennial budget uncertainty clouded the outlook, and the faculty made implementation contingent on adequate funding. However, retreat would be damaging. As the convenor of the university's Academic Board said: 'To abandon the reforms would have a negative impact on the way in which the Law School was viewed.'[33] The phasing-in of the new curriculum began in 1999.[34]

The new legal skills subjects, ambitious in their combination of doctrine and praxis, were among the first to be introduced. They did not begin well. 'Now, having gone in at the deep end, some good things have emerged, and some bad', the dean reported.[35] Specialist legal skills teachers were hard to find, and the rotation of doctrinal and skills teachers in the same classes created problems. In Criminal Law, third-year students had to work in research teams with first-year students, and the work of the groups was assessable. 'In practice the later year students were generally extremely hostile to the scheme', John Keeler wrote.[36] Two law students on the board of the university's student union (one of them its president, Elysia Turcinovic) sent a memorandum, 'The State of the Law School', to the school's Executive Committee, detailing shortcomings in teaching, course materials, administration, computerisation and the transition to the new curriculum. The memorandum concluded: 'The real issue here seems to be one of communication.'[37] For whatever reasons (staff discontent may have been one), many students were unpersuaded about the merits of some of the changes and participated unwillingly in their implementation. Adjustments to the scheme alleviated some concerns. One of the three legal skills subjects was discontinued in 2000, and the new curriculum was gradually bedded down.

§

The financial situation underlying these difficulties was affected by policy changes at federal level and within the university. Beginning in 1990, academic disciplines were grouped in five bands, notionally based on teaching costs, which determined their allocations under the Commonwealth's relative funding model. A smaller fund, the Research Quantum, was allocated according to measures of research performance, and other federal funds were redirected to competitive research grants. Law schools fared badly under these arrangements. Law was placed in the lowest funding band, continuing the longstanding perception among university and government policymakers that it was cheap to teach. As in most universities, internal budget allocations soon followed, with some variations, the patterns of the relative funding model. Law schools were challenged by the Research Quantum, which rewarded research books and refereed articles, and put lower valuations on publications commonly produced by legal academics, such as textbooks, casebooks and government reports. Competitive research income, too, was rewarded under the Research Quantum, but most law schools had a scanty record in attracting it, not least because the pool of funding available for legal research was far smaller than in some other disciplines, such as medical sciences. The Law School's Research Quantum income fell by 12% in 1997, a result (as Rob Fowler saw it) of 'misplaced notions concerning levels of publication and grant income which are appropriate only in the sciences'.[38] The Law School fought a rearguard action seeking recognition for the distinctive forms of legal research, but without success. In the longer term, Adelaide, like other law schools, had to move towards the forms of research that brought the greatest financial rewards.[39]

Some cross-subsidisation between disciplines was involved in the original HECS scheme, as students paid the same contribution whether the cost of providing their courses was high or low. This aspect of the scheme changed in 1996, when student contributions, like funding levels, were placed in bands. Some courses, such as medicine, were in the top band for both the level of student contributions and the level of government funding. Law, however, was placed in the highest band for student contributions (thanks to the comparatively high incomes of graduates) while remaining in the lowest band for federal funding. The funding model took contributions from students according to their probable future capacity to pay and provided funding to law schools according to their deemed needs, but it did nothing to placate dissatisfied students and staff. Resistance was futile, as Rob Fowler reported after a meeting of the Committee (later Council) of Australian Law Deans in 1998: 'It has been the common experience of most Deans that efforts to secure an improved funding level on the grounds that LLB students are now paying more for their education have proved entirely fruitless.'[40] The Law School sought an increase in funding per student from the university, but the vice-chancellor rejected the idea as not politically feasible.[41]

The university faced a 5% cut in federal operating grants for 1997, and, as Fowler put it, 'the position looks very grim'.[42] He presented a plan to revitalise the Law School and stabilise its budget. It sought increased enrolments, enhanced research performance, and curriculum reform, supported by new or augmented sources of funding. Federal policy changes allowed universities to enrol domestic fee-paying undergraduate students, for the first time since the abolition of university tuition fees in 1974. Such students could bring additional funding, as could an increase in HECS-supported enrolments. Cooperative arrangements with the university's Malaysian partner, Sepang Institute of Technology, might lift international student fee income. (Changes in Malaysian professional admission requirements frustrated this initiative.) Offshore postgraduate teaching was another possibility. Regardless of the success of these initiatives, the Law School had to face the prospect of rising, or stubbornly high, student–staff ratios, as Fowler had warned: 'The Faculty will have to explore new and innovative ways of teaching the LLB with proportionately less resources per student. This could include the use of video and multi-media technology, innovations which are now being considered widely throughout all spheres of the tertiary education sector.'[43] Technological innovation was particularly alluring, as networking and the World Wide Web grew exponentially in the late 1990s, but early adopters faced significant technical challenges.[44]

The introduction of domestic fee-paying students was controversial. Student representatives protested to the dean: 'They were extremely forceful in their opposition to the proposed option for Law and saw it as an erosion of the Law degree.'[45] Overcrowding and the decline of equitable access to the law course were among their concerns. Amrita Dasvarma, a law student who was president of the Students' Association, told the *Advertiser* that students had to sit on the floor in lectures and that teachers were hard to find outside class: 'You are better off standing in the stairwell from the staff carpark and trying to ambush them when they arrive for work.'[46] Andrew Ligertwood was the Law School's associate dean (teaching): 'The University has cut our resources and students are being asked to pay higher fees and we have reached something of a crisis in this respect, with students beginning to vent their anger.'[47] But the imperative to find additional sources of revenue overrode such concerns. The university introduced a pilot scheme for undergraduate fee-paying places in 1998. The numbers were small (only twenty-five places across Law, Commerce, Dentistry and Architecture), but applicants for Law accepted offers at an unexpectedly high rate. Fee-paying enrolments spiked, then fell as the number of HECS places increased. The university chose to make no offers of fee-paying places in 2001, but numbers rose thereafter.[48]

Full fees changed the landscape for postgraduate coursework in the Law School. Fees could make the coursework program a source of growing revenue, if a market could be found, and boosting postgraduate enrolments was part of the university's strategic plans. In the early 1990s, the postgraduate coursework program enrolled both fee-paying and Commonwealth-supported students. The number of fee-paying places was limited, but the Law School received the full amount of the fees they paid. Joining existing LLM specialisations, the Graduate Diploma in Environmental Law and the LLM (Environment), introduced in 1993, attracted many students and soon made up around one-third of postgraduate coursework enrolments. The program drew on the expertise of Law School scholars including Adrian Bradbrook and Rob Fowler, a pioneer in the study of legal responses to climate change in Australia. By 1995 the Law School earned about $100,000 a year from its fee-paying postgraduate students, but looming policy changes threatened this income. Postgraduate coursework programs in the Law School became fully fee-paying in 1996, and the university, having lost Commonwealth funding for such courses, decided to retain for central purposes some of the fee income previously paid in full to the Law School. The dean flagged more vigorous marketing to potential students to sustain the program, but competition was growing, and postgraduate students from overseas tended to seek higher degrees by research rather than by coursework. The changing environment made the future of the program doubtful, unless it grew.[49]

The needed growth did not eventuate. Enrolments in the environmental law program declined, as pent-up demand was satisfied. The federal Training Guarantee Levy, which had previously encouraged law firms to pay for postgraduate coursework undertaken by their staff, was abolished in 1996. Law firms were slow to encourage postgraduate study for their employees. The faculty echoed earlier experience: 'Advancement in the legal profession is not normally linked to postgraduate study.'[50] There were only seventeen new applicants for the postgraduate coursework program in 1997. Meanwhile, initiatives in practical legal training and continuing legal education were competing for the Law School's resources. The faculty took the painful step of suspending new enrolments in the postgraduate coursework program from 1998. The decision was unpopular with higher management in the university, but the dean, faced with falling enrolments and deteriorating finances, could only offer the hope of reviving the program sometime in the future.[51]

§

Later-year entry to the LLB was a signature innovation of the Law School in the 1980s, but difficulties mounted in the following decade. The policy had warm support from some students and staff, who applauded the aims of broadening the Law School's intake and reducing the importance of school results. Students Katherine Dellit and Beverli Newbold wrote in 1995: 'Increases in the numbers of mature-age students, women, Aboriginal students, students from working class backgrounds and non-English speaking backgrounds have seen the gradual diversification of the law school student population and this diversification has filtered through to the profession.'[52] John Keeler saw weaknesses in the earlier selection of entrants using only their Tertiary Entry Rank (TER) in Year 12: 'Given the difference in the resources, backgrounds and educational facilities available at different schools TERs are not the outcome of level playing fields of educational competition.'[53] About two-thirds of South Australian school leavers came from government schools. Between 1985 and 1992–95, the proportion of Law School entrants from government schools increased, but it was still disproportionately low, at 38%.[54]

The Flinders Law School, which allowed entry direct from school, offered high-achieving school leavers an attractive alternative to deferred entry at Adelaide, to the disquiet of university management. A university-wide decline in Adelaide's share of top-scoring matriculants caused concern in the Vice-Chancellor's Committee. The dean, Adrian Bradbrook, reported in 1995:

> At the Deans' retreat, the Vice-Chancellor and the Registrar put it to me very strongly that they had a [sic] irrefutable evidence that we were losing top quality school leavers to Flinders and that as a matter of urgency we need to amend our current admission rules. They further stated that when considering this issue, the Faculty of Law should realise that if they changed the policy in order to reserve a number of places for school leavers we would not only be improving the quality of our own students, but would be providing a benefit for other participating faculties, particularly the Faculty of Arts. It was suggested that we were being selfish in adhering to our present rule.[55]

A staunch critic of later-year entry was Justice John Perry, who became a member of the university council in 1995. He disagreed with the 'micro social engineering' he saw in the faculty's efforts to change the social mix of entrants, and he criticised the development of 'idiosyncratic entry procedures', which differed from the widespread use of TERs.[56] The university's selection procedures would soon become more diverse. A specialised aptitude test, in conjunction with an interview and a TER in the top 10%, took the place of TER alone for selection into the medical course in 1997. The rejection of some applicants with exceptionally high TERs proved controversial, but, in the case of Medicine, the vice-chancellor publicly defended the new procedures.[57]

The Law School's Selection Committee investigated elite matriculants (in the top 7%) among law students and found that in 1994 less than half of the elite matriculants studying law in South Australia (44%) were at Adelaide. Although the two law schools were taking roughly equal shares (the figures varied considerably from year to year), the faculty decided to reserve twenty-five places for elite matriculants, who would be selected for later entry using their matriculation scores. The deputy vice-chancellor (academic) subsequently increased the number of offers, without consulting the faculty. Selection swung back towards non-government schools: of the 1996 elite selection, 79% attended non-government schools; only 46% of later-year entrants did so. When the deputy vice-chancellor (academic) proposed to increase the elite quota further, the faculty rejected the proposal unanimously, with the strong support of student representatives. Combining reserved places and later-year entry was unfair, a student focus group said. 'Students who have not performed particularly well in first year are going into Law with those who have had to work hard in first year to qualify.'[58] But the increase stood, despite an appeal by the faculty to the university council, and the elite quota rose to about one-quarter of the LLB cohort.[59]

The prestige and high performance associated with top school leavers were irresistible. The faculty, too, wanted to 'address this haemorrhage', as Rob Fowler put it, 'in order to ensure that a significant component of these elite students are maintained within our undergraduate mix. This in turn is essential to the maintenance of the necessary broad spectrum intellectual milieu within the Law School.'[60] Widely divergent marking practices undermined the use of tertiary results for selection, and applications for later-year entry were in decline, dropping by nearly half in 1996–98. The causes of the decline were unclear, but they may have included the increase in HECS charges for law courses and the attraction of direct entry at Flinders. The elite-matriculant quota continued to expand. Selection based on TERs, with entry direct from school, replaced later-year entry to the

LLB in 2003, under decisions of the Vice-Chancellor's Committee and the executive dean of the new Faculty of the Professions.[61]

§

The Law School's status as a separate faculty of the university, integral to its work since its foundation, came into question as the university reviewed its system of governance in the 1990s. The review took its cue from federal policy, which now favoured 'strong managerial modes of operation', 'streamlined decision-making processes' and 'maximum flexibility', in the words of John Dawkins's foundational policy statement.[62] The review was headed by Peter Karmel, an economist who became the founding vice-chancellor of Flinders University and later chaired the Commonwealth Tertiary Education Commission. Karmel had led a CTEC inquiry into efficiency and effectiveness in higher education, and he became an adviser to Dawkins, despite his criticism of some of Dawkins's proposals. The Adelaide inquiry, which reported in 1990, advocated stronger roles for faculties and deans, with 'as many decisions as possible pushed down as near the work face as possible'. It found that decision-making by the Executive Committee and the Education Committee sidelined the vice-chancellor and was 'slow, tortuous and expensive'. (The Education Committee, which now included all department heads along with many other representatives, had 128 members.) Fred McDougall, director of the Graduate School of Management, was a member of the inquiry panel. 'Academics had abdicated their right to lead, by just simply not making decisions', he later said.[63] The inquiry's solution, adopted by the university, was to re-establish the role of the vice-chancellor as chief executive. Decision-making would be concentrated in the hands of the vice-chancellor, the registrar and two deputy vice-chancellors, who later became known as the Senior Management Group. The Executive Committee would be abolished, Education Committee membership would shrink (it was later renamed the Academic Board), and committee activities would decrease in order to provide 'a capacity for fast response'.[64]

CTEC's *Efficiency and Effectiveness* report counselled against election of deans and heads, doubting that it produced leaders with the necessary skills. In recognition of divided opinion on campus, the governance review recommended allowing faculties to choose for themselves between election and appointment of deans. The law faculty opted for election, which would now be by a two-thirds majority in secret ballot (the default mode of selection in the amended university statutes). The governance review recommended that the posts of dean and head of department should be combined in the university's single-department faculties, Architecture and Planning, Dentistry, Law, and Music. The committee expected that the workload of deans would drop significantly, once the Executive Committee (of which they were members) was abolished. The Department of Law, like its counterparts in single-department faculties, objected. The duties of the head of a large department like Law were so onerous that they should not be combined, even with a slimmed-down deanship. But the merger of the two offices went ahead, hastened by a temporary need. When the dean, Adrian Bradbrook, went on study leave in 1994, the only volunteer to serve as acting dean was the head of department, John Keeler, who thus filled both offices. Bradbrook took over these combined duties on his return, and the new arrangement continued when Rob Fowler was separately appointed both dean and head in July 1995.[65] The dean's workload was alleviated to some extent by the appointment of associate deans for teaching and research, forming an Executive Committee, but the burden was a heavy one, as Fowler discovered:

> I recall sometimes working almost through the entire night, going to bed at 5 a.m., getting up at 8 to grab breakfast, help get the kids ready for childcare or whatever, and then hop on the bus to be in here by a quarter to nine and start work again.[66]

Other targets for reform were the number of deans and the widely varying size of the university's eleven faculties. A seven-faculty plan, meant to achieve economies of scale, had been considered in the Executive Committee in 1986. In 'a political exercise', as the executive member for staffing put it, the plan also sought fairer representation in central forums.[67] If faculties, through their deans, had an equal say in resource allocation (the renegotiation of the 1981 Compact in the Committee of Deans was the immediate spur for action), the process would be fairer if faculties were of roughly equal size. The governance report of 1990 gave qualified support to faculty mergers. Larger academic units were more flexible and had greater capacity for new initiatives, but merging disparate faculties seemed 'likely to produce inharmonious relationships'.[68] Voluntary mergers were best.

A new vice-chancellor, Gavin Brown, made mergers a high priority on his appointment in 1994. Joint meetings of the deans and the Senior Management Group had fifteen members, too many for efficiency, he argued. Faculties could be grouped into academic divisions; other universities had done so. The dean outlined the plan to the law faculty:

> The proposal is that six Executive Deans be appointed to sit alongside the Senior Management Group. The rationale is that there are grave communication problems. Since the establishment of the Senior Management Group the pendulum has shifted too far and Faculties currently do not have an appropriate say in the governance of the University. The Vice Chancellor feels that a more streamlined executive committee is now the order of the day to address the problem and there was no dissent to this scheme.[69]

The largest existing faculties, Arts and Medicine, stood to gain, as Adrian Bradbrook told a faculty meeting: 'The Deans of the two most powerful faculties support the proposal because this gives them a direct voice into [sic] University affairs which they do not have at the moment. Currently the 11 Deans do not form part of the Senior Management Group, but the six new Deans will.'[70] The smallest faculties, on the other hand, faced being grouped with unrelated disciplines and placed under an executive dean who stood between them and the Senior Management Group. This last objection had been noted in the earlier governance report: 'Grouping Faculties into areas supervised by "super-deans" ... would interpolate another layer of hierarchy in the structure and hardly promote efficiency.'[71] The cost of the new layer would ultimately have to be met from faculty budgets, and executive deans would be selected centrally, like other senior managers. General staff foresaw that they would carry a disproportionate share of the burden of restructuring:

> There is a strong conviction among general staff that their contribution and role are repeatedly ignored by academics who do not see them as stakeholders in the system ...
>
> Within this context, there is grave concern that it will be the general staff who will suffer most from the restructuring.[72]

Some in the Law School liked the idea that academics would be relieved of management responsibilities. 'A scholar manager is a nonsense', Michael Detmold wrote. 'So I think we should welcome the idea of an executive dean both as an end to all our agonies of management and also as the condition of the institution of a real academic freedom.'[73] Pooling administrative resources could provide services in computing, financial planning and marketing that the Law School was too small to fund on its own, as Rob Fowler acknowledged. But it was difficult to see an appropriate slot for the Law School in the new framework. It was too small to stand alone, and it lacked natural affinities with potential partners in other disciplines. Brown dropped his initial idea of grouping Arts with Architecture, Law, and Economics and Commerce, after a joint protest by the three smaller faculties, but they then found themselves with no other home. With effect from 1996, Performing Arts, Law, Architecture and Urban Design, and Economics and Commerce formed a division that became known by its acronym, PALACE. 'I know this was the one thing we seemed not to want, but it happens to be the one thing almost all the other parties want', Fowler told staff.[74] The proposed executive deans were renamed heads of division, and the constituent faculties remained intact. Implementation did not require amendment of the university's statutes, thus bypassing the senate, whose veto had stopped the merger of the Faculties of Medicine and Dentistry in 1988.[75]

Gavin Brown soon left the university to become vice-chancellor of the University of Sydney. His successor, Mary O'Kane, who (like Brown) had been deputy vice-chancellor (research), took office in October 1996. One of her first major initiatives was to commission the former vice-chancellor of the University of Melbourne, David Penington, to review the management of the university. Speed in decision-making was a guiding value of the review. As Penington told the university magazine: 'The University has to be able to move with rather faster footwork than hitherto and it has to do that with consultation so people understand why things are changing.'[76] The review coincided with a reduction in the size of the university council. Its new statutory functions would (as O'Kane put it) 'bring the role of the Council more into line with the functions of a company board'.[77]

Penington's report addressed staff discontent arising from the dominance of the Senior Management Group. He recommended giving it a new name (it became the Vice-Chancellor's Committee) and strengthening the role of the Academic Board. He saw problems in the multi-faculty divisions, which had caused confusion of roles and duplication of committees between faculty and division. Some faculty deans were heads of division and others were not, with the result that some faculties had direct representation in the Senior Management Group (albeit in the capacity of division heads) and others felt excluded. Penington recommended that the divisions should become faculties, and the old faculties should become schools. The current confusion and duplication would be reduced by diminishing the role of school boards and deans, whose functions would be handled at the new faculty level. Penington acknowledged that the new structure created difficulties in professional schools, whose faculty boards had hitherto served not only as governing bodies but also as links with the practising professions. He hoped that school boards could continue to perform this role: 'Such a Board would not represent an additional layer of management in terms of broader governance issues or financial or staffing accountability, but rather would have clearly defined roles relating to the external constituency, particularly in relation to the professions.'[78] The interest of the professions extended to questions of resourcing that would normally be outside the remit of the school boards, but these matters could be delegated to the boards of professional schools.

How a school board of this kind would interact with the faculty of which it was part was unresolved in Penington's report. The restructuring proposal put by O'Kane to the Academic Board in 1998 rejected the professional-liaison function of the school boards and created separate advisory boards for professional schools. Responsibility for academic courses would rest with the new faculty boards, although it could be delegated to the schools. The proposal queried the faculties' value in maintaining links with the professions:

> None of the current Boards provide a particularly good mechanism for interaction with an input from the external community, especially the professions, because much of what Faculties do is focussed on internal issues that are not of interest to outside members, and outside members are a very small percentage of Faculty Board membership.[79]

So far as the Law School was concerned, the comment was an indication that the school's relationship with the profession had become more distant, rather than a diagnosis of anything inherent in the existing faculty structure. The history of the faculty provided abundant examples of the interest of the judges and the practising profession in the internal affairs of the Law School, sometimes to the annoyance of the full-time staff. The faculty board had once embodied a sense of shared ownership of the Law School, but interaction with the profession was now moving from the faculty to other bodies (notably the new accreditation body under discussion at the time). This shift was accelerated by the restructuring, as it had been by the ending of Adelaide's position as the state's only law school.

A law faculty meeting unanimously opposed the new faculty structure, as had the PALACE Executive Committee, but the matter was out of the faculty's hands, and the changes came into effect at the start of 1999. The Law School had three representatives on the board of what was initially known as the Faculty of PALACE: the dean, the associate dean (teaching) and the senior executive officer. In 2002 PALACE became the Faculty of the Professions, now including Education but losing Music. The new Law School Board had no external members, other than a representative of the Flinders Law School. The planned advisory board proved difficult to establish, either through lack of willing members (the judges cited a conflict of interest, owing to their responsibility to review the Law School through the accreditation process) or through lack of action by the university. The school board became largely a clearing house for reports and information.[80]

Amalgamation was unpopular, as the faculty vote showed, although faculty status had not ensured independence for the Law School or achieved what its members saw as due recognition of its needs. The Law School's small size, distinctive professional culture and lack of obvious allies on campus had long weakened its claims on the university's attention and resources. The sense of participation, and even autonomy, that some staff remembered had as much to do with the prevailing mode of university management in the 1970s and 1980s as with the separate existence of the Faculty of Law. Before the era of collegiate management, close control by the registrar and the council bound the school more tightly to central power in the university. It is unclear whether the loss of faculty status was felt more strongly in Law than in other small faculties. Nevertheless, abolition of the Faculty of Law was painful. In Rob Fowler's view, amalgamation led to 'a loss of standing on the part of the Law School within the university governance system ... PALACE was, in many respects, a disaster for the Law School, because we lost our voice within the university community.'[81] The perception was not limited to the staff. 'The Law School particularly suffered', Sam Jacobs said; 'it lost its identity as a faculty.' Becoming part of PALACE 'was an absolute disaster'.[82] Andrew Ligertwood compared the old meetings of the department and the faculty with what replaced them:

> In a way, it was extremely time-consuming and probably very inefficient, and we didn't always want to be there, but, in retrospect, it was necessary, if we were going to be running the place in the way that we ran the place ... But to take that responsibility away from the Law School made one's life really different, as an academic. That's how I feel about it. You just feel helpless. You can make decisions in a departmental meeting, but they really have no effect. Perhaps it's a bit like having a voice and nothing else.[83]

The Faculty of Law had been part of the Law School's identity and an enduring framework for collective deliberation. It would have to operate, and see itself, in different ways.

§

The last days of the Faculty of Law and the first year of the Faculty of PALACE were difficult for the Law School. The need for additional income was pressing, and teachers were introducing the new curriculum, with its innovative integration of skills and doctrine. Michael Detmold, an Adelaide graduate and a scholar in constitutional law and jurisprudence, was elected dean from mid-1998 until a newly recruited professor could take office in 2000. He saw great opportunities in a new medium: the internet. These were the early, heady days of the World Wide Web, when opportunities for communication and commercial enterprise seemed boundless and the dot.com boom was building. Universities were caught up in this protean activity. In her history of the modern Australian university, Hannah Forsyth observed: 'The web was associated with some manic enthusiasms, from both technological and theoretical angles.'[84] There were also lasting successes. The establishment of AustLII (the Australasian Legal Information Institute) by two Sydney universities in 1995 was a pioneering initiative in free access to legal information that endured and thrived.

In a planning document for staff, Detmold looked to the future:

> For a flourishing law school in the environment of the next 20 years there are two strategic imperatives: get on the Net and get out into the legal profession. Both things are virtues in themselves; but there are no other ways of generating the required independence of income. Without this we cannot survive at a viable level. We should plan to heed these imperatives whenever the opportunity arises whether or not we can see the exact way they are going to work for us.[85]

His plans to meet these needs crystallised in three projects. The first built on work already done to integrate information technology into teaching and research. The university computer network had been extended to the Ligertwood Building in 1992, and computer-assisted legal research was added to the first-year curriculum in 1995. So few students used laptop computers in lectures that they were 'asked to sit together in one row as other students find the noise distracting'.[86] Computer laboratories in the Law School facilitated access, and the university introduced email accounts for students at the start of 1998.[87]

Michael Detmold and his son Henry, an information technology specialist, had initiated an online system for study materials and learning modules, known as ALICE (Adelaide Law School Intranet for Collaborative Education). The idea was prescient, anticipating features of the learning management systems of later decades, and it fitted in well with university strategy. In what would become a familiar theme, the university supported the use of IT to economise staff teaching time, as the Law School's Executive Committee noted: 'The University was deeply concerned with the decline in its funding base which it believed could be significantly alleviated by reducing teaching (especially through IT), without reducing quality and also preserving research time.'[88] The vice-chancellor funded the second stage of the ALICE project in 1997, in which a small group of students would take a tutorial using the system. The Law School introduced online delivery of course materials, online storage for students' work, and capacity for collaborative learning, through discussion and sharing of revision questions.[89]

But ALICE was a small, bespoke system, built from scratch. Remote access to university systems was unreliable, and the systems themselves were not robust. Students struggled with online reading materials; reading them exclusively on computer was unviable and printing them came at a cost. Difficulties in coordination between staff caused tension when ALICE components were integrated into substantive subjects. The system became overburdened at busy times, leading to a dispute over allegations of deliberate overloading by students in order to disadvantage their competitors. ALICE was forward-looking and innovative, but it failed to live up to its full promise, although acceptance and usage by staff and students grew. It was overtaken by large-scale commercial services when it was integrated into the university-wide MyUni learning management system (based on the commercial Blackboard platform) in 2002.[90]

Detmold's second project recognised growing interest in alternatives to litigation for the resolution of legal disputes. He had discussions with legal academic Dave Brown, who had worked at the Melbourne Law School and ran an independent law school in Melbourne, the Australian College of Law. Brown offered courses in 'dispute avoidance lawyering—teaching lawyers and commercial people how to construct contracts and institute commercial systems characterised by good faith'.[91] The Law School had recently introduced a successful course in arbitration and mediation, run in collaboration with the Institute of Arbitrators and Mediators and the university's Office of Continuing Education. Brown aimed to expand his program in collaboration with an established law school. The courses would be offered to external, fee-paying students (the project was independent of the LLB curriculum). The fee income was alluring to the Law School, as it searched for new sources of revenue; Detmold hoped at one stage that the project could increase the Law School's funding by 20%. Two pilot courses (re-branded as Preventative Legal Practice) were planned for mid-1999, but negotiations between Brown and a Law School advisory committee broke down over monitoring and provision of information. The program never eventuated.[92]

A third initiative aimed to give students practical experience and to use networked collaboration to build a database of legal research. As Detmold put it:

> All our students should have sufficient practical projects undertaken with the legal profession and in wider industry contexts as part of their Legal Skills work that they no longer experience discontinuity between theory and practice … Much of the work should be special project research work made available to individual practitioners and legal institutions and more widely.[93]

Practical experience had obvious potential in the skills component of the new curriculum, and working placements harmonised with efforts being made by the vice-chancellor to strengthen links between the professions and the university. The project was led by Bob Moles, who had worked at the Australian National University's law school. He was appointed to a three-year associate professorship at Adelaide in 1998, to lead computerised materials delivery and the teaching of online research, and to develop 'strategic initiatives in the construction and commercialisation of courses and research in IT mode, particularly with the practising legal profession'.[94]

Moles moved quickly to arrange student work-experience placements in a wide range of roles, in the profession and elsewhere, in what became known as the Adelaide Partnership Program. Detmold was enthusiastic about Moles's work:

> He has been working hard in the past five months establishing contacts in the profession, the courts, government and industry to produce a (to me amazing) portfolio of agreements under which it will be possible to have every student working every year on a major external project. This is an undoubted good, and is one of the keys to professional honour—the social responsibility (skill) of seeing academic things in their real environment, the protocols involved (e.g. organising and carrying out meetings in the wider community, respecting confidentiality), and the spin-off from these for academic integrity.[95]

The activities envisaged by Moles embraced practitioners, courts, judges, industry, government, politicians, police, correctional services, schools, community law centres and the media. Online collaboration could remove geographical barriers: 'We can work with practitioners in London and New York—without having met them. We can support barristers in Sydney and Melbourne in the same way.' Students could generate commercially valuable publications, 'which will give rise to new revenue streams for us all'.[96]

Many practitioners and students welcomed the program. A student participant told the Law School Board that 'he was pursuing it for experience, skills and to network for a prospective job'. He 'felt it represented an enormous opportunity for Law students ... The program allowed students to gain opportunities they would otherwise not have had, due to the few clerkships and work-experience placements available.'[97] Detmold wrote: 'The students love it, particularly those without uncles in legal firms who regard it as a great opportunity to find routes into something that is otherwise very forbidding.'[98] The Law Society praised the initiative, for bringing students into closer contact with the profession.[99]

However, other academic staff regarded the program with growing unease. It had not gone through the vetting required for other academic programs, and it was not integrated into the curriculum. When it was discussed by the Law School Board, staff voiced concern, and a degree of anger, at a perceived lack of accountability and control. 'A Board member said it seemed there were 2 parallel law schools, the Law School and Dr Moles' APP.'[100] The board resolved that the program should be suspended; there would be no new projects, and existing projects would be wound up. The decision attracted unfavourable news coverage and affected the Law School's relationship with the profession. Years later, it was portrayed as the result of the Law School's conservatism. Giving students practical experience seemed, on the face of it, such a good idea that the board's decision was hard for outsiders to understand. But the board's concerns had substance. Kath McEvoy, who took over as dean at the start of 2000, noted problems concerning the position of students in the program (such as uncertainty about insurance cover) and the status of placement work in the degree course. The partnership program closed, and Moles's appointment ended in acrimony.[101]

The projects of 1998–99 showed imagination and ambition. In some ways, they were ahead of their time. They identified growing trends in legal education: the harnessing of information technology; the teaching of dispute resolution beyond the technical details of litigation; and the integration of practical experience into legal study. The Law School's early commitments to the use of technology had lasting effects. A student of the 2010s wrote: 'Having had various overseas study opportunities, I am astonished at how well IT facilities were integrated into the Law School—both physically within the building and in terms of the curriculum.'[102] But ALICE frustrated students when vision outran the capacity to deliver, and the short life of the Adelaide Partnership Program left some in the profession disappointed and puzzled. The Law School's difficulties were conspicuous. It would have to regroup.

Epilogue

In 2000 the deputy vice-chancellor (education), Penny Boumelha, appointed a committee to conduct the first external review of the Law School. Reviews—of departments, courses and individual performance—were a familiar feature of Australian higher education. Part of a burgeoning machinery for evaluation of quality and performance, rolling reviews of departments had been recommended by successive government reports since the late 1970s. Many universities were slow to act, but Adelaide adopted procedures for regular departmental reviews in 1984. They were the responsibility of the vice-chancellor, and the Law School did not find a place in the cycle, although a university review had been expected in the mid-1980s and staff themselves proposed an external review in 1996. As this last initiative hinted, a review might benefit a department, by attracting the university's attention to its achievements and needs. The 2000 review came after the Law School's problems had been much debated internally and sometimes criticised publicly, but positive recommendations might set future directions that both the school and the university could support.[1]

The review was conducted by a committee of four, headed by Cheryl Saunders, associate dean for graduate studies at the Melbourne Law School. She was best known in South Australia for her report to the federal minister for Aboriginal and Torres Strait Islander affairs on Indigenous heritage in the area of the contentious Hindmarsh Island (Kumarangk) bridge in 1994. Saunders joined Justice David

Bleby of the Supreme Court and the deans of law at Monash and the University of New South Wales, Stephen Parker and Paul Redmond. Their report staked a claim for the importance of the Law School within the university, based on the social significance of the discipline: 'A university that undervalues its law school does so at significant cost.'[2] The panel deliberately avoided post-mortems on the troubles of the past few years, but it criticised recent performance. The school's flagship initiatives in teaching, practical content and computerisation had heavy costs in time and money, and they had been implemented only partially. Later-year entry at Adelaide gave Flinders a competitive advantage. The curriculum, renewed with such effort over recent years, did not impress: 'Our basic observations are that the curriculum is a relatively standard offering, perhaps a bit tired, and does not make enough use of the profession in teaching.'[3] The number of active researchers among the teaching staff was low.

The report's most critical comments concerned administration and relations with the profession. The Adelaide Partnership Program, the subject of many submissions to the review, was singled out as an example: 'Neither the way it was introduced, its management while it lasted, nor its suspension reflect well on the effectiveness of the Law School.'[4] The school's merger into PALACE 'has contributed to confusion, demoralisation and ineffectiveness'.[5] The Law School Board was not functioning effectively. The profession perceived the Law School as 'remote, self-indulgent, inefficient, lacking direction and providing a low standard of teaching'.[6] To address these shortcomings, the report recommended a series of internal reviews of problem areas, the reintroduction of entry direct from school, and the re-establishment of an independent faculty of law. The committee had been told by the university that an increase in funding for the Law School was unlikely, but the report nevertheless recommended special funding for five years, to address 'the serious nature of the problems'.[7]

The report and the university's response appeared in the media before they were given to the Law School. The dean, Kath McEvoy, protested: 'It is difficult for us in the Law School not to feel alienated from the University as a result of the way in which it appears to be outside the loop of communication of these crucial matters.'[8] A formal response by the school affirmed that it was open to all the recommendations, although it disagreed with some of the findings on which they were based. It argued that the school's small size made it difficult for it to perform at the same level as the larger schools used for benchmarking. In research, for example, the Law School argued that its performance in proportion to staff numbers was more creditable than the report implied, although more external grants and graduate students were needed. It contested the report's findings about student dissatisfaction with teaching, but student focus groups organised by an external consultant only confirmed the bad news. They revealed high levels of disappointment and unhappiness; most of the participants said that they would switch to another university if they could do so quickly and easily. When the report was delivered, relations with the university were not helped by a bruising wrangle over student complaints that assessment in Corporate Law went beyond the topics covered in lectures.[9]

Critique by the Law School had little effect when the university threw its weight behind the report. The executive dean of PALACE told the Law School Board: 'There was no point in continuing to argue whether the conclusions of the Review were right or wrong: the perceptions in the community concerning the LS were negative, and needed to be addressed.'[10] The university established a Review Implementation Committee to advise the executive dean on the next steps. It also provided special funding of $2 million over three years, which continued, at a reduced rate, until 2006. Law would remain part of a larger faculty, but recovery plans included new leadership, in the shape of an external, professorial dean holding a five-year appointment, as recommended by the report. However, recruitment was disrupted by the university's broader financial troubles, as it slid into deficit. The first appointee withdrew before taking up the post, citing the university's 'financial predicament'.[11] In July 2002 the vacancy was filled by Paul Fairall, dean of law at James Cook University in Queensland. For a time, the university's financial difficulties put Law School staffing on a rollercoaster. In 2002 a major infusion of new academic staff was followed by a round of redundancies. In the longer term, a new relative funding model, adopted in 2001 for the internal allocation of university funds, placed additional strain on the Law School budget, by reducing the weight given to law enrolments in calculating allocations.[12]

As government funding declined as a proportion of university revenue, philanthropic income became increasingly important, but attracting it was difficult. A long drought in major donations to the Law School followed Sir John Langdon Bonython's endowment of the chair of law in 1926, although smaller gifts for prizes, scholarships and the Law Library continued. Commonwealth scholarships supported a growing number of high-achieving school leavers in the law course from the 1950s to the 1970s, and the abolition of tuition fees in 1974 probably reinforced a perception among potential donors that the Commonwealth government was providing all the support that was needed. The results of the Law School's centenary fundraising drive, though gratefully received by the Law Library, were hardly transformative. A renewed effort in 1988 elicited donations from law firms to support projects that would carry the donors' names. Refurbishment of the moot court room, a lecture series, and a student prize were among the results. A bequest by Dame Roma Mitchell in 2000 led, after long delay, to the establishment of the Dame Roma Mitchell chair in law.

Gifts were acknowledged with much gratitude, but their sources sometimes drew critical attention, as they did at many other universities. The Law School formed a special relationship, extending over decades, with the Malaysian state of Sarawak. Two successive chief ministers of Sarawak, Abdul Taib Mahmud and Adenan Satem, were Law School alumni, and Alex Castles strengthened the connection by writing about the state's legal history. Sarawak graduates made a series of donations to the Law School and the wider university. Taib's personal donations, commencing in 1987, supported mooting, refurbishment in the Ligertwood Building and the establishment of the Australian Centre for Environmental Law, among other projects. But the sources of Sarawak's private fortunes were highlighted in Adelaide by reports of widespread forest logging there. Student activism on these and related issues had a new focus when the plaza outside the Law School was named in honour of Taib in 2008. Further allegations against Taib were reported in Australia in 2015, based on a report by a Swiss non-government organisation. The university renamed the plaza in honour of the Colombo Plan, the scholarship scheme that brought Taib, and many others, to study in Australia.[13]

Specialisation in research concentrated the Law School's firepower and added heft to its distinctive strengths. Two notable initiatives built on earlier work. The South Australian Law Reform Institute, established in 2010, continued the Law School's long involvement in law reform projects. Its first major collaborative effort in this area had been a report on consumer credit and moneylending, commissioned by the national Standing Committee of Attorneys-General in 1966 and produced by a team coordinated by Arthur Rogerson. In 1968 the state government established the Law Reform Committee of South Australia. Chaired by Justice Howard Zelling of the Supreme Court, it included a Law School representative, and other Law School staff assisted with some of the many reports it produced before its abolition in 1987. The Law School also had close connections with the Australian Law Reform Commission. Alex Castles became a foundation commissioner in 1975, and among his successors were David Kelly and James Crawford. Other staff members acted as consultants.[14]

The abolition of the Law Reform Committee left a gap noted in the review of the Law School in 2000. It recommended exploratory discussions for the establishment of a law reform commission, but the expense of a new statutory agency with little public appeal made a commission unattractive to successive governments. A different, collaborative model succeeded when John Williams, soon to become dean of the Law School, proposed it in 2010. The South Australian Law Reform Institute was established by the Law School, the Law Society and the South Australian government. By relying on a cooperative agreement, it differed from law reform agencies created by statute in many jurisdictions. Law reform institutes in Alberta and Tasmania were comparable. Unlike them, however, the South Australian institute drew on the work of students, in an invitation-only LLB elective, Law Reform. It became pivotal to the institute's success. The institute linked teaching, research and policy engagement in a new structure that strengthened the Law School's links with government, the profession, and communities affected by laws under review. For the government, the institute had the advantage of subsisting on relatively inexpensive, project-based funding. Handling references from the attorney-general alongside some undertaken on its own initiative, the institute moved beyond the technical bent of the Law Reform Committee to consider topics with a strong social-policy aspect, such as abortion and surrogacy. Its researchers sought broad community consultation, with an emphasis on impartiality and open questions. The institute achieved an enviable record of success in legislative implementation of its recommendations, most of its reports being adopted in South Australian legislation.[15]

The Research Unit on Military Law and Ethics, established in 2015, was a successor to work on military and naval law by earlier generations of Law School staff. Daniel O'Connell joined the Australian Army Legal Corps as a reserve officer soon after he arrived in Adelaide in 1953. In 1966 he began seven years of service in the Royal Australian Naval Reserve, advising, training, researching, and going to sea whenever possible. His commission as a reserve officer gratified a lifelong interest in the sea and put to practical use his expertise in maritime law. Indeed, his interest in international law has been said to originate in his interest in the navy. On O'Connell's departure in 1972, much of his naval work fell to Ivan Shearer, who had been an officer in the Citizen Air Force since his mandatory national service in the 1950s. Shearer moved from the air force to the navy, which he continued to advise on international law after he left the Law School in 1974. The Research Unit on Military Law and Ethics broadened the work of O'Connell and Shearer on international law and rules of engagement to embrace questions of strategic policy, national security, and ethics in the use of force. It grew out of the Law School's work in training military lawyers, and its inaugural director, Dale Stephens, came to the Law School after a career in the Royal Australian Navy, including service as director of operational and international law. The unit's flagship project was the Woomera Manual on the International Law of Military Space Operations. Developed in collaboration with the universities of Exeter, Nebraska and New South Wales, the manual is a comprehensive statement of international law applicable to military space operations, with a particular emphasis on state practice. International interest was evidenced by the representation of twenty-four states and the International Committee of the Red Cross at a state engagement process presenting the project at The Hague in 2022. The manual takes the Law School's longstanding record of research in international law into the new arena of space operations and adds to its profile and recognition beyond Australia.[16]

§

The governance changes of the 1990s and 2000s brought the university's departments increasingly into line with federal government policies and university strategies. They favoured rapid change, responsiveness to central direction, and achievement of goals determined far from the academic coalface. Successive university strategic plans, responding to the policy environment of the day, sought growing enrolments (especially in the fee-paying cohorts that best assisted the university's bottom line), better research performance (increasingly tied to metrics of competitive grant income and publication impact) and assurances of teaching quality. Rapid increases in student numbers across the university provided a financial boost. Law enrolments grew from just over 700 in 1999 to around 1440 in 2017, in full-time terms. Teaching space became hard to find, and classes were sometimes relegated to the deskless moot court room or the Masonic Centre in North Terrace. Full-time equivalent staff rose to forty in 2017, but the growth in student load kept the student–staff ratio high. It stood at 36:1, against a university average of 20:1. The Faculty of the Professions, with easily the university's largest enrolments, also had the worst student–staff ratio, at 31:1.[17]

Limited funding is a persistent theme of reviews of Australian legal education. Australia is not alone; American law schools, too, have a history of low staffing levels. Few, if any, schools have received as much as they would like. In 1964 the Martin report observed: '"Law", it has been said, "can be taught under a gum tree", and for much of Australia's history it might as well have been so taught.'[18] At Adelaide, law staff sometimes saw the university's strength in science as a disadvantage for other disciplines. Andrew Ligertwood was one: 'As a non-scientific faculty, we were always fighting for money and never being resourced in the way that we should have been, we should be, and never have been, and never will be resourced.'[19] It was an old pattern. Vice-Chancellor William Mitchell remarked in 1917: 'The University should be a scientific club.'[20] He was urging collegiality in research, but the university channelled development largely into scientific disciplines during Mitchell's long vice-chancellorship. In 1974 (as law staff ruefully noted) Adelaide had the highest science-based student load of any of Australia's older universities. Research in the humanities and social sciences differed from empirical scientific discovery to such an extent that some had difficulty recognising it as research at all. As Gwilym Croucher and James Waghorne have shown, Australian scepticism about the scholarly value of vocational courses goes back at least to the early twentieth century. A.P. Rowe, Adelaide's first salaried vice-chancellor, had little respect for research outside the sciences, although it benefited from the additional funding he secured for the university. In his outspoken memoir, as his biographer, Hugh Stretton, observed, 'Rowe expressed contempt for research in the humanities and scarcely mentioned the social sciences'.[21] Even lawyers sometimes remarked that law was late to be established as a fully academic discipline in Australia. Their usual reason was the late growth of full-time academic staff, but such comments sat awkwardly with the depth of scholarship of many of Australia's early law professors, among them Adelaide's John Salmond, Jethro Brown and Coleman Phillipson.[22]

Rankings of universities, and of disciplines within them, loomed steadily larger. Moving up was sometimes explicitly acknowledged as a goal, and sometimes left implicit as a hoped-for outcome of improved performance, but it was never far from observations about how the university was travelling. Occasionally, rankings could be a goad, as when the University of South Australia's law school appeared in the Times Higher Education list of the world's top 100 law schools in 2017. The Adelaide Law School dropped out of the top 100, and the news was noted at the next university council meeting. Rankings were volatile and contestable, but their impact on the attractiveness of institutions for prospective students and staff was acknowledged by their frequent use in marketing. Visitors to the Law School's website in 2018 were told that it was South Australia's highest-ranked law school and in the top 100 worldwide, in the more favourable QS world rankings. As the number of law schools burgeoned, such marks of distinction grew in importance. The attractions of the city of Adelaide became part of the university's appeal to prospective students.

Those students were increasingly likely to travel in order to study. In 2017 the vice-chancellor told the university community's annual meeting about 'the threat from interstate Go8s', other members of the Group of Eight research-intensive universities who were recruiting students in South Australia. The University of Adelaide was running a pilot program of its own for interstate recruitment. Graduates were more willing and able than school leavers to cross state (and national) borders. In 2018 international students made up around 5% of the Law School's LLB student load, but over 40% of its higher-degree load. The need for practitioners to have local expertise constrained the portability of law degrees. National recognition of legal qualifications, advocated by Frederick Pennefather in 1890, was still not fully realised over a century later. Once admitted in one jurisdiction, lawyers could practise elsewhere under the intergovernmental mutual recognition scheme implemented in the 1990s and, later, under a national practising certificate regime. However, South Australia stood outside the Legal Profession Uniform Law of 2015, which coordinated admission and regulation in New South Wales and Victoria. States with smaller populations were wary of regulatory domination by the larger professions, and larger law firms, of Melbourne and Sydney. In South Australia, recognition of interstate degrees for admission purposes still depended on a case-by-case assurance (albeit easily provided) that the course covered the Priestley Eleven subjects. The national profession remained a work in progress, its cumbersome machinery shaped by the necessity for separate admission laws in each jurisdiction.[23]

The Law School marked its 135th birthday in 2018 with a public dinner at the Adelaide Town Hall. In the vice-chancellor's speech, a roll call of prominent graduates displayed the Law School's deep connections with the courts, government and the profession. Chief justices, premiers, judges, attorneys-general and academics with Adelaide law degrees made an impressive list. It was a reassuring sign of continuity. A similar list could have been celebrated on any of the Law School's earlier anniversaries, as its graduates permeated the profession in South Australia and beyond. But the school, and its setting, had changed. One of two Australian law schools at its foundation, by 2018 it had become one of thirty-eight, less conspicuous in the pack. Its trajectory was in large part determined by its setting. The population of South Australia grew, but the other mainland states grew faster. University budgets were strongly influenced by the size of enrolments, and modest scale brought inevitable constraints. The Law School was unable to mount the multiple programs that drew revenue and students to the largest schools. Its limited resources were noticeable in graduate studies. It did not offer a *Juris Doctor* (JD), the graduate-entry law degree that contributed significant fee income to some of the Law School's competitors. Its postgraduate coursework offerings were similarly constrained, although they continued a history of noteworthy innovations, such as an Access to Justice LLM stream, offered in partnership with the profession. Having friends in high places was a characteristic of old-established law schools whose graduates went on to win glittering prizes, but it did little for the Law School's bottom line.

Growth was a way to ease these constraints, and if organic growth was slow, a university merger could provide a rapid boost. The University of Adelaide and the University of South Australia, the state's two largest universities, had neighbouring campuses in central Adelaide and obvious potential for combined growth, in an era when bigger was generally deemed to be better. They explored a merger, without result, in 2012 and 2018. A discussion paper for the 2018 proposal pointed to a 'growing gap between the large and medium sized universities' in performance, and saw opportunities for a new, larger university.[24] The creation of the merged University of Manchester in 2004 was cited as a successful example, but talks ended when the councils of the two universities were unable to agree on terms. Speculation about the underlying reasons for the disagreement included possible effects on rankings and the question of who would lead the new university. But interest persisted. In 2022 a new state government included investigation of university mergers in its education policy, and in December 2022 Adelaide and UniSA announced that they would again commence merger discussions. If choosing leaders had been a sticking point four years earlier, it was no longer an obstacle. The new agreement included arrangements for a transitional chancellor and co-vice-chancellors in the merged university, along with a prospective merger date, in January 2026, and a name: Adelaide University. The prospects, including government support, were favourable. When the universities affirmed their agreement in 2023, some scepticism in state parliament's upper house, which could impede the necessary legislation, seemed the only obstacle in the path. The law schools of the two universities could find themselves newly united, and potentially transformed.[25]

Notes

Preface

1   V.A. Edgeloe, *Annals of the University of Adelaide* (Adelaide: Barr Smith Press, 2003), 71; V.A. Edgeloe, 'The Adelaide Law School 1883–1983', *Adelaide Law Review* 9, no. 1 (1983): 1.

2   FLM, 5 April 1982, UAA, S131, item 14, 188.

3   W. Wesley Pue, *Lawyers' Empire: Legal Professions and Cultural Authority 1780–1950* (Vancouver: UBC Press, 2016), 152.

1   Foundations: 1883–1896

1   Patrick Polden and Michael Lobban, 'The Education of Lawyers', in *The Oxford History of the Laws of England: Volume XI: 1820–1914 English Legal System*, ed. William Cornish et al. (Oxford University Press, 2010), 1179; 'Entertainment in the Court', *Register*, 21 December 1914, 6.

2   'The Law Reform Bill', *South Australian Register*, 5 November 1898, 7.

3   'Our City Letter', *Kapunda Herald*, 22 November 1881, 3.

4   Application for the Position of Professor of English Literature, 9 August 1881, UAA, S169, item 183/13; F.A. d'Arenberg to Registrar, 11 March 1897, UAA, S200, item 212/1897; A.E. Spooner to J.W. Tyas, 29 October 1884, UAA, S169, item 230/23.

5   'The University Ceremonial', *South Australian Register*, 31 July 1879, 4.

6   Augustus Short to William Barlow, 15 June 1877, UAA, S169, item 68/31; Proposal for a Law Degree, 1877–78, UAA, S169, item 68.

7   Report of the Legal Education Committee, 14 May 1878, UAA, S169, item 68/44; Josiah Boothby, *Statistical Sketch of South Australia* (Adelaide: W.C. Cox, 1876), 13, 26; 'Special Meeting of the South Australian Law Debating Society', *South Australian Register*, 11 July 1877, 3.

8   Report of the Legal Education Committee, 22 June 1877, UAA, S169, item 68/28; University Council Minutes, 30 May 1878, UAA, S18, item 1, 341; 'In the Supreme Court of South Australia', *South Australian Government Gazette*, 5 October 1876, 2019.

9   Paul Sendziuk, 'No Convicts Here: Reconsidering South Australia's Foundation Myth', in *Turning Points: Chapters in South Australian History*, ed. Paul Sendziuk and Robert Foster (Kent Town, SA: Wakefield Press, 2012), 45–46.

10   Progress Report of the Law and Biology Committee, 30 September 1881, UAA, S169, item 184/15; Report of the Law and Biology Instruction Committee, 28 October 1881, UAA, S169, item 184/19.

11   'The Advertiser', *South Australian Advertiser*, 19 November 1881, 5.

12   R. Barr Smith to Vice-Chancellor, 22 March 1882, UAA, S169, item 184/41.

13   *Adelaide University Act 1874* (SA), s. 11; A.J. Hannan, 'The History of the University', 1964, 41–42, Barr Smith Library, University of Adelaide.

14   'The University of Adelaide', *South Australian Register*, 19 October 1882, 4.

15   'Our City Letter', *Kapunda Herald*, 22 November 1881, 3.

16   'Opening of the New University Building', *South Australian Advertiser*, 6 April 1882, 5.

17   ibid.

18   University Council Minutes, 18 August 1882, UAA, S18, item 3, 1.

19   S.J. Way to Jethro Brown, 15 February 1893, SLSA, PRG 258/1.

20   W.M. Manning to Chancellor, University of Adelaide, 1 December 1887, NLA, MS 6710, folder 1.

21   Clifford Turney, Ursula Bygott, and Peter Chippendale, *Australia's First: A History of the University of Sydney, Volume 1, 1850–1939* (Sydney: University of Sydney in association with Hale & Iremonger, 1991), 115, 123–24, 236–41; Peter Spiller, 'The History of New Zealand Legal Education: A Study in Ambivalence', *Legal Education Review* 4, no. 2 (1993): 227–31; Alfred S. Konefsky, 'The Legal Profession: From the Revolution to the Civil War', in *The Cambridge History of Law in America, Volume 2: The Long Nineteenth Century (1789–1920)*, ed. Christopher Tomlins and Michael Grossberg (Cambridge: Cambridge University Press, 2008), 83–84; Philip Girard, Jim Phillips, and R. Blake Brown, *A History of Law in Canada, Volume 1: Beginnings to 1866* (University of Toronto Press, 2018), 471–80.

22   George Murray to Herbert Mayo, 14 March 1935, UAA, S200, item 121/1935.

23   University Council Minutes, 18 August 1882, UAA, S18, item 3, 3.

24   Arthur M. Hardy to Law Society members, 4 November 1881, UAA, S169 item 184/1.

25   Progress Report of Law Regulations Committee [August 1882], UAA, S169, item 217/6.

26   Report of the Legal Education Committee, 22 June 1877, UAA, S169, item 68/28; Letter to Ascertain the Number of Students Likely to Study Law, 27 June 1877, UAA, S169, item 68/27; Progress Report of Law Regulations Committee [August 1882], UAA, S169, item 217/6; University Council Minutes, 29 September and 27 October 1882, UAA, S18, item 3, 13–17, 21.

27 'The Advertiser', *South Australian Advertiser*, 3 October 1882, 4.

28 'The Advertiser', *South Australian Advertiser*, 9 October 1882, 4.

29 'Law Course for the University', *South Australian Register*, 18 October 1882, 4.

30 Faculty of Law Statutes and Regulations, 1882, UAA, S169, item 352.

31 Daniel R. Coquillette and Bruce A. Kimball, *On the Battlefield of Merit: Harvard Law School, the First Century* (Cambridge, Massachusetts: Harvard University Press, 2015), 309; John Mackinolty and Judy Mackinolty, eds., *A Century Down Town: Sydney University Law School's First Hundred Years* (Sydney: Sydney University Law School, 1991), 21–22.

32 Progress Report of Law Regulations Committee [August 1882], UAA, S169, item 217/6.

33 'Rules of the Supreme Court', *South Australian Government Gazette*, 1 February 1883, 366.

34 University Council Minutes, 18 August 1882, UAA, S18, item 3, 1–3; Hannan, 'The History of the University', 18; Application of E.E. Morris for Hughes chair, October 1882, UAA, S183, item 1/8; R.J.W. Selleck, *The Shop: The University of Melbourne 1850–1939* (Carlton, Vic.: Melbourne University Press, 2003), 200.

35 'Law Lecturers Wanted', *South Australian Register*, 5 February 1883, 4.

36 'The Advertiser', *South Australian Advertiser*, 3 March 1883, 4.

37 Walter Phillips to Registrar, 28 February 1882, UAA, S169, item 199/36.

38 University Council Minutes, 7 March 1883, UAA, S18, item 3, 52; 'Deaths at St Ives', *Cambridge Independent Press*, 29 January 1915, 8; 'Union Society', *Cambridge Independent Press*, 9 February 1878, 5; S.J. Way to H.W. Horwill, 24 October 1905, SLSA, PRG 30/5/9, 187; Testimonial, G.W. Waterhouse, 28 February 1882, UAA, S169, item 199/36; Walter R. Phillips, '"The Kung Yung" of K'ung-Foo-Tsze; or, the Moral Mean', *Victorian Review* 5, no. 26 (1 December 1881): 147–60; F.M. Goadby, 'The Late Dr. W.R. Phillips', *Journal of the Society of Public Teachers of Law* 1931: 34.

39 Walter Phillips to Registrar, 5 May 1883, UAA, S169, item 226/27; University of Cambridge, *Calendar*, 1874, 221; J.A. Venn, *Alumni Cantabrigienses: A Biographical List of All Known Students, Graduates and Holders of Office at the University of Cambridge, from the Earliest Times to 1900* (Cambridge: Cambridge University Press, 1922), pt. 2, vol. 4, p. 456; 'Obituary', *South Australian Register*, 9 December 1890, 3; 'The Advertiser', *Advertiser*, 5 December 1890, 4.

40 FLM, 27 February 1883, UAA, S131, item 1.

41 'The University', *South Australian Register*, 4 March 1889, 4.

42 University of Adelaide, *Calendar*, 1884, clx; University of Adelaide, *Calendar*, 1894, 48–49; University of Adelaide, *Calendar*, 1895, 55; Edgeloe, *Annals*, 138–41.

43 'General News', *Express and Telegraph*, 22 September 1883, 2.

44 'Professors and Their Ways', *News*, 22 September 1931, 6.

45 'The Advertiser', *South Australian Advertiser*, 29 December 1887, 4; FLM, 1883–89, UAA, S131, item 1, 1, 17–18, 24; R.W. Hall and others to Registrar, 18 September 1883, UAA, S169, item 226/38.

46 R.M. Gibbs, *Under the Burning Sun: A History of Colonial South Australia, 1836–1900* (Adelaide: Peacock Publications for Southern Heritage, 2013), 225.

47 'Died on Ferry Boat', *Sun* (Sydney), 10 June 1916, 6; 'Obituary', *Evening Journal*, 22 March 1892, 2; 'Obituary', *Chronicle*, 26 June 1915, 16.

48 FLM, 1883–89, UAA, S131, item 1, 58, 79, 83–84, 95; Albert Jones to Registrar, 5 August 1886, UAA, S200, item 259/1886.

49 University of Adelaide, *Calendar*, 1899, 440.

50 University of Adelaide, *Calendar*, 1883, 81; FLM, 21 June 1895, UAA, S131, item 2, 186; FLM, 27 March 1897, UAA, S131, item 3, 34–35.

51 University of Adelaide, *Calendar*, 1886, ccii; University of Adelaide, *Calendar*, 1887, cci.

52 University of Adelaide, *Calendar*, 1884, cv.

53 Frederick Pollock, *Principles of Contract*, 3rd ed. (London: Stevens & Sons, 1881), 326.

54 'The Law Examinations', *South Australian Register*, 26 March 1886, 7.

55 'The Recent University Examinations in Law', *South Australian Advertiser*, 18 March 1886, 5; 'The University Law Examinations', *South Australian Advertiser*, 19 March 1886, 5; 'The Law Examinations', *South Australian Register*, 18 March 1886, 4; 'The Advertiser', *South Australian Advertiser*, 18 March 1886, 4; G.E. DeMole to W.R. Phillips, 24 March 1886, UAA, S169, item 270.

56 Walter Phillips to Chief Justice, 5 April 1886, UAA, S200, item 164/1886, 4.

57 FLM, 27 May 1890, UAA, S131, item 2, 10.

58 FLM, 21 September 1914, UAA, S131, item 4, 133–34.

59 'The University', *Register*, 4 March 1924, 11; FLM, 1890–95, UAA, S131, item 2, 100–102, 160, 177–78, 193–94.

60 University of Adelaide, *Calendar*, 1886, 116–17; University of Sydney, *Calendar*, 1883–84, 108–09; University of Melbourne, *Calendar*, 1883–84, 146–47; Barry Nicholas, 'Jurisprudence', in *The History of the University of Oxford, Volume VII: Nineteenth-Century Oxford, Part 2* (Oxford: Oxford University Press, 2000), 395; University of Dublin, *Calendar*, 1867, 13; University of Dublin, *Calendar*, 1881, 165–66, 168.

61 Albert Jones to Registrar, 27 January 1891, UAA, S200, item 33/1891.

62 Albert Jones to Registrar, 11 December 1891, UAA, S200, item 543/1891.

63 F.W. Pennefather to George Murray, 25 June 1891, UAA, S200, item 308/1891.

64 FLM, 1890–95, UAA, S131, item 2, 117, 125.

NOTES

65 University of Adelaide, *Calendar*, 1893, 130–31; Albert Jones to Registrar, 19 May 1894, UAA, S200, item 263/1894; Albert Jones to Registrar, 3 November 1900, UAA, S200, item 1087/1900; 'Secret History of the Day', *Smith's Weekly*, 3 May 1930, 23.

66 FLM, 5 July 1886, UAA, S131, item 1, 81–82.

67 W.A. Norman, Random Reminiscences of the South Australian Bench and Bar (1929), Barr Smith Library, University of Adelaide, 3.

68 J.A. Salmond to Registrar, 5 August 1902, UAA, S200, item 797/1902.

69 Particulars of the Accommodation to be Provided in the University Buildings, UAA, S169, item 45; FLM, 1905–17, UAA, S131, item 4, 13–14, 85.

70 'Farewell Luncheon to His Excellency the Governor', *South Australian Register*, 6 January 1883, 5, 6.

71 C.W. Holgate, *An Account of the Chief Libraries of Australia and Tasmania* (London: C. Whittingham, 1886), 14.

72 *Catalogue of the Library of the Supreme Court of South Australia* (Adelaide: E. Spiller, Government Printer, 1883); 'Law Students and the Law Library', *South Australian Advertiser*, 31 March 1888, 7; John Morphett to William Barlow, 2 February 1876, UAA, S169, item 24; 'The Faculty of Law', *South Australian Register*, 2 May 1883, Supplement.

73 University of Adelaide, *Calendar*, 1878, 121; FLM, 1883–89, UAA, S131, item 1, 5–7, 10; G.E. DeMole to Chief Justice, 10 December 1886, UAA, S200, item 489A/1886; Correspondence with Minister of Education, 1883, UAA, S169, item 215; Correspondence Concerning Statutes of Other Colonies, UAA, S169, items 216 and 226; University Council Minutes, 21 December 1883, UAA, S18, item 3, 111; University Council Minutes, 24 February 1888, UAA, S18, item 4, 209; University Council Minutes, 30 July 1897, UAA, S18, item 6, 119; Arthur Blyth to Walter Tyas, 25 July 1888, UAA, S200, item AG10/1888; Edgeloe, 'The Adelaide Law School', 5, 11.

74 'Banquet to Professor Phillips, LL.B.', *Express and Telegraph*, 3 December 1887, 3.

75 Walter Phillips to Chief Justice, 10 March 1904, SLSA, PRG 30/3.

76 Walter Phillips to Chief Justice, 16 December 1918, UAA, S200, item 83/1919.

77 Walter Phillips to Council, 30 November 1885, UAA, S169, item 262; FLM, 1883–89, UAA, S131, item 1, 81, 84; William Mitchell to Sir George Murray, 13 August 1919, UAA, S200, item 633/1919; Goadby, 'The Late Dr. W.R. Phillips'; Leonard Wood, *Islamic Legal Revival: Reception of European Law and Transformations in Islamic Legal Thought in Egypt, 1875–1952* (Oxford: Oxford University Press, 2016), 30, 153–54.

78 F.W. Pennefather to William Barlow, 23 July 1881, UAA, S169, item 183/2.

79   F.W. Pennefather to Chancellor, 19 October 1887, UAA, S200, item
     451/1887; Venn, *Alumni Cantabrigienses*, pt. 2, vol. 5, p. 84; 'Ecclesiastical
     Intelligence', *Times*, 5 January 1897, 10; 'Church of England Synod', *South
     Australian Advertiser*, 2 May 1888, 5, 6; University of Cambridge, *Calendar*,
     1874, 209; University of Cambridge, *Calendar*, 1876, 43; University of
     Dublin, *Calendar*, 1881, 159, 369; University of Cambridge, *Calendar*,
     1892–93, 91.

80   'The Late Dr F.W. Pennefather', *Spectator*, 19 February 1921, 233; F.W.
     Pennefather to William Barlow, 23 July 1881, UAA, S169, item 183/2; Greg
     Taylor, 'Dr Pennefather's Criminal Code for South Australia', *Common
     Law World Review* 31, no. 1 (2002): 64; F.W. Pennefather and E. Balcombe
     Brown, *The Code of Civil Procedure in the Supreme Court of New Zealand*
     (Wellington: Edwards & Green, 1885); 'The New Zealand Herald', *New
     Zealand Herald*, 14 January 1886, 4; F.W. Pennefather, *Colonial and Indian
     Exhibition, 1886: New Zealand, A Field for Emigration: Lecture* (London:
     William Clowes & Sons, 1886); F.W. Pennefather, *On the Natives of New
     Zealand* (London: Harrison and Sons, 1886); *Colonial and Indian Exhibition,
     1886: Official Catalogue* (London: William Clowes & Sons, 1886), xxiii;
     'Second Edition', *Evening Post* (Wellington), 22 February 1887, 3.

81   FLM, 7 November 1887, UAA, S131, item 1, 104.

82   University Council Minutes, 11 November 1887, UAA, S18, item 4, 175;
     List of Candidates for Law Lectureship, UAA, S183, item 7.

83   Memorandum from Sir James Hector to F.W. Pennefather, 17 October
     1887, UAA, S200, item 451/1887.

84   C.W. Richmond to Chief Justice, 17 October 1889, UAA, S200, item
     451/1887.

85   William Cullen to Registrar, 29 November 1887, UAA, S200, item
     495/1887; FLM, 5 December 1887, UAA, S131, item 1, 109; University
     Council Minutes, 16 December 1887, UAA, S18, item 4, 189–90; Cecil
     Sharp to Walter Tyas, 19 December 1887, UAA, S200, item 551/1887;
     Telegram from Pennefather to Registrar, 19 December 1887, UAA, S200,
     item 554/1887.

86   'Magister', 'The Law Lectureship', *South Australian Advertiser*, 31 December
     1887, 5.

87   'Alumnus', 'The Law Lectureship', *South Australian Advertiser*, 29 December
     1887, 7.

88   'The Advertiser', *South Australian Advertiser*, 29 December 1887, 4.

89   'Cui Bono?', *Lantern*, 14 January 1888.

90   'The University', *South Australian Register*, 5 January 1888, 4; University
     Council Minutes, 1885–90, UAA, S18, item 4, 197, 202.

91   'The Advertiser', *South Australian Advertiser*, 29 December 1887, 4.

92   J.J. Bray, 'Way, Sir Samuel James (1836–1916)', Australian
     Dictionary of Biography, 2006, http://adb.anu.edu.au/biography/
     way-sir-samuel-james-9014.

93   Lecture on International Law, UAA, S169, item 290.

94   F.W. Pennefather, *A Visit to India* (Adelaide: J.L. Bonython & Co., 1894), 129.

95   F.W. Pennefather to Walter Tyas, 11 February 1889, UAA, S200, item 58/1889; Memorandum by F.W. Pennefather, 26 June 1889, UAA, S200, item 245/1889; S.J. Way to William Jervois, 16 December 1889, NLA, Papers of Sir William F.D. Jervois (microform): M1822–M1824, 1874–1897, https://nla.gov.au/nla.obj-2352573399.

96   F.W. Pennefather to Sir William Jervois, 29 April 1889, NLA, Papers of Sir William F.D. Jervois (microform): M1822–M1824, 1874–1897, https://nla.gov.au/nla.obj-2352570259/view.

97   F.W. Pennefather to Sir William Jervois, 9 August 1889, NLA, Papers of Sir William F.D. Jervois (microform): M1822–M1824, 1874–1897, http://nla.gov.au/nla.obj-2352571814.

98   ibid.

99   Faculty Report 19/90, UAA, S141, 110.

100 'Adelaide University', *Advertiser*, 24 December 1890, 6; 'University of Adelaide', *South Australian Advertiser*, 12 April 1888, 6; Faculty Report 14/89, UAA, S141, 83; University Council Minutes, 28 March 1890, UAA, S18, item 4, 372; Letter from Registrar, University of Adelaide, in Council Minute Book, vol. 11, University of Melbourne Archives, 1993.0044.00011, 40; John Salmond to Registrar, 22 May 1900, UAA, S200, item 540A/1900. The professor of music's £500 salary was supplemented by student fees.

101 'The Australian Universities', *South Australian Register*, 22 December 1890, 5.

102 'The University Commemoration', *South Australian Register*, 22 December 1890, 7.

103 Edmund Burke, *Reflections on the Revolution in France*, ed. Frank M. Turner (New Haven: Yale University Press, 2003), 81. Pennefather misattributed the quotation to Lord Thurlow.

104 'The Advertiser', *Advertiser*, 22 December 1890, 4; Joseph L. Gerken, *The Invention of Legal Research* (Getzville, NY: William S. Hein & Co., 2016), 187–91, 195–96.

105 F.W. Pennefather to Chief Justice, 26 June 1888, UAA, S200, item 253/1888.

106 Faculty Report 7/88, UAA, S141.

107 'The Advertiser', *South Australian Advertiser*, 29 December 1887, 4; FLM, 13 February 1889, UAA, S131, item 1, 160.

108 'In the Supreme Court of South Australia', *South Australian Government Gazette*, 5 October 1876, 2019; 'Rules of the Supreme Court', *South Australian Government Gazette*, 1 February 1883, 366.

109 FLM, 5 July 1886, UAA, S131, item 1, 81; Martha Wright, 'Ad Eundem Gradum', *AAUP Bulletin* 52, no. 4 (1966): 436; 'Public Notices', *South Australian Register*, 18 December 1876, 2; Invitation to Apply for Ad Eundem Degree, UAA, S169, item 98/2; *An Act to Extend to Graduates of Other Universities Certain Privileges Enjoyed by Graduates of the University of Sydney* (NSW) (1859); 'In the Supreme Court of South Australia', *South Australian Government Gazette*, 5 October 1876, 2019; Victoria, *Rules of the Supreme Court*, Parliamentary Paper no. 98, 1887, 2–3; B.H. McPherson, *The Supreme Court of Queensland 1859–1960: History, Jurisdiction, Procedure* (Sydney: Butterworths, 1989), 229–31.

110 *Re Albert Edward Jones* (1889) 15 VLR 497, 501.

111 University of Melbourne Council Minutes, 4 February 1889, University of Melbourne Archives, 1993.0044, vol. 8, 239; Faculty Report 6/88, UAA, S141; F.W. Pennefather to Dean of Law, 14 December 1892, UAA, S200, item 20/1893.

112 'The Melbourne University', *South Australian Register*, 4 April 1889, 4.

113 'The University', *South Australian Register*, 20 February 1890, 4.

114 'Adelaide Law Degrees', *South Australian Register*, 19 September 1889, 4; University of Sydney, *Calendar*, 1889, 164. The degree was awarded to Albert Jones.

115 FLM, 10 September 1888, UAA, S131, item 1, 132.

116 FLM, 1883–89, UAA, S131, item 1, 126–31, 134–38.

117 'University Senate', *South Australian Register*, 29 November 1888, 7.

118 FLM, 15 September 1890, UAA, S131, item 2, 22.

119 'University of Adelaide', *Advertiser*, 18 September 1890, 7.

120 'University Senate', *South Australian Register*, 9 October 1890, 7.

121 'University Senate', *Advertiser*, 9 October 1890, 5.

122 'University Senate', *South Australian Register*, 9 October 1890, 7.

123 George Murray to Josiah Symon, 27 March 1924, NLA, MS 1736/25/160; Faculty Report 22/90, UAA, S141.

124 'University Senate', *South Australian Register*, 9 October 1890, 7.

125 ibid.

126 'University Senate', *Advertiser*, 9 October 1890, 5.

127 'University Senate', *South Australian Register*, 9 October 1890, 7; Tamson Pietsch, *Empire of Scholars: Universities, Networks and the British Academic World, 1850–1939* (Manchester: Manchester University Press, 2013), 21; Selleck, *The Shop*, 187–92; University of Adelaide, *Calendar*, 1891, cclxxxiv.

128 W. Ross Johnston, *History of the Queensland Bar* (Brisbane: Bar Association of Queensland, 1979), 12–13; J.M. Bennett, ed., *A History of the New South Wales Bar* (Sydney: Law Book Company, 1969), 220–29; Philip Phillips, 'Legal Education and Admission to Practice', in *A Multitude of Counsellors: A History of the Bar of Victoria*, ed. Arthur Dean (Melbourne: Cheshire for the Bar Council of Victoria, 1968), 272–78; 'Supreme Court Library',

Queensland Government Gazette, 15 February 1890, 536; Patrick Polden, 'Barristers', in *The Oxford History of the Laws of England: Volume XI: 1820–1914 English Legal System*, ed. William Cornish et al. (Oxford University Press, 2010), 1022–23; Polden and Lobban, 'The Education of Lawyers', 1195–97.

129 'In the Supreme Court of South Australia', *South Australian Government Gazette*, 5 October 1876, 2019.

130 'University Degrees', *South Australian Register*, 17 September 1890, 4.

131 'University Senate', *South Australian Register*, 9 October 1890, 7; FLM, 20 November 1890, UAA, S131, item 2, 32–33; University of Adelaide, *Calendar*, 1891, 121–25.

132 'The Collapse of the Law School', *South Australian Register*, 8 December 1890, 6.

133 'The University Examination', *South Australian Register*, 10 December 1890, 7.

134 'University Senate Meeting', *Advertiser*, 11 December 1890, 6.

135 'Professor Pennefather's Interview', *South Australian Register*, 5 February 1894, 3.

136 F.W. Pennefather to Registrar, undated, UAA, S200, item 87/1893; F.W. Pennefather to Chancellor, 20 June 1893, UAA, S200, item 262/1893; FLM, 18 November 1895, UAA, S131, item 3, 3; F.W. Pennefather to Chancellor, 28 June 1895, UAA, S200, item 322/1895; S.J. Way to Sir William Jervois, 26 March 1895, NLA, Papers of Sir William F.D. Jervois (microform): M1822–M1824, 1874–1897, https://nla.gov.au/nla.obj-2352616961; Faculty Report 19/95, UAA, S141.

137 F.W. Pennefather to Chancellor, 19 July 1897, UAA, S200, item 709/1897.

138 F.W. Pennefather to Charles Hodge, 28 February 1896, UAA, S200, item 105/1896; Telegram from F.W. Pennefather to Registrar, 20 August 1896, UAA, S200, item 352/1896; F.W. Pennefather to Charles Hodge, 28 January 1897, UAA, S200, item 120/1897; Taylor, 'Dr Pennefather's Criminal Code for South Australia'.

2 Scholars: 1897–1925

1 FLM, 18 November 1895, UAA, S131, item 3, 3.

2 Faculty Report 17/95, UAA, S141; 'House of Assembly', *South Australian Register*, 5 October 1893, 3; 'General Elections', *Express and Telegraph*, 24 March 1893, 3.

3 'Law Reform', *South Australian Register*, 12 December 1895, 3.

4 'The Parliament', *Advertiser*, 11 December 1895, 7; Michael Burrage, *Revolution and the Making of the Contemporary Legal Profession: England, France, and the United States* (Oxford: Oxford University Press, 2006), 253–57; Victoria, *Parliamentary Debates* (Legislative Assembly, 8 July 1891), 288–89; New South Wales, *Parliamentary Debates* (Legislative Assembly, 14 December 1891), 3610–28.

5   Greg Taylor, *A Great and Glorious Reformation: Six Early South Australian Legal Innovations* (Kent Town, SA: Wakefield Press, 2005); 'The Parliament', *Advertiser*, 13 November 1895, 3, 3 (Henry Grainger).

6   'The Law Reform Bill', *Advertiser*, 31 August 1896, 5.

7   'Law Reform', *South Australian Register*, 7 November 1895, 7.

8   'Current Notes', *Punch*, 4 September 1902, 3.

9   'Law Reform', *South Australian Register*, 7 November 1895, 7.

10   'The Parliament', *Advertiser*, 11 December 1895, 7.

11   South Australia, *Parliamentary Debates* (House of Assembly, 11 November 1896), 726.

12   South Australia, *Parliamentary Debates* (House of Assembly, 16 November 1898), 874.

13   'The Law Society and the Law Reform Bill', *Advertiser*, 13 November 1895, 3.

14   South Australia, *Parliamentary Debates* (Legislative Council, 18 January 1899), 588; 'The Parliament', *Advertiser*, 13 November 1895, 3; South Australia, *Parliamentary Debates* (House of Assembly, 6 December 1898), 456–58.

15   'The Ministerial Policy', *South Australian Register*, 3 April 1896, 6.

16   Petition of the University of Adelaide, UAA, S169, item 321, 2.

17   South Australia, *Parliamentary Debates* (House of Assembly, 27 October 1898), 756.

18   FLM, 1895–1905, UAA, S131, item 3, 79, 82; South Australia, *Parliamentary Debates* (Legislative Council, 18 January 1899), 587–88.

19   'The Ministerial Policy', *South Australian Register*, 31 March 1899, 6; 'The Law Reform Bill', *Advertiser*, 13 November 1895, 4; 'The Law Reform Bill', *South Australian Register*, 18 October 1898, 4.

20   Jethro Brown to Registrar, 6 September 1896, UAA, S200, item 374/1896; Michael Roe, 'Brown, William Jethro (1868–1930)', Australian Dictionary of Biography, 2006, http://adb.anu.edu.au/biography/brown-william-jethro-5393; Arnold D. Hunt, 'Torr, William George (1853–1939)', Australian Dictionary of Biography, 2006, http://adb.anu.edu.au/biography/torr-william-george-8831; 'Bible Christian Conference', *South Australian Advertiser*, 27 February 1886, 6.

21   The academic record of Brown and Torr is derived from the university calendars of Cambridge, Dublin and Oxford, and from 'Mr W.G. Torr', *South Australian Register*, 18 September 1891, 5.

22   FLM, 16 December 1896, UAA, S131, item 3, 28.

23   F.W. Pennefather to Chancellor, 25 November 1892, UAA, S200, item 528/1892; S.J. Way to Jethro Brown, 11 December 1896, SLSA, PRG 258/1; University Council Minutes, 11 December 1896, UAA, S18, item 6, 76; Jethro Brown to Registrar, 6 February 1897, UAA, S200, item 68/1897; S.J. Way to Sir T. Fowell Buxton, 9 January 1906, SLSA, PRG 30/5/10,

62; Michael Roe, *Nine Australian Progressives: Vitalism in Bourgeois Social Thought, 1890–1960* (St Lucia, Qld: University of Queensland Press, 1984), 24.

24   John Salmond to Registrar, 26 September 1896, UAA, S200, item 429/1896.

25   S.J. Way to Registrar, 7 May 1897, UAA, S200, item 341/1897.

26   S.J. Way to F.W. Pennefather, 8 November 1897, SLSA, PRG 30/5/4, 410.

27   Alex Frame, *Salmond: Southern Jurist* (Wellington: Victoria University Press, 1995), 56–57.

28   S.J. Way to W.R. Phillips, 9 August 1904, SLSA, PRG 30/5/8, 344.

29   R F.V. Heuston, 'Sir John Salmond', *Adelaide Law Review* 2, no. 2 (1964): 221; FLM, 27 March 1897, UAA, S131, item 3, 35.

30   'In Society's Moods', *Critic*, 15 July 1899, 23; 'A Lady's Letter', *Express and Telegraph*, 18 November 1893, 4.

31   Frame, *Salmond*, 55–56; John Salmond to Charles Hodge, 6 January 1907, UAA, S200, item 54/1907.

32   FLM, 17 May 1897, UAA, S131, item 3, 42; Edgeloe, 'The Adelaide Law School', 39–42; 'Benham, Edward Warner', UAA, S587; F.A. d'Arenberg to Registrar, 11 March 1897, UAA, S200, item 212/1897; E.W. Benham to Registrar, 16 September 1919, UAA, S200, item 547/1919.

33   Norman, Random Reminiscences, Barr Smith Library, University of Adelaide, 4.

34   Margaret J. Jennings, 'Benham, Edward Warner (1872–1948)', Australian Dictionary of Biography, 2006, http://adb.anu.edu.au/biography/benham-edward-warner-9485.

35   Sally O'Neill, 'Kelly, David Frederick (1847–1894)', Australian Dictionary of Biography, 2006, http://adb.anu.edu.au/biography/kelly-david-frederick-3932; Sir Bruce Ross, Interview, 17 November 1982, Barr Smith Library, University of Adelaide, Law School Oral History Archives; Catherine Barron, 'Reclining Connected Forms', Adelaidia, 2018, https://adelaidia.history.sa.gov.au/things/reclining-connected-forms.

36   'Commemoration Day', *South Australian Register*, 10 December 1898, 5.

37   Circular letter from John Salmond, 1 July 1898, UAA, S200, item 553/1898; 'The University Dinner', *Evening Journal*, 19 August 1898, 3; 'University Law School Dinner', *Advertiser*, 28 November 1901, 8; John Salmond to Vice-Chancellor, 20 March 1902, UAA, S200, item 343/1902; Kym Anderson and Bernard O'Neil, *The Building of Economics at Adelaide, 1901–2001* (School of Economics, University of Adelaide, 2004), 1–2, 8; Memorandum from Professor Salmond, 21 December 1898, UAA, S200, item 1168A/1898.

38   Sir John Salmond, *Jurisprudence*, ed. Glanville L. Williams, 10th ed. (London: Sweet & Maxwell, 1947), 9.

39 Gerald J. Postema, *Legal Philosophy in the Twentieth Century: The Common Law World*, Treatise of Legal Philosophy and General Jurisprudence, vol. 11 (Dordrecht: Springer, 2011), 21.

40 Mark Lunney, 'Professor Sir John Salmond (1862–1924): An Englishman Abroad', in *Scholars of Tort Law*, ed. James Goudkamp and Donal Nolan (Oxford: Hart Publishing, 2019), 105.

41 FLM, 1895–1905, UAA, S131, item 3, 47–49, 53, 94–95.

42 Telegram from Robert Stout to S.J. Way, 18 December 1905, UAA, S200, item 999/1905.

43 Frame, *Salmond*, 72–73; John Salmond to Registrar, 14 December 1905, UAA, S200, item 989/1905.

44 'Professorships at the University', *Register*, 3 January 1906, 6.

45 S.J. Way to T. Ruddle, 16 March 1906, SLSA, PRG 30/5/10, 276; Telegram from S.J. Way to Agent-General, 23 December 1905, UAA, S200, item 1906/AG1; 'Concerning People', *Register*, 6 January 1906, 5; Roe, *Nine Australian Progressives*, 36.

46 Jethro Brown to S.J. Way, 21 January 1906, UAA, S200, item 245/1906.

47 W. Jethro Brown, 'The American Law School', *Law Quarterly Review* 21, no. 1 (1905): 69.

48 ibid., 78.

49 Victoria, *Royal Commission on the University of Melbourne: Minutes of Evidence*, Parliamentary Paper no. 20 (2nd session, 1903), 5.

50 James Bryce, *The American Commonwealth*, 2nd ed., vol. 2 (London: Macmillan, 1891), 503.

51 'Law and Lawyers', *Daily Telegraph* (Sydney), 3 December 1909, 5; A.V. Dicey, 'The Teaching of English Law at Harvard', *The Contemporary Review* 76 (1899): 742–43; W. Harrison Moore, 'Legal Education in the United States', *Journal of the Society of Comparative Legislation* 13, no. 2 (1913): 207–12.

52 Jethro Brown to George Murray, undated, SLSA, PRG 259/20.

53 'Law Reforms', *Register*, 6 December 1906, 4.

54 S.J. Way to F.W. Pennefather, 15 August 1907, SLSA, PRG 30/5/11, 318.

55 Norman, Random Reminiscences, Barr Smith Library, University of Adelaide, 3; W. Jethro Brown, 'The Purpose and Method of a Law School: Part I', *Law Quarterly Review* 18, no. 1 (1902): 78; 'The Study of Law', *Register*, 13 June 1906, 4.

56 W. Jethro Brown, 'Law Schools and the Legal Profession', *Commonwealth Law Review* 6, no. 1 (1908): 13.

57 ibid., 12.

58 Jethro Brown to S.J. Way, 21 January 1906, UAA, S200, item 245/1906.

59 Jethro Brown, Law School Report, UAA, S200, item 669/1906.

60 ibid., 4.

NOTES

61 'Democratising the University', *Advertiser*, 1 November 1911, 9.

62 'The University', *Register*, 28 November 1911, 6.

63 'Extension of University', *Register*, 11 June 1914, 9; Gwilym Croucher and James Waghorne, *Australian Universities: A History of Common Cause* (Sydney, NSW: NewSouth Publishing, 2020), 14–18; Western Australia, *Report of the Royal Commission on the Establishment of a University*, Parliamentary Paper (Perth, 1910), 15; Fred Alexander, *Campus at Crawley: A Narrative and Critical Appreciation of the First Fifty Years of the University of Western Australia* (Melbourne: F.W. Cheshire, for the University of Western Australia Press, 1963), 59–62.

64 Julia Horne and Geoffrey Sherington, *Sydney: The Making of a Public University* (Carlton, Vic.: Melbourne University Publishing, 2012), 54; 'Regulations Made by the Council of Education', *South Australian Government Gazette*, 7 January 1876, 37, 44; University of Adelaide, *Calendar*, 1890, 173.

65 Craig Campbell, 'Inventing a Pioneering State High School: Adelaide High, 1908–1918', *Journal of the Historical Society of South Australia*, no. 29 (2001): 6–7; Colin Thiele, *Grains of Mustard Seed* (Adelaide: Education Department, 1975), 83–84; 'Education Regulations', *South Australian Government Gazette*, 14 October 1909, 739, 740; 'Education Regulations', *South Australian Government Gazette*, 16 January 1913, 81, 99; Susan Magarey and Kerrie Round, *Roma the First: A Biography of Dame Roma Mitchell* (Kent Town, SA: Wakefield Press, 2007), 35.

66 South Australia, *Progress Report of the Select Committee of the House of Assembly on the Adelaide University and Higher Education*, Parliamentary Paper no. 113, 1910, 18.

67 S.J. Way to F.W. Pennefather, 16 October 1906, SLSA, PRG 30/5/10, 225.

68 S.J. Way to H.W. Horwill, 22 January 1907, SLSA, PRG 30/5/11, 185–86.

69 Jethro Brown to S.J. Way, 21 January 1906, UAA, S200, item 245/1906; Education Committee Minutes, 8 June 1906, UAA, S23, item 7, 8; Alex Martin and T.E. Barr Smith to C.R. Hodge, 13 March 1907, UAA, S200, item 224/1907; Alex Martin and T.E. Barr Smith to C.R. Hodge, 4 March 1912, UAA, S200, item 112/1912.

70 'The University of Adelaide', *Advertiser*, 3 December 1906, 9; 'Mr W.J. Isbister Dies At 84', *Advertiser*, 18 December 1950, 2.

71 Law School Report, 1906: Registrar's Copy, UAA, S141, 4.

72 Sir Bruce Ross, Interview, Barr Smith Library, University of Adelaide, Law School Oral History Archives.

73 Jethro Brown to S.J. Way, 24 December 1909, SLSA, PRG 30/3.

74 Jethro Brown to S.J. Way, 26 September 1911, SLSA, Jethro Brown Papers, 2.

75 Jethro Brown to S.J. Way, 18 December 1914, SLSA, Jethro Brown Papers, 3.

76 S.J. Way to Jethro Brown, 22 December 1914, SLSA, PRG 30/5/19, 81.

77 Roe, *Nine Australian Progressives*, 31–32; University of Adelaide, *Calendar*, 1907, 190.

78 W. Jethro Brown, *The Underlying Principles of Modern Legislation* (London: John Murray, 1912), 205.

79 Jethro Brown to Council, 28 August 1912, UAA, S200, item 441/1912.

80 Jethro Brown to Chancellor, 27 October 1911, UAA, S200, item 630/1911; 'Sugar Commission', *Register*, 31 October 1911, 7; *Colonial Sugar Refining Co. Ltd v. Attorney-General (Cth)* (1912) 15 CLR 182; Roe, *Nine Australian Progressives*, 41–42.

81 Julja I. Szuster, 'The Injustice of the 1914 Assault on Hermann Heinicke', *Journal of the Historical Society of South Australia*, no. 43 (2015): 104, 106.

82 University of Adelaide, *Calendar*, 1918, 39, 104.

83 'University Honors for German Subjects', *Advertiser*, 28 November 1917, 6.

84 'A Call for Patriotism', *Register*, 29 April 1915, 4; Peter Moore, *A Legal Cohort: South Australia's Legal Community and the First World War* (Darlinghurst, NSW: Australian Legal Heritage, 2018), 144–47, 198–99.

85 Jethro Brown to Vice-Chancellor, 26 January 1916, UAA, S200, item 37/1916.

86 Jethro Brown to Chancellor, 7 October 1918, UAA, S200, item 456/1918.

87 Registrar to Jethro Brown, 1 February 1916, UAA, S200, item 37/1916; Jethro Brown to Chancellor, 29 September 1916, UAA, S200, item 370/1916; 'Mr President Brown: Criticism in Parliament', *Advertiser*, 22 September 1916, 10; Jethro Brown to Chancellor, 14 November 1916, UAA, S200, item 428/1916; Registrar to Jethro Brown, 16 December 1918, UAA, S200, item 456/1918; Jethro Brown to Registrar, 26 November 1919, UAA, S200, item 456/1918.

88 University of Adelaide, *Calendar*, 1877, 58; University of Adelaide, *Calendar*, 1882, cv. An *ad eundem* BSc was conferred on schoolteacher Edward Wainwright in 1883.

89 Catherine Helen Spence, *An Autobiography*, ed. Jeanne F. Young (Adelaide: W.K. Thomas & Co., 1910), 59.

90 Moore, *A Legal Cohort*, 126; 'Rules of the Supreme Court', *South Australian Government Gazette*, 5 June 1890, 1513; *Language of Acts Act 1872* (SA), s. 33; Mary Jane Mossman, *The First Women Lawyers: A Comparative Study of Gender, Law and the Legal Professions* (Oxford: Hart Publishing, 2006), 40–54; *In Re Edith Haynes* (1904) 6 WAR 209.

91 Alison Mackinnon, *The New Women: Adelaide's Early Women Graduates* (Netley, SA: Wakefield Press, 1986), 26; Helen Jones, *Nothing Seemed Impossible: Women's Education and Social Change in South Australia, 1875–1915* (St Lucia, Qld: University of Queensland Press, 1985), 50. Details of Emily Moulden's career are derived from university calendars and contemporary newspapers.

92 South Australia, *Parliamentary Debates* (House of Assembly, 7 November 1911), 879.

93 D. Egerton Jones, *The Year Between* (London: Cassell, 1918), 30.

94 ibid., 243.

95 Jones, Doris Egerton: Student Card, UAA, S1117; Suzanne Edgar, 'Jones, Doris Egerton (1889–1973)', Australian Dictionary of Biography, 2006, https://adb.anu.edu.au/biography/jones-doris-egerton-6870.

96 Doris Jones to Jethro Brown, undated, SLSA, PRG 258/1.

97 Frame, *Salmond*, 55.

98 Justice Roma Mitchell, Interview, 3 July 1981, Barr Smith Library, University of Adelaide, Law School Oral History Archives.

99 Margaret M. Press, *Three Women of Faith: Gertrude Abbott, Elizabeth Anstice Baker and Mary Tenison Woods* (Kent Town, SA: Wakefield Press, 2000), 107–25; Anne O'Brien, 'Tenison Woods, Mary Cecil (1893–1971)', Australian Dictionary of Biography, 2006, https://adb.anu.edu.au/biography/tenison-woods-mary-cecil-8772; 'Professions for Women', *Register*, 6 July 1918; Moore, *A Legal Cohort*, 127–28.

100 Dorothy Somerville, 'Vocations for Girls', *Advertiser*, 8 December 1931, 14.

101 'Women at the Bar', *News*, 7 February 1929, 9.

102 'Women Lawyers', *Sydney Morning Herald*, 16 November 1936, 4; Mary Tenison Woods, 'Careers for Girls', *Advertiser*, 5 September 1933, 14; Magarey and Round, *Roma the First*, 86–87; Alison Mackinnon, *Love and Freedom: Professional Women and the Reshaping of Personal Life* (Cambridge: Cambridge University Press, 1997), 89.

103 'A Girl's Letter', *Quiz*, 27 March 1903, 7.

104 Eileen [sic] Bond, Interview, 14 June 1981, Barr Smith Library, University of Adelaide, Law School Oral History Archives; Mossman, *The First Women Lawyers*, 37–38; Hugh C. Macgill and R. Kent Newmyer, 'Legal Education and Legal Thought, 1790–1920', in *The Cambridge History of Law in America: Volume 2: The Long Nineteenth Century (1789–1920)*, ed. Christopher Tomlins and Michael Grossberg (Cambridge: Cambridge University Press, 2008), 64.

105 Gillian [sic] Goode, Interview, 17 June 1981, Barr Smith Library, University of Adelaide, Law School Oral History Archives.

106 'Judge on Students' No-Women Law', *Mail*, 9 July 1938, 1.

107 'Law Men Amend Constitution', *On Dit*, 28 June 1938.

108 Gillian [sic] Goode, Interview, Barr Smith Library, University of Adelaide, Law School Oral History Archives.

109 University of Adelaide, *Calendar*, 1920, 252; 'Law Students' Society', *Adelaide University Magazine*, November 1920, 14; 'Law Society', *On Dit*, 26 March 1936; 'Law Men Amend Constitution', *On Dit*, 28 June 1938; 'Women Repulsed', *On Dit*, 12 July 1938; 'Women Students Allowed to Debate', *On Dit*, 8 April 1941; 'Women In At Last', *On Dit*, 29 June 1956,

1; E.P. Mullighan, 'Before the Bench', in *Dame Roma: Glimpses of a Glorious Life*, ed. Magarey, Susan (Adelaide: Axiom, 2002), 41.

110 'Signs of the Times', *On Dit*, 13 May 1932; 'Women Law Students' Association', *On Dit*, 26 April 1939; Roma Mitchell to Peter Kelly, 25 November 1982, Barr Smith Library, University of Adelaide, MSS 0130, series 6/4.

111 University of Adelaide, *Calendar*, 1918, 387.

112 Advertisement for Chair of Law, UAA, S200, item 633/1919; 'Professional Engagements', *Register*, 20 December 1919; Applications for Chair of Law, UAA, S280, item 39; Turney, Bygott, and Chippendale, *Australia's First, Volume 1*, 246.

113 *Who Was Who 1951–1960* (London: Adam and Charles Black, 1961), 872; John William Leonard, *Who's Who in Jurisprudence: A Biographical Dictionary of Contemporary Lawyers and Jurists, 1925, with a Complete Geographical Index* (Brooklyn, NY: John W. Leonard Corporation, 1925), 130; University of Toronto, *President's Report*, 1924, 2; Coleman Phillipson, *The International Law and Custom of Ancient Greece and Rome* (London: Macmillan, 1911); John Waugh, 'Controversy and Renown: Coleman Phillipson at the Adelaide Law School', *Adelaide Law Review* 42, no. 1 (2021): 147–71.

114 Telegram from Lord Birkenhead to Agent-General, 26 September 1919, UAA, S280, item 39.

115 Frederick Smith, *International Law*, ed. Coleman Phillipson, 5th ed. (London: Dent, 1918), 7.

116 Lord Reading to Edward Lucas, 30 September 1919, UAA, S280, item 39; 'Law Report, March 22', *Times*, 23 March 1918, 4; A. Lentin, 'Isaacs, Rufus Daniel, First Marquess of Reading (1860–1935), Politician and Judge', *Oxford Dictionary of National Biography*, January 2011, https://www.oxforddnb.com.

117 Notes dictated by A.G. Rymill to his son, UAA, S280, item 369, 2.

118 Reference from Sir John Macdonell, 19 March 1913, UAA, S280, item 39; Coleman Phillipson: Additional Information, UAA, S280, item 39.

119 General Register Office: 1891 Census Returns, The National Archives of the UK, RG 12/3688, 111; General Register Office: 1901 Census Returns, The National Archives of the UK, RG 13/4229, 89; Nigel Grizzard, 'Demographic: The Jewish Population of Leeds—How Many Jews?', in *Leeds and Its Jewish Community: A History*, ed. Derek Fraser (Manchester: Manchester University Press, 2019), 35, 36–37; Wilfrid Prest, 'How We Got Here from There: History in a "Scottish" University', in *Pasts Present: History at Australia's Third University*, ed. Wilfrid Prest (Kent Town, SA: Wakefield Press, 2014), 7, 9–10; Leonie Star, *Julius Stone: An Intellectual Life* (Melbourne: Oxford University Press, 1992), 42–43, 50–51, 59–64.

120 J.F. Downer to Registrar, 26 September 1919, UAA, S280, item 39.

121 J.G. Latham to W.J. Isbister, 17 November 1919, UAA, S280, item 39.

NOTES

122 William Mitchell to Sir George Murray, 25 September 1919, UAA, S200, item 564/1919.

123 William Mitchell to George Murray, 3 December 1919, SLSA, PRG 259/15.

124 Sir Frederick Young and J.F. Downer to W.J. Isbister, 26 September 1919, UAA, S280, item 39; J.F. Downer to W.J. Isbister, 25 September 1919, UAA, S280, item 39; Coleman Phillipson, *Termination of War and Treaties of Peace* (London: Sweet & Maxwell, 1916), vi; Minute of Council, 28 November 1919, UAA, S200, item 71/1920.

125 Moore, *A Legal Cohort*, 13.

126 FLM, 1917–24, UAA, S131, item 5, 18, 41–42; Registrar to N. Lockyer, 29 April 1918, UAA, S200, item 74/1918; *Australian Soldiers' Repatriation Act 1920* (Cth), s. 46(2); *Australian Soldiers' Repatriation Regulations 1920* (Cth), reg. 92–94.

127 'Proposals for Revision of the Course and Curriculum', UAA, S280, item 179; FLM, 18 October 1920, UAA, S280, item 5, 67–68.

128 FLM, 19 February 1917, UAA, S131, item 4, 173; FLM, 1917–24, UAA, S131, item 5, 77–79, 88; FLM, 1924–44, UAA, S131, item 6, 20; Harry Thomson to Registrar, 20 September 1922, UAA, S200, item 528/1922; 'Supreme Court Rules, 1925', *South Australian Government Gazette*, 19 November 1925, 1359.

129 E.J.R. Morgan, *The Adelaide Club, 1863–1963* (Adelaide Club, 1963), 13, 117, 126; 'L'Alliance Francaise', *Mail*, 7 May 1921, 13; 'Adelaide Repertory Theatre', *Critic*, 3 May 1922, 19.

130 University of Adelaide, *Calendar*, 1925, 97.

131 Faculty Report 1/98, UAA, S141; 'Value of Special Coaching', *News*, 11 April 1925, 5; 'The Lure of the Open', *News*, 11 July 1925, 5; FLM, 12 February 1937, UAA, S131, item 6, 186; David Hogarth to Acting Registrar, 23 September 1949, UAA, S280, item 421.

132 Edgeloe, 'The Adelaide Law School', 26; Registrar to Coleman Phillipson, 2 July 1923, UAA, S200, item 325/23; Registrar to A.L. Campbell, 15 September 1925, UAA, S200, item 70/1925.

133 Transcript of Subcommittee Hearings, UAA, S280, item 369, 10–11, 39; University of Adelaide, *Calendar*, 1928, 98; Distribution of Fees, 1876, UAA, S169, item 59; University of Sydney, *Calendar*, 1852–53, 68; Doreen Bridges, 'Ives, Joshua (1854–1931)', Australian Dictionary of Biography, 2006, http://adb.anu.edu.au/biography/ives-joshua-6807; Edgeloe, 'The Adelaide Law School', 26.

134 Transcript of Subcommittee Hearings, UAA, S280, item 369, 26–28, 41; Agnes Rymill to Vice-Chancellor, 3 March 1925, UAA, S200, item 61/25; A.G. Rymill to Vice-Chancellor, 4 March 1925, UAA, S200, item 61/25; H.J. Gibbney and Ann G. Smith, eds., *A Biographical Register 1788–1939: Notes from the Name Index of the Australian Dictionary of Biography*, vol. 2 (Canberra: Australian Dictionary of Biography, 1987), 236; 'Business Leader and Pastoralist', *Advertiser*, 11 September 1934, 15.

135 Transcript of Subcommittee Hearings, UAA, S280, item 369; Eva Phillipson to Justice Poole, 22 March 1925, UAA, S280, item 369; Comments on Two Letters Addressed to the Vice-Chancellor, UAA, S280, item 369; Agnes Rymill to Vice-Chancellor, 3 March 1925, UAA, S200, item 61/25; A.G. Rymill to Vice-Chancellor, 4 March 1925, UAA, S200, item 61/25.

136 Transcript of Subcommittee Hearings, UAA, S280, item 369, 53.

137 Comments on Two Letters Addressed to the Vice-Chancellor, UAA, S280, item 369; Report to the Council of the University of Adelaide of Sub-committee re Professor Phillipson, UAA, S200, item 61/1925, 8.

138 Coleman Phillipson to Justice Poole, 18 April 1925, UAA, S280, item 369.

139 Comments Received 6th May with Letter to Mr Justice Poole, UAA, S280, item 369.

140 Transcript of Subcommittee Hearings, UAA, S280, item 369, 56.

141 ibid.

142 Comments on Two Letters Addressed to the Vice-Chancellor, UAA, S280, item 369; Transcript of Subcommittee Hearings, UAA, S280, item 369, 45.

143 Report to the Council, UAA, S200, item 61/1925.

144 Note Concerning Dismissal of a Professor, UAA, S280, item 369.

145 Report to the Council, UAA, S200, item 61/1925, 4; Transcript of Subcommittee Hearings, UAA, S280, item 369, 11–13, 29–32; Remarks on Mr Hardy's Statement, UAA, S280, item 369.

146 Coleman Phillipson to Vice-Chancellor, 13 May 1925, UAA, S200, item 106/1925.

147 Vice-Chancellor to Coleman Phillipson, 15 May 1925, UAA, S200, item 106/1925; University Council Minutes, 11 May 1925, UAA, S18, item 13, 53–54.

148 'Professor Phillipson's Resignation', *Register*, 18 May 1925, 7.

149 'Professor Phillipson', *Advertiser*, 19 May 1925, 13.

150 Eleanor Wemyss to Coleman Phillipson, 22 April 1925, UAA, S280, item 369.

151 John Qualtrough Ewens, Interview, 8 March 1982, Barr Smith Library, University of Adelaide, Law School Oral History Archives.

152 Cyril M.A. Brown, *William Jethro Brown: A Personal Biography and a Bibliography* (South Perth, WA: The Author, 1983), 50; 'Professor Phillipson's Departure', *Register*, 6 August 1925, 15.

153 Coleman Phillipson, *The Trial of Socrates (with Chapters on His Life, Teaching, and Personality)* (London: Stevens & Sons, 1928), v–vi.

154 'Outstanding Women', *Advertiser*, 27 May 1930, 14.

155 'Obituary', *Register*, 23 March 1926, 9; 'Obituary', *Times*, 18 December 1958, 12; 'World Law Expert Dies at Torquay', *Herald Express*, 16 December 1958, 7.

156   Edgeloe, 'The Adelaide Law School', 26; J.F. Downer to W.J. Isbister, 23 September 1919, UAA, S280, item 39.

157   William Mitchell to Sir George Murray, 25 September 1919, UAA, S200, item 564/1919.

158   Ivan Shearer, 'James Crawford: The Early Years', in *Sovereignty, Statehood and State Responsibility: Essays in Honour of James Crawford*, ed. Christine Chinkin and Freya Baetens (Cambridge: Cambridge University Press, 2015), xv.

159   W.R. Crocker, 'The University of Adelaide in the 1920s', *Journal of the Historical Society of South Australia*, no. 3 (1977): 7.

3   Community: 1926–1957

1   Darnley Naylor to Vice-Chancellor, 27 June 1925, UAA, S200, item 70/1925.

2   Howard Zelling to Peter Kelly, 12 November 1982, Barr Smith Library, University of Adelaide, MSS 0130, series 6/4.

3   J.G. Latham to W.J. Isbister, 19 June 1925, UAA, S200, item 169/1925.

4   Draft Report of Committee on Chair of Law, September 1925, UAA, S280, item 179; Wilfred Fullagar to W.J. Isbister, 17 August 1925, UAA, S200, item 169/1925.

5   A.L. Campbell to Mr Justice Parsons, 11 August 1925, UAA, S200, item 70/1925; G.V. Portus, 'Vale Arthur', *On Dit*, 4 April 1949, 4; 'Central Chancery of the Orders of Knighthood', *London Gazette*, 14 January 1921, 372; Registrar to A.L. Campbell, 15 September 1925, UAA, S200, item 70/1925; Edgeloe, *Annals*, 58–59.

6   J. Langdon Bonython to Sir George Murray, 25 March 1926, UAA, S200, item 37/1926.

7   W.B. Pitcher, 'Bonython, Sir John Langdon (1848–1939)', Australian Dictionary of Biography, 2006, http://adb.anu.edu.au/biography/ bonython-sir-john-langdon-5286; University of Adelaide, *Calendar*, 1922, 288; Draft letter to Chancellor, UAA, S200, item 37/1926; E.J. Prest, *Sir John Langdon Bonython: Newspaper Proprietor, Politician and Philanthropist* (North Melbourne, Vic.: Australian Scholarly Publishing, 2011), 216; 'Chair of Law Endowed', *News*, 30 March 1926, 1.

8   H.J. Katekar, The Law School in the 1930s, Barr Smith Library, University of Adelaide, MSS 0130, series 6/4.

9   Nugent Wallman to Peter Kelly, 25 November 1982, Barr Smith Library, University of Adelaide, MSS 0130, series 6/4; Trevor McFarlane to Peter Kelly, 9 November 1982, Barr Smith Library, University of Adelaide, MSS 0130, series 6/4.

10   Margaret M. Finnis, *The Lower Level: A Discursive History of the Adelaide University Union* (Adelaide University Union, 1975), 134.

11   ibid., 135.

12   W.A. Wynes, Interview by Janet Robertson, 1973, SLSA, J.D. Somerville Oral History Collection, OH 561/63, transcript, 4.

13   John Qualtrough Ewens, Interview, Barr Smith Library, University of Adelaide, Law School Oral History Archives.

14   Law School Undergraduate Handbook, 1988, UAA, S950, item 45, 16.

15   'South Australian Debating Club', *South Australian Advertiser*, 6 December 1858, 2; 'Topics of the Day', *South Australian Advertiser*, 4 December 1863, 2; Minute Book, South Australian Law Students' Society, 1870–74, SLSA, SRG 785; 'University Law Debating Society', *Advertiser*, 25 April 1898, 6; 'Adelaide University Law Debating Society', *Register*, 18 May 1901, 3; 'Adelaide University Law Students' Society', *Adelaide University Magazine*, June 1919, 107.

16   Adelaide University Law Students' Society Programmes, 1934–35, Barr Smith Library, University of Adelaide, MSS 0130, series 6/5; Adelaide University Law Students' Society Programmes, 1936–39, UAA, S1118, item 38; 'Lawyers at Play', *News*, 14 December 1928, 15; 'Law Students' First Dance', *Advertiser*, 27 July 1938, 11; 'Jury Disagrees', *On Dit*, 26 July 1938.

17   'Uproar in Court', *On Dit*, 10 August 1934.

18   'Pre-Election Tussle', *On Dit*, 13 September 1934.

19   'Liberty', *On Dit*, 4 April 1939.

20   'The University Dinner', *South Australian Register*, 18 August 1898, 4.

21   'The Week', *Observer*, 23 December 1905, 4.

22   Alex Castles, Andrew Ligertwood, and Peter Kelly, eds., *Law on North Terrace, 1883–1983* (Faculty of Law, University of Adelaide, 1983), 38–39, 41–43.

23   Keith Edmunds to Peter Kelly, 12 November 1982, Barr Smith Library, University of Adelaide, MSS 0130, series 6/4, 6.

24   'Reports of Societies', *On Dit*, 13 May 1932.

25   'Editorial: Chaos in the Law School', *On Dit*, 30 September 1932.

26   'AULSS Annual Meeting', *On Dit*, 6 April 1937.

27   'Correspondence', *On Dit*, 13 April 1937.

28   A.L. Campbell to A.W. Cocks, 11 November 1936, UAA, S200, item 263/1936.

29   Castles, Ligertwood, and Kelly, *Law on North Terrace*, 43–44.

30   'Law Students v. The Council', *On Dit*, 28 April 1937.

31   'Protest Against Initiations', *On Dit*, 5 April 1948, 7.

32   'Varsity Initiations May End', *News*, 2 May 1932, 1; 'Floggings at Roseworthy', *Advertiser*, 11 February 1932, 10; 'Students Tarred and Thrown Into Torrens', *Advertiser*, 22 April 1948, 1; 'Criminal Sittings', *Advertiser*, 1 June 1951, 5.

33   'In the Faculties', *On Dit*, 29 June 1956, 2.

34   Norval Morris to J.V. Barry, 19 August 1958, NLA, MS 2505/1/3449.

NOTES

35 John Basten, 'Illegal Precedents (and, Past Scandals)', *Lux Gentium*, 1966, no. 2, 14–15.

36 John Waugh, 'The Legal Profession Between the Wars', in *The First World War, the Universities and the Professions in Australia 1914–1939*, ed. Darian-Smith, Kate and James Waghorne (Carlton, Vic.: Melbourne University Publishing, 2019), 227–28; John Waugh, *First Principles: The Melbourne Law School, 1857–2007* (Carlton, Vic.: Miegunyah Press, 2007), 113–24.

37 George Murray to Herbert Mayo, 14 March 1935, UAA, S200, item 121/1935.

38 University of Adelaide, *Calendar*, 1936, 172–73; C.C. Brebner to A.L. Campbell, 16 April 1935, UAA, S200, item 121/1935; Report of Sub-Committee, 20 November 1933, UAA, S200, item 121/1935.

39 'Many Lawyers', *News*, 6 March 1928, 7; 'Professions Less Crowded Than Last Year', *News*, 22 October 1932, 4; Eugene Gorman, 'The Legal Profession and the Community', *Australian Law Journal* 10, no. 13 (1936): 32, 35; 'Too Many S.A. Lawyers', *Mail*, 8 August 1936, 9; 'Population/Lawyers/Law Students in South Australia', UAA, S1118, item 115.

40 'Law Students and Bar', *Advertiser*, 13 April 1938, 33; FLM, 20 September 1943, UAA, S131, item 6, 280; F.B. McBryde to Law Society Secretary, 18 July 1939, UAA, S200, item 151/1939; 'Degrees Awarded' and 'Final Certificates Awarded', Barr Smith Library, University of Adelaide, MSS 0130, series 6/3; 'Rules of Court Regulating the Admission of Practitioners, 1955', *South Australian Government Gazette*, 14 July 1955, 73; FLM, 1965–72, UAA, S131, item 8, 176, 184; Horst Lücke to W.F. Sharpe, 14 October 1970, UAA, S1118, item 114/1.

41 'A Lady of the Law', *Bulletin: Law Society of South Australia*, March 1998, 30.

42 Dorothy Somerville and Sesca Zelling, Interview, 13 October 1982, Barr Smith Library, University of Adelaide, Law School Oral History Archives.

43 'The Law School Dinner', *Advertiser*, 3 December 1903, 6.

44 Lecture Notebook, Law of Evidence, Barr Smith Library, University of Adelaide, MSS 0130, series 4; Pue, *Lawyers' Empire*, 196–97; Peter Moore, *Fisher Jeffries: The First 125 Years* (Darlinghurst, NSW: Australian Legal Heritage, 2010), 56; 'Late Sir John Salmond', *Register*, 23 September 1924, 11.

45 'The Examination System', *Daily Herald*, 23 November 1920, 5; '"Lecturing System Is Too Important A Thing For Us To Worry About Finance"', *On Dit*, 6 July 1937; 'Law Teaching Methods', *Advertiser*, 4 March 1936, 18.

46 'How Long, O Lord?', *On Dit*, 15 June 1937.

47 'Kriewaldt Leads the Way', *On Dit*, 22 June 1937.

48 'Culture', *On Dit*, 7 September 1937.

49 Andrew Ligertwood, Interview by John Waugh, 24 July 2019.

50 A.P. Moore to R.W.F. Tait, 14 September 1979, UAA, S1118, item 51/7; Law Library Report, 1981, UAA, S204, item 1981/82-1, 2.

51 'University Graduates', *News*, 9 February 1926, 6; T. Spencer Shore, ed., *The Savitar 1923* (Columbia, Missouri: Junior Class of the University of Missouri, 1923), 223; Martin R. Kriewaldt to Registrar, 26 May 1923, UAA, S200, item 331/1923; Cases and Materials in Elements of Law and Legal Method, 1963, Barr Smith Library, University of Adelaide, MSS 0156, series 2.

52 Committee on the Future of Tertiary Education in Australia, *Tertiary Education in Australia*, vol. 2 (Canberra: Government Printer, 1964), 57.

53 'Introductions and Valete', *Lux Gentium*, Autumn 1965, 2; 'Professor A.C. Castles', *Lux Gentium*, 1967, no. 2, 3.

54 Jeff Goldsworthy, Interview by John Waugh, 18 October 2018.

55 Rick Sarre, Response to Adelaide Law School History Questionnaire, 2019.

56 General Assessment Comments, UAA, S1511, item 3.

57 John Bray to Peter Kelly, 10 November 1982, Barr Smith Library, University of Adelaide, MSS 0130, series 6/4.

58 University of Adelaide, *Calendar*, 1908, 121.

59 Francis Knowles to Registrar, 22 October 1910, UAA, S200, item 710/1910.

60 Pitt Cobbett to Registrar, 24 March 1910, UAA, S200, item 250/1910; Report of examiners for the degree of LLD, 5 December 1910, UAA, S200, item 842/1910; Harrison Moore to Registrar, 5 February 1910, UAA, S200, item 80/1910.

61 F.L. Stow to Registrar, 23 June 1909, UAA, S200, item 462/1909.

62 FLM, 10 August 1909, UAA, S131, item 4, 65.

63 Report of Examiner on Thesis Submitted by Mr Francis Leslie Stow, UAA, S200, item 661/1909.

64 'Late Dr F.L Stow', *West Australian*, 15 May 1935, 12.

65 FLM, 14 December 1908, UAA, S131, item 4, 55; Howard Zelling to Dean, 26 November 1941, UAA, S200, item 50/1942.

66 'Dr T.J. Browne Dead', *Advertiser*, 23 April 1949, 3; Harrison Moore to Faculty of Law, 13 November 1917, UAA, S200, item 362/1917; FLM, 1917–24, UAA, S131, item 5, 45, 48; Thomas Hewitson: Certificate of Academic Registrar and Biographical Notes, Barr Smith Library, University of Adelaide, MSS 0130, series 6/3.

67 University of Adelaide, *Postgraduate Calendar*, 2008, 9. Statistics are derived from university calendars and List of Doctors of Law, University of Melbourne Archives, University of Melbourne, Faculty of Law, 1996.0065, item UM420/9.

68 'Last Day of the Royal Visit', *Advertiser*, 5 May 1927, 13; University of Adelaide, *Centenary Commemoration: Faculty of Law: 1983* (Adelaide: University of Adelaide, 1983), 8.

69 FLM, 5 November 1973, UAA, S131, item 9, 71; Higher Degrees Committee, Report No. 6/74, UAA, S131, item 10, 223; University of Adelaide, *Calendar*, 1979, vol. 1, 204; Special Degrees Rules, August 2004,

NOTES

https://web.archive.org/web/20080806102231/http:/www.adelaide.edu.
au/policies/676; Special Degrees Rules, February 2017, https://web.archive.
org/web/20170522155759/http://www.adelaide.edu.au:80/policies/676.

70 University of Adelaide, *Centenary Commemoration: Faculty of Law: 1983*, 8; University of Adelaide, 'Former Officers & Honorary Degree Holders of the University', University Archives, 2020, https://www. adelaide.edu.au/records/university-archives/online-resources/ former-officers-honorary-degree-holders#honorary-university-fellows.

71 FLM, 9 May 1927, UAA, S131, item 6, 53.

72 FLM, 12 July 1926, UAA, S131, item 6, 39; University of Adelaide, *Calendar*, 1929, 168.

73 FLM, 9 December 1929, UAA, S131, item 6, 88.

74 Report on Miss Bleby's Thesis for Bonython Prize (November 1929), UAA, S200, item 238/1929.

75 FLM, 15 July 1929, UAA, S131, item 6, 79; Thelma Evelyn Bleby, 'Law of Trusts and Trustees in Australia', Thesis submitted for Bonython Prize, 1929, Law Library, University of Adelaide.

76 'Women Lawyers', *Sydney Morning Herald*, 16 November 1936, 4; FLM, 1924–44, UAA, S131, item 6, 94, 98, 102; Mary Tenison Woods, 'Some Reforms in Law Affecting Women and Children Over the Last Hundred Years', in *A Book of South Australia: Women in the First Hundred Years*, ed. Louise Brown et al. (Adelaide: Rigby for the Women's Centenary Council of SA, 1936), 127–34.

77 Press, *Three Women of Faith*, 113–14; 'Struck Off Roll', *Register*, 22 June 1927, 10; M.C.T. Woods, *Juvenile Delinquency, with Special Reference to Institutional Treatment*. (Melbourne: Melbourne University Press, 1937), 5–6; Woods, Mrs M. Tenison: Thesis for Bonython Prize, UAA, S200, item 22/1934; Ernestine Hill, 'Children and the Law', *Advertiser*, 12 July 1934, 8; 'Helping Children to Help Themselves', *Advertiser*, 14 November 1934, 10.

78 'Child Welfare Reformer Dies', *Sydney Morning Herald*, 21 October 1971, 10; 'Tenison Woods, Mary Cecil (1893–1971)', https://adb.anu.edu.au/ biography/tenison-woods-mary-cecil-8772; Boutros Boutros-Ghali, 'Introduction', in *The United Nations and the Advancement of Women 1945–1996* (New York: United Nations, 1996), 15.

79 R.M. Hague to Acting Registrar, 20 September 1949, UAA, S280, item 421.

80 R.M. Hague to Registrar, 16 May 1936, UAA, S200, item 53/1936.

81 Law Faculty Report 2/1936, UAA, S150, item 18.

82 Helen Whitington, 'Ralph Meyrick Hague: Biography', in *Hague's History of the Law in South Australia, 1837–1867*, by Ralph M. Hague (Adelaide: Barr Smith Press, 2019), 837–38, 840–41; FLM, 1924–44, UAA, S131, item 6, 172, 177; University Council Minutes, 29 May 1936, UAA, S18, item 14, 377.

83 Whitington, 'Ralph Meyrick Hague: Biography', 840–43.

84 University of Melbourne, *Calendar*, 1920, 221; University of Tasmania, *Calendar*, 1920, 67.

85 *Conference of Australian Universities*, University of Melbourne, 30–31 May 1922 (Carlton, Vic.: Ford & Son, 1922), 4; FLM, 1917–24, UAA, S131, item 5, 92, 93, 132; 'Adelaide University', *Register*, 27 November 1924, 3; FLM, 1924–44, UAA, S131, item 6, 45; Fraser, Harry Lovat: Student Card, UAA, S1117.

86 'Introducing Mr Johnston', *On Dit*, 18 March 1941, 1.

87 'University Student Activities', *Advertiser*, 18 April 1939, 14; Penelope Debelle, *Red Silk: The Life of Elliott Johnston QC* (Mile End, SA: Wakefield Press, 2011), 13, 29–32, 38.

88 A.L. Campbell, 'Foreword', *Obiter Dicta*, no. 1 (1939): 3.

89 'Scholarship System Criticised', *Advertiser*, 6 April 1939, 26; 'The Bursaries Again', *On Dit*, 4 July 1939, 1; J.A. La Nauze, 'Some Aspects of Educational Opportunity in South Australia', in *Australian Educational Studies (Second Series)*, by J.D.G. Medley et al. (Melbourne: Melbourne University Press, 1940), 27–61.

90 La Nauze, 'Some Aspects of Educational Opportunity in South Australia', 47.

91 'Regulations under the Education Act, 1915–1935', *South Australian Government Gazette*, 31 August 1939, 616, 628–29; 'Increases in Bursaries', *Advertiser*, 5 February 1947, 2.

92 Alec H. Chisholm, *Who's Who in Australia*, 13th ed. (Melbourne: Herald and Weekly Times Ltd, 1947), 202–03.

93 *Sands & McDougall's South Australian Directory 1939* (Adelaide: Sands & McDougall, 1939), 1933–36; Magarey and Round, *Roma the First*, 82–83; University of Adelaide, *Calendar*, 1943, 421–23.

94 FLM, 1924–44, UAA, S131, item 6, 262, 264–68, 276, 284.

95 John Emerson, *First Among Equals: Chief Justices of South Australia since Federation* (Adelaide: Barr Smith Press, 2006), 222; FLM, 22 November 1945, UAA, S131, item 7, 10; Michael Esposito, 'Recollections of a WWII Bomber', *Bulletin: Law Society of South Australia*, April 2014, 16.

96 FLM, 23 January 1943, UAA, S131, item 6, 264.

97 University Council Minutes, 9 December 1938, UAA, S18, item 14, 134; *Official Year Book of the Commonwealth of Australia, 1942 and 1943* (Canberra: Government Printer, 1944), 170; Stuart Macintyre, *Australia's Boldest Experiment: War and Reconstruction in the 1940s* (Sydney: NewSouth Publishing, 2015), 383.

98 Neil Hargrave, Interview by Rob Linn, 21 July 1997, SLSA, Law Society of South Australia Legal Assistance Scheme 1933–1972: An Oral History, transcript, 32; *Official Year Book of the Commonwealth of Australia, 1946 and 1947* (Canberra: Government Printer, 1949), 245–46, 251; Macintyre, *Australia's Boldest Experiment*, 327–28.

NOTES

99   Macintyre, *Australia's Boldest Experiment*, 331–32.

100 Gillian [sic] Goode, Interview, Barr Smith Library, University of Adelaide, Law School Oral History Archives; University of Adelaide, *Calendar*, 1948, 379; Emerson, *First Among Equals*, 221–22; Samuel Jacobs, Interview by Rob Linn, 23 August 2007, UAA, S1345, item 9, transcript, 14.

101 Rob Linn, *ETSA: The Story of Electricity in South Australia* (Adelaide: Historical Consultants for ETSA, 1996), 54–72; Bruce Muirden and Dean Jaensch, 'The Electricity Trust Affair', in *The Flinders History of South Australia: Political History* (Adelaide: Wakefield Press, 1986), 275–76.

102 Katekar, The Law School in the 1930s, Barr Smith Library, University of Adelaide, MSS 0130, series 6/4; 'A Lady of the Law', *Bulletin: Law Society of South Australia*, March 1998, 30; Miah O'Callaghan to Peter Kelly, 20 December 1982, Barr Smith Library, University of Adelaide, MSS 0130, series 6/4.

103 Ralph Hague to Peter Kelly, 11 November 1982, Barr Smith Library, University of Adelaide, MSS 0130, series 6/4.

104 Magarey and Round, *Roma the First*, 48.

105 'Funeral of Prof. Campbell Today', *Advertiser*, 22 March 1949, 2; 'Funeral of Prof. A.L. Campbell', *Advertiser*, 23 March 1949, 4; Andrew Parkinson, 'The Regret of Sir Samuel Way', *Australian Journal of Legal History* 1, no. 2 (1995): 239–57; Police Report to the Coroner, State Records of South Australia, GRG 1/44, no. 101 of 1949; Affidavit of E.W. Williamson, 23 September 1949, Public Record Office Victoria, VPRS 28/P0003, 416/763.

106 Chair of Law 1949: Unsuccessful Applicants, UAA, S280, item 421.

107 A.P. Rowe to J.H.C. Morris, 6 June 1949, UAA, S200, item 403A/1949.

108 A.P. Rowe to T.S.R. Boase, 6 June 1949, UAA, S200, item 403A/1949; Bruce Debelle, Interview by Lindy McNamara, 4 July 2014, Law Society of South Australia Oral Histories, https://www.lawsocietysa.asn.

109 'Extension of Law Studies Favored Here', *Advertiser*, 26 June 1950, 2; University of Adelaide, *Calendar*, 1950, 443–49.

110 FLM, 1924–44, UAA, S131, item 6, 221, 225; FLM, 19 June 1946, UAA, S131, item 7, 19; Hyman Tarlo, 'Law Schools and Law Teachers in Australia: 1946–1974', *University of Queensland Law Journal* 9, no. 1 (1975): 26–27.

111 FLM, 1945–64, UAA, S131, item 7, 20, 22.

112 University of Adelaide, *Calendar*, 1955, 447–48.

113 FLM, 1895–1905, UAA, S131, item 3, 120–21; FLM, 1945–64, UAA, S131, item 7, 74; FLM, 7 August 1967, UAA, S131, item 8, 87; University of Adelaide, *Calendar*, 1952, 144.

114 University of Adelaide, *Calendar*, 1947, 355.

115 University of Adelaide, *Calendar*, 1949, 282–90; University of Adelaide, *Calendar*, 1958, 381; A.P. Rowe, *If the Gown Fits* (Carlton, Vic.: Melbourne

University Press, 1960), 191; Stewart Cockburn and John Playford, *Playford: Benevolent Despot* (Kent Town, SA: Axiom, 1991), 194–99.

116 Australia, *Report of the Committee on Australian Universities*, Parliamentary Paper 1958, no. 12, 24–25; Croucher and Waghorne, *Australian Universities*, 83–84; W.G.K. Duncan and Roger Ashley Leonard, *The University of Adelaide, 1874–1974* (Adelaide: Rigby, 1973), 193. Funding details are in the successive *States Grants (Universities) Acts* and *Universities (Financial Assistance) Acts* (Cth).

117 'National Union to Act on Com. Scholarships', *On Dit*, 9 August 1956; 'Move for Higher Living Allowances', *On Dit*, 12 June 1959.

118 University of Adelaide, *Calendar*, 1952, 307; FLM, 16 April 1956, UAA, S131, item 7, 142; Development in 1955, FLM, 19 July 1954, UAA, S131, item 7, 113.

119 Kirsty Gover and Eddie Cubillo, 'The Challenge of Indigenous Polities', in *The Cambridge Legal History of Australia*, ed. Peter Cane, Lisa Ford, and Mark McMillan (Cambridge: Cambridge University Press, 2022), 232.

120 R.A. Blackburn to Vice-Chancellor, 9 November 1956, UAA, S200, item 403A/1949; *Milirrpum v Nabalco Pty Ltd* (1971) 17 FLR 141.

121 'Clubs and Societies', *On Dit*, 24 April 1950, 7.

122 Samuel Jacobs, Interview by Rob Linn, 11 August 1997, SLSA, Law Society of South Australia Legal Assistance Scheme 1933–1972: An Oral History, 111.

123 'Many Students Studying Law', *Advertiser*, 28 September 1949, 10; 'Plea for More Law Students', *News*, 26 April 1955.

124 FLM, 1945–64, UAA, S131, item 7, 60, 62, 67, 70, 108; 'Freed Lithuanians' Ideas of the Future', *Mail*, 15 October 1949, 8; 'Their Celebration Was Just Like Home', *Mail*, 30 October 1954, 8.

4 On the Move: 1958–1967

1   'A.W.L.S.S.', *On Dit*, 1 July 1932.

2   University of Adelaide, *Calendar*, 1913, 367; Castles, Ligertwood, and Kelly, *Law on North Terrace*, 35; FLM, 19 August 1946, UAA, S131, item 7, 22; Horst Lücke, Interview by Rob Linn, 17 October 2006, UAA, S1345, transcript, 10.

3   'Future Accommodation of the Law School', FLM, 28 July 1958, UAA, S131, item 7; Provisional Report on Accommodation Requirements, FLM, 14 April 1958, UAA, S131, item 7.

4   Norval Morris to J.V. Barry, 19 August 1958, NLA, MS 2505/1/3449.

5   FLM, 1945–64, UAA, S131, item 7, 178, 180.

6   Arthur Rogerson, 'The Ligertwood Building', *Obiter Dicta*, August 1968, 7.

7   'What Next?', *On Dit*, 10 July 1961, 1.

8   'Editorial', *Lux Gentium*, Autumn 1964, 2.

9   FLM, 12 December 1963, UAA, S131, item 7, 344.

10   John W. Salmond, 'The Literature of Law', *Columbia Law Review* 22, no. 3 (1922): 198.

11   Report on Proposed New Building, North Terrace, 1959, UAA, S564, item 217, 8.

12   'Staff Development in 1965 and 1966', FLM, 4 May 1964, UAA, S131, item 7.

13   University of Adelaide, *Calendar*, 1956, 507; University of Adelaide, *Calendar*, 1960, 676.

14   'Student Cut at University "Unthinkable"', *Advertiser*, 29 December 1956, 3; FLM, 4 April 1966, UAA, S131, item 8, 34; Australia, *Fourth Report of the Australian Universities Commission*, Parliamentary Paper no. 81, 1969, 19–20; University of Adelaide, *Calendar*, 1967, 352; Selection Committee Report, 1967, UAA, S131, item 8, 74.

15   Norval Morris to J.V. Barry, 26 April 1960, NLA, MS 2505/1/4424.

16   Zelman Cowen to Erwin Griswold, 13 May 1952, NLA, MS 6736/3/17, 4.

17   Mark Finnane, 'Norval Morris (1923–2004)', *Current Issues in Criminal Justice* 15, no. 3 (2004): 267–71; Bonython Chair of Law 1957, UAA, S183, item 72.

18   'Professor Appears for Killer', *Advertiser*, 3 December 1957, 11; *R. v. Taylor and O'Meally* [1958] VR 285.

19   Geoffrey Tebbutt, 'He Hates Whippings Even More than Hangings', UAA, S163, item 35.

20   Norval Morris, Interview by Mark Finnane, 16 December 2003, NLA, ORAL TRC 5119, 64; Castles, Ligertwood, and Kelly, *Law on North Terrace*, 60.

21   Norval Morris to J.V. Barry, 17 July 1959, NLA, MS 2505/1/3935.

22   'Flogging "Not Useful"', *Advertiser*, 31 March 1958, 1; Norval Morris, 'Sentencing Convicted Criminals', *Australian Law Journal* 27, no. 3 (1953): 205.

23   Norval Morris, Interview by Mark Finnane, 16 December 2003, NLA, ORAL TRC 5119, 58.

24   Norval Morris to J.V. Barry, 7 July 1960, NLA, MS 2505/1/4612.

25   Norval Morris to J.V. Barry, 6 March 1961, NLA, MS 2505/1/5524.

26   Ceylon, *Report of the Commission of Inquiry on Capital Punishment*, Parliamentary Paper no. 14, 1959; Norval Morris to J.V. Barry, 8 November 1961, NLA, MS 2505/1/6138.

27   'A Freshman's Guide to the Staff', *Obiter Dicta*, August 1968, 56, 56.

28   Wilfrid Prest, 'Alex Castles: An Adelaide Perspective', *Legal History* 7, no. 1 (2003): 29–36; Alex Castles: CTEC Questionnaire Response, UAA, S1118, item 43/2.

29   Report on the Future Academic Shape of the Law School, FLM, 5 February 1962, UAA, S131, item 7, 4.

30 I.A. Shearer, ed., 'Daniel Patrick O'Connell, 1924–1979', 32, Typescript, 1981, Barr Smith Library, University of Adelaide.

31 FLM, 1895–1905, UAA, S131, item 3, 261–62, 282.

32 Memorandum on the Working of the Law Curriculum, FLM, 14 June 1955, UAA, S131, item 7; FLM, 1945–64, UAA, S131, item 7, 148, 195, 201.

33 'Lawyer and Language', *News*, 7 June 1939, 7.

34 FLM, 20 September 1943, UAA, S131, item 6, 280; FLM, 12 August 1957, UAA, S131, item 7, 161.

35 Memorandum on Options in the Curriculum, FLM, 12 May 1958, UAA, S131, item 7, 2, 5.

36 FLM, 1945–64, UAA, S131, item 7, 228, 231.

37 Shearer, 'Daniel Patrick O'Connell, 1924–1979', 30.

38 Bill Othams, Response to Adelaide Law School History Questionnaire, 2019; D.P. O'Connell, 'The Quality of (South) Australian Education', *Quadrant*, April 1971, 32.

39 I.A. Shearer, 'Obituary: Professor D.P. O'Connell', *Australian Year Book of International Law* 7 (1981): xxiv; FLM, 4 December 1961, UAA, S131, item 7, 279; C.H. Bright and Alex C. Castles, 'A New School of International Law', *Adelaide Law Review* 1, no. 3 (1962): 339–42; Staff Memorandum 16/75, John Keeler Papers, Departmental Committee Minutes 1975; Shearer, 'Daniel Patrick O'Connell, 1924–1979', 32–33, 37–40.

40 James Crawford, Interview, 19 January 1983, Barr Smith Library, University of Adelaide, Law School Oral History Archives.

41 Annual Report to AULSA, 1970, UAA, S1118, item 115.

42 Matthew Stubbs, 'The *Adelaide Law Review* at (Volume) 40: Reflections and Future Directions', *Adelaide Law Review* 40, no. 1 (2019): 3.

43 ibid., 2–3; 'Adelaide Law Review', *Obiter Dicta*, August 1968, 51; Adelaide Law Review Association Financial Statements, UAA, S1118, items 85/3 – 85/8.

44 Keith Sangster, Note on Refresher Training for Legal Profession (1975), Barr Smith Library, University of Adelaide, MSS 0130, series 6/4; 'Legal Seminar in Adelaide', *Law Council Newsletter*, May 1967, 21; Sentencing Institute Program, UAA, S1118, item 99; Horst Lücke to S.J. Jacobs, 23 November 1972, UAA, S1118, item 103; Horst Lücke to E.S. Barnes, 9 September 1977, UAA, S1118, item 60/2.

45 'A Freshman's Guide to the Staff', *Obiter Dicta*, August 1968, 56, 57.

46 Regular reports on the TV Project appeared in Law Students' Society publications. See also TV Project: Report to Law Society, September 1971, UAA, S1118, item 119; Lindy McNamara, 'Life Beyond the Law', *Bulletin: Law Society of South Australia*, July 2012, 32.

47 'Brief Pardoned', *On Dit*, 17 April 1959, 10.

48 Anonymous response to Adelaide Law School History Questionnaire, 2019.

NOTES

49 Olssen, E.A.: Appointment as Part-Time Assistant in Law Library, UAA, S200, item 46/1932; Olssen, Edwin Alexander: Staff Card, UAA, S587; 'Adult Education', *New Zealand Herald*, 23 March 1940, 13; 'University Staff', *Otago Daily Times*, 17 September 1947, 4.

50 Richard J.M. Finlay, 'Gwenda Fischer at the University of Adelaide Law Library' (typescript), Barr Smith Library, University of Adelaide, MSS 0158, series 1.

51 Richard J.M. Finlay, 'Funeral' (typescript), Barr Smith Library, University of Adelaide, MSS 0158, series 1.

52 Gwenda Sargeant, 'Libraries, Librarians and Society', Barr Smith Library, University of Adelaide, MSS 0158, series 5, 4.

53 Horst Lücke to Alex Castles, 28 September 1968, Horst Lücke Papers.

54 Gwenda Fischer to Registrar, 1 November 1968, Barr Smith Library, University of Adelaide, MSS 0158, series 5; Barr Smith Library: Librarian's Report, 1968, Barr Smith Library, University of Adelaide, MSS 0158, series 5; G.L. Fischer, *In Memoriam: Gwenda Clare Fischer, 1921–1998* (Brighton, SA: Pump Press, 1999); Gwenda Fischer, Curriculum Vitae, 1970, Barr Smith Library, University of Adelaide, MSS 0158, series 6; Gwenda Sargeant to Mrs C.M. Sargeant, 6 May 1962, Barr Smith Library, University of Adelaide, MSS 0158, series 5.

55 Brief to Architects for Stage I of a New Building for the Faculty of Law, UAA, S1118, item 157.

56 Australia, *Third Report of the Australian Universities Commission: Australian Universities 1964–1969*, Parliamentary Paper no. 330, 1966, 98–132.

57 'Fashion Feature', *Testis*, 1972, no. 2, 5.

58 Rogerson, 'The Ligertwood Building', *Obiter Dicta*, August 1968, 7.

59 Gwenda Fischer, 'The Law Library at the University of Adelaide, 1959–68', *Australian Library Journal* 8, no. 6 (1969): 215.

60 Brian Magarey, 'President's Report', *Law Society Bulletin*, September 1971.

61 Ron Newbold, 'Classics at the University of Adelaide (1874–2012)', in *A History of the Faculty of Arts at the University of Adelaide 1876–2012*, ed. Nick Harvey et al. (University of Adelaide Press, 2012), 101; Correspondence with Cheesman Doley Brabham and Neighbour, 1965–66, UAA, S564, item 198.

62 'A Coke's Tour of the Law School', *Lux Gentium*, 1967, no. 1, 13, 13.

63 Horst Lücke to Jacqueline Elliott, 31 March 1977, UAA, S1118, item 59.

64 R.F. Luxton to Chairs of Departments, 10 March 1977, UAA, S1118, item 72/1.

65 DCM, 26 February 1979, UAA, S1118, item 1/1, 4; Australia, *Fifth Report of the Australian Universities Commission*, Parliamentary Paper no. 120, 1972, 149; Law School Board Minutes, 4 June 2007, Adelaide Law School, 2.

66 Roy Green, Response to Adelaide Law School History Questionnaire, 2019.

67   Bill Othams, Response to Adelaide Law School History Questionnaire, 2019.

68   Callum Di Sario, Response to Adelaide Law School History Questionnaire, 2019.

69   'Building Works Anger Uni Staff', *Advertiser*, 8 March 1991, 8; Notice of Building Closure, March 1991, UAA, S1118, item 157; 'Building Blues', *Law Students Society Newsletter*, March 1991, 17.

70   Geoff Lindell, Interview by John Waugh, 31 May 2018.

71   'Obiter Dicta', *Hilarian*, 1994, no. 3, 23; I.A. Shearer, 'O'Connell, Daniel Patrick (1924–1979)', Australian Dictionary of Biography, 2006, https://adb.anu.edu.au/biography/oconnell-daniel-patrick-11280; Arthur Rogerson to V.A. Edgeloe, 27 February 1967, University of Adelaide Correspondence Files, 1967/305; Horst Lücke, 'Obituary: Alex Castles', *Adelaide Law Review* 24, no. 2 (2003): 147–48.

72   F.H. Lawson to Registrar, 13 June 1963, University of Adelaide Correspondence Files, 1963/218.

73   Arthur Rogerson to Registrar, 21 May 1963, University of Adelaide Correspondence Files, 1963/218.

74   Shearer, 'Daniel Patrick O'Connell, 1924–1979', 34.

75   Alex Castles to Horst Lücke, 11 September 1968, Horst Lücke Papers.

76   Horst Lücke to Alex Castles, 28 September 1968, Horst Lücke Papers.

5 A First-Class Fight: 1968–1979

1   Anonymous response to Adelaide Law School History Questionnaire, 2019.

2   'Fresher's Guide to Faculties', *On Dit*, 6 March 1968, 15.

3   Bill Othams, Response to Adelaide Law School History Questionnaire, 2019.

4   Finnis, *The Lower Level*, 173; 'Students Want Council Representation', *On Dit*, 9 July 1941, 2; 'Adelaide Behind Other Aust. 'Varsities', *On Dit*, 8 July 1960, 1.

5   FLM, 1965–72, UAA, S131, item 8, 139–40, 144, 146–47, 154, 157, 164.

6   University of Adelaide, *Calendar*, 1974, vol. 3, 1048.

7   Annual Report to AULSA, 1971, UAA, S1118, item 110/1, 2.

8   Lücke, 'Obituary: Alex Castles', 149; 'The Gilbert Jessop Society', Barr Smith Library, University of Adelaide, MSS 0130, series 6.

9   Paul N. Savoy, 'Toward a New Politics of Legal Education', *Yale Law Journal* 79, no. 3 (1970): 445.

10   Submission on Increased Student Membership, FLM, 7 August 1972, UAA, S131, item 8.

11   FLM, 7 August 1972, UAA, S131, item 8, 300–301.

12   Rex Hunter to Law School Liaison Committee, 9 February 1978, UAA, S1515, item 1; FLM, 7 February 1972, UAA, S131, item 8, 273; FLM, 7 June

NOTES

1976, UAA, S131, item 11, 475; DCM, 16 June 1983, UAA, S1118, item 1/2, 3.

13   Adelaide Law School, *Student Guide*, 1979, 17.

14   'Letter to the Editor', *Cobwebs*, 1980, no. 1, 4.

15   University of Adelaide, *Calendar*, 1969, 130.

16   ibid., 112.

17   David Kelly, Submission on Administration of the Law School, 6 August 1969, John Keeler Papers, DCM 1969–71, 2.

18   Bonython Chair of Law: Terms of Appointment, University of Adelaide Correspondence Files, 1963/218.

19   Horst Lücke, Interview by Rob Linn, 17 October 2006, UAA, S1345, transcript, 14.

20   Horst Lücke to Ivan Shearer, 30 July 1969, John Keeler Papers, DCM 1969–71.

21   Staff Association Sub-Committee on University Government: Position Paper, UAA, S1118, item 61, 6.

22   John Keeler, Interview by John Waugh, 4 September 2018.

23   Horst Lücke to Alex Castles, 28 September 1968, Horst Lücke Papers.

24   John Keeler, Interview by John Waugh, 4 September 2018.

25   Horst Lücke to Ivan Shearer, 30 July 1969, John Keeler Papers, DCM 1969–71, 1; Memorandum from Alex Castles to Staff, 19 March 1969, John Keeler Papers, DCM 1969–71.

26   John Keeler, Interview by Stephen Beaumont, May 2013, UAA, S1345.

27   Proposals for Revision of the Administrative Structure of the Law School, 1969, John Keeler Papers, DCM 1969–71.

28   ibid., 7.

29   Report of the Committee on the Departmental Structure of the Law School, 1969, UAA, S1118, item 61, 8–9, 15.

30   Horst Lücke to Ivan Shearer, 30 July 1969, John Keeler Papers, DCM 1969–71.

31   Memorandum from M.J. Trebilcock to All Staff, 27 June 1969, UAA, S1118, item 61.

32   Arthur Rogerson, Comments on Proposed Administrative Structure of the Department of Law, 17 October 1969, John Keeler Papers, DCM 1969–71.

33   Arthur Rogerson to Vice-Chancellor, 16 October 1969, University of Adelaide Correspondence Files, 1963/218.

34   Horst Lücke to Alex Castles, 4 March 1970, Horst Lücke Papers.

35   Horst Lücke, Interview by Rob Linn, 17 October 2006, UAA, S1345, transcript, 12.

36   University Council Minutes, 6 February 1970, UAA, S18, item 34, 6–7.

37   Alex Castles to Horst Lücke, 25 January 1970, Horst Lücke Papers.

38   Horst Lücke to Alex Castles, 3 November 1970, Horst Lücke Papers.

39 Alex Castles to Horst Lücke, 17 September 1970, Horst Lücke Papers.

40 Horst Lücke to L.W. Cox, 29 September 1972, John Keeler Papers, DCM July 1971–September 1972.

41 FLM, 1 October 1973, UAA, S131, item 9, 62; Departmental Government: Report of Standing Sub-Committee of the Education Committee, UAA, S1118, item 61; DCM, 1 September 1972 and 29 September 1972, John Keeler Papers.

42 Report on Governance and Management of the Law School, DCM, 26 March 1997, S1118, item 2/15, 2.

43 Response to CTEC Questionnaire, October 1985, UAA, S1118, item 43/3, 5–6.

44 A.P. Moore to G. Nash, 14 September 1979, UAA, S1118, item 95/1.

45 Prest, 'How We Got Here from There', 25.

46 P.B. Mayer, 'The Revolution of 1981: The Corbett Report and After', *Vestes: The Australian Universities Review* 26, no. 1 (1983): 45.

47 'Review of the Structure of the Central Administration: Interim Report', *University of Adelaide Bulletin*, 21 September 1979.

48 Andrew Ligertwood, Interview by John Waugh, 24 July 2019.

49 University of Adelaide, *Annual Report*, 1981, 14; John Keeler, Interview by Stephen Beaumont, May 2013, UAA, S1345.

50 DCM, 27 October 1975, UAA, S1118, item 63/1, 4.

51 Horst Lücke to Gwenda Fischer, 24 January 1972, Barr Smith Library, University of Adelaide, MSS 0158.

52 'Law School Development for the Triennium 1973–1975', UAA, S1118, item 46/2, 5.

53 FLM, 19 April 1971, UAA, S131, item 8, 224–25.

54 FLM, 6 September 1971, UAA, S131, item 8, 246.

55 Horst Lücke to L.W. Cox, 20 September 1971, in Faculty of Law Minutes, 4 October 1971, UAA, S131, item 8.

56 University Council Minutes, 1 October 1971, UAA, S18, item 35, 113.

57 David Kelly to G.M. Badger, 4 October 1971, in Faculty of Law Minutes, 4 October 1971, UAA, S131, item 8.

58 FLM, 4 October 1971, UAA, S131, item 8, 249–51.

59 FLM, 18 October 1971, UAA, S131, item 8, 253.

60 Samuel Jacobs, Interview by Rob Linn, 23 August 2007, UAA, S1345, item 9, transcript, 32.

61 FLM, 18 October 1971, UAA, S131, item 8, 253; University of Adelaide, *Calendar*, 1972, vol. 2, 467; Adelaide Law School, *Student Guide*, 1979, 3.

62 Horst Lücke to S.J. Jacobs, 11 January 1972, UAA, S1118, item 114/2.

63 'From the President', *Law Society Bulletin*, July 1973, 1.

64 Notice to students, 28 January 1972, UAA, S1118, item 114/2.

65 DCM, 12 November 1971, John Keeler Papers.

NOTES

66   FLM, 1 November 1971, UAA, S131, item 8, 258; FLM, 5 March 1973, UAA, S131, item 9, 12.

67   Horst Lücke to P.M. Nickolls, 19 May 1972, UAA, S1118, item 114/2.

68   John Keeler to Chief Justice, 10 September 1975, UAA, S1118, item 107; Chief Justice to President, Law Society, 13 November 1972, FLM, 15 December 1972, UAA, S131, item 8; R.G. Matheson to Chief Justice, 3 June 1975, FLM, 4 August 1975, UAA, S131, item 10.

69   R.G. Matheson to John Keeler, 23 September 1975, FLM, 6 October 1975, UAA, S131, item 10, 367.

70   John Keeler to M.F. O'Loughlin, 7 October 1975, UAA, S1118, item 107; Council of Legal Education: Summary of Meeting, 27 November 1975, UAA, S1118, item 73; FLM, 1 March 1976, UAA, S131, item 11, 422–25; P.R. Morgan, 'Legal Practitioners Bill', *Law Society Bulletin*, February 1975, 4.

71   Selection Committee Report, FLM, 4 June 1973, UAA, S131, item 9.

72   'From the President', *Law Society Bulletin*, February 1974, 1; Chief Justice to Alex Castles, 28 May 1973, FLM, 4 June 1973, UAA, S131, item 9; John Keeler to M.F. O'Loughlin, 22 November 1976, UAA, S1118, item 59.

73   FLM, 3 July 1972, UAA, S131, item 8, 298.

74   South Australia, *Parliamentary Debates* (House of Assembly, 12 June 1975), 3363; Horst Lücke to I.A. Shearer, 8 May 1974, UAA, S1118, item 113; 'President's Report', *Law Society Bulletin*, September 1976, 1.

75   'Law School Development for the Triennium 1973–1975', UAA, S1118, item 46/2, 5.

76   ibid.

77   Annual Report to AULSA, 1971, UAA, S1118, item 110/1, 2.

78   President, Law Society, to Alex Castles, 28 November 1972, FLM, 15 December 1972, UAA, S131, item 8.

79   FLM, 19 February 1973, UAA, S131, item 9, 9.

80   ibid.

81   FLM, 3 March 1975, UAA, S131, item 10, 239.

82   Meeting of Law Students, 1 October 1974, UAA, S1118, item 113.

83   'The Case for a Course of Practical Legal Instruction', UAA, S1118, item 75/2, 3; G.J. Mathiesen to John Keeler, undated, UAA, S1118, item 107; R.G. Matheson to Minister of Education, 21 August 1975, FLM, 1 September 1975, UAA, S131, item 10; J.W. von Doussa, '20 Years PLT in South Australia', UAA, S204, Meeting 2/96, 71–72; 'Rules of Court Amending the Supreme Court Admission Rules', *South Australian Government Gazette*, 13 October 1977, 1072.

84   FLM, 7 August 1967, UAA, S131, item 8, 88.

85   Academic Registrar to Faculty Members and Chairs of Committees, 9 October 1969, in Faculty of Law Minutes, 6 October 1969, UAA, S131, item 8.

86   FLM, 6 October 1969, UAA, S131, item 8, 158.

87   FLM, 6 April 1970, UAA, S131, item 8, 177; FLM, 3 November 1969, UAA, S131, item 8, 162–63.

88   FLM, 16 April 1970, UAA, S131, item 8, 180.

89   Horst Lücke to Alex Castles, 23 April 1970, Horst Lücke Papers.

90   Alex Castles to Horst Lücke, 12 May 1970, Horst Lücke Papers.

91   Report of Sub-Committee on Supplementary Exams and Legal Ethics and Accounts, FLM, 7 September 1970, UAA, S131, item 8; FLM, 1965–72, UAA, S131, item 8, 181–82, 189–90.

92   Alex Castles to J.E. Richardson, 30 April 1973, UAA, S1118, item 85/5.

93   Rex Hunter to Colin Howard, 13 June 1978, UAA, S1118, item 45/2; Alex Castles to Registrar, 26 September 1974, UAA, S1118, item 46/2.

94   Selection Committee Report, 1967, UAA, S131, item 8, 74; FLM, 1976, UAA, S131, item 11, 481, 522–23; Matthew Goode, Report on Role of Course Advisor, 27 August 1980, UAA, S131, item 13, 237–38.

95   Report of Committee on Future Accommodation, 1964, UAA, S131, item 7, 366.

96   FLM, 16 April 1970, UAA, S131, item 8, 181.

97   Horst Lücke to Alex Castles, 4 March 1970, Horst Lücke Papers.

98   Alex Castles to Horst Lücke, 15 September 1970, Horst Lücke Papers.

99   FLM, 2 November 1970, UAA, S131, item 8, 203–04.

100 Flinders University Submission to the Australian Universities Commission, 1976–1978 Triennium: Proposal for a School of Law, UAA, S1118, item 63/1, 4.

101 Australia, *Sixth Report of the Australian Universities Commission*, Parliamentary Paper no. 271, 1975, 106; Australia, *Universities Commission: Report for Triennium 1977–1979*, Parliamentary Paper no. 23, 1977, 87.

102 Dean's Notes on Agenda, FLM, 4 October 1976, UAA, S131, item 11, 535.

103 C.H. Bright to Dean, Faculty of Law, 10 April 1973, UAA, S1118, item 53.

104 Cedric Thomson to I.A. Shearer, 18 September 1973, UAA, S1118, item 114/2; FLM, 6 December 1976, UAA, S131, item 11, 577.

105 Horst Lücke to P.H. Glow, 23 May 1978, UAA, S1118, item 46/1.

106 Horst Lücke to A.E. Shields, 29 September 1976, UAA, S1118, item 46/1, 4.

107 Student/Staff Ratios, 1971, UAA, S1118, item 115; Notes on the Sixth Report of the Universities Commission, FLM, 4 August 1975, UAA, S131, item 10, 333, 333; 'Staff and WSUs as at 30 April Each Year', UAA, S204, item 1983/84-2; Australia, *Sixth Report of the Australian Universities Commission* (1975), 171.

108 Alex Castles to Horst Lücke, 22 June 1970, Horst Lücke Papers.

109 Horst Lücke to Illa Nicholls, 11 September 1972, UAA, S1118, item 113.

110 Alex Castles to Registrar, 26 September 1974, UAA, S1118, item 46/2; DCM, 28 April 1980, UAA, S1118, item 1/1.

111 Adelaide Law School, *Student Guide*, 1974, 7.

112 FLM, 6 December 1971, UAA, S131, item 8, 266; 'Poor Persons Legal Relief in South Australia', *Law Institute Journal*, 1 October 1934, 162; Magarey and Round, *Roma the First*, 105; Jack Beards, 'Law Students' Legal Aid Group', *Testis*, Orientation 1972, 23, UAA, S1118, item 153/1; David Pearce to Academic Staff, 24 April 1972; UAA, S1118, item 114/2; 'Auction Shop Show: Second Act', *On Dit*, 1 April 1973, 5; 'Legal Aid Society', *Just Quietly: Law Students' Society Newsletter*, March 1985, 6.

113 Tim Reeves, 'Duncan, George Ian (1930–1972)', Australian Dictionary of Biography, 2006, https://adb.anu.edu.au/biography/duncan-george-ian-10063; Tim Reeves, 'Dr Duncan Revisited', *Journal of the Historical Society of South Australia*, no. 44 (2016): 117–26.

114 Tim Reeves, *The Death of Dr Duncan* (Adelaide: Wakefield Press, 2022), 13, 31; 'Ads & Information', *Gay News* (London), 28 June 1973, 19.

115 Dino Hodge, *Don Dunstan: Intimacy & Liberty: A Political Biography* (Kent Town, SA: Wakefield Press, 2014), 96–97.

116 Reeves, *The Death of Dr Duncan*, 35–42, 84–85; Report to Commissioner of Police on Death of Dr George Ian Ogilvie Duncan, by Criminal Investigation Department of New Scotland Yard, October 1972, SLSA, D 8754(L)/1, paras 45–84.

117 Horst Lücke, Interview by Rob Linn, 17 October 2006, UAA, S1345, transcript, 21.

118 'Text of Letters in Torrens Drowning Case', *Advertiser*, 2 June 1972, 8.

119 'Reward May Be Offered on Duncan Killing', *Advertiser*, 6 July 1972, 1.

120 'Police Officers May Be Questioned', *Advertiser*, 8 June 1972, 6; Bob Whitington, 'Police Questioned Over River Death', *Advertiser*, 20 May 1972, 1, second edition; 'Approach to Police Chief on Drowning', *Advertiser*, 29 May 1972, 1; Reeves, *The Death of Dr Duncan*, 72–76.

121 Scotland Yard Report, SLSA, D 8754(L)/1, para. 50.

122 Graham Willett, *Living Out Loud: A History of Gay and Lesbian Activism in Australia* (St Leonards, NSW: Allen & Unwin, 2000), 42–45; 'Opinion', *On Dit*, 24 March 1961, 8; 'Abreast of the Times', *On Dit*, 1 August 1962, 6; 'The Homosexual Villain', *On Dit*, 25 September 1964, 8; 'Four Essays upon Aspects of Homosexuality', *On Dit*, 5 August 1969, 5; 'SAUA Elections', *On Dit*, 11 September 1972, 6.

123 Tim Reeves, 'The 1972 Debate on Male Homosexuality in South Australia', in *Gay Perspectives II: More Essays in Australian Gay Culture*, ed. Robert Aldrich (Sydney: University of Sydney, 1993), 170.

124 *Criminal Law Consolidation Act Amendment Act 1972*, no. 94 (SA), s. 3.

6 Gatekeeping: 1980–1989

1 Jen Marshall, 'Abschol', *On Dit*, 19 April 1962, 7; Tom Gara, 'The Aboriginal Presence in Adelaide, 1860s–1960s: From Exclusion to Assimilation', in *Colonialism and Its Aftermath: A History of Aboriginal South*

Australia, ed. Peggy Brock and Tom Gara (Mile End, SA: Wakefield Press, 2017), 101, 103; Jennifer Clark, *Aborigines & Activism: Race, Aborigines & the Coming of the Sixties to Australia* (Crawley, WA: UWA Press, 2008), 140–45.

2   Edmund Wanganeen, ed., *Justice Without Prejudice: The Development of the Aboriginal Legal Rights Movement in South Australia* (Underdale, SA: Aboriginal Studies and Teacher Education Centre, SACAE, 1986); Bernard J. O'Neil, 'Beyond Trinkets and Beads: South Australia's Aboriginal Legal Rights Movement, 1971–1978', *Aboriginal History* 6, no. 1 (1982): 28–38; FLM, 3 February 1975, UAA, S131, item 10, 216; Course Proposal: Aborigines and the Law, UAA, S1513, item 6/1.

3   FLM, 5 November 1973, UAA, S131, item 9, 70; John Keeler to John Goldring, 14 January 1976, UAA, S1118, item 45/1.

4   Irene Watson, 'Colonial Logic and the Coorong Massacres', *Adelaide Law Review* 40, no. 1 (2019): 171.

5   ibid., 167.

6   Stewart Motha, 'The History of a Lie: The Mabo Case after 30 Years', Countersign—A Podcast, accessed 31 May 2022, https://countersignisapodcast.com/podcasts/ the-history-of-a-lie-the-mabo-case-after-30-years/.

7   Lindy McNamara, 'History a Turning Point for Irene', *Bulletin: Law Society of South Australia*, October 2017, 14; Alison Mackinnon, *A New Kid on the Block: The University of South Australia in the Unified National System* (Carlton, Vic.: Melbourne University Publishing, 2016), 82; 'Student Lounge', *Law Students Society Newsletter*, April 1989.

8   Andrea Mason, 'Where Do a Bird and a Fish Build a House? An Alumna's View on a Reconciled Nation', *Adelaide Law Review* 40, no. 1 (2019): 181.

9   Stuart Macintyre, Gwilym Croucher, and André Brett, *No End of a Lesson: Australia's National System of Higher Education* (Carlton, Vic.: Melbourne University Publishing, 2017), 117–18; Harry Hobbs and George Williams, 'The Participation of Indigenous Australians in Legal Education, 2001–18', *UNSW Law Journal* 42, no. 4 (2019): 1308; Nicole Watson, 'Indigenous Legal Traditions and Australian Legal Education', in *The Cambridge Legal History of Australia*, ed. Peter Cane, Lisa Ford, and Mark McMillan (Cambridge: Cambridge University Press, 2022), 719–64.

10   University of Adelaide, *Annual Report*, 1982, 10.

11   DCM, 23 September 1982, UAA, S1118, item 1/2, 3; University of Adelaide, *Review of Governance: Final Report*, 1990, 62, 74–76; University of Adelaide, *Annual Report*, 1987, 88.

12   Adelaide Law School, *Student Guide*, 1984, 24.

13   'Hitler Burnt the Books …', *40%*, 1983, No. 5, 2.

14   Law Society Submissions to CTEC Review of Australian Law Courses (1985), UAA, S1118, item 43/3, Appendix; J. Parham, 'Women and Law', *Law Students Society Newsletter*, April 1989; Adelaide Law School, *Handbook of Studies for the Bachelor of Laws*, 1995, 66; Kamini Davenport,

'Davenport in a Storm', *Hilarian*, 1996, no. 1, 5, UAA, S950, item 85; FLM, 16 September 1996, UAA, S204, Meeting 4/96, 1.

15   Hilary Charlesworth, Interview by John Waugh, 26 July 2018.

16   Judith Gardam, Interview by John Waugh, 19 October 2018; Margaret Allen and Susan Magarey, 'Gender Studies and Social Analysis', in *A History of the Faculty of Arts at the University of Adelaide 1876–2012*, ed. Nicholas Harvey et al. (University of Adelaide Press, 2012), 209–20.

17   University of Adelaide, 'University of Adelaide Announces ICAC Response', Newsroom, 24 June 2021, https://www.adelaide.edu.au/newsroom/news/list/2021/06/24/university-of-adelaide-announces-icac-response.

18   Robyn Layton, Interview, 15 June 1981, Barr Smith Library, University of Adelaide, Law School Oral History Archives.

19   ibid.

20   'It's Academic Rape', *55%*, 1981, no. 2, 12.

21   University of Adelaide, *Annual Report*, 1982, 10–11.

22   Australia, *Sixth Report of the Australian Universities Commission* (1975), 91–92.

23   R.E. Bogner, 'Development without Growth', *Lumen*, 28 November 1975, 6.

24   University of Adelaide, *Annual Report*, 1982, 3; University of Adelaide, *Annual Report*, 1984, 5; Compact Discussions 1984: Faculty of Law Submission, UAA, S204, item 1983/84-1, 5; Faculty of Law 1988–90 Triennial Submission, UAA, S204, item 1985/86-4, 5.

25   University of Adelaide, *Annual Report*, 1981, 11; Compact of Deans, FLM, 13 July 1981, UAA, S131, item 14, 61; Mayer, 'The Revolution of 1981: The Corbett Report and After', 47; DCM, 18 June 1981, UAA, S1118, item 1/2, 5.

26   Compact Discussions 1984: Faculty of Law Submission, UAA, S204, item 1983/84-1, 1.

27   Faculty of Law Report no. 2/85, UAA, S204, item 1985/86-1, 1–2.

28   Compact Discussions 1984: Faculty of Law Submission, UAA, S204, item 1983/84-1, 8.

29   ibid., Appendix A.

30   Faculty of Law Report no. 2/85, UAA, S204, item 1985/86-1, 1.

31   Compact Discussions 1984: Faculty of Law Submission, UAA, S204, item 1983/84-1, 9; Draft Response to Law Society Letter, 8 July 1986, UAA, S204, item 1985/86-2, 3.

32   FLM, 13 July 1981, UAA, S131, item 14, 62.

33   ibid., 67.

34   ibid., 70.

35   DCM, 30 July 1981, UAA, S1118, item 1/2, 1; Michael Detmold to Faculty Members, 6 July 1981, UAA, S131, item 14, 66.

36 Tony Moore to Michael Detmold, 31 July 1981, UAA, S131, item 14, 77.

37 FLM, 10 August 1981, UAA, S131, item 14, 83.

38 'The Student Opinion on the Quota', UAA, S131, item 14, 79.

39 FLM, 10 August 1981, UAA, S131, item 14, 83.

40 Faculty of Law 1988–90 Triennial Submission, UAA, S204, item 1985/86-4, 4.

41 Dean to Staff, 18 September 1984, UAA, S1511, item 11/2.

42 Louise Boylen, 'Law Faculty Calls for Quota Cuts', *Australian*, 17 October 1984, 15.

43 Faculty of Law Report no. 4/82, UAA, S204, item 1981/82-1, 2; FLM, 1 October 1984, UAA, S204, item 1983/84-2, 12.

44 FLM, 1 October 1984, UAA, S204, item 1983/84-2, 8.

45 University Council Minutes, 14 December 1984, UAA, S204, item 1985/86-4, 19.

46 Chief Justice to Donald Stranks, 30 October 1984, UAA, S204, item 1985-86/4.

47 Donald Stranks to Chairman, Education Committee, and others, 18 October 1984, UAA, S204, item 1985/86-4.

48 DCM, 9 July 1981, UAA, S1118, item 1/2, 3.

49 'Teaching Initiatives in 1986: Quota Reduction', UAA, S204, item 1985/86-4, 1; Jim Hambrook to Members of Faculty, February 1985, and Harry Medlin to Jim Hambrook, 11 April 1985, UAA, S204, item 1985/86-4; Harry Medlin correspondence with Jim Hambrook, 1985, UAA, S631, item 211.

50 Selection Committee Report, FLM, 4 June 1973, UAA, S131, item 9.

51 Rob Fowler, Interview by John Waugh, 28 March 2019.

52 Anonymous response to Adelaide Law School History Questionnaire, 2019.

53 'WWJD? What Would Jay Do?', *Hilarian*, 2015, no. 1, 7; J.R. Bradsen and J.A. Farrington, 'Student Selection and Performance in the Faculty of Law, the University of Adelaide', *Australian Universities Review* 29, no. 1 (1986): 31.

54 Bradsen and Farrington, 'Student Selection and Performance in the Faculty of Law', 30.

55 ibid.; Faculty of Law Report no. 4/85, UAA, S204, item 1985/86-1, 5.

56 'Curriculum Reform 1985/86', UAA, S204, item 1985/86-1, 4–5.

57 Ingmar Taylor, 'President's Welcome', *Testis*, 1987, no. 1.

58 University Council Minutes, 9 August 1985, UAA, S18, item 49, 150–52; Faculty Report 10/89, UAA, S1118, item 10.

59 Andrew Ligertwood, Interview by John Waugh, 24 July 2019.

60 Students Enrolling for the First Time in the Faculty of Law, 1985 to 1989, UAA, S950, item 74, 7, 17; University Council Minutes, 9 August 1985,

UAA, S18, item 49, 152; Law Society Submissions to CTEC Review of Australian Law Courses, UAA, S1118, item 43/3, 17–18; Rodney Burr, Interview by Lindy McNamara, 4 July 2014, Law Society of South Australia Oral Histories, https://www.lawsocietysa.asn.au/Public/About/Oral_ Histories/Burr.aspx.

61   FLM, 5 April 1982, UAA, S131, item 14, 185.

62   'University Law Library Sponsorships', UAA, S1118, item 158; DCM, 17 March 1983, UAA, S1118, item 1/2, 1; E.G. Whitlam, 'The Machinery of Democracy', *Adelaide Law Review* 9, no. 2 (1983): 229–34; Horst Lücke, A Short History of the Adelaide Law School, Horst Lücke Papers.

63   'Faculty of Law: Overall Resources', UAA, S204, item 1983/84-3, 10.

64   Extract from Faculty of Law Report No. 6/76, UAA, S1176, item 7; Australia, *Sixth Report of the Australian Universities Commission* (1975), 136.

65   'Items of Interest', *Law Society Journal* (Sydney), March 1965, 19.

66   Curriculum Committee Report on AUC Submissions 1976–78, UAA, S1118, item 42, 2.

67   Extract from Faculty of Law Report No. 6/76, UAA, S1176, item 7; FLM, 1 October 1979, UAA, S131, item 13, 92; Dennis Pearce, Enid Campbell, and Don Harding, *Australian Law Schools: A Discipline Assessment for the Commonwealth Tertiary Education Commission* (Canberra: Australian Government Publishing Service, 1987), vol. 1, 245.

68   FLM, 1 October 1984, UAA, S204, item 1983/84-2, 6.

69   FLM, 1 October 1979, UAA, S131, item 13, 84; DCM, 18 November 1982, UAA, S1118, item 1, 2; FLM, 8 August 1983, UAA, S204, item 1983/84-2, 5–6; Report on Reform of the Master of Legal Studies, UAA, S204, item 1985/86-2, 6–7; Pearce, Campbell, and Harding, *Australian Law Schools*, vol. 1, 232.

70   Proposed Postgraduate Degrees and Diplomas, UAA, S204, item 1985/86-1, 8.

71   Rob Fowler to Jim Hambrook, 13 March 1986, UAA, S204, item 1985/86-4.

72   Report on Reform of the Master of Legal Studies, UAA, S204, item 1985/86-2, 2; Law School Strategic Plan 1992–95, UAA, S950, item 4, 17.

73   Pearce, Campbell, and Harding, *Australian Law Schools*, vol. 1, 209.

74   ibid., 209–10.

75   'Students to Give Their Opinion of Lecturer', *News*, 11 May 1954, 9; Macintyre, Croucher, and Brett, *No End of a Lesson*, 173–75; Pearce, Campbell, and Harding, *Australian Law Schools*, vol. 4, 166.

76   Dennis Pearce, 'The Past Is a Different Country', in *The Future of Australian Legal Education: A Collection*, ed. Kevin Lindgren, François Kunc, and Michael Coper (Sydney: Lawbook Co., 2018), 53.

7 School and Faculty: 1990–1999

1 von Doussa, '20 Years PLT in South Australia', UAA, S204, Meeting 2/96, 72–73.

2 John Keeler, 'Practical Legal Training', UAA, S1118, item 142/1, 4.

3 Katherine Dellit and Beverli Newbold, 'Get a Job!', *Hilarian*, 1995, no. 1, 4; Macintyre, Croucher, and Brett, *No End of a Lesson*, 158; Jane Dargaville, 'Fee Proposal Reconsidered', *Canberra Times*, 11 August 1994, 7; Justice Mullighan to the Judges, 13 September 1995, UAA, S1118, item 142/1, 2.

4 Law Students' Society Media Release, 7 August 1995, UAA, S1118, item 142/1.

5 FLM, 15 December 1995, UAA, S204, Meeting 9/95, 2; Admission Procedures Review Committee Report, UAA, S1118, item 144/2.

6 'PLT at Flinders: Reaching a Decision', UAA, S1118, item 142/2; 'Post LLB Teaching in the Law School: A Discussion Paper', UAA, S1118, Meeting 7/95; 'Proposal Concerning Practical Legal Training', UAA, S204, Meeting 2/96; Meeting of Law School Representatives, 6 November 1996, UAA, S204, Meeting 5/96; Meeting of PLT Advisory Group, 22 January 1997, UAA, S1118, item 142/3.

7 Rob Fowler to Mary O'Kane, 26 June 1996, UAA, S1118, item 142/2.

8 David Meyer to Rob Fowler, 25 February 1997, UAA, S1118, item 142/3; Agreement between Law Society and University of Adelaide, December 1998, UAA, S1118, item 142/5.

9 Background paper by Justice Perry, November 1995, UAA, S1118, item 142/1, 10–11; John Doyle to Rob Fowler, 27 May 1997, UAA, S1118, item 142/4.

10 John Doyle to Dean Clayton, 29 September 1995, UAA, S1118, item 144/1.

11 Memo from John Perry to Admission Procedures Review Committee, 29 March 1996, UAA, S1118, item 144/1, 2.

12 'The Position of the Law Society', UAA, S1118, item 144/1, 1; 'From the Prez', *Law Students Society Newsletter*, March 1989.

13 Katherine Dellit and Nick Gallus to Admissions Procedures Review Committee, 26 March 1996, UAA, S1118, item 144/1.

14 John Doyle to Trevor Griffin, 31 July 1996, UAA, S1118, item 144/2, 3.

15 John Doyle to Kath McEvoy, 27 August 2001, UAA, S1118, item 14.

16 Paul Fairall to John Doyle, 22 June 2004, UAA, S204, item 2004.

17 John Keeler to Larry Frakes, draft, 15 January 1990, UAA, S1118, item 157; Adelaide Law School, *Annual Report*, 1993, 7.

18 Law School Strategic Plan 1992–95, UAA, S950, item 4, 3.

19 Macintyre, Croucher, and Brett, *No End of a Lesson*, 156–57; FLM, 6 October 1986, UAA, S204, item 1985/86-3, 6–7; Adelaide Law School, *Annual Report*, 1996, 24; William and Mary Summer Law Program,

NOTES

1992–98, UAA, S1118, item 164; Law School Executive Minutes, 16 August 1999, UAA, S204, EEC 3/99, 1–2.

20 Mike Rann, Interview by Kerrie Round, 7 May 2003, Barr Smith Library, University of Adelaide, MSS 0125, series 3, transcript.

21 Hilary Charlesworth, Interview by John Waugh, 26 July 2018.

22 'Editorial', *Hilarian*, April 1996, 2; Mark Clisby, 'Battle of the Law School Funding', *Bulletin: Law Society of South Australia*, March 1992, 10; Memo by Rob Fowler: Academic Staff Retreat, 1996, UAA, S1118, item 2/9.

23 The New Adelaide Law School: Planning, UAA, S204, EEC 2/99, 1.

24 Meeting Notes: Student Focus Group, 3 September 1997, UAA, S1118, item 3/4; 1994 Course Experience Questionnaire: Summary of Results for Law, UAA, S1118, item 13; DCM, 12 August 1996, UAA, S1118, item 2/11; FLM, 25 November 1996, UAA, S204, Meeting 5/96, 5–6.

25 Dean's Report, 29 July 1996, UAA, S204, Meeting 3/96, 2.

26 DCM, 16 December 1998, UAA, S204, Meeting 1/99, 3.

27 Law School Board Minutes, 3 May 1999, UAA, S204, Meeting 2/99, 4.

28 Dean's Report, 4 May 1998, UAA, S204, Meeting 2/98, 4; DCM, 16 February 1998, UAA, S1118, item 2/23, 2.

29 G.E. Dal Pont, *Lawyers' Professional Responsibility in Australia and New Zealand*, 1st ed. (Sydney: LBC Information Services, 1996), 23.

30 Dean's Report, 29 July 1996, UAA, S204, Meeting 3/96, 4.

31 LLB Curriculum Working Party Report, UAA, S204, FLM, February 1997, 4.

32 Rachel Spencer, Response to Adelaide Law School History Questionnaire, 2019.

33 FLM, 6 April 1998, UAA, S204, Meeting 1/98, 3.

34 FLM, 20 October 1997, UAA, S204, Meeting 4/97, 3–4; LLB Curriculum Review: Outline of Revised Proposals, UAA, S204, Meeting 4/97; Pearce, Campbell, and Harding, *Australian Law Schools*, vol. 4, 166.

35 Dean's Report, 21 June 1999, UAA, S204, Meeting 3/1999.

36 Submission by JFK (John Keeler), UAA, S1540, item 2/2, 13.

37 Memo from Ben Allgrove and Elysia Turcinovic to Executive Committee, 6 October 1999, UAA, S204, EEC 3/99, 10.

38 'Revitalising the Law School: A Funding Strategy', UAA, S950, item 5, 9.

39 Macintyre, Croucher, and Brett, *No End of a Lesson*, 144–47, 196–98.

40 Meeting of Committee of Australian Law Deans, 23–24 April 1998, UAA, S204, Meeting 2/98, 1.

41 DCM, 3 November 1997, UAA, S1118, item 2/21, 1.

42 Dean's Report, 25 November 1996, UAA, S204, Meeting 5/96, 1.

43 ibid., 2.

44 'Revitalising the Law School: A Funding Strategy', UAA, S950, item 5.

45 FLM, 25 November 1996, UAA, S204, Meeting 5/96, 2.

46 Michelle Daw, 'Uni Bid for Fee-Paying Students Under Fire', *Advertiser*, 14 August 1997, 5.

47 'Curriculum Reform: What Decisions Do We Need to Make?', UAA, S1118, item 2/18, 1.

48 University of Adelaide, *Annual Report*, 1998, 11; Selection Committee Report, 1998, UAA, S204, Meeting 1/98, 3; Selection/Admissions 2000, UAA, S204, Meeting 2/2000, 2; Background Information for Law School Review Committee, UAA, S1540, item 2/1, 27–28; Law School Board Minutes, 12 March 2001, UAA, S204, Meeting 2/2001, 7.

49 'Post LLB Teaching in the Law School: A Discussion Paper', UAA, S1118, Meeting 7/95; Dean's Report, 29 July 1996, UAA, S204, Meeting 3/96, 3.

50 Draft Research Management Plan, UAA, S204, Meeting 7/95, 1.

51 Postgraduate Coursework Program, UAA, S204, Meeting 6/96; FLM, 20 December 1996, UAA, S204, Meeting 6/96, 6; Memo from Rob Fowler to Doug McEachern, 6 May 1998, UAA, S203, item 6.

52 Dellit and Newbold, 'Get a Job!', *Hilarian*, 1995, no. 1, 4.

53 Submission by JFK (John Keeler), UAA, S1540, item 2/2, 18–19.

54 Robert Fowler to John Perry, 28 June 1996, UAA, S204, Meeting 3/96.

55 Dean's Report, 27 March 1995, UAA, S204, Meeting 3/95, 2.

56 John Perry to Vice-Chancellor, 21 July 1995, UAA, S204, Meeting 7/95.

57 Planning Issues: A Discussion Paper, May 1994, UAA, S1118, item 6/1, 7; Christopher Richards, 'Medical Schools Aim for Students a Cut Above', *Age*, 17 November 1998, 26; Mary O'Kane, 'Student Selection Procedures Row', *Advertiser*, 16 January 1999, 22.

58 Meeting Notes: Student Focus Group, 3 September 1997, UAA, S1118, item 3/4, 4.

59 Selection Committee Report: Direct Selection of Elite Matriculants, UAA, S204, Meeting 5/95; Selection Committee Report, 1997, UAA, S204, Meeting 2/97, 4–5; FLM, 25 November 1996, UAA, S204, Meeting 5/96, 4; FLM, 20 December 1996, UAA, S204, Meeting 6/96, 5.

60 Robert Fowler to John Perry, 28 June 1996, UAA, S204, Meeting 3/96, 5.

61 Selection Committee Report, 1997, UAA, S204, Meeting 2/97, 1; Selection Committee Report, 1998, UAA, S204, Meeting 1/98, 2; Kath McEvoy, 'Selection and Related Issues for 2002 and Beyond', UAA, S204, Meeting 5/2001.

62 Australia, *Higher Education: A Policy Statement*, Parliamentary Paper no. 202, 1988, 103.

63 Fred McDougall and Gary Martin, Interview by Rob Linn, 7 June 2010, UAA, S1345, item 18.

64 University of Adelaide, *Review of Governance*, 12, 20, 21; Commonwealth Tertiary Education Commission, *Review of Efficiency and Effectiveness in Higher Education*, Parliamentary Paper no. 415, 1986; Macintyre, Croucher, and Brett, *No End of a Lesson*, 69–70.

NOTES

65   Procedures for Election of Dean, 1993, UAA, S1118, item 159; Review of Governance: Submission of the Department of Law, UAA, S1118, item 159, 1–2; University of Adelaide, *Review of Governance*, 59; Memo from Adrian Bradbrook to Teaching Staff, 20 September 1993, UAA, S1118, item 159.

66   Rob Fowler, Interview by John Waugh, 28 March 2019.

67   Executive Committee Position Paper on Faculty Structure and Proportional Representation, EX 8/86/3/12/348, John Keeler Papers, Appendix I.

68   University of Adelaide, *Review of Governance*, 30.

69   FLM, 16 December 1994, UAA, S204, Meeting 1/95, 7.

70   ibid., 8.

71   University of Adelaide, *Review of Governance*, 30.

72   Notes from Consultations with General Staff, UAA, S1043, Academic Board 2/95.

73   Michael Detmold, 'The Restructuring of the Faculties: Law' (1995), John Keeler Papers.

74   'Restructuring', *Law School News*, 3 July 1995, 1, UAA, S1526, item 2.

75   Dean's Report, 31 August 1995, UAA, S204, Meeting 7/95, 1; 'Restructuring Proposals', *Law School News*, 13 June 1995, 1, UAA, S1526, item 2.

76   'Adelaidean Interview: Professor David Penington', *Adelaidean*, 10 March 1997, 6.

77   Mary O'Kane, 'Voice: Wise Counsel', *Adelaidean*, 24 March 1997, 2.

78   'Review of Management and Administration: Report', UAA, S204, Meeting 1/97, 21.

79   Academic Board 7/98: Faculties and Divisions, UAA, S204, Meeting 6/98, 1.

80   DCM, 10 February 1997, UAA, S1118, item 2/13, 2; FLM, 4 August 1997, UAA, S204, Meeting 3/97, 5; Law School: Committees 1999, UAA, S204, EEC 1/99; Background Information for Law School Review Committee, UAA, S1540, item 2/1, 38; Law School Board Minutes, 2 September 2002, UAA, S204, Meeting 5/2002, 3; Law School Board Minutes, 8 March 2004, UAA, S204, Meeting 1/2004, 1; Law School Board Minutes, 18 October 2004, UAA, S204, item 2004, 1.

81   Rob Fowler, Interview by John Waugh, 28 March 2019.

82   Samuel Jacobs, Interview by Rob Linn, 23 August 2007, UAA, S1345, item 9, 29, 32.

83   Andrew Ligertwood, Interview by John Waugh, 24 July 2019.

84   Hannah Forsyth, *A History of the Modern Australian University* (Sydney: NewSouth Publishing, 2014), 187.

85   The New Adelaide Law School: Planning, UAA, S204, EEC 2/99, 1. Emphasis in the original.

86   Adelaide Law School, *Handbook of Studies for the Bachelor of Laws*, 1995, 57.

87 Law School Strategic Plan 1992–95, UAA, S950, item 4, 12; Dean to Pamela Lyon, 28 February 1996, UAA, S1118, item 12, 3; University of Adelaide, *Annual Report*, 1997, 6.

88 Law School Executive Minutes, 25 May 1998, UAA, S1118, item 3/7, 3.

89 Bernadette Richards, 'Alice Comes to Law School: The Internet as a Teaching Tool', *Legal Education Review* 14, no. 1 (2003): 117–25; DCM, 26 May 1997, UAA, S1118, item 2/15, 4; The New Adelaide Law School: Planning, UAA, S204, EEC 2/99, 4, 6.

90 Law School On Line Publishing Committee: Position Paper, UAA, S204, Meeting 2/2000; Consumer Market Research: Law School, September 2001, UAA, S1118, item 14, Group 3, 7; Law School Executive Minutes, 9 August 1999, UAA, S204, EEC 2/99; Correspondence Concerning Law of Crime, UAA, S204, Board of Examiners, 16 August 2001.

91 Dean's Report: Professional Certificates in Dispute-Avoidance Lawyering, UAA, S204, Law School Board Meeting 1/99.

92 Vicki Waye to Tim Scroop, 30 August 2000, UAA, S1540, item 2/2; Preventative Legal Process Advisory Committee Report, 21 June 1999, UAA, S204, Meeting 3/99.

93 The New Adelaide Law School: Planning, UAA, S204, EEC 2/99, 10.

94 Dean's Report, 18 December 1998, UAA, S204, Meeting 6/98, 2.

95 Dean's Report, 21 June 1999, UAA, S204, Meeting 3/1999.

96 External Law Program Management Plan, UAA, S204, Meeting 2/2000, 2, 12, 17–19.

97 Law School Board Minutes, Special Meeting, 31 January 2000, UAA, S204, 9.

98 Michael Detmold, The Adelaide Law Partnership Program, UAA, S204, Law School Board, Special Meeting, 31 January 2000.

99 Law Society of South Australia: Submission to Review of the Adelaide Law School, UAA, S1540, item 2/2, 3.

100 Law School Board Minutes, Special Meeting, 31 January 2000, UAA, S204, 8.

101 ibid., 10; Graham Archer, *Unmaking a Murder: The Mysterious Death of Anna-Jane Cheney* (North Sydney: Penguin Random House Australia, 2017), 110–13; Kath McEvoy to Tim Scroop, 3 October 2000, UAA, S1540, item 2/1, 15; Thea Williams, 'Laying Down the Law to Students', *Advertiser*, 27 April 2000, 7.

102 Anonymous response to Adelaide Law School History Questionnaire, 2019.

Epilogue

1 Macintyre, Croucher, and Brett, *No End of a Lesson*, 174; Michael Detmold to Faculty Members, 6 July 1981, UAA, S131, item 14, 71; University of Adelaide, *Annual Report*, 1984, 12; Academic Staff Retreat 1996: Finances/Resources Priorities/Objectives, UAA, S1118, item 2/9.

NOTES

2   Review of the Adelaide University Law School, December 2000, UAA, S1118, item 14, 10.

3   ibid., 25.

4   ibid., 29.

5   ibid., 30.

6   ibid., 32.

7   ibid., 39.

8   Kath McEvoy to Penny Boumelha, 19 April 2001, UAA, S204, Meeting 2/2001.

9   Law School Response to Review Report and Recommendations, UAA, S1118, item 14; Consumer Market Research: Law School, September 2001, UAA, S1118, item 14, 22.

10   Law School Board Minutes, 23 April 2001, UAA, S204, Meeting 2/2001, 3.

11   'Academic's Decision Blow for Law School', *Advertiser*, 1 December 2001, 5.

12   Vice-Chancellor's Committee, Meeting 8/01, Item 4, UAA, S204, item 2001; Law School Board Minutes, 25 March 2002, UAA, S1118, item 188, 3; Law School Draft Financial Plan 2006–2008, UAA, S1118, item 163.

13   'Soon There May Just Be Pictures', *On Dit*, June 1990, 12; 'New Court Honours Chief Minister', *Adelaidean*, December 2008, 3; 'Protest Rally: Malaysia MP Alarm Bells', *Advertiser*, 25 March 2011, 9; Kylar Loussikian, 'Student Protest over Taib Plaza', *Australian*, 18 September 2013, 27; Michael West, 'Tycoon's Family under Investigation', *Age*, 2 November 2015, 21.

14   Adelaide Law School, *Report on the Law Relating to Consumer Credit and Moneylending* (Adelaide: Law School, University of Adelaide, 1969); D. St L. Kelly, 'The South Australian Law Reform Committee', *Adelaide Law Review* 3, no. 4 (1970): 481–86; Andrew Ligertwood, 'Law Reform in South Australia: An Overview', *Legal Service Bulletin* 2, no. 2 (1976): 35–38; Adelaide Law School, 'Law Reform Committee of South Australia Reports Archive (1968–1987)', accessed 19 April 2022, https://law.adelaide.edu. au/research/south-australian-law-reform-institute/archive; 'Law Reform Appointment Maintains Links', *Lumen*, 18 December 1981, 24.

15   Sarah Moulds, 'Community Engagement in the Age of Modern Law Reform: Perspectives from Adelaide', *Adelaide Law Review* 38, no. 1 (2017): 441–62.

16   'Australian Military Forces', *Commonwealth of Australia Gazette*, 1 April 1954, 1007, 1009; Shearer, 'Daniel Patrick O'Connell, 1924–1979', 10, 56–57.

17   John Edge, *The McWha Years: The University of Adelaide, 2002–2012* (University of Adelaide, 2012), 3; University of Adelaide, *Annual Report*, 2017, 14, 16.

18   Committee on the Future of Tertiary Education in Australia, *Tertiary Education*, 2:57.

19 Andrew Ligertwood, Interview by John Waugh, 24 July 2019.

20 William Mitchell, *Lecture on the Two Functions of the University and Their Cost* (Adelaide: G. Hassell & Son, 1917), 19. Mitchell was quoting government analyst William Hargreaves.

21 Hugh Stretton, 'Rowe, Albert Percival (1898–1976)', Australian Dictionary of Biography, 2006, https://adb.anu.edu.au/biography/rowe-albert-percival-11572.

22 Peter de L. Swords and Frank K. Walwer, *The Costs and Resources of Legal Education: A Study in the Management of Educational Resources* (New York: Council on Legal Education for Professional Responsibility, 1974), 47–48; Croucher and Waghorne, *Australian Universities*, 14–15; Duncan and Leonard, *The University of Adelaide*, 77; Notes on the Sixth Report of the Universities Commission, FLM, 4 August 1975, UAA, S131, item 10, 333; Vivienne Brand, 'Decline in the Reform of Law Teaching? The Impact of Policy Reforms in Tertiary Education', *Legal Education Review* 10, no. 2 (1999): 111.

23 G.E. Dal Pont, *Lawyers' Professional Responsibility*, 6th edition (Rozelle, NSW: Lawbook Co., 2017), 23–25, 44–45, 65; *LPEAC Rules* (SA) (2018).

24 Nous Group, *Creation of a New University through Merger: The University of Adelaide and University of South Australia*, 2018, 1, https://web.archive.org/web/20180817030731/http://www.newuniversity.nousgroup.com.au/discussion-paper-1.

25 Robert Bolton, 'University of Adelaide Pulls Plug on Merger', *Australian Financial Review*, 24 October 2018, 10; Robert Bolton, 'Valuable Uni Merger Failed on Minor Issue', *Australian Financial Review*, 5 November 2018, 12.

Bibliography

Archives and Manuscripts

Sources for the history of the Law School are found in many series in the University of Adelaide Archives, as detailed in the endnotes. Among the most important are the Faculty of Law Minutes, 1883–1982 (Series 131), Faculty of Law Minutes and Papers, 1982–2005 (Series 204), Law School Records, 1936–2001 (Series 1118), Faculty of Law Reports, 1883–1900 (Series 141), and Council Minutes (Series 18). Minutes of the Faculty of Law for 1988–94 have not been located; if recovered, they may aid future historians. Much administrative history of the Law School is documented in the Registrar's Department Correspondence, 1872–1939 (Series 169, known as the Envelopes), and Registrar's Correspondence Files, 1886–1960 (Series 200, known as the Dockets).

The manuscript collections of the Barr Smith Library include the University of Adelaide Law School Oral History Archives, 1981–83, Papers Related to the Teaching of Law and the History of the Law School, 1823–1983 (MSS 0130), and the papers of Gerald and Gwenda Fischer (MSS 0158). The State Library of South Australia holds the papers of Jethro Brown (PRG 258), Sir George Murray (PRG 259) and Sir Samuel Way (PRG 30), together with the lecture notebooks of Dame Roma Mitchell (in PRG 778).

University and Student Publications

40%

55%

Adelaidean

Adelaide Law School Annual Report

Adelaide Law School Handbook of Studies

Adelaide Law School Undergraduate Handbook

Adelaide Law School Student Guide

Adelaide Law School Year in Review

Adelaide University Magazine

Cobwebs

Hilarian

Law Students Newsletter

Lumen

Lux Gentium

Mere Puff

Newsletter: Law Students Society

Obiter Dicta

On Dit

Portia

Soliciting Information

Testis

University of Adelaide Annual Report

University of Adelaide Calendar

Other Sources Cited

Adelaide Law School. 'Law Reform Committee of South Australia Reports Archive (1968–1987)'. Accessed 19 April 2022. https://law.adelaide.edu.au/research/south-australian-law-reform-institute/archive.

Adelaide Law School. *Report on the Law Relating to Consumer Credit and Moneylending*. Adelaide: Law School, University of Adelaide, 1969.

Alexander, Fred. *Campus at Crawley: A Narrative and Critical Appreciation of the First Fifty Years of the University of Western Australia*. Melbourne: F.W. Cheshire, for the University of Western Australia Press, 1963.

Allen, Margaret, and Susan Magarey. 'Gender Studies and Social Analysis'. In *A History of the Faculty of Arts at the University of Adelaide 1876–2012*, edited by Nicholas Harvey, Jean Fornasiero, Greg McCarthy, Clem Macintyre, and Carl Crossin, 209–34. University of Adelaide Press, 2012.

Anderson, Kym, and Bernard O'Neil. *The Building of Economics at Adelaide, 1901–2001*. School of Economics, University of Adelaide, 2004.

Archer, Graham. *Unmaking a Murder: The Mysterious Death of Anna-Jane Cheney*. North Sydney: Penguin Random House Australia, 2017.

Australia. *Fifth Report of the Australian Universities Commission*. Parliamentary Paper no. 120, 1972.

Australia. *Fourth Report of the Australian Universities Commission*. Parliamentary Paper no. 81, 1969.

Australia. *Higher Education: A Policy Statement*. Parliamentary Paper no. 202, 1988.

BIBLIOGRAPHY

Australia. *Report of the Committee on Australian Universities*. Parliamentary Paper 1958, no. 12.

Australia. *Sixth Report of the Australian Universities Commission*. Parliamentary Paper no. 271, 1975.

Australia. *Third Report of the Australian Universities Commission: Australian Universities 1964–1969*. Parliamentary Paper no. 330, 1966.

Australia. *Universities Commission: Report for Triennium 1977–1979*. Parliamentary Paper no. 23, 1977.

Barker, David. *A History of Australian Legal Education*. Annandale, NSW: Federation Press, 2017.

Barron, Catherine. 'Reclining Connected Forms'. Adelaidia, 2018. https://adelaidia.history.sa.gov.au/things/reclining-connected-forms.

Bennett, J.M., ed. *A History of the New South Wales Bar*. Sydney: Law Book Company, 1969.

Bleby, Thelma Evelyn. 'Law of Trusts and Trustees in Australia'. Thesis submitted for Bonython Prize, 1929, Law Library, University of Adelaide.

Bond, Eileen [sic]. Interview, 14 June 1981. Law School Oral History Archives. Barr Smith Library, University of Adelaide.

Boothby, Josiah. *Statistical Sketch of South Australia*. Adelaide: W.C. Cox, 1876.

Boutros-Ghali, Boutros. 'Introduction'. In *The United Nations and the Advancement of Women 1945–1996*. New York: United Nations, 1996.

Bradsen, J.R., and J.A. Farrington. 'Student Selection and Performance in the Faculty of Law, the University of Adelaide'. *Australian Universities Review* 29, no. 1 (1986): 25–31.

Brand, Vivienne. 'Decline in the Reform of Law Teaching? The Impact of Policy Reforms in Tertiary Education'. *Legal Education Review* 10, no. 2 (1999).

Bray, J.J. 'Way, Sir Samuel James (1836–1916)'. Australian Dictionary of Biography, 2006. http://adb.anu.edu.au/biography/way-sir-samuel-james-9014.

Bridges, Doreen. 'Ives, Joshua (1854–1931)'. Australian Dictionary of Biography, 2006. http://adb.anu.edu.au/biography/ives-joshua-6807.

Bright, C.H., and Alex C. Castles. 'A New School of International Law'. *Adelaide Law Review* 1, no. 3 (1962): 339–42.

Brown, Cyril M.A. *William Jethro Brown: A Personal Biography and a Bibliography*. South Perth, WA: The Author, 1983.

Brown, W. Jethro. 'Law Schools and the Legal Profession'. *Commonwealth Law Review* 6, no. 1 (1908): 3–15.

Brown, W. Jethro. 'The American Law School'. *Law Quarterly Review* 21, no. 1 (1905): 69–78.

Brown, W. Jethro. 'The Purpose and Method of a Law School: Part I'. *Law Quarterly Review* 18, no. 1 (1902): 78–91.

Brown, W. Jethro. *The Underlying Principles of Modern Legislation.* London: John Murray, 1912.

Bryce, James. *The American Commonwealth.* 2nd ed. Vol. 2. London: Macmillan, 1891.

Burke, Edmund. *Reflections on the Revolution in France.* Edited by Frank M. Turner. New Haven: Yale University Press, 2003.

Burr, Rodney. Interview by Lindy McNamara, 4 July 2014. Law Society of South Australia Oral Histories. https://www.lawsocietysa.asn.au/Public/About/Oral_Histories/Burr.aspx.

Burrage, Michael. *Revolution and the Making of the Contemporary Legal Profession: England, France, and the United States.* Oxford: Oxford University Press, 2006.

Campbell, A.L. 'Foreword'. *Obiter Dicta,* no. 1 (1939): 3.

Campbell, Craig. 'Inventing a Pioneering State High School: Adelaide High, 1908–1918'. *Journal of the Historical Society of South Australia,* no. 29 (2001): 5–20.

Castles, Alex, Andrew Ligertwood, and Peter Kelly, eds. *Law on North Terrace, 1883–1983.* Faculty of Law, University of Adelaide, 1983.

Catalogue of the Library of the Supreme Court of South Australia. Adelaide: E. Spiller, Government Printer, 1883.

Ceylon. *Report of the Commission of Inquiry on Capital Punishment.* Parliamentary Paper no. 14, 1959.

Charlesworth, Hilary. Interview by John Waugh, 26 July 2018.

Clark, Jennifer. *Aborigines & Activism: Race, Aborigines & the Coming of the Sixties to Australia.* Crawley, WA: UWA Press, 2008.

Cockburn, Stewart, and John Playford. *Playford: Benevolent Despot.* Kent Town, SA: Axiom, 1991.

Colonial and Indian Exhibition, 1886: Official Catalogue. London: William Clowes & Sons, 1886.

Committee on the Future of Tertiary Education in Australia. *Tertiary Education in Australia.* Vol. 2. Canberra: Government Printer, 1964.

Commonwealth Tertiary Education Commission. *Review of Efficiency and Effectiveness in Higher Education.* Parliamentary Paper no. 415, 1986.

Conference of Australian Universities, University of Melbourne, 30–31 May 1922. Carlton, Vic.: Ford & Son, 1922.

Coquillette, Daniel R., and Bruce A. Kimball. *On the Battlefield of Merit: Harvard Law School, the First Century.* Cambridge, Massachusetts: Harvard University Press, 2015.

BIBLIOGRAPHY

Crawford, James. Interview, 19 January 1983. Law School Oral History Archives. Barr Smith Library, University of Adelaide.

Crocker, W.R. 'The University of Adelaide in the 1920s'. *Journal of the Historical Society of South Australia*, no. 3 (1977): 3.

Croucher, Gwilym, and James Waghorne. *Australian Universities: A History of Common Cause*. Sydney, NSW: NewSouth Publishing, 2020.

Dal Pont, G.E. *Lawyers' Professional Responsibility*. 6th edition. Rozelle, NSW: Lawbook Co., 2017.

Dal Pont, G.E. *Lawyers' Professional Responsibility in Australia and New Zealand*. 1st ed. Sydney: LBC Information Services, 1996.

Debelle, Bruce. Interview by Lindy McNamara, 4 July 2014. Law Society of South Australia Oral Histories. https://www.lawsocietysa.asn.

Debelle, Penelope. *Red Silk: The Life of Elliott Johnston QC*. Mile End, SA: Wakefield Press, 2011.

Dicey, A.V. 'The Teaching of English Law at Harvard'. *The Contemporary Review* 76 (1899): 742–58.

Duncan, W.G.K., and Roger Ashley Leonard. *The University of Adelaide, 1874–1974*. Adelaide: Rigby, 1973.

Edgar, Suzanne. 'Jones, Doris Egerton (1889–1973)'. Australian Dictionary of Biography, 2006. https://adb.anu.edu.au/biography/jones-doris-egerton-6870.

Edge, John. *The McWha Years: The University of Adelaide, 2002–2012*. University of Adelaide, 2012.

Edgeloe, V.A. *Annals of the University of Adelaide*. Adelaide: Barr Smith Press, 2003.

Edgeloe, V.A. 'The Adelaide Law School 1883–1983'. *Adelaide Law Review* 9, no. 1 (1983): 1.

Emerson, John. *First Among Equals: Chief Justices of South Australia since Federation*. Adelaide: Barr Smith Press, 2006.

Ewens, John Qualtrough. Interview, 8 March 1982. Law School Oral History Archives. Barr Smith Library, University of Adelaide.

Finnane, Mark. 'Norval Morris (1923–2004)'. *Current Issues in Criminal Justice* 15, no. 3 (2004): 267–71.

Finnis, Margaret M. *The Lower Level: A Discursive History of the Adelaide University Union*. Adelaide University Union, 1975.

Fischer, G.L. *In Memoriam: Gwenda Clare Fischer, 1921–1998*. Brighton, SA: Pump Press, 1999.

Fischer, Gwenda. 'The Law Library at the University of Adelaide, 1959–68'. *Australian Library Journal* 8, no. 6 (1969): 213–18.

Forsyth, Hannah. *A History of the Modern Australian University.* Sydney: NewSouth Publishing, 2014.

Fowler, Rob. Interview by John Waugh, 28 March 2019.

Frame, Alex. *Salmond: Southern Jurist.* Wellington: Victoria University Press, 1995.

Gara, Tom. 'The Aboriginal Presence in Adelaide, 1860s–1960s: From Exclusion to Assimilation'. In *Colonialism and Its Aftermath: A History of Aboriginal South Australia,* edited by Peggy Brock and Tom Gara, 86–105. Mile End, SA: Wakefield Press, 2017.

Gardam, Judith. Interview by John Waugh, 19 October 2018.

Gerken, Joseph L. *The Invention of Legal Research.* Getzville, NY: William S. Hein & Co., 2016.

Gibbney, H.J., and Ann G. Smith, eds. *A Biographical Register 1788–1939: Notes from the Name Index of the Australian Dictionary of Biography.* Vol. 2. Canberra: Australian Dictionary of Biography, 1987.

Gibbs, R.M. *Under the Burning Sun: A History of Colonial South Australia, 1836–1900.* Adelaide: Peacock Publications for Southern Heritage, 2013.

Girard, Philip, Jim Phillips, and R. Blake Brown. *A History of Law in Canada, Volume 1: Beginnings to 1866.* University of Toronto Press, 2018.

Goadby, F.M. 'The Late Dr. W.R. Phillips'. *Journal of the Society of Public Teachers of Law* 1931: 33–34.

Goldsworthy, Jeff. Interview by John Waugh, 18 October 2018.

Goode, Gillian [sic]. Interview, 17 June 1981. Law School Oral History Archives. Barr Smith Library, University of Adelaide.

Gorman, Eugene. 'The Legal Profession and the Community'. *Australian Law Journal* 10, no. 13 (1936): 27.

Gover, Kirsty, and Eddie Cubillo. 'The Challenge of Indigenous Polities'. In *The Cambridge Legal History of Australia,* edited by Peter Cane, Lisa Ford, and Mark McMillan, 227–57. Cambridge: Cambridge University Press, 2022.

Grizzard, Nigel. 'Demographic: The Jewish Population of Leeds—How Many Jews?' In *Leeds and Its Jewish Community: A History,* edited by Derek Fraser, 35–48. Manchester: Manchester University Press, 2019.

Hannan, A.J. 'The History of the University', 1964. Barr Smith Library, University of Adelaide.

Hargrave, Neil. Interview by Rob Linn, 21 July 1997. Law Society of South Australia Legal Assistance Scheme 1933–1972: An Oral History. SLSA.

Heuston, R.F.V. 'Sir John Salmond'. *Adelaide Law Review* 2, no. 2 (1964): 220.

Hobbs, Harry, and George Williams. 'The Participation of Indigenous Australians in Legal Education, 2001–18'. *UNSW Law Journal* 42, no. 4 (2019): 1294–1327.

Hodge, Dino. *Don Dunstan: Intimacy & Liberty: A Political Biography*. Kent Town, SA: Wakefield Press, 2014.

Holgate, C.W. *An Account of the Chief Libraries of Australia and Tasmania*. London: C. Whittingham, 1886.

Horne, Julia, and Geoffrey Sherington. *Sydney: The Making of a Public University*. Carlton, Vic.: Melbourne University Publishing, 2012.

Hunt, Arnold D. 'Torr, William George (1853–1939)'. Australian Dictionary of Biography, 2006. http://adb.anu.edu.au/biography/torr-william-george-8831.

Jacobs, Samuel. Interview by Rob Linn, 11 August 1997. Law Society of South Australia Legal Assistance Scheme 1933–1972: An Oral History. SLSA.

Jacobs, Samuel. Interview by Rob Linn, 23 August 2007. S1345, item 9. UAA.

Jennings, Margaret J. 'Benham, Edward Warner (1872–1948)'. Australian Dictionary of Biography, 2006. http://adb.anu.edu.au/biography/benham-edward-warner-9485.

Johnston, W. Ross. *History of the Queensland Bar*. Brisbane: Bar Association of Queensland, 1979.

Jones, D. Egerton. *The Year Between*. London: Cassell, 1918.

Jones, Helen. *Nothing Seemed Impossible: Women's Education and Social Change in South Australia, 1875–1915*. St Lucia, Qld: University of Queensland Press, 1985.

Keeler, John. Interview by John Waugh, 4 September 2018.

Keeler, John. Interview by Stephen Beaumont, May 2013. S1345. UAA.

Kelly, D. St L. 'The South Australian Law Reform Committee'. *Adelaide Law Review* 3, no. 4 (1970): 481–86.

Konefsky, Alfred S. 'The Legal Profession: From the Revolution to the Civil War'. In *The Cambridge History of Law in America, Volume 2: The Long Nineteenth Century (1789–1920)*, edited by Christopher Tomlins and Michael Grossberg, 68–105. Cambridge: Cambridge University Press, 2008.

La Nauze, J.A. 'Some Aspects of Educational Opportunity in South Australia'. In *Australian Educational Studies (Second Series)*, by J.D.G. Medley, R.T. Crosthwaite, H.C. Robinson, Anna Dane, and J.A. La Nauze, 27–61. Melbourne: Melbourne University Press, 1940.

Layton, Robyn. Interview, 15 June 1981. Law School Oral History Archives. Barr Smith Library, University of Adelaide.

Lentin, A. 'Isaacs, Rufus Daniel, First Marquess of Reading (1860–1935), Politician and Judge'. Oxford Dictionary of National Biography, January 2011. https://www.oxforddnb.com.

Leonard, John William. *Who's Who in Jurisprudence: A Biographical Dictionary of Contemporary Lawyers and Jurists, 1925, with a Complete Geographical Index*. Brooklyn, NY: John W. Leonard Corporation, 1925.

Ligertwood, Andrew. Interview by John Waugh, 24 July 2019.

Ligertwood, Andrew. 'Law Reform in South Australia: An Overview'. *Legal Service Bulletin* 2, no. 2 (1976): 35–38.

Lindell, Geoff. Interview by John Waugh, 31 May 2018.

Linn, Rob. *ETSA: The Story of Electricity in South Australia*. Adelaide: Historical Consultants for ETSA, 1996.

Lücke, Horst. Interview by Rob Linn, 17 October 2006. S1345, transcript. UAA.

Lücke, Horst. 'Obituary: Alex Castles'. *Adelaide Law Review* 24, no. 2 (2003): 147–48.

Lunney, Mark. 'Professor Sir John Salmond (1862–1924): An Englishman Abroad'. In *Scholars of Tort Law*, edited by James Goudkamp and Donal Nolan, 103–32. Oxford: Hart Publishing, 2019.

Macgill, Hugh C., and R. Kent Newmyer. 'Legal Education and Legal Thought, 1790–1920'. In *The Cambridge History of Law in America: Volume 2: The Long Nineteenth Century (1789–1920)*, edited by Christopher Tomlins and Michael Grossberg, 36–67. Cambridge: Cambridge University Press, 2008.

Macintyre, Stuart. *Australia's Boldest Experiment: War and Reconstruction in the 1940s*. Sydney: NewSouth Publishing, 2015.

Macintyre, Stuart, Gwilym Croucher, and André Brett. *No End of a Lesson: Australia's National System of Higher Education*. Carlton, Vic.: Melbourne University Publishing, 2017.

Mackinnon, Alison. *A New Kid on the Block: The University of South Australia in the Unified National System*. Carlton, Vic.: Melbourne University Publishing, 2016.

Mackinnon, Alison. *Love and Freedom: Professional Women and the Reshaping of Personal Life*. Cambridge: Cambridge University Press, 1997.

Mackinnon, Alison. *The New Women: Adelaide's Early Women Graduates*. Netley, SA: Wakefield Press, 1986.

Mackinolty, John, and Judy Mackinolty, eds. *A Century Down Town: Sydney University Law School's First Hundred Years*. Sydney: Sydney University Law School, 1991.

Magarey, Susan, and Kerrie Round. *Roma the First: A Biography of Dame Roma Mitchell*. Kent Town, SA: Wakefield Press, 2007.

Mason, Andrea. 'Where do a Bird and a Fish Build a House? An Alumna's View on a Reconciled Nation'. *Adelaide Law Review* 40, no. 1 (2019): 173–86.

Mayer, P.B. 'The Revolution of 1981: The Corbett Report and After'. *Vestes: The Australian Universities Review* 26, no. 1 (1983): 45–51.

McDougall, Fred, and Gary Martin. Interview by Rob Linn, 7 June 2010. S1345, item 18. UAA.

BIBLIOGRAPHY

McPherson, B.H. *The Supreme Court of Queensland 1859–1960: History, Jurisdiction, Procedure.* Sydney: Butterworths, 1989.

Mills, Helen, and Charles Bagot. 'The Early History of the Law Faculty', *Obiter Dicta*, 1968, 32–34.

Mitchell, Justice Roma. Interview, 3 July 1981. Law School Oral History Archives. Barr Smith Library, University of Adelaide.

Mitchell, William. *Lecture on the Two Functions of the University and Their Cost.* Adelaide: G. Hassell & Son, 1917.

Moore, Peter. *A Legal Cohort: South Australia's Legal Community and the First World War.* Darlinghurst, NSW: Australian Legal Heritage, 2018.

Moore, Peter. *Fisher Jeffries: The First 125 Years.* Darlinghurst, NSW: Australian Legal Heritage, 2010.

Moore, W. Harrison. 'Legal Education in the United States'. *Journal of the Society of Comparative Legislation* 13, no. 2 (1913): 207–12.

Morgan, E.J.R. *The Adelaide Club, 1863–1963.* Adelaide Club, 1963.

Morris, Norval. Interview by Mark Finnane, 16 December 2003. ORAL TRC 5119. NLA.

Morris, Norval. 'Sentencing Convicted Criminals'. *Australian Law Journal* 27, no. 3 (1953): 186–200.

Mossman, Mary Jane. *The First Women Lawyers: A Comparative Study of Gender, Law and the Legal Professions.* Oxford: Hart Publishing, 2006.

Motha, Stewart. 'The History of a Lie: The Mabo Case after 30 Years'. Countersign—A Podcast. Accessed 31 May 2022. https://countersignisapodcast.com/podcasts/the-history-of-a-lie-the-mabo-case-after-30-years/.

Moulds, Sarah. 'Community Engagement in the Age of Modern Law Reform: Perspectives from Adelaide'. *Adelaide Law Review* 38, no. 1 (2017): 441–62.

Muirden, Bruce, and Dean Jaensch. 'The Electricity Trust Affair'. In *The Flinders History of South Australia: Political History*, 270–82. Adelaide: Wakefield Press, 1986.

Mulligan, E.P. 'Before the Bench'. In *Dame Roma: Glimpses of a Glorious Life*, edited by Magarey, Susan, 39–56. Adelaide: Axiom, 2002.

Neave, Marcia. Interview by John Waugh, 25 June 2019.

Newbold, Ron. 'Classics at the University of Adelaide (1874–2012)'. In *A History of the Faculty of Arts at the University of Adelaide 1876–2012*, edited by Nick Harvey, Jean Fornasiero, Greg McCarthy, Clem Macintyre, and Carl Crossin, 81–107. University of Adelaide Press, 2012.

Nicholas, Barry. 'Jurisprudence'. In *The History of the University of Oxford, Volume VII: Nineteenth-Century Oxford, Part 2*, 385–96. Oxford: Oxford University Press, 2000.

Nous Group. *Creation of a New University through Merger: The University of Adelaide and University of South Australia*, 2018. https://web.archive.org/web/20180817030731/http://www.newuniversity.nousgroup.com.au/discussion-paper-1.

O'Brien, Anne. 'Tenison Woods, Mary Cecil (1893–1971)'. Australian Dictionary of Biography, 2006. https://adb.anu.edu.au/biography/tenison-woods-mary-cecil-8772.

O'Neil, Bernard J. 'Beyond Trinkets and Beads: South Australia's Aboriginal Legal Rights Movement, 1971–1978'. *Aboriginal History* 6, no. 1 (1982): 28–38.

O'Neill, Sally. 'Kelly, David Frederick (1847–1894)'. Australian Dictionary of Biography, 2006. http://adb.anu.edu.au/biography/kelly-david-frederick-3932.

Parkinson, Andrew. 'The Regret of Sir Samuel Way'. *Australian Journal of Legal History* 1, no. 2 (1995): 239–57.

Pearce, Dennis. 'The Past Is a Different Country'. In *The Future of Australian Legal Education: A Collection*, edited by Kevin Lindgren, François Kunc, and Michael Coper, 49–56. Sydney: Lawbook Co., 2018.

Pearce, Dennis, Enid Campbell, and Don Harding. *Australian Law Schools: A Discipline Assessment for the Commonwealth Tertiary Education Commission*. 5 vols. Canberra: Australian Government Publishing Service, 1987.

Pennefather, F.W. *A Visit to India*. Adelaide: J.L. Bonython & Co., 1894.

Pennefather, F.W. *Colonial and Indian Exhibition, 1886: New Zealand, A Field for Emigration: Lecture*. London: William Clowes & Sons, 1886.

Pennefather, F.W. *On the Natives of New Zealand*. London: Harrison and Sons, 1886.

Pennefather, F.W., and E. Balcombe Brown. *The Code of Civil Procedure in the Supreme Court of New Zealand*. Wellington: Edwards & Green, 1885.

Phillips, Philip. 'Legal Education and Admission to Practice'. In *A Multitude of Counsellors: A History of the Bar of Victoria*, edited by Arthur Dean, 271–87. Melbourne: Cheshire for the Bar Council of Victoria, 1968.

Phillips, Walter R. '"The Kung Yung" of K'ung-Foo-tsze; or, the Moral Mean'. *Victorian Review* 5, no. 26 (1 December 1881): 147–60.

Phillipson, Coleman. *Termination of War and Treaties of Peace*. London: Sweet & Maxwell, 1916.

Phillipson, Coleman. *The International Law and Custom of Ancient Greece and Rome*. London: Macmillan, 1911.

Phillipson, Coleman. *The Trial of Socrates (with Chapters on His Life, Teaching, and Personality)*. London: Stevens & Sons, 1928.

Pietsch, Tamson. *Empire of Scholars: Universities, Networks and the British Academic World, 1850–1939*. Manchester: Manchester University Press, 2013.

BIBLIOGRAPHY

Pitcher, W.B. 'Bonython, Sir John Langdon (1848–1939)'. Australian Dictionary of Biography, 2006. http://adb.anu.edu.au/biography/bonython-sir-john-langdon-5286.

Polden, Patrick. 'Barristers'. In *The Oxford History of the Laws of England: Volume XI: 1820–1914 English Legal System*, edited by William Cornish, J. Stuart Anderson, Ray Cocks, Michael Lobban, Patrick Polden, and Keith Smith, 1017–62. Oxford University Press, 2010.

Polden, Patrick, and Michael Lobban. 'The Education of Lawyers'. In *The Oxford History of the Laws of England: Volume XI: 1820–1914 English Legal System*, edited by William Cornish, J. Stuart Anderson, Ray Cocks, Michael Lobban, Patrick Polden, and Keith Smith, 1175–1222. Oxford University Press, 2010.

Pollock, Frederick. *Principles of Contract*. 3rd ed. London: Stevens & Sons, 1881.

Postema, Gerald J. *Legal Philosophy in the Twentieth Century: The Common Law World*. Treatise of Legal Philosophy and General Jurisprudence, vol. 11. Dordrecht: Springer, 2011.

Press, Margaret M. *Three Women of Faith: Gertrude Abbott, Elizabeth Anstice Baker and Mary Tenison Woods*. Kent Town, SA: Wakefield Press, 2000.

Prest, E.J. *Sir John Langdon Bonython: Newspaper Proprietor, Politician and Philanthropist*. North Melbourne, Vic.: Australian Scholarly Publishing, 2011.

Prest, Wilfrid. 'Alex Castles: An Adelaide Perspective'. *Legal History* 7, no. 1 (2003): 29–36.

Prest, Wilfrid. 'How We Got Here from There: History in a "Scottish" University'. In *Pasts Present: History at Australia's Third University*, edited by Wilfrid Prest, 6–28. Kent Town, SA: Wakefield Press, 2014.

Pue, W. Wesley. *Lawyers' Empire: Legal Professions and Cultural Authority 1780–1950*. Vancouver: UBC Press, 2016.

Rann, Mike. Interview by Kerrie Round, 7 May 2003. MSS 0125, series 3, transcript. Barr Smith Library, University of Adelaide.

Reeves, Tim. 'Dr Duncan Revisited'. *Journal of the Historical Society of South Australia*, no. 44 (2016): 117–26.

Reeves, Tim. 'Duncan, George Ian (1930–1972)'. Australian Dictionary of Biography, 2006. https://adb.anu.edu.au/biography/duncan-george-ian-10063.

Reeves, Tim. 'The 1972 Debate on Male Homosexuality in South Australia'. In *Gay Perspectives II: More Essays in Australian Gay Culture*, edited by Robert Aldrich, 149–92. Sydney: University of Sydney, 1993.

Reeves, Tim. *The Death of Dr Duncan*. Adelaide: Wakefield Press, 2022.

Richards, Bernadette. 'Alice Comes to Law School: The Internet as a Teaching Tool'. *Legal Education Review* 14, no. 1 (2003): 115–38.

Roe, Michael. 'Brown, William Jethro (1868–1930)'. Australian Dictionary of Biography, 2006. http://adb.anu.edu.au/biography/brown-william-jethro-5393.

Roe, Michael. *Nine Australian Progressives: Vitalism in Bourgeois Social Thought, 1890–1960*. St Lucia, Qld: University of Queensland Press, 1984.

Ross, Sir Bruce. Interview, 17 November 1982. Law School Oral History Archives. Barr Smith Library, University of Adelaide.

Rowe, A.P. *If the Gown Fits*. Carlton, Vic.: Melbourne University Press, 1960.

Salmond, John W. 'The Literature of Law'. *Columbia Law Review* 22, no. 3 (1922): 197–208.

Salmond, Sir John. *Jurisprudence*. Edited by Glanville L. Williams. 10th ed. London: Sweet & Maxwell, 1947.

Savoy, Paul N. 'Toward a New Politics of Legal Education'. *Yale Law Journal* 79, no. 3 (1970): 444–504.

Selleck, R.J.W. *The Shop: The University of Melbourne 1850–1939*. Carlton, Vic.: Melbourne University Press, 2003.

Sendziuk, Paul. 'No Convicts Here: Reconsidering South Australia's Foundation Myth'. In *Turning Points: Chapters in South Australian History*, edited by Paul Sendziuk and Robert Foster, 33–47. Kent Town, SA: Wakefield Press, 2012.

Shearer, I.A., ed. 'Daniel Patrick O'Connell, 1924–1979'. Typescript, 1981, Barr Smith Library, University of Adelaide.

Shearer, I.A. 'Obituary: Professor D.P. O'Connell'. *Australian Year Book of International Law* 7 (1981): xxiii–xxx.

Shearer, I.A. 'O'Connell, Daniel Patrick (1924–1979)'. Australian Dictionary of Biography, 2006. https://adb.anu.edu.au/biography/oconnell-daniel-patrick-11280.

Shearer, Ivan. Interview by John Waugh, 5 September 2018.

Shearer, Ivan. 'James Crawford: The Early Years'. In *Sovereignty, Statehood and State Responsibility: Essays in Honour of James Crawford*, edited by Christine Chinkin and Freya Baetens, xiii–xix. Cambridge: Cambridge University Press, 2015.

Shore, T. Spencer, ed. *The Savitar 1923*. Columbia, Missouri: Junior Class of the University of Missouri, 1923.

Smith, Frederick. *International Law*. Edited by Coleman Phillipson. 5th ed. London: Dent, 1918.

Somerville, Dorothy, and Sesca Zelling. Interview, 13 October 1982. Law School Oral History Archives. Barr Smith Library, University of Adelaide.

South Australia. *Progress Report of the Select Committee of the House of Assembly on the Adelaide University and Higher Education*. Parliamentary Paper no. 113, 1910.

Spence, Catherine Helen. *An Autobiography*. Edited by Jeanne F. Young. Adelaide: W.K. Thomas & Co., 1910.

Spiller, Peter. 'The History of New Zealand Legal Education: A Study in Ambivalence'. *Legal Education Review* 4, no. 2 (1993): 223–54.

Star, Leonie. *Julius Stone: An Intellectual Life*. Melbourne: Oxford University Press, 1992.

Stretton, Hugh. 'Rowe, Albert Percival (1898–1976)'. Australian Dictionary of Biography, 2006. https://adb.anu.edu.au/biography/rowe-albert-percival-11572.

Stubbs, Matthew. 'The *Adelaide Law Review* at (Volume) 40: Reflections and Future Directions'. *Adelaide Law Review* 40, no. 1 (2019): 1–14.

Swords, Peter de L., and Frank K. Walwer. *The Costs and Resources of Legal Education: A Study in the Management of Educational Resources*. New York: Council on Legal Education for Professional Responsibility, 1974.

Szuster, Julja I. 'The Injustice of the 1914 Assault on Hermann Heinicke'. *Journal of the Historical Society of South Australia*, no. 43 (2015): 99–110.

Tarlo, Hyman. 'Law Schools and Law Teachers in Australia: 1946–1974'. *University of Queensland Law Journal* 9, no. 1 (1975): 26–38.

Taylor, Greg. *A Great and Glorious Reformation: Six Early South Australian Legal Innovations*. Kent Town, SA: Wakefield Press, 2005.

Taylor, Greg. 'Dr Pennefather's Criminal Code for South Australia'. *Common Law World Review* 31, no. 1 (2002): 62–102.

Tenison Woods, Mary. 'Some Reforms in Law Affecting Women and Children Over the Last Hundred Years'. In *A Book of South Australia: Women in the First Hundred Years*, edited by Louise Brown, Beatrix Ch. de Crespigny, Mary P. Harris, Kathleen Kyffin Thomas, and Phebe N. Watson, 127–34. Adelaide: Rigby for the Women's Centenary Council of SA, 1936.

Thiele, Colin. *Grains of Mustard Seed*. Adelaide: Education Department, 1975.

Turney, Clifford, Ursula Bygott, and Peter Chippendale. *Australia's First: A History of the University of Sydney, Volume 1, 1850–1939*. Sydney: University of Sydney in association with Hale & Iremonger, 1991.

University of Adelaide. *Centenary Commemoration: Faculty of Law: 1983*. Adelaide: University of Adelaide, 1983.

University of Adelaide. 'Former Officers & Honorary Degree Holders of the University'. University Archives, 2020. https://www.adelaide.edu.au/records/university-archives/online-resources/former-officers-honorary-degree-holders#honorary-university-fellows.

University of Adelaide. *Review of Governance: Final Report*, 1990.

University of Adelaide. 'University of Adelaide Announces ICAC Response'. Newsroom, 24 June 2021. https://www.adelaide.edu.au/newsroom/news/list/2021/06/24/university-of-adelaide-announces-icac-response.

Venn, J.A. *Alumni Cantabrigienses: A Biographical List of All Known Students, Graduates and Holders of Office at the University of Cambridge, from the Earliest Times to 1900.* 10 vols. Cambridge: Cambridge University Press, 1922.

Victoria. *Royal Commission on the University of Melbourne: Minutes of Evidence.* Parliamentary Paper no. 20. 2nd session, 1903.

Victoria. *Rules of the Supreme Court.* Parliamentary Paper no. 98, 1887.

Wanganeen, Edmund, ed. *Justice Without Prejudice: The Development of the Aboriginal Legal Rights Movement in South Australia.* Underdale, SA: Aboriginal Studies and Teacher Education Centre, SACAE, 1986.

Watson, Irene. 'Colonial Logic and the Coorong Massacres'. *Adelaide Law Review* 40, no. 1 (2019): 167–71.

Watson, Nicole. 'Indigenous Legal Traditions and Australian Legal Education'. In *The Cambridge Legal History of Australia,* edited by Peter Cane, Lisa Ford, and Mark McMillan, 719–64. Cambridge: Cambridge University Press, 2022.

Waugh, John. 'Controversy and Renown: Coleman Phillipson at the Adelaide Law School'. *Adelaide Law Review* 42, no. 1 (2021): 147–71.

Waugh, John. *First Principles: The Melbourne Law School, 1857–2007.* Carlton, Vic.: Miegunyah Press, 2007.

Waugh, John. 'The Legal Profession Between the Wars'. In *The First World War, the Universities and the Professions in Australia 1914–1939,* edited by Darian-Smith, Kate and James Waghorne, 220–34. Carlton, Vic.: Melbourne University Publishing, 2019.

Western Australia. *Report of the Royal Commission on the Establishment of a University.* Parliamentary Paper. Perth, 1910.

Whitington, Helen. 'Ralph Meyrick Hague: Biography'. In *Hague's History of the Law in South Australia, 1837–1867,* by Ralph M. Hague, 811. Adelaide: Barr Smith Press, 2019.

Whitlam, E.G. 'The Machinery of Democracy'. *Adelaide Law Review* 9, no. 2 (1983): 229–34.

Willett, Graham. *Living Out Loud: A History of Gay and Lesbian Activism in Australia.* St Leonards, NSW: Allen & Unwin, 2000.

Wood, Leonard. *Islamic Legal Revival: Reception of European Law and Transformations in Islamic Legal Thought in Egypt, 1875–1952.* Oxford: Oxford University Press, 2016.

Woods, M.C.T. *Juvenile Delinquency, with Special Reference to Institutional Treatment.* Melbourne: Melbourne University Press, 1937.

Wright, Martha. 'Ad Eundem Gradum'. *AAUP Bulletin* 52, no. 4 (1966): 433–36.

Wynes, W.A. Interview by Janet Robertson, 1973. J.D. Somerville Oral History Collection, OH 561/63, transcript. SLSA.

Index

INDEX

INDEX

INDEX

Wakefield Press is an independent publishing and
distribution company based in Adelaide, South Australia.
We love good stories and publish beautiful books.
To see our full range of books, please visit our website at
www.wakefieldpress.com.au
where all titles are available for purchase.
To keep up with our latest releases, news and events,
subscribe to our monthly newsletter.

Find us!

Facebook: www.facebook.com/wakefield.press
Twitter: www.twitter.com/wakefieldpress
Instagram: www.instagram.com/wakefieldpress

www.ingramcontent.com/pod-product-compliance
Ingram Content Group UK Ltd.
Pitfield, Milton Keynes, MK11 3LW, UK
UKHW050631030125
452892UK00009B/52

9 781923 042391